ANATOMY OF THE ORCHESTRA

ANATOMY
of the
ORCHESTRA

Norman Del Mar

University of California Press
Berkeley and Los Angeles

University of California Press
Berkeley and Los Angeles
Printed in Great Britain

© 1981, 1983 by Norman Del Mar

First Paperback Edition, with revisions, 1983

ISBN 520–05062–2

Library of Congress Catalog Card Number
81–11559

FOR THEA MUSGRAVE

Dear friend and colleague
exhilarating and challenging companion
warm and deeply sympathetic composer
with love.

Contents

(The chapters are summarized in detail on the pages immediately following.)

Contents

SECTION I: **THE STRINGS**

Contents

SECTION II: **THE WOODWIND**

Contents

Contents

SECTION III: **HORNS**

SECTION IV: **THE HEAVY BRASS**

SECTION V: **TIMPANI AND PERCUSSION**

Contents

SECTION VI: **KEYBOARD AND OTHER INSTRUMENTS**

Contents

Dedicatory Introduction

My dear Thea,

Here at last is your book. At least I hope it is your book, because it has been through so many rewritings that you may no longer recognize it. My hope is, nevertheless, that it will give you at least some of the answers, or details, or views, or ideas, that were in your mind when you urged me to persevere with it, despite my endless feelings of discouragement.

And it has remained ever after 'Thea's orchestra book' because the title has been a virtually insoluble problem. In the event the one it bears was the inspiration of Barrie Iliffe, who like yourself has been enormously helpful and encouraging. He has, moreover, read the typescript section by section and produced many excellent (and often hilarious) comments and suggested corrections.

I was grateful that Barrie proposed a satisfactory title because the reason for my difficulty in finding one was bound up with the very fact that I have never been able to explain to any of my interested friends just exactly what the book was about. The only thing I felt clear about was that no such book existed so far, a state of affairs repeatedly apparent when I went to the local library to search for details or verification of material, only to come away saying to myself, 'Of course I can't find it; I keep forgetting, it doesn't yet exist'—which also explains, of course, the absence of a bibliography even though I do occasionally mention some specialist book which I possess or have consulted.

This then has been my motivation for writing, against what I often felt to be my better judgement. For I know only too well that not only can the book never be complete, but also that it can never be completely correct or up to date. As I open the scores of my own library, often at random, or study a new work for my next conducting

21

assignment, further exceptions or contradictions or additions to something I have said, stare me in the face, and I wonder how (or whether) I should find a place for them. Ultimately I fully accept that in allowing my work to be published I expose myself to colleagues and experts refuting something I have said, or charging me with omitting some vital piece of information, or (most likely of all) insisting that my view of the state of the orchestral world vis-à-vis one or other instrument or some aspect of professional practice is not true of all countries, or is no longer true in Britain. If this does happen, let me state here and now that I shall not be chagrined, but highly interested and delighted.

For there is no escape: to question every one of my countless associates on point after point would not only be a hopelessly long drawn out process, but would also land me in precisely the quicksands of over-specialization that it has been my constant vigilance to avoid as outside my terms of reference. The very viewpoint of this book is and must remain opposed to each and every specialist, even over points of fact. For often enough the truth is less important than what some composer believed to be the truth, or meant when he was actually ignorant of the whole truth. Hence my percussion section is, for example, absolutely not in competition with James Blades's masterly compendium[1], for Jimmy and books like his really do give the truth in every specialized and historical detail, whereas this is not a book of instruments, nor of instrumentation, nor of orchestration, though some elements of all of these inevitably intrude.

The hardest task has been to decide at each stage as much what to omit as what has got to be said in the sheer interests of intelligibility. At one point it even seemed necessary to state that the instruments of the string orchestra are normally played with the hairs of the bow. Unless I somehow planted this commonplace it seemed impossible to get to the point of discussing Mahler's daring in prescribing a legato style of bowing with the wooden back, and so progress towards the extraordinary techniques to be found in Berg's *Lyric Suite*, techniques nowhere mentioned in conventional books of orchestration.

If this is not a book of orchestration, one of the most important differences seems to me to lie in the angle of approach. Its purpose has never been in the smallest degree to advise the student how to write for the orchestra; my interest lies the opposite way round—from the point of view of either the performer or the score-reader, especially the

---

[1] *Percussion Instruments and their History*, Faber, London, 1970.

conductor, who wants to know what the composer meant, thought he meant, or even maybe should—in my opinion—have meant. And in the course of this I hope I have unravelled at least some of the confusions and contradictions which occur in almost every score—whether over the matter of the notation of string harmonics, what tuba really plays 'Bydlo' in the Mussorgsky/Ravel *Pictures from an Exhibition* as well as the transposing B♭ tuba of Bax's *Overture to a Picaresque Comedy*, or what the harpist thinks Mahler meant when he wrote 'Mediator' against certain notes; for none of these problems can be solved through recourse to any available reference books or textbooks of orchestration.

I have also included other aspects of orchestral practice, whether public—such as platform presentation; or theoretical—as the confusingly different ways composers lay out the arrangements of instruments in the score, so that it is by no means always possible for a conductor to pick up the score of any work and obtain an instinctive impression of the sound at a glance.

Yet at the same time the idiosyncratic style of a composer's layout should not be interfered with, as it may also have a value of comprehension and background. As you know, Thea, I hate scores to be presented with all the transposing instruments rewritten to appear at actual pitch. This can cause waste of time at rehearsal as well as impediments of reading, since the parts of instruments such as piccolos or horns then appear quite differently to the score-reader (or again conductor) from the way they do to the player, and so give a false impression of the sound and technical aspect. Yet a score of Prokofiev (who habitually wrote all his scores in C throughout) set out in the usual way with clarinets, horns and trumpets conventionally notated, looks curiously odd; see, for example, the Second Piano Concerto.

This leads me to a question I have been repeatedly asked: who am I addressing? And to this I have no straightforward answer; naturally I am to some extent addressing you, Thea; it has been suggested —by the clarinettist Colin Bradbury—that I might be addressing the string chapter to him, and the wind chapter to the violinist Eli Goren; while Barrie Iliffe and others have indicated that although the sheer technicality of some parts suggests that it is surely aimed at the composer/ performer fraternity, a great deal of it will be of absorbing interest to the concert goer. Gratifying as this would undeniably be, I cannot accept the credit for this being my intention and purpose in writing the book which is, I must confess, a compendium of the things that interest me, which I have failed to find elsewhere, and in which I have a yen to interest others, whosoever they may be. Some of these things are of quite a general nature, applicable to all the orchestral sections equally like the notation symbols which I discuss in my closing quasi-appendix section.

There are many more subjects of this kind or others parallel; I could perhaps have tried to cover them all, or as many as I could think of—such as, for example, some of the controversial tempo markings—the difference between 'rit.', when it might indicate 'ritenuto', and 'rall.', this latter always a gradual process—the meaning of Andantino, the exact opposite when Mozart uses it to the meaning attributed to it by Tchaikovsky—the true significance of Largo, usually but by no means necessarily a slow mark—and so on; but these all really belong to another book, and to one not primarily concerned with the orchestra.

Yet such details are constantly in dispute during orchestral work because of what is commonly described as the imperfections of our musical notation. Nor is this as bad as it is so often made out to be. The flexibility and hidden variations of meaning implicit in different points of view would be largely destroyed if music were a science capable of being set down with absolute precision. Interpretation would cease to exist, and the tape-recorder/synthesizer milieu would finally triumph. Already players often consider that in contemporary music they are less and less expected to exercise their artistry and individuality, since either they are required to work to a mathematical exactness to which only a computer could hope to do justice, or, on the contrary, given a freedom of choice that makes nonsense of their métier, which is the sheer business of getting the notes, which are on the stand in front of them, right. This question of correctness is crucial; an orchestral musician is outraged if for any reason at all it can be shown not to matter. Such a suggestion strikes at the root of his whole training and consequentially the ethic by which he works and lives. Players will discuss amongst themselves, or hotly and at length with the conductor, points of phrasing and interpretation, the details of which virtually no member of the audience will be even remotely aware. And the extent to which they are allowed to matter is one of the responsibilities which must eventually devolve on the conductor, that is to say, my own métier; and yet this is a subject hardly touched upon in this book. For that is, of course, another book and one I do not feel myself yet ready to write. Perhaps I will one day; but meantime I hope this one will please and interest you, Thea.

In addition to the numerous publishers listed on page 27 from whose works I have quoted with their kind agreement, my warmest thanks are due to countless expert colleagues whose brains (whatever I may have said above) I have at various times picked.

But I must in particular record my profound and affectionate appreciation to Patrick Carnegy—most encouraging and uplifting of editors; to that enormously gifted composer David Matthews, who has torn himself away from his creative activities to prepare for publication this alarmingly complicated endeavour; and, as so often in the past, to Barrie Iliffe who has read and proof-read the book at various stages of its gestation with infinite patience and refreshing humour.

It has been just such friends who have enabled me to bring the task to any possibility of conclusion in reasonably good spirits and some semblance of sanity.

Hadley Common   N.R.D.M.
January, 1981

Preface to revised edition, 1983

In preparing this new edition I have taken the opportunity of correcting as many as possible of the more glaring errors. Some of these were easily and quickly spotted, others pointed out by critics and friends whose comments and contributions I continue to welcome but not all of which has it been practicable to incorporate. One correspondent, for example, raised a thorny issue over the nature and meaning of the Italian 'Cimbasso'. Here the different editions of *Grove* are at odds with one another and the whole subject is full of surmise. There does indeed seem to be a case for believing it to have often been one of the larger members of the trombone family, but I am still not to be persuaded that a tuba never was used and that Anthony Baines (of all people) was in ignorance when he wrote in *Grove 5* of the cimbasso often being applied to the Italian narrow-bore tuba as used in La

Scala, Milan. Perhaps ultimately the word may well have been more generic than specific, rather like 'continuo'.

One of my strongest misgivings concerns the definition of the term 'grosses Orchester' as specifying the presence of trombones. I should have remembered that Tovey committed himself positively and quite otherwise as follows: 'The term "full orchestra" implies the use of trumpets or drums; trombones are not necessary.' Other authorities are less precise and I wonder from where Tovey derived his certainty on the subject, although there is no question but that he is borne out by Brahms's use of 'grosses' and 'kleines' in the two Serenades (which he is discussing in the above quotation).

N.R.D.M.

Acknowledgements

Thanks are due to the following publishers for permission to reproduce copyright music:

Anglo-Soviet Music Press Ltd. (Shostakovich, Symphonies 1, 3 & 7)

M. P. Belaieff, Frankfurt (Glazunov, Symphony No. 5)

Boosey & Hawkes Music Publishers Ltd., London (Bartók, *Concerto for Orchestra*, Suite Op. 4, Violin Concerto; Britten, *Les Illuminations, Nocturne, Peter Grimes, The Rape of Lucretia*; Delius, *The Walk to the Paradise Garden*; Elgar, *Cockaigne*; Mussorgsky-Ravel, *Pictures from an Exhibition*; Prokofiev, *Ala and Lolly, Classical Symphony, Peter and the Wolf*, Symphony No. 5; R. Strauss, *Ariadne auf Naxos, Daphne, Elektra, Feuersnot, Die Frau ohne Schatten, Intermezzo, Der Rosenkavalier, Salome*; Stravinsky, *Agon, Chant du Rossignol, Orpheus, Petrouchka, Pulcinella, Le Sacre du Printemps*; Xenakis, *Pithoprakta*)

Bosworth & Co. Ltd., London (R. Strauss, *Burleske*)

Edition Bote & G. Bock, Berlin (R. Strauss, *Sinfonia Domestica*)

Breitkopf & Härtel, Wiesbaden (Sibelius, *En Saga*, Symphony No. 4, *Valse Triste*)

J. & W. Chester/Edition Wilhelm Hansen London Ltd. (Falla, *El Amor Brujo, The Three-cornered Hat*; Poulenc, *Sinfonietta*; Rossini-Respighi, *La Boutique Fantasque*; Stravinsky, *Firebird* Suite)

L. Doblinger (B. Herzmansky), Vienna (Dohnányi, Suite in F♯ minor)

Editions Max Eschig, Paris (Falla, *Nights in the Gardens of Spain*; Milhaud, *La Création du Monde;* Ravel, *Alborado del Gracioso*; Szymanowski, *Sinfonia concertante*)

Faber Music Ltd. (Curwen Edition), London (Holst, *The Planets*)

Carl Fischer, Inc., New York (Webern, *Im Sommerwind*)

Rob. Forberg-P. Jurgenson Musikverlag, Bonn (Prokofiev, Piano Concerto No. 1)

Carl Gehrmans Musikförlag, Stockholm (Wiren, Serenade for Strings)

Edition Wilhelm Hansen, Copenhagen (Nielsen, Symphony No. 4; Schoenberg, Serenade; Sibelius, Symphonies No. 5 & 6)

Haydn-Mozart Presse (Alfred A. Kalmus Ltd.) (Haydn, Symphony No. 51)

F. E. C. Leuckart, Munich (R. Strauss, *Alpensinfonie, Le Bourgeois Gentilhomme, Ein Heldenleben, 'Wiegenlied'*)

Novello & Co. Ltd. (Bantock, *Fifine at the Fair*; Elgar, *Falstaff, Grania and Diarmid*, Symphony No. 2)

Oxford University Press, London (Delius, *Summer Night on the River*; Rawsthorne, Symphony No. 3; Vaughan Williams, *Job*, Symphony No. 4; Walton, *Façade, Scapino*, Symphony No. 1)

Peters Edition Ltd., London (Schoenberg, *5 Orchesterstücke*; R. Strauss, *Also Sprach Zarathustra, Don Juan, Don Quixote*)

G. Ricordi & Co., Milan (Respighi, *Feste Romane, Fontane di Roma, Trittico Botticelliano*)

Editions Salabert, Paris (Honegger, *Horace Victorieux, Jeanne d'Arc au Bûcher*)

Samfundet Til Udgivelse af Dansk Musik (Nielsen, Symphony No. 6)

G. Schirmer, Inc., New York (Schoenberg, Violin Concerto)

Schott & Co., Ltd., London (Blomdahl, *I Speglarnas Sal*; Tippett, *Concerto for Double String Orchestra*, Ritual Dances from *The Midsummer Marriage*, Symphony No. 2)

B. Schott's Söhne, Mainz (Françaix, *Sérénade*; Henze, *Novae de Infinito Laudes*; Hindemith, *Kammermusik No. 1*; Nono, *Y su sangre*; R. Strauss, *Ariadne auf Naxos, Daphne, Elektra, Feuersnot, Die Frau ohne Schatten, Intermezzo, Der Rosenkavalier, Salome*; Stravinsky, *Firebird Ballet, Jeu de Cartes*, Violin Concerto)

Skandinavisk Musikforlag, Copenhagen (Nielsen, Symphony No. 5)

Supraphon (Alfred A. Kalmus Ltd.) (Janáček, *Taras Bulba*)

Stainer & Bell Ltd., London (Delius, *Eventyr*)

United Music Publishers Ltd. (Durand: Debussy, *La Mer, Iberia; L'Apprenti Sorcier, La Péri*; Messiaen, *Turangalîla-Symphonie*; Ravel, *Daphnis et Chloé, Ma mère l'Oye, Rapsodie Espagnole, Schéhérazade, Le Tombeau de Couperin, La Valse*; Roussel, *Le Festin de L'Araignée*, Symphony No. 3. Enoch: Enesco, *First Romanian Rhapsody*. Heugel: Pierné, *Les Enfants à Bethléem*. Jobert: Debussy, *L'après midi d'un faune, Fêtes*)

Universal Edition (Alfred A. Kalmus Ltd.), Vienna (Berg, *Kammerkonzert, Lulu, 3 Orchesterstücke, 3 Stücke aus der Lyrischen Suite*, Violin Concerto, *Wozzeck*; Delius, *Dance Rhapsody No. 1*; Janáček, *Sinfonietta*; Milhaud, *Sérénade*; Schoenberg, *Erwartung*, Suite Op. 29, *Gurrelieder, Kammersymphonie No. 1, Variations for Orchestra*; Webern, Passacaglia, *Variations* Op. 30)

Universal Edition (London) Ltd. (Bartók, *Dance Suite, Music for Strings, Percussion and Celesta*; Boulez, *Le marteau sans maître*; Kodály, *Dances from Galanta, Háry János*; Mahler, *Das Lied von der Erde*, Symphony No. 9)

Section I

THE STRINGS

1 DEFINITIONS

The string body occupies a primary position in the constitution of the orchestra. This is not merely so in a visual sense—their position at the front of the concert platform—but because the very presence of multiple strings can be taken to determine whether a group of instruments should be described as an orchestra at all. Even the presence of single strings (that is, one player of each department) is barely sufficient to qualify an ensemble as an orchestra, though borderline cases exist such as Jean Françaix's *Sérénade* which, scored for twelve instruments including five solo strings, is actually—if perhaps incorrectly—described as being 'pour petit orchestre'.

In English, an instrumental group entirely without strings is always a band; wind, brass, percussion, or military band, the latter being made up of all the other groups. This corresponds with such Italian formations as are to be found in, for example, Verdi's *Rigoletto* which contains passages for 'Banda interna' conventionally laid out in short score on two staves. In French and German, however, a wind ensemble containing either or both woodwind and brass is termed *Harmonie*, while French military bands may be simply *Musique*—e.g. Musique de la Garde Républicaine.

The French *les cordes* parallels the English 'strings' but the Germans with typical punctiliousness specify *Streichinstrumente*, i.e. stroked instruments as distinct from *Saiteninstrumente* which is, on the contrary, a blanket term including equally those whose strings are not only bowed but plucked, hammered or whatever, such as the instruments in Section VI: harp, piano, harpsichord, mandoline, guitar etc. Hence Bartók's *Musik für Saiteninstrumente, Schlagzeug und Celesta* is a title hard to translate since the straightforward English equivalent (*Music for*

29

Strings, Percussion and Celesta) fails to indicate that the score includes harp and piano. In the German title only the celesta has to be singled out, since its keyboard operates hammers that strike not on strings but metal bars.

The Italian term for the string group presents a curious anomaly. Although the word for string is *corda* (similar to the French) the section as a whole is called not *le corde* but *gli archi*, i.e. not the strings, but the bows.

2 NOMENCLATURE OF THE SECTION'S COMPONENTS

It can next be laid down for purposes of definition that the standard string section of the orchestra consists of four members of a single family subdivided according to size, and hence register: violins, violas, cellos and basses.

Although many scores use their language of origin in giving the names of the instruments, the international custom is generally to preserve the Italian. There is, however, no question of uniformity and different composers and publishers have their own idiosyncrasies, the languages even being mixed up at times.

Thus violins may be: *Violini* (It.), *violons* (Fr.), or *Violinen* (Ger.), though the Germans also sometimes use *Geigen*, a word derived from the old Italian *giga*, since in its early days the instrument was closely associated with the jig (= the French *gigue*). The English 'fiddle' is also sometimes used, though primarily as a colloquial term (Percy Grainger's attempt to introduce it into printed scores gives a quirky appearance and has had no following). The Germans also have *Fiedel*, which came to acquire a folky flavour and was exploited by Mahler to depict the macabre country fiddler of his Fourth Symphony:

Ex. 1

The purpose of the raised tuning is to add a more wiry, penetrating, unsophisticated quality to the playing (see also p. 103).

Violas may be: *Viole* (It.), *altos* (Fr.) or *Bratschen* (Ger.). The French use of *alto* is certainly logical, though unexpected since all other French names are in line with the Italian, while *Bratsche*, the most common of German deviations from Italian, has in fact an Italian origin—i.e. *[viola da] braccio* (= arm) as opposed to *viola da gamba* (= leg).

Cello seems to be the one word to have been taken over universally without exception. The full form 'violoncello' is of course widely used and this will be found with numerous endings, such as the French *violoncelle*, or without one at all as in one German form, *Violoncell*. Occasionally the howler 'violincello' does still make the odd appearance. For 'Cello' is in fact merely an all-purpose diminution (as in *vermicelli*), just as the suffix '-one' is an augmentation (e.g. *padrone*). Thus violoncello (literally) means 'a little violone'—i.e. a little big viola.

The violone, the precursor of our modern double bass, was strictly a double-bass viol and will often be found in scores by Bach and other early composers, though they may also include all the bottom string instruments within the blanket term 'continuo' or (as in Monteverdi) *bassus generalis.*

There are many differences between the members of the consort of viols and of the violin family both in shape and in methods of playing. Only in the evolution of the orchestral bass have some of these differences survived, such as the curvature of the shoulders and the so-called Dragonetti bow. The Italian *basso* or *contrabasso*, or even— strangely enough—*contrabbasso*, converts naturally into *contrebasse* (Fr.), or *Kontrabass* (Ger., spelt either with a C or a K). In English, in addition to the usual 'bass' or 'double bass,' the term 'string bass' is sometimes used, especially in groups like dance or military bands in which string instruments are a minority.

3 EARLY INSTRUMENTS

Although violins, violas, cellos and basses constitute the body of the string section, a few of the more interesting historical string instruments may sometimes be encountered in the symphony orchestra though these are never to be found in sections, only as solo players. The most familiar are the viola d'amore and the viola da gamba, the latter principally introduced as a continuo instrument or for purist performances of Monteverdi, Schütz or other early music. Perhaps its chief claim to a repertoire status in the orchestra derives from the parts in Bach's Sixth Brandenburg Concerto, in the Passions and in some of the Cantatas. Bach's notation for it is generally similar to that of the cello, but in Cantata No. 106, *Gottes Zeit ist die allerbeste Zeit*, the first of the two gambas is notated in the alto clef and the second in the tenor and bass clefs:

Ex. 2

The viola da gamba has six strings and unlike the cello has no spike, being gripped between the knees. Moreover, as with all viols, the bow is held from beneath much like the Dragonetti bass-bow. A disconcerting feature of this gamba bow-style is that the bow strokes work the opposite way to the regular strings—i.e. the down bow travels from point to heel.

The gamba has not been revived in nineteenth- and twentieth-century music, unlike the viola d'amore which makes periodic reappearances, such as the obbligato at the beginning of Raoul's aria from Act 1 of Meyerbeer's *Les Huguenots*, the offstage solo in Act 2 of Puccini's *Madama Butterfly*, or Pfitzner's inclusion of it in *Palestrina*. Yet even in the latter opera it oddly appears only briefly in a not particularly exposed passage, whereas the many obbligatos which portray a sixteenth-century instrument in the hands of one of the characters on stage are taken by one—or at times two—ordinary violas. This is perhaps because players of the extraordinary viola d'amore, with its seven strings plus a further seven sympathetic strings, are extremely rare; in practice all such examples of these are usually played by the conventional viola, which is even given as an *ossia* for the solo in the 'Parting of Romeo and Juliet' from Prokofiev's ballet. In the case of the Puccini at least, it must be admitted that the imaginative subtlety in the composer's choice of colour for Butterfly's touching night vigil largely goes for nothing, played as it is behind the scene in unison with the offstage chorus.

None of the other ancestors of the violin family have sufficient status orchestrally speaking to warrant inclusion here despite their appearance in scores by Schütz or other Baroque composers. The *violino piccolo* of Bach's First Brandenburg Concerto, Schütz's *violetta* and the numerous other instruments listed and described by Terry in his book *Bach's Orchestra*[1], belong wholly to the specialist and to history.

4 PERSONNEL

While the orchestral string section consists of groups of four related instruments, it has a basic fivefold organization. This arises out of the standard division of the violin strength into 1sts and 2nds, which are as much complete and self-contained units as are the violas, cellos and basses. The Germans refer to the strings equally as the *Streichquartett* or *Streichquintett* according to whether or not the 1st and 2nd violins are considered collectively as a single instrument genus. In this context these terms, normally associated with the solo string quartet or quintet of chamber music, are occasionally usurped in the instrumental lists at the beginning of orchestral scores, or in analyses. The abbreviation 'Q' may thus also be found in piano arrangements or vocal scores in German editions where these give indications of the instrumentation.

However true it may be that the repertoire ranging from early to contemporary music can be found to show similar divisions for instruments other than the violins, or different divisions (into three, etc.), or *no* divisions whether for violins or any of the others, these variations are far less frequent and do not affect the constitution or administration of the orchestra.

Professional orchestral musicians are employed on three scales of seniority: principals, sub-principals and rank-and-file. Of these, the last group only applies to the strings and does not exist in any other

---

[1] Charles Sanford Terry, *Bach's Orchestra*, Oxford University Press, London, 1932.

department. The players so designated are the lowest paid for they bear the least individual responsibility. Moreover, although rank-and-file players are all administratively equal in status, they may compete avidly for desk positions, outside or inside, nearer the front or back, first or second violin etc., and this often causes strife and discontent within a badly disciplined orchestra.

Experiments have been made in some organizations with a rotation system of rank-and-file players. This has some clear advantages but there are also equally serious drawbacks. Certainly there is an obvious overall increased responsibility, but the apparent gain in incentive through being rescued from the oblivion of the back desks is offset by the loss of potential reward through promotion. And the conductor's valuable gain in personal contact with players he otherwise only sees and controls from a distance is counteracted by the unsettling effect upon the players of being required to readjust to new partners and environment. Apart from training orchestras, therefore, such schemes remain the exception rather than the standard practice.

The principal and sub-principal players of each section, i.e. the two players at the first desk, are especially selected and auditioned both as personalities and with a view to their heavy artistic responsibility. The 1st violins are, however, a special case with the principal and sub-principal of the section the no. 2 and 3 players respectively. For the no. 1 1st violin is the Leader, that is, not just of the 1st violins, or even of the string department, but of the whole orchestra. The Americans, for whom the word 'Leader' may often signify the conductor, call this primary figure 'Concertmaster', a direct translation of the German *Konzertmeister*. The French use either *Chef d'attaque* (a splendidly graphic title) or simply *Premier violon*, corresponding with the Italian *Primo violino*, although *la spalla* is also in current use, *spalla* meaning shoulder, i.e. for the conductor to lean on (figuratively, perhaps) since the leader, with his overall authority, is the liaison between conductor and orchestra. He may also act as spokesman for the orchestra *vis-à-vis* the management, except in matters that properly fall into the province of an appointed union steward. But in addition the leader may share this role with the chairman of a representative committee formed by the members of the orchestra in such duties as addressing the assembled players on points of procedure or internal dispute.

Should the leader have extended solos to play during the course of a work, the second player automatically assumes the leadership of the section; if both players of the first desk are playing solo lines, the tutti has to be led by no. 3 and so on. One may find as many as four solo violins used (as in the 'Gretchen' movement of Liszt's *Faust Symphony*), thus putting the onus of temporary leadership further and further back.

In recognition of the leader's position and responsibility it is the custom in Britain for him to receive special mention, as it is also to make a solo entrance on to the platform, both at the beginning of the concert and after the interval. He also takes the initiative of choosing the strategic moment to lead his colleagues off at the end. These marks of distinction are nevertheless not universal, and on the Continent the leader will mostly take his place together with the rest of the orchestra, though he may stand up to obtain silence and either give or request the A for the orchestra to tune (see also p.169).

One world-wide tradition is that the conductor shakes hands with the leader at the end of the concert. This courtesy, sometimes viewed cynically as savouring of a Mutual Admiration Society, in fact provides the conductor with the opportunity to show his appreciation of the whole orchestra, as well as the leader's cooperation. Many conductors signify their enthusiasm by shaking hands also at the very beginning of the proceedings before a note is played, or even shaking hands with all the other leaders of the sections in his immediate environment, though this last is less customary in Britain.

String players always sit in pairs at their desks, including the larger instruments up to the cellos and basses. Only in amateur orchestras does one find individuals who have managed to insist on having a desk to themselves on account of bad eyesight or whatever. This pair-seating is one reason why left-handed players are exceedingly uncommon, as their back-to-front movements are disruptive.

Single players will be seen in professional orchestras, however, when a section contains an odd number of players, either because the composer has so stipulated in the score or because such is the orchestral strength, whether through illness or otherwise. The single player will then generally occupy the last desk, but this may well prove unsatisfactory either on geographical grounds or because the programme contains passages directed to be played by precisely the last desk or desks, each presupposing a pair of players.

Pair seating automatically gives rise to two ranks of players, outside and inside—that is, nearer and further respectively from the audience. Accordingly some orchestras, preferring that the deputy leader should be an outside player, engage their no. 3 1st violin in that capacity, thus leaving the subleader (no. 2) undisturbed in the event of a change of leader. On the other hand, some top-line international orchestras actually engage two leaders who share that extremely exacting office. They may then either sit together on the first desk (taking turn and turn about with the outside leading and inside supporting positions) or only appear at all in alternation if they feel that their prestige might otherwise be compromised.

5 DIVIDED PLAYING

Each string section is frequently required to be divided into numerous different parts and this can be carried out in various ways. Even the simplest *divisi a 2*[1] can be executed either at the desk or by desks. *Divisi* at the desk signifies that the file of outer players takes the upper line, that of the inner players the lower, and is the manner normally adopted by players for any two-fold division unless instructed otherwise. *Divisi* by desks, on the other hand, denotes that the two players at each desk play in unison, the odd numbered desks taking the top, the even numbered the bottom part. This is a very convenient method for page turns where the music continues without rests, as the outside player can keep the line going while the inside player turns.

Where *divisi* at the desk is adopted it is only natural that the foremost outside and inside players should represent the leaders of their respective files. But this may be confused when not only are the tutti *divisi* but at their head there is an odd number (1, 3, 5 etc.) of players with solo lines. The leader of tne remainder (*gli altri, die Übrigen*) will then inevitably be seated on the inside at the head of those players with the lower line, though he himself will play the upper. An example may help to clarify this complicated state of affairs:

---

[1] This is often indicated in the score simply by 'a 2' producing a confusingly different use of this mark from its application to the wind; see p. 191.

Ex. 3 Strauss, 'Wiegenlied', Op. 41 no. 1

In this instance no. 4 1st violin will be the leader of the tutti section throughout the song (for the figure and *divisi* persist) playing the upper line although he sits at the head of the file playing the lower—the leader of whom will be no. 6.

Ex. 3 also shows the German equivalent, *geteilt*, to the standard Italian term *divisi*. The abbreviation *div.* is clear enough but the German abbreviation *geth.*, short for the old German form *getheilt* found especially in Wagner, is not always understood by players. The German contradiction *Alle* corresponds with the Italian *tutti*, while *zusammen* is the equivalent of *unisoni*.

It is rare to find one or other form of *divisi* actually specified in scores but the Germans do have the indication *Pultweise geteilt*. Unfortunately this, meaning literally 'deskwise', is misleading since it is in fact used to signify *divisi* at the desk as in Strauss's *Salome*:

Ex. 4

Here the extra stave for the first desk, introduced for the sake of a solo passage a few bars later, confirms the meaning of the instruction. This is furthermore in keeping with normal practice in octave passages of this kind.

A third method of *divisi a 2* is by blocks, front and back. Composers sometimes force this method upon players and conductors by having two different parts printed carrying the music for only the front or back desks. Although this form of dividing may naturally be applied to any section it may have special relevance to the cellos, whose lower line will often be in unison with the basses, and so is best played by the back desks who sit nearest to them. The cello parts of Smetana's *Vltava*, for example, are printed in this way.

It cannot be said that any one of these methods is the best in all contexts. Each is freely used and the different forms of *divisi* may replace each other even within the span of a single work or movement. The choice will depend on various practical considerations arising from the musical layout, or in response to specific instructions in the score.

One outstanding example of such a choice arises when only half the section is required to play. This may be indicated by the Italian *metà*, or by the German *die Hälfte*. (The French equivalent *la moitié* is very rarely seen.) Except in the few instances where the score stipulates the front desks, it is usual for the file of outside players to take the passage by themselves. The virtue of this is not just to reduce the weight of tone but to thin out the actual quality.

Divisi a 3 (*en trois parties, dreifach geteilt*) can also be handled in different ways. Left to themselves the players for simplicity's sake generally take a desk a line, thus:

Ex. 5

But as can be seen from Ex. 5 this places the players of the third line very far back, as well as keeping each of the desks with the same line to play almost out of earshot of one another. If therefore the musical context is one of harmonic or chordal textures a better mixture is effected with a *divisi* by players:

Ex. 6

(Ex. 5 and 6 show arrangements of players at their desks as seen to the right of the conductor. Those on the left would, of course, appear mirror-wise.)

Fourfold *divisi* (*a 4, vierfach*, etc.) is on the face of it a simpler affair since it is an obvious derivative of *divisi a 2* by desks, each line of which is then subdivided again. Looked at from this point of view it can be seen to equate with a *divisi a 4* by players:

Ex. 7

This is especially clear when the part is printed on two staves each bearing a pair of lines, but is less obvious when the publisher has been conscientious enough to lay out the whole scheme on four staves. This apparently enlightened practice in the event occupies so much space on the printed page that it carries with it the hazard of frequent and awkward, even impossible, page turns in busy extended passages. In such cases it may be necessary to condone the 'desk a line' method even here, where the disadvantages of ensemble already inherent in threefold *divisi* are rendered still more acute. An example occurs in the last movement of the Sibelius Symphony No. 5:

Ex. 8

and so on for a further 73 bars. The page turns *can* only be executed with a *divisi* by desks although the closely-knit effect is sacrificed.

Insufficiently considered layout on the part of composers as well as publishers or copyists may pose quite knotty problems to the players and conductor. There is a notorious passage in Wagner's *Tannhäuser* Overture, beginning with what seems a simple *divisi*:

Ex. 9

Ex. 9 shows the 1st violin lines exactly as they appear in the full score with the change of system occurring at the *Un poco ritenuto* three bars before letter D. The new layout (where Wagner asks for the violins to be disposed in four equal parts) gives the half strength, corresponding with the upper divided line of the previous bars, on the first two staves. Accordingly the initial *divisi* will need to be not at the desk, as would normally take place, but by desks, since the second player is shown subsequently to be in unison with the first. Unfortunately in the parts the change of line occurs at a different place and the fourfold *divisi* is laid out from the very beginning of the passage, with the upper line of the first two bars given only to the topmost of the four staves. This error is also taken over in the Eulenburg miniature score, thus adding further currency to a faulty reading.

Nor is this the only problem; a few bars later the upper two lines take over from the clarinet the melodic interest:

Ex. 10

Here the passage would only be practicable if all the players with the top lines were sitting together, i.e. the first part given to desks 1 and 2, the second to desks 3 and 4 and so on. Nor is this procedure inconsistent with the music of Ex. 9 and it may well be what Wagner had in mind. But what by tradition actually happens is quite different: for the melodic lines in Ex. 10 are always given to two solo violins, the lower parts being taken by the remainder divided at the desk. The change of *divisi* effected at this point is then organized in each player's copy through a system of arrows hurriedly scribbled in as a reminder where to go next.

Another example, this time a real Wagnerian conundrum of *divisi*, occurs at the very beginning of the Prelude to *Lohengrin*. Here the music is for four solo violins plus the broad mass of all the remaining violins (1st and 2nd) divided into four equal parts, though nothing in the score identifies exactly who plays what. For after four bars the solo violins play each in unison with one of the divided tutti lines, after a further eight bars they detach themselves and play together to form a fifth equal strand which itself merges five bars later again to form four equal groups. After yet another sixteen bars the first and third, and the second and fourth lines join up so that with the turn of the page of score 1st and 2nd violins are found in the conventional positions. It would be an intriguing exercise to try to make it all work and to sort out just what Wagner could possibly have envisaged. Certainly the Breitkopf editors of the orchestral parts completely failed to find the right answer and were forced to bowdlerize Wagner's part-writing in order to retrieve their error at the point where the lines finally merge into simple 1st and 2nd violins.

These Wagnerian problems are perhaps extreme cases, but simpler, relatively straightforward issues are no less important. One of the commonest is exemplified by a passage from Kodály's *Dances of Galanta*:

Ex. 11

In the interest of clarity the copyist has laid out the parts with the passage after the eight-bar rest on three staves. But this automatically leads to equally distributed threefold divisions whereas Kodály's clear intention was that the strength of the lower line should continue to equal that of the upper, divided itself as it is. Without a misleading arrangement in the copy this would be easily carried out through a *divisi* by desks. Where the upper line then subdivides, the odd-numbered desks to whom this becomes allocated then further divide at the desk while the even-numbered desks continue to play the lower line in unison.

Some of the most perplexing situations arise when the composer keeps changing the *divisi* between two, three, four, five and even six or more lines, often within the space of a few bars, causing players to search out their way amidst a maze of shifting parts.

Ex. 12

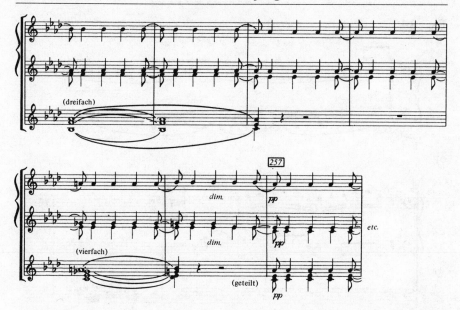

Ex. 12 gives the 2nd violin part of an excerpt from Strauss's opera *Intermezzo*, an excerpt that also occurs as one of the Symphonic Interludes under the title 'Am Kamin'. The score specifies a section of nine violins divided up as shown above with the first three players detached and the remainder split into five, into three, into four and then (for what is in fact an extended period) into two, with the lower line subdivided. Exactly how this all works with a total of nine players Strauss did not bother to explain; in practice decisions have to be made over which line should be doubled by the remaining back-desk players, or whether it might be better for these to be silent in certain bars.

Nor is this the only *divisi* headache in *Intermezzo* for, having fixed upon viola and cello sections comprising five players each, Strauss writes for the three desks in different ways, as if it were alternately the first and the back desk which has the single player, viz:

Ex. 13

Solo Desk 2 Desk 3   and   Desk 1 Desk 2 Player 5

so that the only way to carry out his instructions to the letter is to carry six players with either the second or the sixth remaining silent in such passages as:

Ex. 14

Over the whole repertoire every kind of *divisi* will of course arise ranging from the simplest block divisions, equal or unequal (as in the first movement of Bartók's Divertimento), to the elaborate desk by desk layouts of Schoenberg's *Gurrelieder* or the *ne plus ultra* of Xenakis's compositions, in some of which every single player has a different line to play.

6 SCORE LAYOUT

In a full orchestral score the strings are normally to be found grouped together at the foot of the page or system. The violins, 1st and 2nd, will mostly be bracketed, as will the cellos and basses, these last often even put on a single stave as 'Vc e Cb' in classical scores, since much of what they have to play is identical. They may then be termed simply *Bassi*, this being assumed to include the cellos. Scores of Beethoven's B♭ Piano Concerto ('No. 2' of 1785) are printed in this way as are some (Peters and the earliest Eulenburg) of the C Major Concerto, Op. 15, but by the Third Concerto in C minor the combined line is always shown as 'Violoncello e Basso'.

Works whose scores give no more than the single word *Bassi* often cause considerable uncertainty and controversy. In Mozart's Serenades and Divertimenti, for example, cellos might very well not form part of the ensemble, in which case *Bassi* would mean literally no more than double basses. Hence, from such precedents, in a piece like the *Masonic Funeral Music* the indications are that here too Mozart intended the basses to stand alone without cellos, especially in view of the unusual instrumentation, as well as the arrangement of the part-writing. Certainly the music is less opaque as well as more original in texture, when played in this way.

The combining of cellos and basses on a single stave also takes for granted that, although written in unison, the basses in fact sound an octave lower than the cellos. This custom of treating the basses as transposing instruments is bound up with the character of their tone which in turn reacts upon the visual impression of their appearance in the score. A passage like the great melody of Beethoven's Choral Symphony both looks and is much more a true unison as Beethoven wrote it:

Ex. 15

than if he had written:

Ex. 16

Yet it could legitimately be claimed that the *sound* of Ex. 15 is actually:

Ex. 17

and that only Ex. 16 gives a scientifically true unison.

45

Nevertheless, not only does Ex. 16 reveal the technical reality of the high positions on the basses necessary to produce such a unison, but also that taking quality of timbre into account this does not give any true musical (as opposed to scientific) unison of sonority.

Yet, as a result of the bias in recent years against the use of transposing instruments in the conductor's score, many composers are writing for basses at actual pitch and are consequently tending to misjudge this aspect of timbre and technique. The basses thus continually find themselves clambering about in uncongenial and ineffective registers as in the following:

Ex. 18

Even Schoenberg, the initiator of this line of thought and from whose *Variations for Orchestra*, Op. 31 the above fragment is taken, might have been influenced to reconsider the question of unison pitch had the score been laid out as the players see their lines:

Ex. 19

While the layout of the full score is broadly standardized, with the strings at the foot of the page, there are exceptions to be found mostly derived from earlier practices. Until the early nineteenth century all kinds of arrangement were in current use and the manuscripts of Mozart, Beethoven and even Schubert will often show the upper strings at the top of the score, the bass line at the bottom, and the wind and brass in the middle. Modern editions have brought uniformity to scores as a matter of policy but a curious survivor of older methods exists in the Prelude to Wagner's *Tristan und Isolde*. One system—but only one—is given in archaic manner on the second page of the music (page 4 of the actual score):

Ex. 20

The score as shown in Ex. 20 reproduces the layout of Wagner's manuscript precisely. Wagner was in many ways a traditionalist and his operatic scores present another analogous remnant from earlier custom: that of placing the vocal line within the string block at the foot of the score above the bass or cello/bass line.

This derives from *basso continuo* in which for the sake of the keyboard performer playing from score the solo line was placed immediately above the figured bass. The custom was also carried over at times into instrumental concertante works with the result that well-established editions of the classical concerto repertoire may be found with the solo line (including piano) in that position. Very occasionally it may even be placed between the violins and violas, but this has no historical or any other justification.

The normal placing of the solo line, instrumental or vocal, in modern scores is, however, immediately above the string group, although keyboard (*Klavier*) concertante parts are also to be found below all the strings, at the very bottom of the score, a style that can be seen to date back to Bach's Concertos.

When solo lines occur within the string section itself the usual custom is for each solo to appear in the score at the head of its respective section (i.e. solo viola above the violas, then solo cello above the cellos, etc.); on the other hand examples are to be found where all the solo instruments are placed together above the tutti:

Ex. 21   Blomdahl, *I Speglarnas Sal*

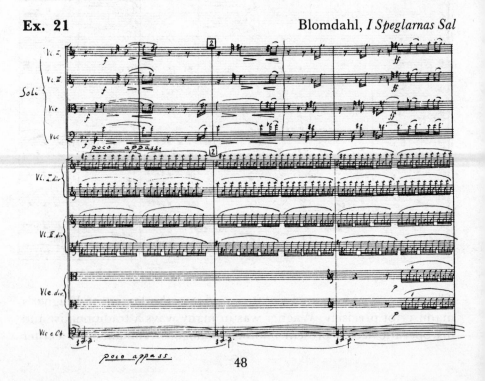

This is also the usual layout where the solo lines are fully concertante for the duration of the work, as in Stravinsky's *Pulcinella*; but it may be adopted for short periods of obbligati, especially if the solo instruments are playing parts similar in style and texture to each other but different from the tutti as in the Blomdahl example just quoted.

Even in such cases, however, there is no inflexible rule and Ex. 22 gives a parallel instance in which the opposite layout is presented:

Ex. 22   Dohnányi, Suite in F♯ Minor, Op. 19

7 PLATFORM PLANNING

On the concert platform the string section normally occupies the frontmost position of the orchestra with the groups of instruments organized according to recognized formulae to which orchestras all over the world conform. Of these the oldest established formation is:

Ex. 23

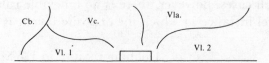

This is the classical grouping favoured by most of the past generation of traditionally minded conductors such as Toscanini, Furtwängler, Klemperer, etc. and militantly championed, to the point of letters to *The Times*, by Sir Adrian Boult.

An important variant of Ex. 23 has the virtue of keeping the basses in what has become their more usual position, to the conductor's right:

Ex. 24

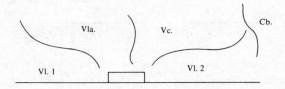

At one time these formations, with their primary feature of the violins seated nearest the audience along the entire length of the platform, fell seriously into abeyance; but they have had something of a return to favour. Nevertheless, the most widely adopted seating plan in current use remains:

Ex. 25

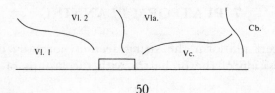

Advocates of this arrangement hold it advantageous that all the higher sound is on one side and all the lower on the other, while others oppose it for this very reason.

A fourth arrangement would seem to complete the range of possibilities by putting the violas in the disputed place to the conductor's right:

Ex. 26

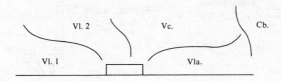

This is beloved of some conductors in the belief that it spotlights the violas which, of all the string departments, have the least penetrating power. At the same time, however, they are facing away from the audience, and all in all they gain less from the position than either the 2nd violins or the cellos.

A further variant to all the foregoing, much favoured in America, stretches the basses out in a line along the rear of the platform. Undeniably impressive as the basses look, featured in this way, they are seriously separated from the rest of the strings and especially from the cellos with whom they have so many passages in common. That inveterate experimenter Leopold Stokowski once tried putting the cellos in a row at the back as well, just in front of the basses. But this was not a success, each cellist feeling unbelievably isolated up there facing the audience, a growling doublebass at his back, his colleagues strung out on either side, and the whole woodwind block between him and the other strings with whom he was trying to play in ensemble.

The arguments in favour of Ex. 23 and 24, featuring the 2nd violins on the right, are not only historical but musical. For a key factor in the development of two such groups of a single instrument is the to and fro of antiphonal writing that is to be found not only in classical times but also in the world of the romantics. A passage such as the following from Rimsky-Korsakov's *Capriccio Espagnol* is reduced to nonsense if the violins are all bundled together on one side of the platform:

Ex. 27

This is no more than an extreme example out of hundreds of cases where the composers' intention is a play between two alternating sections, such as:

Ex. 28   Elgar, Symphony No. 2

A particularly interesting and subtle use of interplay between the two violin sections, and which goes for very little when they are seated together, is the famous overlapping passage at the beginning of the finale of Tchaikovsky's *Symphonie Pathétique*:

Ex. 29

Adagio lamentoso (♩ = 54)

In the recapitulation the identical notes recur but with the lines straightened out, giving an entirely different, more immediate effect, since the 1st violins carry the whole of the melody.

Mahler wrote passages for the 1st and 2nd violins, which, while completely in unison as far as the notes are concerned, are widely at variance in their dynamic markings:

Ex. 30

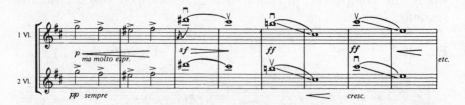

Effects like this example from Mahler's Ninth Symphony are totally negated if the violins are seated together in a single composite group; whereas if they are placed according to the traditional formula for which Mahler was writing, the conception is fascinating and original. It is moreover a device of which he was particularly fond, for it appears in very many of his works.

One objection often raised to seating the 2nd violins on the right is that their quality is substantially weakened owing to the tilt of their instruments away from the audience. Yet the apparent loss of tone is an illusion since, like all matters of balance, it is instinctively rectified by the players; whereas on the contrary a certain variation of timbre can indeed be detected and must surely be a positive gain.

More serious is the purely practical consideration that the wide separation of the 1st and 2nd violins causes difficulties of ensemble especially in the numerous passages they play together. The undue width of platform in some halls, the bad acoustics of others, certainly create difficulties for the back desks of the respective groups when antiphonal seating is insisted upon in all circumstances as a matter of principle. With training, and where lavish rehearsal time is available, difficulties of ensemble can certainly be overcome; but in our less than ideal professional world the loss of time and the frustrations caused may prove overriding factors unless there is a positive desire to make it work on the part of both conductor and players.

There is also the side issue of the psychological impact on the 2nd violins. Many a passage that is merest drudgery when they are no more than a subsidiary section of a great mass of fiddlers can become of liveliest interest when they are in opposition to their colleagues as well as in full view of the audience; it is surprising how much better they can sound when seated separately.

However, the seating plan of Ex. 25 also has strong points in its favour apart from the attractive ease it offers in obtaining good ensemble. The histrionic aspect as the conductor turns across for broad contrast to a richly prominent body of cellos (or, though surely less so, of violas) must certainly have been one of the chief factors in the rising popularity of Exx. 25 and 26. With the cellos on the right in particular, the rotating swing round the orchestra of passages such as Ex. 31 from Schumann's Fourth Symphony makes splendid visual as well as aural effect.

Ex. 31

Moreover, in view of the prevalence of this arrangement in present-day orchestras, a number of works have entered the standard repertory which take it so much for granted that it is for all intents and purposes indispensable. In Shostakovich's Fifth Symphony, for example, the violins are re-divided *for the slow movement only* into an exactly equal number of 1sts, 2nds and 3rds, the three lines being printed in full in both the 1st and 2nd violin parts to enable the distribution to be made. In the antiphonal formations of Exx. 23 and 24 this would clearly be unworkable with any degree of accuracy.

Richard Strauss laid out the scores of both *Elektra* and *Josephslegende* with 1st, 2nd and 3rd violins, and in the former he further arranged that in the case of the violas, who are also divided into three, the first players should 'muta in IV Violinen' (i.e. 'change to', not to be confused with muting). This doubling of the two instruments creates an unusual problem, but whether or not carried out to the letter the whole disposition of the parts with their various groupings is clearly only practicable on the assumption that the violins are seated in a single body adjacent to the violas, although this was not Strauss's normal practice in the concert hall.

Conversely, many works treat all or varying quantities of violins as a single group throughout. In such cases there can patently be no possible purpose in antiphonal seating whether the total body of violins is used, as in Hindemith's *Konzertmusik* for strings and brass; or only a few, such as the six in Strauss's *Bourgeois Gentilhomme/Ariadne auf Naxos* music, or the three of Stravinsky's 'Dumbarton Oaks' Concerto and Ibert's *Divertissement*.

Here the problem is rather how best to utilize the leader and subleader of the 2nd violins who are permanently engaged in this capacity regardless of such special circumstances, and who are by definition the best players after the leaders of the 1sts.

Yet another seating situation arises where there are no violins at all. Brahms's Serenade in A, Op. 16, is written for an ensemble led by the violas, who must then occupy the place to the left of the conductor otherwise always occupied by the 1st violins. Stravinsky's *Symphony of Psalms* has no other strings than cellos and basses and requires an entirely individual formation centred around the two pianos which play a primary role in the unusual orchestration.

Whatever seating is adopted, the players nearest to the audience always form the outside, the others the inside file. Sometimes, however, the leader of the section to the conductor's right elects to change over with his partner, thus taking the inside position although still playing the top line. The reason for this is that some players consider that they are in a better position to see the conductor and his beat, regardless of the odd appearance from the audience's point of view as well as the irregularities that must arise in *divisi* passages. For this change is purely a matter of the first desk which will thus differ from the remainder of the section.

In the case of the instrumental groups in front of the conductor the identification of outside and inside players may be a little less regular. In principle the left-hand group is organized like the 1st violins, viz:

Ex. 32

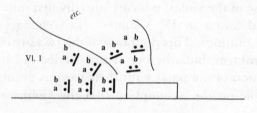

But the right-hand groups are not always arranged as the exact mirror of this:

Ex. 33

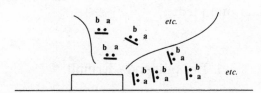

for the section to the right front of the conductor, whether violas or cellos, often elect to seat themselves in conformity with their colleagues to his left front, leaving only those on the extreme right as the exceptions:

Ex. 34

However confusing this may be for the conductor—and he may have to take care to know who is who of the players in front of him—he does not interfere with the players' preferences in such matters.

When the strings are permanently divided for the whole of a work or movement it is often a good idea—platform permitting—to arrange each section in two clear files:

Ex. 35

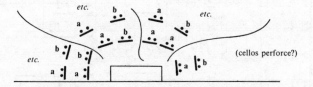

Generally the cellos are found to require too much space to enable this formation to be extended to them also. But in a piece like Stravinsky's *Apollon Musagète* which is scored throughout for 1st and 2nd cellos it is of such great advantage to be worthwhile trying to make it possible.

Works that benefit from this kind of seating are those in which the *divisi* is best organized by desks, as for example Elgar's *Introduction and Allegro* or, in particular, Reger's *Four Tone Poems after Böcklin*, in the first of which half the players form a muted string group while the other half remain unmuted:

Ex. 36

1. Der geigende Eremit.

A fully separate division of the strings into dual formation is not possible in this work because for the subsequent movements Reger returns to a normal disposition. When, however, a composer stipulates a double string orchestra as integral to his overall design, the layout normally adopted is one of mirror-wise symmetry, thus, in the most practical way, emphasizing the identity of each group:

Ex. 37

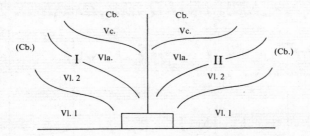

The placing of the cellos and basses along the back clearly presupposes the absence of woodwind and brass, and in the majority of cases this is indeed so. Bantock's monster setting of the *Omar Khayyám Ruba'iyat* provides a very rare instance of a full orchestral score with the strings divided throughout into two orchestras.

Normally, therefore, the rostra vacated by the wind can be occupied by the cellos, and this is very necessary as their tone is otherwise easily lost in being pushed so far to the back of the platform. The positions of the basses shown in brackets in Ex. 37 indicate alternatives sometimes found unavoidable where space is limited. But the disadvantage of the two groups of basses being so very far apart is made acute, when, as often, composers write for the basses of both orchestras in unison (or parallel) (See Ex. 38, overleaf).

The standard formation of Ex. 37 has, naturally, to be adapted with some degree of flexibility if the double string orchestra is part of a larger ensemble, as in Frank Martin's *Petite Symphonie Concertante*, which uses the two string orchestras as the concerto grosso to a concertante of harp, harpsichord and piano. Bartók's *Music for Strings, Percussion and Celesta* also presents problems, the solution to which the composer has tried to indicate in a kind of map at the beginning of the score.

Examples 36 and 38 both show the conventional notation of the double orchestra in two complete units, one above the other; but as the Reger indicates, this need not necessarily mean that the players will actually be seated in double formation. Such a divergency between platform and score layouts can be very confusing to the conductor.

Ex. 38   Tippett, *Concerto for Double String Orchestra*

A similar divergency (if the other way round) occurs in another work by Tippett, his *Fantasia Concertante on a theme of Corelli*. Here the tutti strings are disposed as a double orchestra and are so laid out in the score everywhere except in the central Andante and the subsequent fugue, which are, on the contrary, notated for a single body though with all parts *divisi* except the basses. In practice the lower line of each part should be allocated, in the interest of clarity, to the players of the second orchestra placed on the conductor's right, even though this is not made clear in the score. Moreover, the work includes in addition a concertino of three solo players (two violins and cello, as in the classical concerto grosso) placed in front, and here again no provision is made in the layout of the central fugue for these soloists. The result of this conflicting score planning is that, contrary to the composer's express intentions, performances take place in which the players are allowed to remain in the conventional single orchestral seating as for the rest of the programme. It is in fact Tippett's intention that the two concertino violinists should stand, and this too is based on concerto grosso tradition although it is no longer the invariable custom today. In Handel or Corelli, etc., these solo players will often have individual parts and, whether they stand or not, will require desks to themselves involving reseating of the whole of their sections. They will also need careful platform placing so that each soloist-leader is not too far from his respective tutti even though the concertino group remains closely enough knit for obbligato ensemble passage-work. A solo double bass (as in *Pulcinella*) also adds substantially to the problem, being quite difficult to place satisfactorily.

Nor is there a standard score layout for the classical concertino, as it may be given in a block above the main body or with each soloist above his own section. The Handel Concerti Grossi, Op. 6, can be found in both styles, the former in Peters edition, the latter in Eulenburg.

An ingenious multiple grouping was planned by Luigi Nono in his *Y su sangre* whereby, as my additions to Nono's own diagram show, he was able to subdivide his players not only into two, but three orchestras in the uninterrupted course of the continuous work:

Ex. 39

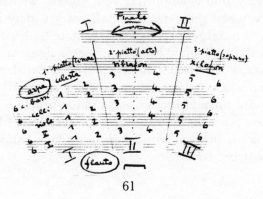

In theory it is clear that the six players can be subdivided into either two or three formations but at the same time this can only be at the expense of the instrumental divisions arranged as they are in five receding lines. The violas and cellos especially will suffer severely from being relegated to the back of the platform unless they can be raised on rostra.

But all these special formations are to a large extent dependent on local conditions. The same is true, with perhaps even greater force, of the opera pit which, with its comparative lack of depth and its extensive width, poses different problems even where the orchestration is simple and straightforward. Hence, in addition to the layouts already discussed, other methods are often tried, such as that of placing all the strings on one side and all the wind on the other, an arrangement which Stokowski at one time introduced experimentally into the concert hall, though its disadvantages of balance and ensemble seem finally to have told against it.

At Bayreuth there is a unique situation arising from the reflected acoustics of the pit. Accordingly the positions of the 1st and 2nd violins are reversed, the 1sts actually sitting on the right of the conductor, from whom a fine degree of adaptability is certainly required.

8 NUMERICAL STRENGTH

There is no absolute number of strings that constitutes a symphony orchestra, but the full strength aimed at for prestige concerts in the capital cities of the world may be said to be: sixteen 1st violins, fourteen 2nd violins, twelve violas, ten cellos and eight basses. At other times one desk less all round is very common, although every conceivable variation is employed and, indeed, written for.

Composers, when they specify at all, vary widely in their preferences. Berlioz's habitual practice was to state 'at least 15, 15, 10, 11, 9', a curious strength since it presupposes a single player at most of the back desks, a situation generally found unsatisfactory (see p. 35 above). Also it will be noticed that Berlioz was specifying more cellos than violas—an unusual though not unique practice. Debussy in *La Mer* asks at one point for no less than sixteen cellos, although nowhere else in the score is there any indication that he is thinking in terms of an abnormal string strength:

Ex. 40

Wagner, in *The Ring*, lists a string body of 16, 16, 12, 12, 8 against a wind body that might have been thought to require more extravagant forces. The largest string body actually prescribed on the assumption that it must and will be made available, is in Schoenberg's *Gurrelieder*.

The numbers quoted are: 20, 20, 16, 16 plus an unspecified number of basses, the whole—he says—to be further reinforced. Even London's Royal Festival Hall platform had to be measured carefully to see if it could accommodate such a vast gathering of players, without any 'further reinforcement'.

Although it is by no means regular practice to give exact figures of string strength, there are a surprising number of scores where they are in fact noted, especially when the composer is anxious that the force should not be too large for good balance in accompaniment. Thus most of Strauss's operas and orchestral Lieder are carefully adjusted and detailed with this in mind. Again Stravinsky stipulated no more than 8, 8, 6, 4, 4 *players* (not desks) for his Violin Concerto, whilst a similarly small group is insisted upon by Poulenc as the background to a solo harpsichord in his *Concert Champêtre*.

Where the composer leaves no instructions the conductor's responsibility and artistry begin. For example, Honegger gives no indication in his *Pastorale d'Eté*, but only a hopelessly insensitive conductor would play this delicate fragment with a body of strings worthy of Strauss's *Ein Heldenleben*. Programmes can easily come to mind that could benefit from variations of string strength for every item.

And fashion can also play a part: classical works—Haydn, Mozart, Schubert, etc.—which would once have been played by the full orchestra under every international conductor from Bülow to Toscanini will generally be played today with greatly reduced strings in the pursuit of stylistic purity. Yet Mozart once wrote to his father in delighted excitement on hearing one of his symphonies played by forty violins with the rest of the orchestra augmented in proportion. Performances of the Beethoven symphonies have recently been given, on grounds of authenticity, with an orchestra of reduced strings such as Beethoven himself would have found at his disposal. But it is far from sure that what he actually had was, at the same time, what he really would have liked, in particular for the odd-numbered, more considerable symphonies. In any case opinions will always differ over the right artistic demands of every work whilst also bearing in mind the acoustics of each individual hall.

One has also to remember that the fewer the players the higher the standards of execution must be. Far less than a full symphony orchestra can a chamber orchestra afford to have passengers in the rank-and-file strings, since any imperfection is the more immediately perceived. Moreover, personal responsibility is likely to be greater since as soon as the lines divide each may be played by only two or even a single solo player.

The fewer the number of players on any one line the harder it is to match the tone quality. Two players—i.e. a single desk—is certainly the hardest of all. Yet composers have been known to choose precisely this effect, such as Liszt in his E♭ Piano Concerto:

Ex. 41

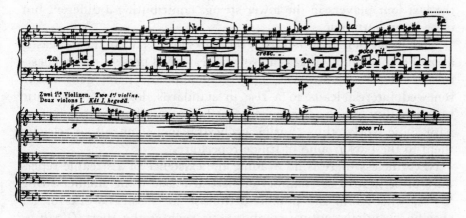

—a device Tchaikovsky echoes with his two cellos in the popular B♭ minor Piano Concerto:

Ex. 42

Players tend to shun this all too revealing problem when they can, and such passages are sometimes wrongly taken by a single musician. But there is certainly no need to court disaster by trying, for instance, to play the *Siegfried Idyll* with two players to each string part, as was once advocated in all seriousness by an eminent critic.

Elgar specified the use of the two players only of each *back* desk for subdued effects in his First Symphony, saying that the object was 'to

get a widely diffused tone, though not prominent: the desks chosen',
he adds significantly, 'should be as far apart as possible'. In this he
was following Strauss's example in *Don Quixote* where the oboe's first
day-dreaming reference to Dulcinea is accompanied by only the back
players from the 1st violins, with magically distant otherworldly
effect. Britten extended this idea of using only back players in the
closing bars of his Passacaglia from *Peter Grimes*, though here the
purpose is to create a mysterious background as the result of each of
the last four players in the lower strings contributing a different but
close-lying harmonic.

Such usage of individuals from the ranks forms part of the increased
area of responsibility that is a growing feature of present-day orchestral life. There is, however, both gain and loss here: gain where
renewed interest leads to a rise in standards, loss where soloistic
responsibility may lead to special fees being laid down in connection
with some works, thus causing orchestral managements to relegate
them to the background of fringe repertoire.

Nevertheless there is no evading the existence of a sizeable repertoire of orchestral or chamber-orchestral music using smaller string
forces, whether in the pursuit of finesse in classical works or for
specific twentieth-century compositions such as the Ibert *Divertissement* or Stravinsky's 'Dumbarton Oaks' Concerto, both of which
require as few as three violins (written as a single line), three violas
and two each of cellos and basses, down to Schoenberg's *Kammersymphonie*, Op. 9, scored for single strings, that is to say, none other than a
solo string quintet.

9 SOLO WORK ON VIOLINS

The timbre of a single string player is so different from the mass
quality of the section that its use in apposition to the string body is
often comparable with the contrasting use of a solo wind instrument.
Members of each of the string family can be found spotlighted in this
way, including the double bass.

Perhaps it is only to be expected that the commonest single string
colour is that of the solo violin, ranging from the briefest of melodic
strands to concertante sections as those in Strauss's *Ein Heldenleben*.
This exploits double-stoppings in two-part counterpoint as well as
complicated chordal passages *à la* Paganini, while similar and other

spectacular techniques are introduced by Rimsky-Korsakov in his *Capriccio Espagnol* and *Scheherazade*. In addition to these, works like Strauss's *Bourgeois Gentilhomme*, Stravinsky's *Apollon Musagète* or *Agon*, and others too numerous to list but no less exacting, are famous for their solos and provide virtuoso shop-windows for which no leader or prospective leader can afford to be unprepared.

An interesting use of the leader's solo timbre occurs in Stravinsky's Violin Concerto where he is given a duet with the actual soloist:

Ex. 43

One of the most striking examples of ensemble playing between a soloist and leaders of the string groups occurs in the slow movement of Tchaikovsky's Piano Concerto No. 2 in G, Op. 44. For much of the length of the movement the solo piano is joined by the leader and first cellist in a piano trio, both string players enjoying short cadenzas. Although violin cadenzas are quite a feature of Tchaikovsky's orchestral music (as, for example, the Theme and Variations from the Suite No. 3, the *Mozartiana* Suite and numerous places in the ballets), this is such an exceptional instance that the leader often stands to perform it, as he has also been known to do in the beautiful extended cantilena in the Benedictus of Beethoven's *Missa Solemnis*.

A solo violin is sometimes required to stand offstage, as in the 'Colloquy' of Hindemith's *Sinfonia Serena*. Here a solo violin in the wings plays in alternation with the leader (a process later repeated on the other side of the platform or stage with violas) after the manner of the 'Deposuit' from the Magnificat of Monteverdi's *Vespers* of 1610.

It could be argued that such effects belong more in the province of the theatre than the concert platform, but there is a legitimate element of theatricality in symphonic music that should not be underestimated, least of all derided, although taste and changing fashion will always be factors to be taken into account. It is by no means unknown for the whole string group to play standing (excluding the cellos, who do not even attempt to stand for National Anthems). Sir Henry Wood used to play the Third Brandenburg Concerto with the massed body of strings standing, and just as this practice was coming to be regarded as mere exhibitionism, quite out of keeping with the classicism of Baroque music, along came the Adolf Busch Chamber Players. Busch offered a style of Bach presentation, thought in the 1930s to be particularly purist, in which all the players (admittedly far fewer than Wood used) performed standing.

Rachmaninov conceived the solo part in his instrumental version of the *Vocalise* for the entire 1st violin section playing standing in front of the accompanying orchestra, while Toscanini made a justly famous gramophone record in which all the 1st violins stood to play in unison, and at breakneck speed, Paganini's notorious *Perpetuum Mobile*. Today such experiments have fallen into abeyance, although some chamber orchestras such as the Lucerne Strings do still specialize in standing formations; and except of course for individual solo work, string players try (not always successfully) to oppose attempts by contemporary composers who direct them to stand up whilst playing.

Sometimes passages may be written with more than one independent obbligato violin part. In cases of a second solo this may fall either to no. 2 1st violin, as in Mahler's Ninth Symphony:

Ex. 44

or to the leader of the 2nd violins. Handel's Concerti Grossi, Op. 6, present a curious situation, since the solo 2nd violin plays sometimes in unison with the tutti 1sts, and sometimes with the tutti 2nds, in addition to his duo-concertante work with the solo 1st player.

In the event such obbligati are normally played by the leader of the 2nd violins, who also automatically takes on the 2nd violin solo in such works as Elgar's *Introduction and Allegro* or Stravinsky's *Pulcinella*. On the other hand the no. 2 1st violin does also come into his own whenever the composer simply asks for a pair of solo players, as in Strauss's *Ariadne auf Naxos,* or the solo sextet that opens the same composer's opera *Capriccio*.

Sometimes, however, the composer fails to make it clear whom he was writing for, and the conductor and players become dependent upon a decision made by the publishers when preparing the orchestral material. To refer once again to the Prelude to *Lohengrin*, for instance, Wagner merely specified '4 einzelne Violinen' in the opening bars, which could most conveniently all come from the firsts. But in the parts the lines are actually given to the first desks each of 1sts and 2nds and so perforce it is always performed.

Confusingly enough, the word 'solo' is not infrequently added in the parts and/or score to indicate that the *line* is of solo importance, not that it is to be rendered by a single player. This (which naturally occurs also in solo passages for the lower strings) may need a decision from the conductor – aided perhaps by whether or not the word 'tutti' appears by way of contradiction later.

Further confusion in this respect may, moreover, be created in concertos where the words 'solo' and 'tutti' are repeatedly added to the orchestral parts, not, however, with reference to these at all but purely to identify sections in which the concerto soloist is or is not playing, and hence as a guide to where the tone should be moderated in the interests of accompaniment.

10 SOLO WORK ON LOWER STRINGS

Viola solos are comparatively rare, but when they occur they are greatly treasured for their mellow and gracious quality. In consequence, brilliant viola solos are the exception, though the snatch in Liszt's E♭ Piano Concerto gives a good example:

Ex. 45

Executed with the appropriate *élan* this never fails to receive a shuffle of feet in approbation from the rest of the orchestra. Sibelius's *En Saga* also provides a characterful instance; but the more usual kinds, for which the viola is especially well suited, are such solos as Elgar writes for it in 'Dorabella' from the 'Enigma' Variations or in the serenade section from the Concert Overture *In The South*.

Of extensive solos for the principal viola, those in Hugo Wolf's *Italian Serenade*, Aennchen's Aria from Weber's *Der Freischütz*, Bantock's *Fifine at the Fair*, and particularly Strauss's *Don Quixote* stand out for the rewarding opportunities they offer. The latter contains possibly the most famous orchestral viola obbligato of all, with its splendid characterization of Sancho Panza. In practice, however, the viola is generally made too subordinate to the solo cello who, taking the role of the Don himself for much—though by no means all—of the work, is in many performances placed in the hands of an international solo artist. On the contrary, the score reveals that it was not planned in concerto form, but with the solo passages for both instruments set equally for the first players of their respective orchestral sections.

The principal cellist, with his evocative utterance and spectacular compass, naturally comes in for a very considerable share of extended solos. Haydn's Symphony No. 95, Beethoven's *Prometheus* ballet music, Brahms's B♭ Piano Concerto, Reger's *Ballett Suite*, or the Overture to Rossini's *William Tell* provide only a handful out of the wide range of works with important virtuoso solos for the 1st cello. The Rossini Overture also shows the use of an ensemble of further solo cellos together with the leader of the section, a device also exploited by Wagner in the First Act of *Die Walküre* as well as by Puccini in *Tosca*.

Few and far between as double bass solos may be, examples can certainly be found in the repertoire, both fragmentary and of quite substantial length and importance. The grotesque duet for solo bass and trombone in Stravinsky's *Pulcinella* is unquestionably one of the most notorious challenges to the leader of the bass section, but pride of place must surely go to the muted solo bass of Mahler's First Symphony with its parody of 'Frère Jacques':

Ex. 46

11   THE BOW AND ITS STANDARD USAGE

If in a score no specific mark stands against a string line, it is assumed that the instrument is played in the conventional manner with the hair of the bow (It., *arco*; Fr., *archet*; Ger., *Bogen*, abbreviated to *Bog.*). The hair is generally from white horses' tails, but these are becoming alarmingly scarce and plastic hair has been tried, though with indifferent success. Bass bows have for some time been occasionally fitted with black hair and this is beginning to appear in the other strings as well. To make the bow grip the strings, a player will rub the hair with resin.

Bows all conform essentially to the same basic design although varying progressively in length and width from the long slender bow of the violins to the very short high bows of the basses, which unlike the others' are sometimes held from beneath in what is called Dragonetti style.

The English word used in orchestral scores for the end of the bow held by the hand is generally 'heel'. The Germans use *Frosch* which corresponds to the English 'frog', but this and yet another English term 'nut' are rarely used by composers as they refer more specifically to the mechanism located at that end to adjust the tightening or loosening of the hair. Copland writes 'at the frog' in *Appalachian Spring*, however. The French and Italians share the word *Talon* (= *talone*). The opposite end is universally known as the point (Fr., *pointe;* It., *punto*; as well as Ger., *Spitze*—the direct translation), although 'at the end of the bow' (fr., *au bout de l'archet*) does also appear.

These terms appear in scores where composers have definite ideas on styles of playing to be adopted that specifically need to be executed at one or other end of the bow. For example, heavy, rough or emphatic passages will be played at the lower half nearest to the heel:

Ex. 47   Stravinsky, *Firebird Suite*, 1919

while the upper half of the bow—i.e. towards the point—is asked for in pursuit of lightness, delicacy or extreme softness:

Ex. 48

This gives an example of imaginative use of playing at the point from Prokofiev's *Classical Symphony* whilst many instances of the soft shimmer it can also provide may be found, in particular amongst French composers. Debussy, in his opera *Pelléas et Mélisande,* also uses the effect in *forte* playing for its gentler colouring, but this is rare.

Since up- and down-bow may provide differences of character in phrasing, and the amount of bow length used will materially affect style and technique, a skilful bowing plan becomes a salient facet of orchestral work. Not even in warm melodic passages is the full length of the bow necessarily required, and one of the points to be borne in mind is how important it is for the players to arrive at the right part of the bow for what lies ahead.

This organizational work, with its appropriate knowledge and skill, falls properly to the leader's responsibility and through him to the leaders of the other string sections. But both composers and conductors, in order to clarify their requirements and save rehearsal time, sometimes mark scores and parts with bowing indications using the standard symbols ⊓ and ∨ to represent down and up-bow respectively (down-bow travelling from heel to point). These signs may be found inverted for use below the notes, viz: ⊔ and ∧ , but are then often confusing and are even mistaken for other similar symbols.

Conductors in particular, however, know all too well that many of the marks representing hours of painstaking labour and thought may come to be changed on the spur of the moment by the players during rehearsal as the result of individual views, style and specialist understanding of the orchestra's leader. Nevertheless it is usually found that the time and trouble has been well spent; leaders and players automatically use as far as possible the bowings they see in front of them, and the hired parts that constitute the vast majority of materials in compulsory circulation these days are mostly full of maddeningly contradictory markings and *ad hoc* decisions that are the legacy of countless previous hirings. A few changes and disagreements with consistent and well-thought out marks can always be solved quickly by a good section, often without even stopping the rehearsal.

Orchestral parts are also to be found printed with bowing added by editors employed (anonymously) for the purpose by publishers. Such parts may as a result conflict with the scores of the self-same editions (Dukas' *La Péri* is a dreadful example, but the Leipzig Breitkopf & Härtel edition of the standard repertoire is very often culpable in this respect) and may, moreover, be out of step with each other. Here again preliminary work by the conductor prevents loss of time and frayed tempers. Conductors and soloists sometimes purchase their own material for this purpose as do many of the great orchestras.

Unfortunately, owing to the greatly increased cost of printing, publishers are becoming more and more reluctant to produce orchestral material for sale and prefer to keep a limited number of sets for hire only, so it is becoming ever less possible to build such a library of orchestral materials except in the case of the more popular classical and non-copyright works.

Composers are apt to be discouraged from putting bowing marks into their scores after experiencing the often ruthless treatment of players who all too readily regard the results as inconvenient or ill-informed. Yet there remains much to be said for composers' marks as an indication of style and manner, even if they have to be adapted or, at worst, discarded.

The special down-bow sign four bars after Fig. 7 in the 'Menuet' of Ravel's *Tombeau de Couperin* Suite:

Ex. 49

is not just a casual suggestion but an integral part of the composition. For it indicates a gap in sound before the accented *f* third beat, since the phrasing is so planned that the previous two-note phrase already comes on a down-bow, so that the players' bows have to be lifted for a re-attack if the printed sign is to be observed.

Elgar, himself a violinist, very often shows his intentions by means of bowing marks that should thus not be lightly ignored; similarly Britten's marks need to be respected and so with many others. But some composers relied on the views of violinist colleagues or the leaders of orchestras they had occasion to conduct. Stravinsky's bowings, for example, reflect the idiosyncratic style of Samuel Dushkin, which is often greatly at odds with present-day techniques. Mahler worked closely in conjunction with Arnold Rosé, for so many years the revered leader of the Vienna Philharmonic Orchestra. Yet Mahler's bowings are of the utmost importance as an integral expression of his thought even when they are so eccentric as to be virtually impractical without at least some small modifications:

Ex. 50   Mahler, Symphony No. 9

A serious hazard in the adoption of one out of the many possible bowings for a given passage is the fact that the slur serves both for bowing and phrasing, and it is not always clear which the composer had in mind. (In English we make the distinction between a 'tie', when the same sign binds two identical notes, and the 'slur' which indicates the smooth execution of two or more notes of different pitch. In other languages there is no such clear demarcation in the use of, for example, the German *Bindung*, the French *ligature*, etc.). In his attempts to notate his intentions precisely Mahler even uses slurs simultaneously with indications of bow changes, as if to emphasize that the two are not incompatible. The following example from the Andante of the Sixth Symphony shows a particularly fine distinction of this. Compare the different bowings of the 2nd violins and violas:

Ex. 51

Admittedly the inordinately long slurs at the beginning of Wagner's *Siegfried Idyll* are palpably phrasing and give no possible indication of bowing:

Ex. 52

But a passage like the following from Borodin's First Symphony is far from obvious:

Ex. 53

Technically this could in fact be played in a single bow, and, on the evidence of the writing elsewhere in the work, it may possibly have been intended thus. But in practice the players find it too cramped, and some suitable point needs to be found for a bow change where the break in phrasing will least disturb the smooth line of Borodin's intention. Sometimes this is done by making different players of the section change bow on different notes, but such free bowing is the exception rather than the rule and normally string players aim for unanimity of bowing both within their section and the sections with each other, as far as instrumental character and the orchestration of the music will allow.

Free bowing can nevertheless claim to be a device in its own right; for so interested did Leopold Stokowski become in the effects of encouraging every player to change bow wherever it suited his personal style best that the ever-pioneering conductor took the ultimate step of specifically training the strings of his Philadelphia Symphony Orchestra in this way during his long term of office, thereby obtaining an unprecedented quality of warmth and richness. In doing so he deliberately turned a blind eye to the attendant drop in unity and discipline of phrasing, as well as to untidiness of appearance on the platform. This latter consideration, though naturally not in itself a primary matter (one recalls the band sergeant who put his trombone section in the guard-room because their slides were not moving uniformly in and out), is all the same at least partially linked with unanimity of ensemble.

Stokowski encountered considerable opposition when he tried to enforce this total freedom of individual bowing on players of other orchestras not accustomed to such unusual methods. Yet if it may not be a satisfactory general principle, its occasional adoption can still benefit many places in the orchestral repertoire, as for example in long melodic passages where the illusion would be created of one single unbroken phrase.

But there are other reasons for changing the bow in the middle of a phrase than that of an overlong slur. Mention has already been made (p. 73) of the need to exercise forethought in order to arrive at the right part of the bow for some particular technique or effect: for a quick change to pizzicato (needing to be at the heel); for a passage to be played off the string (near the middle of the bow); for a sudden drop to pianissimo (best effected at the point) and so on.

An orchestral player normally follows certain principles when bowing a passage. A crescendo is more naturally phrased on an up-bow, a feminine ending on a down. Hence Tchaikovsky's printed bowing in the first movement of his *Symphonie Pathétique* appears perversely back to front:

Ex. 54

Although this particular example is habitually changed in practice it does in fact work extremely well if observed precisely as printed. Indeed it must be emphasized that the more obvious principles concerning the coordination of technique and phrasing should not be too inflexibly applied, and furthermore a rigid observance of them may very well betray a mere rudimentary knowledge of orchestral string playing. For a good section can, if circumstances dictate, use the reverse of the more natural bowing and still achieve the desired effect.

The device of using successive bow strokes in the same direction, instead of the normal up- and down-bow alternation, may be introduced for a variety of expressive reasons, whether languid:

Ex. 55 Ravel, *Rapsodie Espagnole*

or emphatic:

Ex. 56 Bruckner, Symphony No. 4

A succession of up-bows will by contrast generally be light or spiky:

Ex. 57 Nielsen, Symphony No. 5

Extra up- or down-bows may, however, be taken purely as a matter of convenience in order to come the right way round, especially if the passage is otherwise being taken as it comes:

Ex. 58   Haydn, 'Oxford' Symphony No. 92

or:

Ex. 59

The clearest way to indicate this is by two adjacent down- or up-bow symbols as shown in Ex. 58 and 59. But all too often a slur is used, either by the printers, together with dots (which are easily over-looked), viz: or in haste by the players during rehearsal, a practice leading all too often to an incorrect legato.

12 OTHER COLOURISTIC USES OF THE BOW

The normal method of drawing the bow, with the hair passing across the strings at a point midway between the bridge and the end of the fingerboard, allows the full quality of the instrument to speak and this can be taken for granted if no contrary instruction appears in the score and part. It may, however, need to be specified as a cancellation after some other style of playing has been called for. It will then be termed *in modo ordinario* or *naturale* (abbreviated to *nat.* or even plain *arco*). The German word used is generally *gewöhnlich*, the French, *jeu ordinaire*.

Of other styles, the two most common are with the bow crossing the strings near to the bridge and, conversely, as far as possible away from the bridge—i.e. over the fingerboard. The most common term for the former is the Italian *sul ponticello*, that is to say on the bridge, although taken literally this would produce virtually no sound at all. Yet most of the translations are close to this meaning: *am Steg* (Ger.) or *sur le chevalet* (Fr.); although the French do also say *près du chevalet*. In any case it is as well that the terms constitute exaggeration because in the event it is extraordinarily difficult to make orchestral string players observe the instruction properly. This is further aggravated by the fact that it is to some extent possible to emulate the thin squeaky sound it produces in other ways without struggling to play in what is rather an uncomfortable and unnatural position.

Ponticello is mostly prescribed for the eerie, sometimes magical, atmosphere it conjures up in pianissimo:

Ex. 60   Wagner, *Tristan und Isolde*

Yet, although rarely used in a forte or fortissimo it can be excitingly effective. Britten instructs the violas and 1st violins to play towards the bridge (*poco sul ponticello*) in order to get a nasal, strident quality in the opening fanfares of *Les Illuminations*, one of the many brilliantly imaginative strokes with which this work abounds. Falla also introduces a ferocious use of *ponticello* in his ballet *The Three-cornered Hat*:

Ex. 61

Here, apart from its exotic timbre, the edgy texture has the additional advantage of transparency, allowing the woodwind to penetrate the otherwise dense mass of string sound. For, unless the strings really play as near to the bridge as possible, the wind simply cannot be heard.

Legato melodic passages can also be played *sul ponticello*, though the result is generally rather unreliable, as the upper frequencies tend to predominate over the actual note intended. Debussy uses this effect in *Ibéria*:

Ex. 62

The opposite style of playing with the bow over the fingerboard (It., *sul tasto*; Fr., *sur la touche*; Ger., *am Griffbrett*) has the effect of taking the richness out of the tone—to whiten it, one might say; and it is therefore similar to *flautato* playing (see p. 87).
Sul tasto is in the nature of things an ethereal style and is therefore largely used in soft slower-moving passage-work:

Ex. 63   Ravel, *Rapsodie Espagnole*

Mahler, on the other hand, introduces it as a change of colour, even in the middle of a phrase:

Ex. 64   Mahler, Symphony No. 5

It is, at the same time, a splendid method of lightening the string texture for accompaniment purposes and can therefore be adopted even when not actually prescribed by the composer.

To be strictly accurate, it is possible to draw the bow across the strings on the side of the bridge towards the tail-piece. But this is, of course, contrary to the design of the instrument and is thus not so much a musical as a sonic effect. An unearthly squeaky noise is produced without any controllable note since this part of the string is unaffected by the fingers of the left hand on the fingerboard. The notes are, in fact, totally unpredictable and will vary from one instrument to another; nor will the lower strings necessarily give off a deeper sound than the higher. Nevertheless, it has been used orchestrally as a stochastic effect, for instance, by Blomdahl in the opening bars of his *I Speglarnas Sal*, while Alban Berg in the *Altenberg Lieder*, Op. 4, specifies that the bow should be drawn over the very holes of the tail-piece itself. This is, it may be observed, only practicable at all for instruments without adjusters and produces at best only a faint, indefinite noise. All these unconventional effects are usually notated by means of crosses for the noteheads, viz: together with explanatory footnotes.

Another unconventional, though less rare device, is that of drawing the bow across the strings in the correct place *vis-à-vis* the bridge and fingerboard but with the bow turned upside-down so that the strings are stroked with the wood instead of the hair. This produces very little tone (so is generally derided by the players) but has, nevertheless, a real colouristic validity. A famous early instance of this is in the third movement of Mahler's First Symphony. At the time of composition the idea was so revolutionary that Mahler inserted a footnote into the score saying 'Kein Irrthum! Mit dem Holz zu streichen'. ('No mistake! Stroke with the wood.')

83

Since then the effect has been fairly frequently adopted, especially by the neo-Viennese school, where it is to be found even in lyrical passages:

Ex. 65   Berg, *3 Stücke aus der Lyrischen Suite*

But *col legno* if not qualified as shown in the above example assumes a vertical use of the back of the bow, the wood being struck against the strings with percussive effect. This technique, common as it is and widely encountered in the repertoire, is much dreaded by players as it does no good at all to the varnish on their bows which, like the instruments themselves, are often valuable. It is true that if executed honestly with only the wood of the bow very little actual note is heard; and when composers write important note formations *col legno*, for example:

Ex. 66   Berlioz, *Symphonie Fantastique*

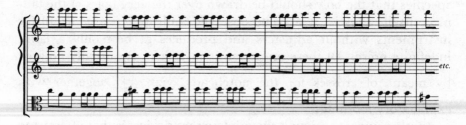

the players will generally cheat to a greater or lesser extent by turning the bows sideways so that a little of the hair also comes into play.

The above example, the dance of the skeletons from the Witches' Sabbath, is often thought to be one of the earliest instances of *col legno*, but it is on the contrary to be found already in the Turkish music of Mozart's A major Violin Concerto, K. 219. Here it appears in the cellos and basses under the unusual instruction 'coll'arco al roverscio', an expression which so foxed the editors of the Breitkopf *Gesamtausgabe* (including such eminent names as Brahms, Joachim,

Köchel, Nottebohm and Reinecke) that they bowdlerized it into the nonsensical 'col arco cresc.' with the result that only recently, and still not invariably, has the magnificent idea come back into its own. Ravel, interestingly enough, elected to adopt Mozart's phraseology in his *Rapsodie Espagnole* where part of the string group is instructed to play 'avec le dos de l'archet'.

If the players cheat to too great an extent, only the hair being brought into contact with the strings, this contributes a quite different device, which is found constantly in Rossini under the term *battuto* and is much beloved of Mahler who termed it *mit dem Bogen geschlagen* ('struck with the bow'). A vivid instance of this can also be found in the second of Webern's *6 Orchesterstücke*, Op. 6.

None of these vertical techniques produce much sheer volume especially in view of the cautious attitude of the musicians, but all are to be found prescribed in dynamics up to *ff* and in fact under pressure a considerable percussive sound can be obtained, so that the following from Mahler's Seventh Symphony is by no means unrealistic:

Ex. 67

Apart from the hair or the wooden back of the bow, other parts have in recent years come to be designated as striking implements, such as the nut itself, with which one can tap the belly of the instrument, the tailpiece, etc., including even the back, again instructions not especially beloved of players (see also p. 100 below).

Conversely the bows can be used, whether with the wood or hair, to strike some object other than the instrument, such as the music desks in Rossini's Overture *Il Signor Bruschino*. In modern scores this is humourlessly indicated by cross-headed notes and 'col legno', although Rossini's intention is well-known. Of course it never occurred to him that the solid wooden desks of his day would give place to metal objects ranging from heavy dull-sounding contraptions to flimsy collapsible affairs quite unsuitable for his splendid idea. Worst of all, he unwittingly initiated the concept of using stringed instruments and their adjuncts as instruments of percussion. Schoenberg even conceived the idea of using cello and bass bows in conjunction with cymbals (see p. 390 below).

13 VARIATIONS OF BOWING STYLE

Should normal bowing require special mention it is referred to as *détaché*, or (Ger.) *Strich für Strich* (lit. 'stroke for stroke'), as Mahler puts in his scores. Sibelius, in the opening of the Third Symphony, writes 'mit liegendem Bogen' (lit. 'with lying bow', i.e. on the string) which actually underlines the firm nature of *détaché* playing in order to avoid the semi-staccato, half-off the string technique players tend to adopt in such passages.

None of these terms concern themselves with the length of bow used. In most cases this is simply not specified, in the assumption that it will vary according to the character and intensity of the music. However, if for example longer strokes are wanted, the notes may be capped with lines: (𝄐𝄐𝄐𝄐) , although this symbol can have the side-effect of separating the notes. For the line is also a form of stress,[1] even if less sharp than the different accent symbols > or ∧ . It was to prevent this kind of ambiguity that Mahler characteristically added verbal injunctions to convey his wishes, such as *lang gestrichen* ('with long strokes'), *viel Bogenwechsel* ('many changes of bow') or the passionate exhortation *'Ton!!'*.

The use of long bows may seem to suggest the automatic result of stronger dynamics, but on the contrary they have a particular validity in soft passage-work where, if executed with a light bow-arm, they give a lucidity to the texture, often called for in practice, though admittedly less usually found in printed scores. One outstanding example requiring light quick strokes in an otherwise lyrical passage occurs in Stravinsky's *Pulcinella*:

Ex. 68

This style is sometimes known as *portato* (not to be confused with *portamento*, see p. 131 below) and is related to *louré*, a technique

---

[1] This is part of a larger area of confusion that is discussed in the closing section, see pp. 502–6.

particularly appropriate for classical works on account of its origin in
viol playing. A characteristic of *louré* is the use of the whole length of
the bow drawn smoothly and swiftly across the strings as for
accompaniment figures in Bach:

Ex. 69   Bach, Brandenburg Concerto No. 3

This in turn is not dissimilar to the technique employed for
flautato—as the name suggests, a style producing a pale flute-like
quality—also achieved by a fast travelling and pressure-less use of the
bow:

Ex. 70   Sibelius, Symphony No. 6

(It is sometimes thought that *flautato* and *sul tasto* are identical and indeed Gardner Read's *Thesaurus of Orchestral Devices*[1] wrongly cites as an example of *sul tasto* Tippett's use of *flautato* in his First Symphony.)

Turning to short bowing styles, the first that arises is *marcato*. Instead of the notes merging easily into one another the sound of each is stopped by the bow before the next is initiated. The edge of the new note is then sharply attacked, irrespective of whether it is taken with a change of bow direction or not. Marcato may be indicated in scores by means of symbols (whether lines, accents or arrow-heads denoting increasing degrees of intensity) or alternatively by the word itself. The French *marqué* can also be found as well as the German *betont*.

In accordance with the above definition a true marcato should always be interpreted on the string, although the situation is often confused through the appearance, in scores, of dots—properly the sign for staccato—over the notes. The same is true of the extreme form of marcato, i.e. *martellato* (= hammered; the French use the same word, *martelé*, but neither English nor German have a standard word of their own).

Conversely a true staccato should be taken off the string though players will by no means always regard the use of dots over the notes as an automatic instruction to this effect: for marcato or *martellato* at the upper half of the bow is often a safer method for difficult ensemble passage-work.

As with marcato, there are different degrees of staccato, ranging from what players understand as 'half-off' (normally used in stronger rapid passages where a *détaché* style might become too heavy in quality) to the *spiccato*. Outside English-speaking countries *spiccato* is the general term used for all off-the-string playing regardless of degree, but we tend to use it for the harder, more brittle form of staccato referred to abroad as *spiccato assai*.

Spiccato, or indeed any off-the-string staccato, is most usually played near the middle of the bow or towards the heel where it becomes increasingly easy to control. As the heel is approached, however, it also becomes gruffer, more aggressive. For light playing therefore, composers sometimes ask for a staccato to be taken at the point in circumstances where the character of the music nevertheless requires that it be played off the string. Difficult as this is for control and ensemble, it can and should be done in Roussel's *Le Festin de l'Araignée*:

---

[1] Putnam, London, 1953, p. 399.

Ex. 71

and Sibelius's *Valse Triste:*

Ex. 72

But Berlioz's similar instruction for the notorious passage near the beginning of the *Symphonie Fantastique* is never observed, being impractical; a *spiccato* in the middle of the bow gives the desired light but pointed effect:

Ex. 73

There is, in fact, little guidance to be found in most scores to indicate whether a passage is to be played on or off the string, and most players will either make their own ad hoc decisions or discuss the matter with the conductor. An instance involving a succession of alternative styles of bowing may be found in Wagner's Prelude to *Die Meistersinger*:

Ex. 74

leading, in due course, to:

In these excerpts, ⌐x⌐ is perhaps obviously rendered *détaché*, ⌐y⌐ *martellato*, while ⌐z⌐ will be taken *spiccato* off the string. But it is clear that Wagner's actual instructions are not free from the possibility of different interpretations in this respect.

Particularly vexing are cases where the string parts have been edited with redundant or even incorrect phrase-marks and bowings. Dukas' *La Péri* is an outstanding instance of this, but the standard Breitkopf parts of the classics are to an enormous extent the product of late nineteenth-century string professors whose added bowings and phrase-marks are based on long out-of-date methods of over-all marcato playing at the point in lieu of a true staccato, since off the string techniques were at the time considered undesirable as well as largely unfeasible for orchestral work. To correct these marks is no simple matter, since the removal of a line or dot may all too easily lead the players to go to the opposite extreme instead of back into neutral, as it were. (It must be added, however, that many works are now being reprinted by the Wiesbaden branch of Breitkopf and Härtel in which the old bowings, fingerings and other editorial marks have been removed.)

Shorter and lighter even than the spiccato is *saltato* (or *saltando*) (Fr., *sautillé*; Ger., *Springbogen*) in which the bow is bounced near the middle, more vertically than laterally, and necessarily with some speed which in turn becomes an integral part of the effect:

Ex. 75   Borodin, *Polovtsian Dances*

This can be executed up or down-bow, and on one string or across the strings as in Sibelius's *En Saga*:

Ex. 76

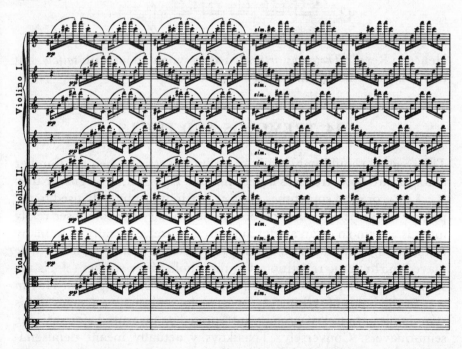

The word *ricochet* is also used for this technique, though more by players than by composers on the printed page. *Ricochet* moreover, is sometimes loosely applied to the extension of *saltato* known as *jeté*, as in Stravinsky's 'Dance of the Firebird':

Ex. 77

The length of the bow is here made to travel across the string in a succession of bouncing down-bows. There is no specific translation in any other language of this French term and German composers, for example, merely draw (as for *saltato*) upon *Springbogen*, as for example Mahler in *Das Lied von der Erde*:

Ex. 78

Hence in Read's *Thesaurus, jeté* is listed as synonymous with *saltato*, but this is again a misleading over-simplification.

14 TREMOLOS AND TRILLS

The tremolo should only really come into question when the number of to-and-fro bow strokes is indeterminate. However, the signs for this: ≢ , ≢ , ⸗ , or even sometimes only ⌐ , are indiscriminately used to the point where it is all too often debatable whether the composer really intends a tremolo or an actual measured figure, especially as in many instances the tempo is slow enough for the exact number of notes to be played in rhythmic repetition. On the whole, three strokes (♪̄) is the standard notation, but this itself can lead to misreadings. For Haydn was in the habit of writing ♪ for tremolo, and many passages in his symphonies are today wrongly interpreted as measured slow-moving semi-quavers. Conversely, Tchaikovsky actually meant demisemi-quavers when he used three strokes and added a fourth when he wanted tremolo.

Sometimes the clue to what might seem an unlikely interpretation is given by the printing out in full of a first specimen group, thus:

Ex. 79

as in the slow movement of Dvořák's D minor Symphony, Op. 70, or Siegfried's Funeral Music from Wagner's *Götterdämmerung*. Very occasionally composers do add 'trem.' but there seems to be no such word indication in use at all for 'non trem.' or 'measured' in the countless borderline cases where either of two essentially different effects is equally possible. For in the absence of any obvious choice players tend automatically to take it all too readily for granted that they should play tremolo.

A hazard of melodic lines to which tremolo is added, whether fast or slow, measured or unmeasured, is that the notation does not allow for phrasing, since the slur serves equally for phrasing and bowing whereas in a tremolo a bowed slur would be a contradiction. Thus in a passage such as the following from Brahms's *Academic Festival Overture*:

Ex. 80

it is only from the woodwind slurs that the correct phrasing and accentuation can be discerned. Poulenc, in his *Sinfonietta*, actually writes:

Ex. 81

but it does cause perplexity amongst players who perhaps reasonably though unimaginatively protest that the slur as marked is unplayable. Yet Poulenc's method has much to commend it. For ties are equally obscured by double-stroke or tremolo notation, so that there is no way for the players to know whether phrase notes should be re-stressed or continued in syncopation. Schumann's perhaps overuse of semi-tremolo is often rendered unnecessarily tedious owing to the unclear appearance of passages such as:

Ex. 82   Schumann, Overture *Manfred*

Tremolos can be played not merely through the repetition of a single note but across two, as in Schumann's Cello Concerto:

Ex. 83

The point here is the absence of slurs in the 2nd violins and violas, for otherwise this passage would correspond with the legato tremolo discussed on p. 95. Indeed these parts are sometimes wrongly taken legato since this effect is rare, although Kodály uses it in his *Summer Evening* (bars 208–18).

Duparc, in his orchestration of the song *L'Invitation au Voyage*, calls for a *trémolo ondulé*. This device was certainly known in the seventeenth and eighteenth centuries and was exploited orchestrally by, for example, Gluck in his opera *Alceste*. Forsyth,[1] in a section of his book on orchestration called 'The Obsolete Undulating Tremolo', describes the action as 'a series of pressures exerted by the fingers of the right hand on the bow during the course of a long legato bow-stroke. The fingers alternately exert and relax the pressure as the bow proceeds on its course'.

[1] Cecil Forsyth, *Orchestration*, Macmillan, London, 1914 (second edition 1935), p. 350.

Today few string players have so much as heard of the technique, and opinions in orchestras tend to be confused over not merely the method of execution but even what effect could possibly be intended.

The legato tremolo is notated like the 2nd violins and violas in Ex. 83 though with slurs whenever the notes are more than a tone apart, whether they are measured or unmeasured. When they are a tone or a semitone apart they are only written in this way if they are to be measured, since otherwise the effect simply corresponds with a trill and is indicated by the sign *tr* or *tr*⁓. Where the trill persists for several bars the *tr* may be found repeated in each bar, viz:

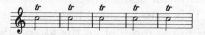

as also in the case of repetitions of the same note for notational reasons in a long bar, as in the slow movement of Beethoven's Pastoral Symphony:

Ex. 84

Such cases should certainly not always be taken to mean that the trill is to be restarted at each new *tr*. As with the use of the tremolo strokes, composers are often unclear in this respect. The clearer notation is the use of a long continuous wavy line or by the use of ties, far more commonly found with the trill than the tremolo.

Composers are also by no means always clear about whether they intend a semitone or a whole-tone trill, though in the absence of any specific indication—such as a tiny accidental above the *tr* sign—the note consistent with the prevailing harmony is normally taken. If a *downward* trill is intended (i.e. trilling with the lower note) a little note-head is conventionally added in brackets after the main trilling note, as is also the case when in the midst of normal trills the shake temporarily extends to notes wider than the interval of a second.

A matter for decision, which of course applies as much to the wind as to the strings, is whether a trill should start with the main or the alternating note. In the bulk of the romantic or more modern repertoire, it is usually taken that the trill is to be started with the printed note, but in seventeenth- and eighteenth-century music it is very often started with the upper note. Here again as so often it becomes a question for artistic judgement on each occasion, like the handling of the trill's end—whether or not with a turn (Ger., *Nachschlag*). This too is by no means standardized and even in Beethoven (in Ex. 84, for instance), uncertainty may exist with differences between scores and parts.

15 PLUCKED AND OTHER NON-BOWED STYLES

When the term *arco* (or *Bog.* etc.) actually appears in the text it assumes a contradiction of some other method of execution in the preceding passage. This may be some less usual style of handling the bow such as *col legno* but is more often the alternative to plucking the strings directly with the fingers. This is always designated by the Italian *pizzicato* (abbreviated to *pizz.*) since strangely enough no equivalents in other languages have ever been introduced (other than the 'plucked' of the eccentric and highly idiosyncratic scores of Percy Grainger).

If no specific instruction is added the string is normally plucked at the nearest convenient place on the edge of the fingerboard by one or sometimes more fingers of the hand holding the bow. The use of extra fingers is relatively rare but is necessitated in passages of exorbitant speed.

When pizzicato is used in rapid alternation with arco—and especially for a single note—the string can be plucked near the scroll by the left hand. When the composer positively wants this to be done the correct method of notation is a cross sign (+) over each note, but players will often adopt this method as a convenience in quick to-and-fro pizzicato even when not so instructed. This is not always as desirable as it is practical, since a different sound emerges, thinner and more twangy. (Although obviously most usual in the case of open string notes, the left-hand pizz. can also be done with one finger stopping the string while another plucks.)

Properly the + sign specifically indicates a left hand pizz., but in the Funeral March from *Grania and Diarmid* Elgar uses it in a cello passage that cannot possibly be played so:

Ex. 85

Perhaps he meant the players to use the vertical method of plucking, away from—instead of across—the instrument: this is mentioned on p. 98 below.

In their pursuit of special effects, contemporary composers sometimes instruct the strings to be plucked with the fingernail, or plucked very near to the bridge, the latter sounding very dry (not at all squeaky like arco *ponticello*) and having little carrying power. Players frequently resist such effects which they regard as unrealistic and frustrating as well as causing disagreeable resin on the finger.

It was once thought integral to pizzicato technique that the thumb should be anchored to the corner of the fingerboard and the index finger used. Nowadays this is no longer invariable practice and the resultant hand freedom allows the middle or other fingers to be used and at different points along the fingerboard. Although there is a consequent loss of firmness and power there is also greater flexibility and variation of colour. Certainly the anchoring thumb has to be dispensed with when two or more strings are plucked with flamboyant effect as in the last fortissimo chord of Elgar's *Introduction and Allegro*.

Chords can also be plucked in rhythmic succession in a to-and-fro motion often appropriately designated *alla chittarra* or *quasi guitara*. This is variously notated, whether by the use of up- and down-bow symbols as in Rimsky-Korsakov:

Ex. 86   Rimsky-Korsakov, *Capriccio Espagnol*

(quasi Guitara, non divisi)

or with arrows:

Ex. 87   Bartók, *Music for Strings, Percussion and Celesta*

The latter is used when a single symbol is required to indicate a chord to be plucked in the opposite to the normal direction, i.e. if it is to sound downwards from the top towards the bottom note. If no instruction appears it is assumed that the direction will be from bottom to top, but this is not always necessarily correct. In the popular 'Marcia' from Dag Wiren's Serenade, the cellos' open string three-note chords could well be thought to be more striking when spread downwards towards the resonant bottom C. Alternatively such cello chords in particular may be plucked in neither the one nor the other direction but vertically *upwards*, away from the instrument using a finger for each string, as suggested in connection with Ex. 85 and here in the coda to the Scherzo from Dag Wiren's work:

Ex. 88

Here again, however, the score gives no guidance over the manner of execution which thus becomes a nice stylistic point.

Sibelius, in the Pastorale from his incidental music to *Pelleas and Melisande*, writes, for the violas, a repeated succession of A♭'s directed to be played 'Mit dem Daumen, Instrument frei', an unusual instruction for a similar manner of execution.

In Roussel's *Suite en Fa* the unusual instruction 'glissez' is used to denote the throwing of the plucking fingers right across the instrument; while Debussy in *La Mer* wrote strong dramatic pizzicato notes for the violins with the injunction 'à vide' (i.e., open string).

If executed over-enthusiastically such vehemence can cause the string to rebound off the fingerboard giving a snapping crack. Mahler was the first actually to prescribe this exaggerated over-plucking in the Scherzo of his Seventh Symphony, while Bartók exploited it to such an extent that he found it convenient to invent a special symbol ↺ :

Ex. 89   Bartók, Violin Concerto (1938)

As this quotation shows, Bartók uses it even in quite soft dynamics, though the string cannot actually be made to snap at less than forte.

An additional aspect of pizzicato is that the sound can be encouraged (by the manner of plucking, by vibrato, etc.) to ring on for long enough to allow the pitch to be altered so as to produce a glissando (upwards or downwards). This is never very loud, especially compared with the initial plucking from which it derives, but it has enough reality to have entered the range of string effects to be found in orchestral literature. One example of the problems associated with this device is that notation often fails to make it clear, as in the passage quoted below, whether the second of each pair of notes is replucked or not. In this instance it is generally considered (rightly or wrongly) that Bartók did mean glissandi even though he did not say so, and that these second notes merely indicate the extent of the plucked sounds' rise or fall:

Ex. 90   Bartók, Concerto for Orchestra

Composers have sometimes written extremely rapid pizzicato passages that are often bowdlerized to arco on the assumption that they are impracticable. But in a large string section the impression may be adequately and effectively conveyed even though each individual is achieving something less than total accuracy, so that the abandoning of a composer's intention is unnecessary and highly regrettable.

Free massed plucking has even been used deliberately as in the 'thrumming' pizzicato tremolo of the *Cadenza accompagnata* in the last movement of Elgar's Violin Concerto, which is directed in a footnote to be executed 'with the soft part of three or four fingers across the strings'.

When a pizzicato continues over an extended period and there are sufficient rests before and after the adjacent arco passages, the players often lay down their bows. This is naturally the custom in movements played wholly pizzicato like the 'Divertissement' from Delibes's *Sylvia* or the Scherzo from Tchaikovsky's Fourth Symphony; it is also obligatory for such devices as in the fête scene from Debussy's *Ibéria* where the violins are instructed to be held under the arm.

Pizzicato is sometimes specially marked muted, but players rarely obey this as they regard the effect as indistinguishable, except for its inferior quality, from an unmuted pizzicato played truly pianissimo.

Whilst pizzicato is of course the most usual alternative to arco, it is certainly not the only one. For example, the strings may be slapped with the whole hand, as in dance-band double bass technique. (Indeed in the context of popular music the bass is rarely played with the bow.) Some contemporary composers, especially American, have experimented with this for the whole string group, though with only moderate success.

Beyond this, most other non-bowed methods are viewed by the players with hostility since they generally consist of various ways of knocking the sides, tailpiece, belly or even the back of the instruments with the knuckles, the nut of the bow, or other more or less lethal objects. Since instruments range in value to astronomic heights (the best Italian examples are worth tens of thousands of pounds) it is understandable that resentment is aroused amongst orchestral players who in avant-garde works may find themselves called upon to handle their precious instruments in a fashion whose purpose would be served equally well if executed upon a nicely made cigar box. Moreover a resistance is aroused against the acceptance of new artistic ethics, however valid in the broad sense, but which set at nought the long years of dedicated training that string players must undergo to acquire the skills necessary to produce beautiful and brilliant sounds in keeping with the design and purposes of their treasured instruments.

16 THE STRINGS AND TUNING

Controversy continues to rage over the actual strings themselves. Once made of sheep or cat-gut, the highest violin string—the E (also designated in scores by the Roman numeral I)—was the first to be replaced by steel wire. The G string—the lowest, and designated IV—came, on the other hand, to be covered spirally with metal, to be followed by the D and A. Today steel strings can be found for all four, although the resultant sacrifice in tonal warmth and beauty is widely deplored by string players.

Steel strings, however, have a factor of convenience that cannot be ignored, such as the screw fitted to the tail-piece, which is only usable in connection with these; this enables fine adjustments of tuning to be carried out quickly and easily even in the course of rehearsal or performance. This can also be of particular advantage in cases where the composer prescribes changes of tuning during a work or movement.

In principle all the orchestral stringed instruments tune in perfect fifths except the basses. The advantage of such a tuning is the particular characteristic ring of a bare fifth, which is, after all, acoustically the truest consonance after the octave. It is usual, therefore, to see the players sounding together two adjacent strings while listening until the unmistakable fifths ring is produced by the adjustment of either or both. The violins work in either direction from A, which by virtue of its central position, both generally in the orchestra and in the range of the violin, is the standard pitch-note announced for tuning purposes.

In the case of the violas and cellos, however, A is the highest string, the open strings of the groups being tuned thus:

Ex. 91

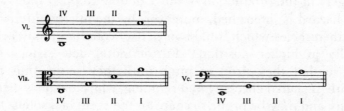

There was a time when, the double bass having been reduced to no more than a 3-stringed instrument, it too was tuned in fifths, viz:

Ex. 92

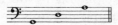

(Hence Elgar's *ossia* in *The Dream of Gerontius* making allowance for basses with no lower open A string—see Fig. 80 in Part II of that work.) But with the disappearance of this inadequate and short-lived variety, the standard double bass tuning established itself not in fifths but in fourths:

Ex. 93

IV   III   II   I

(Ex. 92 and 93 sounding an octave lower.)

Such a tuning naturally lacks the ring of fifths but at the depth of pitch involved this would in any case be very hard to recognize, and in actual fact bass players tune entirely differently from their other string colleagues by means of matching high-sounding harmonics.

The double bass tuning in fourths arises fundamentally from the much wider stretch between the notes of this instrument, intervals of a fourth and upwards being beyond the range of the normal hand. But the fourth lacks the distinctive character of the fifth which, forming part of the basic string ethos, has become an orchestral device of itself, much exploited by composers. Bare fifths can be found everywhere in the repertoire, whether actually playable on open strings or not, yet where the double-stopped fifth is not producible on open strings it is the hardest of all to play in tune. For a single finger placed directly across the strings carries a margin of error far in excess of any use of two fingers in the production of other double-stopped intervals.

This hazard is intensified, moreover, by the innate unreliability of strings themselves which, unless in perfect condition, may be untrue especially in higher positions. Furthermore, new strings tend to stretch so that they drop in pitch until they settle, thus needing constantly repeated checking and retuning, whilst old ones deteriorate in quality and may be prone to snap. In the event of a soloist, or even a leader, suffering a broken string during a concert, a quick substitution of instruments may take place so that a back desk player can scuttle off the platform to replace the broken string, while the players with most responsibility carry on as little disturbed as possible by the emergency. But often enough the unfortunate musician will have to carry on as best he may by playing as much of the part as he can on other strings in unfamiliar and ungainly positions.

Strings are also greatly subject to atmospheric conditions of temperature or humidity. It is generally believed that as hall and instruments warm up the wind will rise in pitch while the strings will drop. In actual practice, however, the strings rise as well, though for a variety of reasons including the psychological fact that players tend to keep adjusting their intonation in an upward direction.

Composers sometimes instruct the strings to adopt unconventional tunings. (This is always an unpopular requirement and is strenuously resisted by players as—with some justice—they say it throws out all the fingerings and that changes in string tension can upset the instrument.) Such re-tunings, known as *scordatura*, have a long and venerable history and may be applied to all four strings, though in this case it usually concerns only a single player, i.e. a soloist or the leader. A well-known solo instance is in Mozart's *Sinfonia Concertante*, K. 364, where the viola is tuned up a semitone and written as a transposing instrument in D. A notorious example for the leader of the orchestra is Mahler's Fourth Symphony (Ex. 1 on p. 30 above): in this case the player has to bring on to the platform a second retuned instrument which he keeps by his side for quick change-over during the Scherzo.

Instances of all sorts of retunings can be found in the repertoire for special purposes or effects such as the fiddling skeleton in Saint-Saëns' *Danse Macabre*, whose E string tuned down to E♭ forms so amusingly grisly a feature of the score.

In fact by far the commonest *scordatura* is for a single string to be retuned and this is the primary requirement in the case of the tutti. Such a change may be required in order to obtain an otherwise non-existent natural harmonic as in Stravinsky's *Firebird*:[1]

Ex. 94

But it is most often a matter of lowering the bottom string so as to extend the range. Hindemith, for instance, instructs the 2nd violins to tune their G strings to F♯ in the slow movement of his *Symphonic Dances*. Here he uses a very unconventional notation; as the only note to be played after retuning is the open string he writes it as a G and adds a footnote to explain that it is to sound F♯. But the more usual and simpler expedient is to keep to conventional notation and simply to use the extended range as Bax does in his First Symphony where his 2nd violins actually tune down to F♮ and his violas to C♭.

---

[1] But see footnote on p. 132.

Similarly the cellos have to tune right down to bottom B♭ in Strauss's *Panathenäenzug* for left hand piano and orchestra.

Strauss, in particular, was so prone to use instruments below their normal range that he came less and less to bother about writing into the score where and when it needs to be done. In *Don Quixote* he does in fact specify where the viola should tune to low B for the famous Sancho Panza solo, but already in *Salome* the violins find themselves confronted with passages such as the following, entirely without warning:

Ex. 95

The story goes that during a rehearsal the players expostulated, only to receive from Strauss the curt retort, 'Well, what did you expect me to write, a G?'.

In point of fact Strauss did not always expect the players to tune down for such instances which abound in his works right up to the end of his long life, as for example in *Metamorphosen*. For there was always in this most professional of composers considerable method in his apparent madness. In his more patient moments he would explain that if the player *thought* the unobtainable note strongly enough and tried hard to look as if he *was* playing it, the audience would never know it was missing.

Where a composer positively intends that the players should tune down he normally allows time with rests for this to be done. But one grotesque yet valid effect must be allowed for, in which the players change the tuning whilst actually playing the string concerned. Haydn characteristically used this joke-effect in his Symphony No. 60, 'Il Distratto':

Ex. 96

∗) The violins tune up from F to G.

17 PROBLEMS OF DOUBLE BASS TUNING

Of all the strings who suffer repeated demands for retuning it is the basses who carry the heaviest burden. Notes below E are frequently to be found in Bach, and Mozart too seems to take the low notes for granted, though opinions differ over the extent to which they were actually played. Cherubini, in *Medée*, composed in 1797, wrote down to low C in circumstances that are unequivocal since the basses are given an individual line—that is to say not merely in unison with the cellos—and he was followed by Beethoven who commonly used the low notes for important bass passages. No doubt players were already then adept as they are today at taking it upon themselves to transpose up an octave either whole passages or even isolated notes in the middle of a phrase in order to obviate the nuisance and hazards of tuning down, should instruments of the necessary range not be available. The great edition of the classical repertoire, Breitkopf & Härtel, actually went so far as to doctor their published bass parts so that no note below E appears at all, the opening bars of Schubert's Unfinished Symphony, for instance, being given thus:

Ex. 97

though the score, like the manuscript, clearly shows the low notes for the basses on a separate stave. Incidentally, Forsyth[1] discusses this very passage, but having had access only to an incorrect Peters score his arguments are as mistaken as his facts.

Composers of the romantic and later eras generally assume the existence of at least some basses in every orchestra capable of producing the low notes down to C. These instruments are actually a sub-species carrying a fifth string originally tuned not in fourths like the other strings but specifically to C:

Ex. 98

---

[1] *Orchestration*, p. 438.

Even Walter Piston[1], writing in the mid-1950s, states that this is the tuning of the 5-string bass but the truth is that these days players find it more practical to preserve uniformity of technique by tuning the extra bottom string to B. Many players, however, insist that the bigger 5-stringer is clumsier as well as less resonant than the conventional 4-string bass and for this reason a compromise can often be seen in the form of a finger-board extension fitted to the neck of the 4-string instrument. This always has the lowest string tuned to C and thus, lacking the open E as well as the overall tuning in fourths, is at best no more than a half measure.

It remains, however, virtually unknown for a large bass section to be entirely made up of 5-string or extended instruments and many composers, such as Mahler, prescribe special low-lying notes or phrases to be played only by those having the extra range, and include insistent instructions that they are not to be played at the upper octave by the other members of the section. Indeed, even today, the 5-string bass has by no means become the universal standard instrument one might have expected, and has failed to render the 4-stringer obsolete as this in its turn once did to the 3-stringer. On the contrary, there are orchestras everywhere to be found that do not possess a single bass capable of playing below E without retuning, and the struggle continues unabated when conductors may try to insist upon the low notes in, for example, Britten's *Serenade* (E♭) or Strauss's *Die Liebe der Danae* (D), to quote only two amongst the myriad scores in which the bottom double bass notes are quite isolated and are thus particularly indispensible.

Nor is it to be supposed that composers have been satisfied with C as the ultimate fundamental tone. Reger, for instance, specifically instructs his 5-string basses to tune the C down to B in his *Hiller Variations*, while the even more demanding Richard Strauss (*Panathenäenzug*) writes as low as B♭. Strauss interestingly adds the old term 'Violone' below the normal *Kontrabass* in this connection, since Baroque scores clearly reflect the fact, now established, that many of these old instruments were tuned like the viola da gamba with the bottom D string tuned down to C or even further as required. (See, for instance, the *violone di ripieno* part of Bach's Second Brandenburg Concerto.)

In some countries players have actually agitated for extra payment

---

[1] *Orchestration*, Gollancz, London, 1955, p. 100.

in return for producing notes below E, though without establishing any lasting custom. The effect of the problem has, however, been to mislead a number of present-day composers, either in response to over-cautious treatises on instrumentation or as a result of bitter experience, into accepting E as the lowest note of the double bass, themselves transposing any potentially lower notes up the octave. In so doing they are thus showing in their very scores the *faute de mieux* situation, to which they might certainly have to be resigned in some circumstances, instead of the musical effect, line or sounds they would really require given willing players and a scrupulous conductor.

Perhaps a case could still be made for Berlioz's *octobass*, wistfully dreamed up in his ideal orchestra and once actually built. Unfortunately, practice proved theory to be at fault and the mighty instrument was abandoned. Could it ever have been played—and this itself is doubtful in the extreme—its sound would have been woefully inadequate. Even the tone of the double bass continues to give surprise, so contrasted is its usually thin wheezy voice, when heard in isolation in any but the bottom register, with its noble and impressive appearance.

18 STRINGS' COMPASS IN THE UPPER REGISTER

It is not easy to fix the upper extent of the strings' compass. In the first place every string of each instrument has a high register of its own, and the strained sounds of high notes on the lower strings of violins and violas (though less so of cellos and basses) are widely exploited for expressive purposes by composers for moments of intensity in preference to the same notes obtained more easily on a higher string. The method of notation used is by designating the string required, whether by name—*sul G, auf der G Saite, sur le sol,* etc.—or by number, the enumeration being ordered from the highest downwards as shown on p. 101 above.

The highest string is thus 'I' or, for the violins, 'sul E', although Chabrier in his *Gwendoline* Overture adds the French term 'chanterelle' to the 1st violin part (though it does not appear in the score) to indicate the use of the E string.

Composers rarely write notes for the lower strings higher than a tenth above the open string (though Britten writes up to

107

on the violins' G strings in his *Prince of the Pagodas*) but on the uppermost the players can be regularly required to continue up into positively stratospheric regions. Opinions differ amongst the various pedagogues as to what is in fact the highest note obtainable on the violin, but the following passage from Strauss's *Also sprach Zarathustra* is one of the highest actually written:

Ex. 99

Theoretically the violas might be assumed to command an identical register a fifth lower, but in practice composers mostly avoid using their extreme upper notes even when the violins are playing at the very top; this is because the extra size of the viola puts these notes out of reach for most players and in any case this is not their purpose in

life. Strauss in *Heldenleben* does admittedly write up to ⟨music⟩ which

A♭ would still only correspond with a top E♭ on the violins, being just under two octaves above the open string. And even so it comes as part of a long tutti played entirely in unison with all the violins and much of the wind and is therefore in no way hazardous.

Where the cellos are concerned composers are once again more adventurous. Elgar, in the first movement of his A♭ Symphony takes

the cellos as high as ⟨musical notation⟩ which is relatively a good deal higher

still above the open string than the violins in the *Zarathustra* quotation, Ex. 99.

Conversely, basses have once again a more limited range, with as much as an octave less at their disposal. These are, however, like the violas, occasionally extended through the use of harmonics (see p. 120 below).

It can be argued that the intonation of the very highest notes can never be really secure when played by a large string section, but they have been most effectively used, especially when supported either by a doubling piccolo or with other violins playing in unison at the lower octave. But it remains a challenge and conductors have even exploited the virtuosity of their violin sections through the mass playing of passages never intended for unison playing (such as the Adagio of Mozart's Divertimento No. 15 in B♭, K. 287, a favourite show-piece of Toscanini, Beecham, Karajan, etc.), however much contemporary opinion may decry the practice as unstylish:

Ex. 100

The highest clef to be used orchestrally is the commonest G-treble

clef:[1] ⟨musical notation⟩ and the violins have no need to know any other clef at all.

Viola players use the C-alto clef: ⟨musical notation⟩ for all normal range passages

but have to be at their ease with the treble clef for the upper register.

Cellists need to be versed in no less than three clefs, the bass (F): ⟨musical notation⟩

the tenor (another C clef): ⟨musical notation⟩ for higher passage-work as well as the

treble clef for high parts. Where this latter is concerned there is sometimes uncertainty due to a few late-romantic composers retaining

---

[1] Other G clefs were once in use: see Ex. 138 on p. 141.

the old cello notation whereby passages in the treble clef were written an octave higher than they sound. The following passage from Bruckner's Third Symphony, for example, looks far more ferocious than it really is (though the need to transpose does in fact continue to give anxiety to many a cello section):

Ex. 101

Dvořák was in the habit of writing the treble clef for cellos in this way until later in life when he had second thoughts. The *ppp* held D at the end of the slow movement of the New World Symphony is clearly written at actual pitch and in the Overture *Carneval* the same passage is written twice, first in the old notation and then immediately after in the new:

Ex. 102

In the musical context there is no question but that the passages should sound identically and it would seem that it was at just this time that Dvořák began to think of changing his method. Mahler, too, a traditionalist at heart, used the old notation in the Fourth Symphony but changed to the new in the original version of No. 5, though rightly considering it necessary to explain himself with one of his characteristic footnotes:

Ex. 103

While this notation is still widely found in standard editions of classical chamber music, in the orchestral repertoire many of the parts have been rearranged so as to avoid the treble clef (generally in favour of the tenor clef) or sometimes transposed to read at pitch.

This octave transposition of cello treble clef notation is to some extent analogous to that of horns in the bass clef (see p. 218) although it has not survived to the same degree, nor is it similarly defended by the players themselves who on the contrary find it misleading.

Basses also need to be at home in the same three clefs although understandably the upper clefs are relatively rarely used. As with the cellos there is a confusion with respect to the treble clef although it is not the same. There is no direct parallel with the cello old and new notations but some mystery surrounds such solos as the 'Obbligato Kontrabass' in Mozart's concert aria 'Per Questa Bella Mano,' K. 612. This notorious piece appears at first sight to be obviously in a similarly transposed notation and indeed is always heard today with the treble clef passages sounding two octaves lower than written (instead of the normal single octave bass transposition). Moreover the Breitkopf printed part is rewritten so altered, even though it has meant actually distorting Mozart's line in the following passage:

Ex. 104

where the last arpeggio is twisted so as to cover a span of one less octave in the interests of sheer possibility. It is hard to imagine how it would have been played in Mozart's time.

Normally, however, the treble clef as used for basses is treated simply as a continuation of the bass (or tenor) clef except in the case of harmonics which are normally notated at concert pitch (see p. 120 below). The whole question of harmonics is nevertheless so complicated in the matter of their constitution and notation alike that it is best tackled without delay and with respect to all the strings.

19 HARMONICS

In all of the foregoing, the only methods considered by which players obtain differences of pitch have been either by tuning with the pegs (or adjusters), or by pressing the string with the finger over the fingerboard, thus altering in the first place the tension, in the second the length, of the vibrating part of the string.

When, however, the finger touches the string lightly at certain clearly defined places along its length, the vibrations are split up and different notes, of a white purity, are obtained. The French and Germans call these sounds *Flageolet* (abbr. *Flag.*), since they are indeed flute-, or rather recorder-like (flageolet being another name for the recorder); but the English term, following the Italian *armonico*, remains 'harmonic'.

The scientific explanation of exactly what harmonics exist on each string and the different ways in which each possible one may be found is extremely complicated and confusing. (There is an extensive account of this in Forsyth on pp. 328-334). But what is really required for practical purposes is the simplest *exposé* of the notes which result from the finger touching a string at each valid point, followed by some discussion on the numerous ways composers have tackled the problem of notation.

First, for purposes of reference, the harmonic series which is the scientific basis of all music (whether for strings or wind) is here laid out in terms of the G string of the violin or viola:

Ex. 105

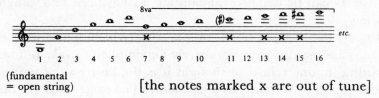

(fundamental
= open string)   [the notes marked x are out of tune]

Theoretically these are obtained by touching the string half-way, two-thirds-way, three-quarters-way, etc. up its length, but in practice by nos. 5 or 6 of the series the finger has approached so near to the bridge that these harmonics become rapidly more and more unfeasible. Nevertheless it so happens that by touching the string lightly in the same way at various other points between nos. 1 and 2 some of these harmonics also result in an irregular order, viz:

(a) a minor 3rd above the open string sounds 2 octaves and a 5th above (= no. 6)
(b) a major 3rd above the open string sounds 2 octaves and a 3rd above (= no. 5)
(c) a 4th above the open string sounds 2 octaves above (= no. 4)
(d) a 5th above the open string sounds 1 octave and a 5th above (= no. 3)
(e) a minor 6th above the open string DOES NOT EXIST (N.B.)!
(f) a major sixth above the open string sounds 2 octaves and a 3rd above (= no. 5)
(g) an octave above the open string sounds 1 octave above (= no. 2)

Set out diagrammatically this will appear (always, by way of example, only in relation to the G string):

Ex. 106

Here *x* represents the open string—i.e. no. 1 of the harmonic series given in Ex. 105—while *g* is in fact no. 2 of that same series. For this reason in both Ⅰ and Ⅱ of Ex. 106 they are notated with the usual round notes with an 'o' placed over the top, for it is general practice to write in this way both open strings and such natural harmonics from Ex. 105 as can be reached (amounting, as has been said, only to the first few).

But all these notes of ⫪ in Ex. 106 (which sound as they are written) are notated thus not merely for simplicity's sake but because according to one school of thought it is the best way of writing any note required to be taken as a harmonic. The executants are then left to work out which way they may prefer to find the notes on their instruments. It is with this method in mind that Forsyth somewhat rashly wrote that 'the notation of harmonics is simplicity itself'. That it is the very opposite even a superficial exploration of the repertoire will disclose.

This is, however, clearly the least confusing method for the score reader as also for the inexperienced composer, although it carries with it the danger of writing impracticable or unrealistic harmonics without perceiving the implications. Certainly it is to be found in orchestral literature to an appreciable extent, though mostly to designate what are perhaps misleadingly known as 'natural harmonics' but are actually Nos. 2–4 of Ex. 105 when they are to be taken at their correct position on the string:

Ex. 107   Rimsky-Korsakov, *Capriccio Espagnol*

In ⫪ of Ex. 106, on the other hand, notes 'a' to 'f' are given with diamond heads, the diamond indicating not the pitch of the note as it sounds but the place on the string where it is to be touched by the finger. This notation has the advantage of simplicity to the player though it requires rapid deciphering by the score reader or conductor before he will know what sounds to expect from a passage such as the following from Ravel's *Le Tombeau de Couperin*:

Ex. 108

In fact the note 'g' in Ex. 106 ⌐I⌐ can also be notated as ♯♪ since this is where the finger is placed in any case, and is thus often written so by composers who are in the habit of using diamonds for harmonics generally.

It is clear that notes 'b' and 'f' in Ex. 106 ⌐I⌐ provide alternative methods of obtaining the same note. This is only one example of the many notes that may be taken as a harmonic in more than one position, sometimes even with a choice of string (as shown by the scrupulous instructions in Ex. 108). Hence this method may also not always be the best, since the players may prefer to find the note a different way from that prescribed, in view of the particular characteristics of their instruments.

Harmonic 'c' provides the basis for what are known as 'artificial harmonics.' For, since the interval of a fourth can be stretched on any of the instruments other than the double bass, the string can be firmly stopped with the first finger (or thumb in the case of the cello) at any point along its length, while the little finger lightly touches the fourth above. This will provide a whole new series of harmonics which are usually notated in double fashion, the lower note representing the stopping finger (or thumb) and the diamond shaped note above indicating the lightly touching little finger:

Ex. 109

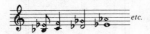

As always when diamond notation is used in this way the sound is not given, which is here two octaves above the lower note. Ex. 109 has been devised to illustrate how in this diamond notation only the lower heads indicate the note-values; as can also be seen in Ex. 108, the diamonds are never filled in for the purposes of the shorter note values (crotchet, quaver, etc.).

This same harmonic 'c', where it is used in relation to the open string (exactly as shown in Ex. 106, in fact,) is sometimes notated in yet another way, especially by Ravel, viz: ♯(*sounding*) Hence the violas in the last bar of 'Petit Poucet' from the Suite *Ma mère l'Oye* are given the following harmonic: ♯ though this is identical with

115

as it would appear in the notation illustrated in Ex. 106.

Of course the existence of alternative notations leads to confusion over which string is meant, what note, which octave, etc. In Milhaud's *Suite Symphonique No 2*, 'Protée', he writes which, somewhat equivocal in context, actually sounds . The following passage from Ravel's *Shéhérazade* never fails to stop a rehearsal for many minutes while players and conductor sort out what sounds are intended:

Ex. 110

The fact that the orchestral parts differ from the score no doubt arose in the first place from attempts by the publishers to interpret Ravel's intentions but scarcely helps the performers. In the event the harmonics in the 2nd violins sound an octave higher than the diamonds, the minim diamonds in both viola parts sound the same despite the different notations(!) i.e. the E two octaves higher, and those in the cello sound one octave, and the basses two octaves, higher.

The situation is further confused by the possibilities arising from the existence of an alternative notation also for harmonic 'd', from Ex. 106. For it is possible, in the case of the violin, to create a further series of 'artificial' harmonics by extending the little finger a *fifth* above the stopping first finger, thereby producing sounds an octave and a fifth

above the lower stopped note, e.g.

Ravel's way of writing so many of his harmonics purely in diamond heads sometimes leads to undiscovered errors or misprints since the relationship between written and sounding notes is by no means obvious and not every conductor or score reader has the knowledge or experience to work out the exact sound effect of a complicated page of divided strings full of diamonds. Yet without this detailed study, a mix-up as occurs in the bass line from *Le Tombeau de Couperin* remains an enigma causing heated controversy and waste of valuable rehearsal time:

Ex. 111

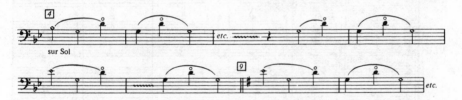

For there is no harmonic (i.e. the minor sixth—see 'e' in Ex.106) and this can therefore only be a misprint, presumably for as at Fig. 4 in the score, though arising because of the perfectly possible E's at Fig. 9. Yet the truth is obscured because of the unreliability on many basses of even those harmonics (in particular 'a', 'b' or 'f') as should exist.

Bartók in his *Dance Suite* mixes up many of the harmonic notations presented simultaneously, including some diamonds in the cellos and basses which unusually indicate the sound and not the position of the finger:

Ex. 112

Because of all these troubles, some composers write all harmonics other than the simplest 'natural' ones by adding the resultant sound at the top of the notes showing the method of execution, viz:

118

Ex. 113   Balakirev, Symphony No. 1

or worse still:

Ex. 114   Schoenberg, *Erwartung*

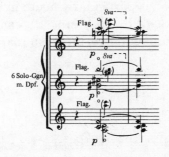

Splendidly self-explanatory and logical at an intellectual level, this actually creates a different and equally perplexing confusion especially for the players who find themselves confronted by a series of complicated patterns that can be most bewildering to the eye in quicker passages:

Ex. 115   Schoenberg, Suite, Op. 29

There is thus no uniformity of notation in harmonics at all. Even so *routiné* a composer as Verdi changed his mind from one work to another. In *Un Ballo in Maschera* he wrote:

119

Ex. 116

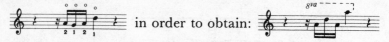

in order to obtain:

whereas in the *Te Deum* the following appears in the violins and violas sounding one octave higher, if the piano reduction is to be believed:

Ex. 117

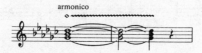

Yet this remains to some extent an open question for I myself possess two recordings, one of which gives the context at pitch, the other sounding two octaves higher.

This octave question is particularly acute in respect of double bass harmonics. Most, though by no means all, composers write these at actual pitch, in contradiction to the customary double bass octave transposition:

Ex. 118   Stravinsky, *Agon*

There are, however, exceptions (Alban Berg, *Wozzeck*; Berkeley, Symphony No. 1, etc.) and bass players will often require the conductor to decide upon the octave to be sounded, the choice being dictated many a time on *ad hoc* grounds of musical logic.

20 OPEN STRINGS AND THEIR NOTATION

Since the open string is the 1st harmonic—i.e. *x* in Ex. 106—it is perhaps only logical that it should be represented by the same notation as that of 'natural harmonics', that is to say, by means of an 'o' over the note. Yet this is less to be found in printed scores than might be expected because composers rarely seem to have strong views on whether a note that is one of the open strings should or should not be taken in this way.

For the string sounding at its full length has quite a different quality—much more ringing, even twangy, and less easily modified by vibrato, though this is not wholly impossible. Hence an open string in the course of a phrase will stand out in a way now generally thought undesirable, except for reasons of technical convenience, as opposed to the days when Breitkopf & Härtel prepared their sets of orchestral materials, adding countless 'o's for open strings as well as harmonics in the classical repertoire in accordance with the interpretation of the time.[1]

Nevertheless, composers well versed in string technique do sometimes specifically prescribe open strings along with the 'flageolet' quality of harmonics as a particular expressionistic effect, both in arco and pizz. Sibelius features pizzicato open strings in alternation with stopped notes in the second movement of his Fifth Symphony, although his notation with tails up and down instead of the conventional 'o' leaves inconclusive, to the point of self-contradiction, which notes are open and which stopped:

Ex. 119

Open strings are sometimes used to simulate an air of primitive simplicity as in this solo from Bantock's *Fifine at the Fair*:

Ex. 120

---

[1] See also p. 90.

But composers do also use them for actual simplicity. Both Vaughan Williams's Concerto Grosso and Britten's *Noye's Fludde*, for example, include parts written entirely on open strings for the benefit of amateurs or young players who need have no left hand technique.

21 THE USE AND APPLICATION OF MUTES

Muting is not merely a device for softening the tone but a colour in its own right. The commonest indication for this and its contradiction is the Italian *con/senza sordini* (abbr. *sord.*), for which the French is *avec/sans sourdines* and the German, *mit/ohne Dämpfer*. The Germans also use *gedämpft* (muted) which is clear enough, but the additional terms *Dämpfer auf* (on) and *Dämpfer ab* (off) are liable to be confused. *Dämpfer weg* is also sometimes found and corresponds with another and graphic Italian indication, *via sordini*—i.e. 'away with mutes'. Tchaikovsky, in his *Symphonie Pathétique,* also gives the rare 'alzate sordini' (literally lift, or raise, the mutes). Advance warning is sometimes given of an approaching muted passage. This is generally obvious, e.g. *préparez les sourdines*, but the German *Dämpfer vorbereiten* should perhaps be documented. Players often put into their copies the symbols ⊓⊓ and ⊔⊔ for mutes on and off, but these are never found in print.

Composers sometimes neglect to indicate where the mutes should come off and *ad hoc* decisions have constantly to be made (see, for example, the last movement of Rachmaninov's Third Piano Concerto, or the 'Scène d'amour' from Berlioz's *Romeo and Juliet*). One result of this is that there are places in the repertoire where it is believed that the unmuting directions have been omitted whereas the composer may well have intended the veiled tone to persist even in loud passages. One of the best known instances of this dilemma is the central climactic passage of the Largo of Dvořák's New World Symphony, which is often played unmuted although there is no such indication, whereas on the contrary the sound of muted strings makes a remarkable and beautiful effect.

The contrast of sheer colour between muted and unmuted strings whether soft or loud has been variously exploited. Reger was particularly fond of dividing his string group for this purpose as in his *Variations and Fugue on a Theme of Mozart*. The opening of 'Der geigende

Eremite' from his *Four Tone Poems after Böcklin* quoted on p. 58 above shows something of this range of possibilities.

Although naturally all the strings can equally be muted, bass mutings are less often scrupulously observed and most basses reckon that conductors hardly ever notice whether mutes are used or not. Nevertheless bass mutes certainly do exist and in the hands of first-class and conscientious players make excellent sense of composers' practice of writing for them. It is perhaps revealing that Mahler elected to write for a muted bass in the 'Frère Jacques' solo from the First Symphony quoted on p. 71 above.

Every conceivable shape and species of mute exists, whether made of wood, metal or plastic. The change of tone from one type or substance to another is, however, very slight and convenience remains the deciding factor.

With the exception of those for basses, mutes are no longer necessarily independent objects placed over the bridge, but may be a sliding contraption that remains permanently on the instrument. This has the clear advantage of speed in application or removal as well as in the matter of storage when not in use. But players consider that there is a noticeable loss of quality in all such modern substitutes even while recognizing their practical value. For composers all too often allow little or no time to put on mutes or to take them off; furthermore there are notorious places in the repertoire where mutes have to be handled at moments of extreme softness or tension:

Ex. 121   Wagner, *Siegfried Idyll*

124

All detachable mutes tend to make little plopping sounds, especially when being removed by a large section, and over-anxiety is a common cause of accidents, with mutes being lost, kicked, or dropped with devastating effect.

Many instances do in fact occur in the repertoire where mutes have to be put on for excessively short periods—even for a single note or chord—and players often simply cheat with a very soft *sul tasto* rather than take risks, and it becomes the conductor's responsibility whether or not to condone such practices. One instance in which he will generally do so is where a movement ends with muted strings but leads *segue* (i.e. without a break) into a new movement to be played unmuted. Rather than lose the dramatic hush and immobility at the all-important moment of transition it is often preferable to allow the players either to remove the mutes early and finish as softly as possible or conversely to unmute only after the new movement has been launched.

All the various devices of string techniques are used and written for in conjunction with mutes—*ponticello, col legno,* harmonics, etc., but in practice the mute merely reduces (if not actually negates) the character of the device. String players thus often try to ignore the muting indication rather than fight against what seems to them unreasonable odds in the pursuit of unrealistic aims.

22 EXTREMES OF TONE: CHORDS AND DOUBLE-STOPPING

The tonal range of the string body is simply enormous. What is particularly remarkable is that a large string orchestra can achieve miracles of pianissimo without even using mutes, which a small body of players would find virtually impossible to emulate. Indeed a chamber group can never really attain that velvety hush so characteristic of the end of nearly every large orchestral work of Delius.

At the other end of the scale, a purely string ensemble, though naturally no match for the full weight of the brass or percussion, can nevertheless command a very considerable body of tone. In order to increase the basic potential, composers commonly make use of the device of double, triple or quadruple-stopping, whether in arco or pizzicato. In scores this is rarely referred to by the English term just cited, the most normal usage being the Italian *non divisi* (the German

correspondingly *nicht get(h)eilt*) or simply a square bracket thus:

But the Germans do also use *Doppelgriff* and the French, *double corde.*

In classical scores or the orchestral parts of standard works, square brackets or verbal indications are on the whole equally rare and it is often a matter of decision for players or conductor whether, or to what extent, chords should be divided in the conflicting interests of tonal weight, panache, dramatic intensity or ensemble, not to mention intonation where the chords lie awkwardly. The most usual way of actually prescribing that a chord should be spread is for the lower notes to be shown with shorter note values indicating that these are to

be released while the upper note is held: . This is, however, less

of an expediency than an effect in its own right, as in bar 21 of the first movement of Beethoven's Fifth Symphony.

On violins and violas it is possible for a three-note or conceivably a

126

four-note chord to be played virtually unspread, although hardly in anything less than a *forte*. Even then a passage like the following from Mozart's Fourth Horn Concerto, K. 495, might very well sound rough and disagreeable:

Ex. 122

With typical thoroughness Forsyth gives an extended list of possible three and four-note chords, but this is of less practical value than it might seem. Where composers write awkward or frankly impossible chords it still gives a better impression of the effect they really want, and players are adept at dividing where necessary. This is generally done by various kinds of overlapping so that the compromise is barely perceptible. The overlap will usually be of two and two in three-note chords, but not in four-note ones which are taken three and three, viz:

Where chords are directed to be spread this is mostly taken to mean from bottom to top and no specific indication is marked. But as has been mentioned in connection with pizzicato, the reverse is of course equally possible and when required is notated either by a vertical arrow to the left of the chord or by spelling out the notes as appoggiaturas:

One of the favourite uses of chords and double-stopping is the combining of stopped and open strings. A device much loved by Mozart is double-stopping on a unison—the open D, for example, sounded simultaneously with the same note stopped on the G string:

Ex. 123   Mozart, Violin Concerto No. 4, K. 218

(Similarly the A is taken on the D and A strings.)

The use of open strings with other notes above produces a splendid resonance, much exploited by, for example, Rimsky-Korsakov:

Ex. 124 Rimsky-Korsakov, *Scheherazade*

Although the fuller harmonic texture that chords supply remains the principal purpose of double-stopping, it can also be introduced for contrapuntal writing. This is, however, so exacting that it is rarely used for a whole section—indeed it is mostly written for a single player as in the famous solo from Strauss's *Ein Heldenleben*:

Ex. 125

Berg, by an ingenious combination of arco and left hand pizzicato contrived a two-part tutti passage for violas in his Violin Concerto, but felt it wise to add an optional indication ('eventuell geteilt' = *divisi* if necessary) condoning the sharing of the lines. This last-minute caution does, however, largely spoil the effect if acted upon:

Ex. 126

23 BROKEN CHORDS, ARPEGGIANDO STYLES, ETC.

The techniques of double-stopping naturally also include those of broken chords, *arpeggiandi*, bowed tremolos or figures across the strings, all of which are to be found copiously exploited in the orchestral repertoire.

Two-note figurations across the strings can be found in classical scores, such as for example, Mozart:

Ex. 127   Mozart, Symphony No. 32, K. 318

In this style of bowing the circulatory movement of the arm makes it convenient for the violins and violas to play the upper string notes with an up-bow whether or not these fall on the beat. Hence a figure such as that in Haydn's 'Military' Symphony, No. 100, which lies the opposite way:

Ex. 128

would also normally be bowed upside-down (i.e. starting on the up-bow). On the cello, however, the whole system is reversed and the upper string is normally taken with the down-bow.

When slurred, this kind of figuration can clearly be considered as a kind of slow melodic tremolo effect. Brahms was particularly fond of this, using it not only in chamber music (see particularly the F major Cello Sonata, Op. 99) but as a tutti effect. It creates a most beautiful shimmering texture in the closing passage of the Third Symphony:

Ex. 129

Brahms also had a penchant for extending the device to the alternation of a single note played legato across two strings, a technique sometimes known by the French term *bariolage*.

Three- and four-note figurations are generally simply broken chords such as abound in the classical literature for the solo stringed instrument. Used orchestrally, however, they become a magical colouristic effect, and one especially beloved by Wagner (see Siegmund's Spring Song from *Die Walküre* or especially the Prelude to *Parsifal*). In these examples it is played fully legato but it can also be effected *saltato* as in the opening pages of Sibelius's *En Saga* (see Ex. 76 above).

Dvořák was also very fond of writing *arpeggiando* passage-work for the strings though often he would produce patterns more suitable for the keyboard, such as the following from *The Golden Spinning Wheel*:

Ex. 130

In contemporary music players are often required to execute rapid and far-flung leaps across the instrument which, though possible perhaps, are hard to achieve with reliable accuracy especially when string-crossing is added to the hazards of rapid left-hand shifts:

Ex. 131   Webern, *Variations,* Op. 30

In these days of chromium-plated purity of style, impeccable cleanliness in shifts of whatever width is considered to be an essential yard-stick of orchestral standard. Yet audible, even quasi-portamento changes of position as well as actual slides between the notes were once a recognized style of orchestral expression. Composers took such *portato* for granted as is shown for example by the performances of his own works conducted by Elgar. This style of playing would therefore not normally be specially indicated, though pronounced slithers or extravagant glissandi wanted for particular effects would be notated by a line drawn between the notes. This would generally be a straight line but in some avant-garde scores wavy lines are substituted to suggest more elaborate smears.

Such *portati* effects might be realized through the deliberate exaggeration of shifts of position, extra ones being taken over and above those actually needed by the normal method of fingering the passage in question. But even greater suggestion of parodied sentiment is made by the use of a single finger sliding up or down the string. Mahler calls specifically for this in, for example, the Fifth Symphony, and even goes so far as to prescribe a smeared shift between two identical notes taken on different strings.

In its more extreme form the portamento turns into an out-and-out glissando (the French use the analogous word *glissez* but the English and Germans have kept the standard Italian). Examples of this can be found extended to cover the entire length of the string or even to continue across the strings, though this requires ingenuity on the part of the players to disguise the inevitable cheating necessary to create the illusion of one gigantic swoop:

Ex. 132   Ravel, *La Valse*

Glissandi present problems of notation, especially when they begin or end in the middle of a bar. In such cases there is no invariable custom and composers differ in their solutions, putting stemless notes in brackets, or bracketed rests, or even noteless stems such as Xenakis in his *Pithoprakta*:

Ex. 133

Although in the score it seems clear enough what is meant, the part can be quite perplexing to the player who loudly protests that there are not enough beats or notes in the bar, etc.

It is rare to find the speed of the slide in a glissando mentioned or indicated in any way. In a quick passage such as the example from Ravel's *La Valse* quoted as Ex. 132 above there is no difficulty and this kind of quick slither in both directions was a favourite colourful device of Ravel's, and was taken over by many subsequent composers. But in slower tempi the speed of the slide may become very much a matter of style or judgement, as also the point in the duration of a longer note when the glissando should begin. Unless the composer specifies to the contrary, as occasionally happens, it is usually assumed that the slide will start only towards the end—i.e. at the up-beat to the end-note—to avoid an ugly, grotesque or at worst comical effect.

In many contemporary works, however, it is precisely the slow glissando that is wanted in the overriding desire to extend the palette of orchestral devices. Many composers are, in this respect, strangely blind to the truth that the effect is so ridiculous and inevitably arouses audience reaction of a most irreverent kind. Any suggestion of this is apt to be rejected indignantly as highly offensive, yet the danger remains and should not be ignored.

Undoubtedly one of the most magical glissando effects is that of harmonics exploited by Stravinsky in *The Firebird*[1] and especially by Britten in *Les Illuminations*:

---

[1] Unfortunately the dazzling effect of this is to some extent spoilt in the 1919 version through one of the myriad misprints of the edition; the instruction at the 2nd bar of Fig. 3, '8va' for the 1st violins who have tuned their E strings down to D, produces an impossibility and should sound *two* octaves higher (cf. the original ballet score). As a result many players ignore the instruction and play on the D string like the 2nd violins.

Ex. 134

This most delicate of effects is produced by gliding the finger gently over the surface of the string with just the least hesitation at the points where the harmonics occur. It can therefore only be done softly although Ravel, who uses it in his *Rapsodie Espagnole,* marks it *mf* and describes it graphically in a footnote: 'Glissez en affleurant la corde . . .' adding '. . . du côté du chevalet', i.e. near the bridge, a most interesting but difficult variant.

The glissando has less often been exploited in staccato since this naturally counteracts the characteristic slither. Nevertheless, Strauss uses a *spiccato* glissando to depict the flowing of gold dust in the ballet *Josephslegende.* His most famous use of the device is, however, for the solo violin in *Till Eulenspiegel,* although this is a borderline case; for the notation is misleading and has more often than not led to a wrong interpretation (see Ex. 135, overleaf).

Here the word 'glissando' describes the effect and not the means of execution. For whereas in a true staccato glissando the players would be left free to play an indeterminate number of notes, in the above passage Strauss prescribed exactly thirty—i.e. falling into five groups of sextuplets so as to correspond with the bottom of the run which he notates as two written-out groups of the new $\frac{6}{8}$ bar.

Ex. 135

The same use of the term can be found in Mahler and also in recent years in the little violin solo at the end of Rawsthorne's *Street Corner Overture*. In all such examples the passages should be actually fingered without true sliding even though the style and rapidity of execution undoubtedly imitates the effect of a glissando.

For, with their ability to play infinite gradations of intonation, the strings can theoretically play intervals finer than the semitone (unlike the wind instruments that are constructed with a view to the twelve-note octave and can only fake smaller gradations by means of artificial adjustment of lip or breath). Composers have during the last decades tried to exploit this string capability, writing either glissandi which stop at points within the semitone, or actually writing quarter-tones, sixth-tones, or other micro-tones. Generally, however, it is accepted that Westerners' ears are not trained to recognize intervals narrower than the semitone, and quarter-tones (by far the commonest of these fine intervals) are usually given to solo players so that the inevitable inaccuracies do not result in poor intonation.

An additional hazard of quarter-tones is the lack of standardized notation, each composer—Bartók, Berg (Violin Concerto), Bloch (Piano Quintet, *Schelomo*), Hába (a specialist in this field with many quarter-tone works to his credit), etc.—inventing his own, every one of which has to be digested and memorized afresh by the executants. Arrows over the notes, sharps with one or three vertical strokes instead of two, reversed flats, accents in place of accidentals—the variants are legion. But micro-tones remain a fringe device and the twelve-note octave continues to form the foundation of our musical system.

24 VIBRATO—AND CONCLUSION

As the portamento was until recently taken for granted, so, since its introduction with the superseding by the violin family of the viols, has the vibrato. This shaking to and fro of the left wrist and hand is the standard method of tone production for all stopped notes and is cultivated by every player in his own way in the pursuit of style and a beautiful quality from his beloved instrument. All forms of legato and sustained playing are subject to vibrato with the exception of harmonics. For the lightly touching finger is less capable of producing a true vibrato and furthermore the narrow places on the string where harmonics can be obtained hardly allow for the fluctuations of pitch on either side of the note which constitute the very nature of vibrato. Indeed vibrato is in a sense the antithesis of the deliberately white, even cold, character of pure harmonics, since its purpose lies in the production of warmth and colourful tone.

Broadly speaking, it is the use and degree of vibrato to which composers are indirectly referring when using such terms as *dolce* (German *zart*, French—though more rarely—*doux*) or *espressivo* (German *ausdrucksvoll*, French *expressif*). Hence when a composer stipulates that a passage be played *senza espress.* (*ohne Ausdruck* etc.) this is often taken to mean 'without vibrato' although this is not necessarily the right interpretation. For when strings really do play absolutely without any vibrato whatsoever a strange bare sound ensues that is quite a special effect in its own right and may or may not represent the composer's intention.

In some contemporary scores, therefore, the specific term *senza vibrato* has come to be used, together with *con* (or *senza*) *vibrato poco a poco* where the warmth of colour is to be added (or withdrawn) gradually (Fricker, Violin Concerto: Goehr, *Little Music for Strings,* etc.).

Moreover, so automatic is the normal use of vibrato that the appearance of the actual word itself generally signifies that more—or perhaps a slower, wider—vibrato is called for than the players would naturally produce. This could be to create a special degree of intensity, or perhaps even for the grotesque, or as a parody:

Ex. 136   Bartók, Suite No. 2, Op. 4

It is to a large extent the combination of many individual vibrati which is the predominant characteristic of the string mass, and which gives it its unique colour, the very colour which identifies the symphony orchestra itself. It is also the one colour of which for some indefinable reason the ear never tires, unlike that of any other group of instruments whether of wind and/or percussion.

The string orchestra can thus be a fully self-contained entity which has indeed a large and splendid repertoire of its own ranging through all periods of musical history from early classical to the contemporary schools. As a result countless string ensembles have come into being and have acquired international reputations without the need for more than the occasionally co-opted wind or timpani players in order to add a particular work for some special concert or programme.

At the same time, although the strings have this clear advantage over the wind, the latter can boast a compensating quality in the carrying power of even quite small groups. This accounts for the specifically outdoor nature of wind ensembles, from the divertimenti and serenades of the Haydn/Mozart era to the entire gamut of military music and brass bands. For string quality disperses hopelessly in the open air and any orchestra or string group depends on some kind of artificial amplification, as the organizers of parks concerts or the creators of open-air auditoriums such as Hollywood Bowl well know.

One outstanding and curious feature of the string timbre is that it cannot be imitated in any way. This is a fact which organ builders and devisers of electronic equipment are reluctant to face since it is contrary to all the theories they most vehemently hold and assert.

Finally the string body is outstandingly flexible and intuitive. Miracles of instinctive and instantaneous response can be achieved by a highly trained string orchestra in which, it should be remembered, most of the members lack that element of individual contribution enjoyed by every wind player. And oddly enough, when groups of wind players take over the string rank-and-file roles, as in the military band, they never achieve any comparable finesse of nuance, whether in interplay to each other in tone and dynamics, to a conductor's freedom of expression or rubato, to variations of style or technique, or even in the matter of the endless give-and-take in accompaniment within the orchestra itself or in concerto and operatic work. And where traditional rhythmic freedom is concerned, such as in the waltzes of Johann Strauss, or the opening of the Scherzo of Dvořák's D Minor Symphony, Op. 70:

Ex. 137

an alert string section can accomplish as one man, and even without rehearsal, subtleties of phrasing which could never be written down or explained and which would require hours of preparation and rehearsal with the soloist-orientated wind groups.

Although, therefore, life as a rank-and-file string player is often berated as soul-destroying in the long run, the corporate string section—made up to some extent though it may be of individuals each aspiring to greater opportunities for self-expression—remains the essential foundation upon which the symphony orchestra firmly rests.

Section II

THE WOODWIND

1 DEFINITIONS

This department comprises all the wind instruments of the orchestra with the exception of the horns and heavy brass. For although today not all the instruments are actually made of wood, they were when the term 'woodwind' first came into general use. However, the term continues to serve even though strictly speaking it has ceased to be accurate, either because wood has to a large extent been superseded by metal—as with flutes—or because newer instruments like saxophones, allied to the section, have been invented which have never been made of wood.

The German equivalent of 'woodwind' corresponds with the English, viz: *Holzbläser* or just *Holz*, while the French and Italians always omit the '-wind', simply saying *les bois* and *i legni* respectively. In English the word 'wind' is used colloquially to mean only the woodwind, but the corresponding words *Bläser, les vents* and *i fiati* on the contrary imply the inclusion of all the brass as well.

It is rare for a work to be written for a symphony orchestra that omits woodwind altogether. Constant Lambert's *Rio Grande* is perhaps the outstanding example, while Hindemith's *Konzertmusik für Streichorchester und Blechbläser* is another well-known instance, although as its title shows it also has no percussion. In general any ensemble qualifying as an orchestra is assumed to carry some woodwind although the section may be quite diminutive.

The woodwind section is constituted of a variety of instruments which normally fall into four main species: flutes, oboes, clarinets and bassoons. Of these all are reed instruments with the notable exception of the flutes, whose sound is produced by the direct application of the mouth blowing across a hole in the head-joint.

Each of these woodwind families has subsidiary members, instruments on which the players may be required to alternate. This demands a degree of agility and adaptability of technique as well as the provision of appropriate aids in the form of furniture designed to make quick changes possible. Flutes, for instance, sometimes can be seen to have a box-like fitment attached to their stands to hold the instrument(s) not in use (for some reason these attachments are rarer than they used to be, and in any case the tiny piccolo can be conveniently kept snugly in the pocket), whereas clarinets and bassoons need more elaborate structures to support the tall and heavy bass members of their species. Composers are not always realistic in allowing sufficient time for the change, which can be quite a cumbersome operation in the case of, for instance, the contrabassoon. In Mahler's 5th Symphony the third clarinettist is instructed to handle no less than five different instruments, often with only three or four bars rest to make the switch. But the ultimate is reached by Janáček who allows no time whatever at certain points in his Rhapsody *Taras Bulba*, so causing the 3rd bassoon, who is directed to double contra, to make *ad hoc* decisions on how to adapt his part by playing some bars on the wrong instrument in order to render the change possible. Players may also choose to make the switch earlier than marked so as to have warmed up the alternate instrument in time for an important solo, a consideration rarely taken into account by composers.

It can be particularly inconsiderate for a composer to require the player to change from the smallest to the largest member of a family (or vice versa), as for example the piccolo and the alto flute, or the little E♭ and the hefty bass clarinet. Such different techniques are involved that players sometimes even refuse to take on such a part alone, insisting that an extra player be engaged.

2 NOMENCLATURE AND SPECIES

FLUTES

Flute

The orchestral flute family has three members of which the flute itself (It., *flauto*; Fr., *flûte*; Ger., *Flöte*) is the middle one in register. Whilst it can be technically shown to be built in D, the flute has never been a transposing instrument and is always notated at concert pitch. It also uses only one clef, the G-treble clef, although in some early scores exceptions are to be found. Bach, for example, wrote the famous flute duet in the aria 'Sheep may safely graze' from the Cantata no. 208, *Was mir behagt* in a different and far less familiar G clef, viz:

Ex. 138

Piccolo

This name for the smallest flute is an abbreviation of the Italian *flauto piccolo*; but whereas this is the international term, the Italians themselves always use *ottavino*. The French and Germans both use direct translations of *flauto piccolo*, i.e. *petite flûte* and *kleine Flöte*.

The piccolo is now always written in C although an octave lower than the actual sound. Transposing piccolos were once widely used, though principally in wind bands; Mozart wrote for piccolo in G in *Die Entführung aus dem Serail* but the part only survives in this form in an appendix to the full score.

Flute in G

This third member of the family is the bass or alto flute. Until comparatively recently the term 'bass flute' was used automatically but a move is now being made to adopt 'alto flute' as being more correct on the grounds that a lower, true bass flute does exist, pitched an octave lower than the ordinary flute. As yet, however, this has no place at all in the repertoire and orchestrally speaking the controversy could therefore be thought to be academic. The fact is that, practically, the 'alto flute' and the 'bass flute' are one and the same; e.g. the bass flute of Britten's *Sinfonia da Requiem* is identical to the alto flute of his later works.

This instrument is pitched a fourth lower than the flute and is notated in the treble clef as a transposing instrument in G. It is the French who consequently avoid any argument by simply calling it *flûte en sol*, and so it appears in all French scores. Stravinsky in the original edition of *Le Sacre du Printemps* gave it the equivalent Italian of *flauto in sol*, but the Italians and Germans very rarely use the instrument at all. The occasional modern Italian score can be found with *flautone*, never *flauto grande*, since this, like the German *grosse Flöte* is already in regular use for the ordinary flute as opposed to the piccolo when the two instruments alternate.

An exception to the alto flute being pitched in G in orchestral literature cannot go unmentioned. This is Glazunov's Eighth Symphony where a 'flauto contralto in F' is listed. This instrument has long since disappeared and players today know nothing about it. Rimsky-Korsakov mentioned it in his *Principles of Instrumentation*, though only *en passant* as an alternative to that in G, and since Glazunov never used its bottom notes (on the contrary writing surprisingly high passages for much of the time) it is hard to know why he should have specified the lower instrument. (It is interesting however, to find that Rimsky-Korsakov already refers to this F instrument as an alto flute.)

OBOES

Oboe

Since, strange to say, no smaller member of the oboe family has been established orchestrally, the oboe itself remains the highest representative. Below come, in turn, the oboe d'amore, the cor anglais and the bass oboe.

The French term *hautbois*—literally 'high wood'—was once in use in England and spelt 'hautboy'; but both English and German have adopted the Italian *Oboe*, although the Germans sometimes restore the H to make *Hoboe* as, for example, in many (but by no means all) of the works of Richard Strauss.

Like the flute, the oboe is written at concert pitch and only in the treble clef.

Oboe d'amore, Cor Anglais

The oboe d'amore is so called internationally although the French translate the name into *hautbois d'amour*. Thus too, for all the controversy over the origin of the curious name, translations of 'cor anglais' agree in preserving the exact meaning, viz: English horn, *corno inglese* (It.,) *Englisches Horn* (Ger.). Wagner led the way in *Parsifal* in trying to make a change to *Althoboe* but failed to break the established usage. In English-speaking countries, however, it is oddly enough the French version that persists and colloquially the instrument is always referred to as the 'cor'.

Theoretically the oboe d'amore and the cor anglais might be said to be the alto and tenor oboes respectively (the original tenor of the family was called the *taille*, a term to be found in Purcell scores), but the oboe d'amore has remained something of a stranger in the orchestra, the cor anglais having supplanted it as the regular alto member of the family.

The cor anglais, pitched a fifth below the oboe, is normally notated in the treble clef as a transposing instrument in F. Bach, however, wrote for it—under the name of *oboe da caccia* (strictly speaking its immediate predecessor)—at actual pitch in the alto clef, an example imitated by Prokofiev for his 'oboe contralta'. Gevaert, in his *Treatise of Instrumentation*, cites two other notations of earlier days, an 'Ancienne notation française' and an 'Ancienne notation italienne'. The former, used by French operatic composers up to Halévy, was an ingenious device which by using the C clef on the second line-up managed to combine the actual pitch with the standard position of the notes on the stave for the sake of ease for the player. The Italian notation, however, again an operatic tradition, was wholly absurd (as Gevaert frankly admits) since the notes are given an octave below the actual sound. Nevertheless this notation survives in so standard a repertoire work as the Overture to Rossini's *William Tell*. In some earlier editions such as Eulenburg's predecessor Donajowski, the *ranz des vaches* cor anglais solo appears in this notation thus:

Ex. 139

The oboe d'amore lies between the oboe and the cor, sounding a minor third lower than notated. Therefore, while Bach again wrote at concert pitch, though in the treble clef, such romantic scores as have revived the instrument (e.g. Mahler's Rückert Lied 'Um Mitternacht' and Debussy's *Gigues*) follow the example of Strauss's pioneering *Symphonia Domestica* and notate it as a transposing instrument in A. (Holst's *Somerset Rhapsody*, where the oboe d'amore solo is admittedly given at concert pitch, hardly counts since the passage is designated for oboe with the oboe d'amore shown in brackets as a highly desirable alternative.)

Bass Oboe

This is again something of a rarity, but unlike the oboe d'amore does not have its origin in earlier music. It first reached the orchestra in the guise of the heckelphone (a very similar instrument specifically invented by Heckel) in Strauss's *Salome* of 1905, which paved the way for the vogue subsequently enjoyed by the bass oboe in England during the first decades of this century, when it was used by Delius in several works (*Dance Rhapsody No. 1*, *Mass of Life*, etc.), by Holst in *The Planets* and Bax in his First Symphony.

Both the bass oboe and the heckelphone sound an octave below the oboe, but composers differ over notation. Strauss wrote for the heckelphone in both *Salome* and *Elektra* as a transposing instrument (in the treble clef sounding an octave lower than written) as did Holst and Bax, whereas Delius wrote at pitch using both treble and bass clefs:

Ex. 140   Delius, *A Dance Rhapsody*

and in the *Mass of Life* he used the tenor clef as well.

CLARINETS

There are more varieties of clarinet in current orchestral use than of any other wind instrument. For a start it is unique in that there are two completely basic instruments before one begins to take into account all the 'odds and sods' as they are vulgarly called amongst the players. The name 'clarinet' is clearly derived from *clarino* (the English 'clarion'), a kind of trumpet, but it has never been anything but a woodwind instrument. Curiously the corresponding English derivative 'clarionet' is still occasionally to be found in early editions and old fashioned tutors for the instrument, but is essentially archaic.

Versions of the name in other languages are all very close to one another (*clarinetto*, *Klarinette*, etc.).

Clarinet in B♭, Clarinet in A

These are the twin standard instruments, which are notated as transposing instruments in the treble clef. Hence they sound respectively a tone and a minor third lower than written. Some scores, such as Sibelius's Symphony No. 7, actually notate clarinets for brief periods in the bass clef when they are in their lowest register, but this is not carried over into the parts.

Both the B♭ and A clarinets are regularly used and are interchanged as convenience of key may dictate; music in flat keys normally being written for the B♭ (which subtracts two flats from the key signature), those in sharp keys for the A (which subtracts three sharps). Composers even instruct the players to change from one to the other during the course of a work or movement—as, for example, in the first movement of Brahms's Third Symphony—and as a result clarinettists usually have at their feet wooden stands with protruding cones on which the instrument not in use at the moment may safely rest. It must be admitted, however, that a player sometimes prefers not to make the prescribed change if it is only for a short period. Instead he will continue on the same clarinet, transposing the part at sight, rather than nurse a cold instrument for an important solo, even though he need not play on a different reed and mouthpiece but can when necessary transfer these from one instrument to the other, as they are easily detachable.

In point of fact the B♭ clarinet is very much the leading partner and is becoming more and more the instrument composers write for as a matter of course, especially with technique at so high a level as well as bearing in mind the contemporary retreat from tonality. As a result in some, especially Latin, countries (including South America) players no longer carry A clarinets at all, although they are often consequently trapped by the formidable problems of transposition which confront them.

Even so, it would be quite wrong to consider that the A clarinet is in danger of becoming extinct. It actually has the more beautiful tone of the two and as a result enjoys a priceless literature all its own, based on Mozart solo pieces (the Concerto and the Quintet) and most of the Brahms chamber works. Nor is it neglected by all present-day composers, as the Ritual Dances from Tippett's *The Midsummer Marriage* illustrate (Ex. 169). On the other hand, Delius in his *Dance Rhapsody No. 1*, written as long ago as 1908, simply did not bother with the A clarinet even though it meant producing the most awkward passages in fantastic keys for the B♭ instrument such as the following:

Ex. 141

Typically, Strauss wrote in *Salome* for pairs of both A and B♭ clarinets giving a fascinating study of his view of their qualities both in apposition and conjunction.

Clarinet in B♮

Of the long list of accessory clarinets the one in B♮ is quickly disposed of, for it no longer exists. Yet it appears in old editions of, for example, Mozart's operas *Idomeneo* and *Così fan tutte*, in the latter especially in Fiordiligi's great aria 'Per pietà'. In all standard editions of the score, however, it is replaced by the A clarinet.

Clarinet in C

Thought to be virtually extinct not so long ago, the C clarinet is actually back in circulation, though it is still comparatively rare. In classical and early romantic times it was as standard as the B♭ and A, so that any work centering around the tonality of C would automatically be written for C clarinets, such as Beethoven's First and Fifth Symphonies, Schubert's Sixth and Great C Major, Bizet's Symphony, Liszt's *Faust Symphony*, etc. to name only a few outstanding examples.

But Strauss and Mahler used the C clarinet differently; that is to say, in its own right and quite opposed to the others, for its individual, rougher quality. It is, however, precisely because of this—as well as the difficulty of obtaining good and reliable instruments—that clarinettists normally try to avoid it, and tend to transpose C parts on the B♭ instrument.

From what has already been said it must be becoming increasingly

clear that the art of instantaneous transposition at sight, complicated—even hazardous—as it sometimes is, has up to a point
become part of the orchestral clarinettist's stock in trade. This fact
unfortunately encouraged Schoenberg to expect players of his ferociously difficult works from Op. 22 onwards to read from material laid
out according to his theories of 'logical' notation exclusively in concert
pitch, 'using any instrument they may prefer'. This, however, carried
the assumption of expertise far beyond the level of practicality, with
the result that the works are usually played from bad and faulty
manuscript copies transposed for B♭ clarinet, the beautifully printed
and spotlessly clean printed copy (in C) lying neglected and abandoned.

Richard Strauss actually turned in later life to the C clarinet in yet
another capacity, that of a substitute for the E♭ or D as the top
instrument of the group. The *Potpourri* (Overture) to the opera *Die
Schweigsame Frau* gives a good example of the virtuosity, range and
reliability of intonation Strauss already took for granted from players
of this relatively unfamiliar and treacherous member of the family.

Clarinet in D and in E♭

The Italians and French refer to these smaller clarinets specifically as
clarinetto piccolo or *petite clarinette*, but this has not been adopted in other
countries. Indeed, where England is concerned, so self-explanatory is
the E♭ clarinet considered today that 'E♭' has become an adjective
colloquially synonymous with 'little' amongst orchestral musicians,
who use it as a diminutive for non-musical objects such as houses or
cars.

The D clarinet has had a short and curious career. At one time it
occupied a position of equality alongside the E♭, especially in Germany. It can be found in Liszt (e.g. *Mazeppa*), Wagner (*Die Walküre*),
Mahler (Fifth and Sixth Symphonies), and in several works of Strauss
though its most famous appearance is certainly in *Till Eulenspiegel*. On
the other hand, it is hardly to be found in Italian or French scores and
the Second Symphony of Enesco is an unexpected exception.

Both the little clarinets are notated as transposing instruments, the
E♭ sounding a minor third higher, the D a tone higher, than written.
Although D clarinets are occasionally to be seen, they have normally
been superseded by the E♭, players once again simply transposing the
parts at sight. The E♭ has in fact established its supremacy because of

its quite individual tonal character, its shrill hard quality giving pronounced drama and incisiveness to the wind band, as in the 'Sunday Morning' opening to the Second Act of Britten's *Peter Grimes*:

Ex. 142

The still smaller clarinets in F and high A♭ once known in continental military bands have never formed any part of the symphony orchestra.

Basset Horn

Turning next to the larger clarinets, the place of the alto clarinet is taken by the basset horn (It., *corno di bassetto*; Ger., *Bassethorn*), since the original alto clarinet—pitched in E flat an octave below the well-known E♭ instrument—is another purely military band member and even there is becoming increasingly rare.

In fact the basset horn represents the orchestral alto clarinet in F and is specifically so called in Stravinsky's *Threni*, where it makes an unexpected reappearance. It was saved from extinction because of the essential parts Mozart wrote for it in works such as the Requiem, *Die Zauberflöte*, the *Masonic Funeral Music*, the Serenade in B♭, K 361, etc., before it aroused the interest of Richard Strauss. Today, included as it is in Strauss works in the standard repertory like *Der Rosenkavalier*—let alone *Elektra* which calls for two—it cannot any more be classified as an archaic curiosity, even though it is by no means a regular member of the basic woodwind section. This unsatisfactory border-line state of affairs is, as with the C clarinet, aggravated by the scarcity of good instruments.

The Italian name *corno di bassetto* is additionally familiar for having been the *nom de plume* of Bernard Shaw when writing as music critic of *The Star* in the 1880s. The German form, as shown above, corresponds with the English, but the French equivalent is academic as no French composers have used it.

The basset horn is written as a transposing instrument sounding a fifth lower. Mozart, and Strauss (ever the traditionalist) after him, used both treble and bass clefs, though the notes in the bass clef jump an octave down in the process, sounding a fourth higher, viz:

Ex. 143   Strauss, *Elektra*

This corresponds with old horn notation (see p. 218 below), an analogy that accentuates the confusion of the name of the instrument and which, like that of the cor anglais, remains unexplained satisfactorily. Forsyth[1] attributes it to its inventor, believed to be a certain Herr Horn, 'basset' being an old but common word for any low pitched instrument. But whatever its origin it has led to a number of false interpretations, such as Mozart's Duos K 487. These, beyond question composed for two horns, were actually published in the Breitkopf *Gesamtausgabe* as duets for basset horns, probably on account of the high range of the parts, although the music is full of obvious French horn characteristics. Conversely, two of the three basset horn parts in the *Masonic Funeral Music* have sometimes been ascribed to French horns.

---

[1] *Orchestration*, p. 282.

Bass Clarinet

The bass clarinet is to the clarinet what the cor anglais is to the oboe; i.e. the most regular extra instrument to be found normally in the hands of the 3rd player.

Its name is virtually the same in all languages except only that Italian composers list it not as *clarinetto basso*, as in international Italian, but as *clarone*.

From the repertoire of printed scores it might appear that, like the ordinary clarinet, the bass clarinet is standardized in both B♭ and A though with a strong leaning this time towards the A instrument. Yet, on the contrary, in actual fact the A is completely superseded and no longer exists at all, the mass of parts for it being automatically played on the standard B♭ instrument. The bass clarinet in C must also once have existed—Liszt writes for it in the symphonic poem *Mazeppa*—but this has utterly disappeared.

The notation of the bass clarinet is by no means a simple matter. Orchestration text-books recognize two methods that admittedly predominate, viz:

(1) the so-called French notation, sounding a ninth (or minor tenth) lower than written. This uses the treble clef, even to the very bottom notes, and is arguably the most common notation in general use, that is to say not merely in France. Richard Strauss used it between *Guntram* and *Ein Heldenleben* after which he reverted to:

(2) the so-called German notation, sounding a tone (or minor third) lower than written. This largely uses the bass clef but—and here is the important point—when the upper register is reached the change is made to the treble clef, the transposition however, remaining the same.

But this is not the end of the story. Quite an assortment of composers use a combination of these notations which is best regarded as a third method, viz:

(3) as notation (2) but on reaching the treble clef jumping up the octave and transposing as in notation (1). This seems to have been initiated by Liszt in his first symphonic poem *Ce qu'on entend sur la montagne* and, although Liszt himself subsequently used only notation (1), was adopted by different composers such as Liadov, Rachmaninov, Busoni and even Stravinsky in *Le Sacre du Printemps*.

The effect of this complex situation is to throw into doubt the intentions of composers using notations (2) and (3) wherever the treble clef appears. For example the opening of the last movement of Sibelius's Sixth Symphony has sometimes been misinterpreted:

Ex. 144

In this context, high as it appears, the bass clarinet should indeed sound a tone and not a ninth below the written note.

Webern's *6 Orchesterstücke*, Op. 6, present a particularly acute instance of this dilemma. In the revised 1928 version only notation (1) is used. But in the 1909 *Urfassung* Webern wrote in both treble and bass clefs and it is quite uncertain which octave the treble clef notes should sound, the question being further confused by an equivocal footnote and by the fact that the part is written in a different notation from the score, making *ad hoc* decisions necessary on each occasion.

There is thus no escaping the frequent ambiguities, the only guides towards correct interpretation of doubtful contexts being knowledge of composers' practice and—one hopes—internal evidence from the score itself.

Pedal Clarinet

Last in the gamut of orchestral clarinets comes the pedal, or contrabass clarinet, an octave lower again than the bass clarinet. This is also found written in B♭ or A (the latter, for example, in Schoenberg's *5 Orchesterstücke*, Op. 16) though it seems doubtful whether an instrument in A has ever actually existed. The notation for the pedal clarinet has always been in the bass clef but sounding an octave lower—i.e. a ninth (or tenth) lower than written.

Its appearance in the orchestral repertoire is extremely rare. Schoenberg, in addition to the *5 Orchesterstücke*, introduced it into his *4 Orchesterlieder*, Op. 22, but not, as one might have expected, in his mammoth *Gurrelieder* even though this is scored for no less than seven members of the clarinet family. D'Indy wrote a part for it in his opera *Fervaal* and Strauss did actually give it a short passage in *Josephslegende* but so little expected it to be used that he wrote in an *ossia* for contrabassoon.

The opinion has often been expressed that the pedal clarinet is so obviously more suited than any member of the bassoon family to supply the bass to the woodwind ensemble that it can only be a matter of time before it sweeps all before it. Yet in the event this has proved an illusion and the few players in possession of an instrument can, like bass oboes, virtually command their own fee for the isolated occasions they may be called upon to produce it.

BASSOONS

If the clarinet is the orchestral woodwind instrument with the greatest number of varieties, the bassoon is the one with the fewest. The smaller tenoroon has never had more than a shadowy existence and has made no appearance in the orchestra at all. Thus only the contra- or double bassoon survives as a regular associated family member.

Bassoon

The English genus name corresponds with the French *basson* but both the Italian and German names describe the instrument's appearance and wooden construction: *fagotto* and *Fagott*. Curiously *basun* is the Scandinavian for trombone (a corruption of *Posaune*), a linguistic mix-up that can lead to magnificent incidents at rehearsals in those countries; but fortunately the term does not normally appear in printed scores.

The bassoon is notated at concert pitch, using predominantly the bass clef but rising through the tenor to occasional uses of the treble clef, though this latter is not very popular with players. Examples, are, however, more widespread than is commonly supposed.

153

Double Bassoon

All other languages give this instrument the prefix 'contra' in its various guises (Fr. *contre-*; Ger. *Kontra-*; It. *contra-*). The Italians, however, also use the spelling *contraffagotto*, as does Beethoven in *Fidelio*, recalling the corresponding Italian spelling for string basses: *contrabbassi* (see p. 31). The simple term 'contra' has actually become by itself the colloquial name for the double bassoon in this country, though it has never been taken to suffice in the printed score.

The contra is normally written in the bass clef, but sounding an octave lower. Some French composers, however, such as d'Indy, Dukas or Debussy (though not Ravel), write for the instrument at pitch usually adding 'octave réelle' to avoid ambiguity. Wagner too, writing for it for the first time in *Parsifal*, notated it in this way as if it were merely a bassoon with extended compass.

On the rare—but not unknown—occasions when the contra is taken into the higher register, the tenor clef is, as with the bassoon, sometimes used as an alternative to the bass, though still sounding the octave lower, but not the treble as such extreme altitudes hardly come into question.

3 COMPASS AND EXTREMES OF RANGE

FLUTES

The range of the flute is normally given as but this is by no means the plain and simple fact of the matter. In earlier years composers wrote no higher than top A, even Schumann distorting melodic phrases to avoid the B♭, viz:

154

Ex. 145   Schumann, Symphony No. 1

but thereafter composers can be seen to be extending the range not merely to C, as stipulated in so many books of orchestration, but to top D, Prokofiev's repeated use of that note in his *Classical Symphony* being notorious (though it is not a particularly difficult note; Forsyth, among others, exposing his conservatism in stating that 'only exceptional players can touch it').

Officially  still remains the bottom note of the flute, though

at the same time a very important section of the repertoire takes the low B for granted, as for example in the Dvořák Cello Concerto:

Ex. 146

and players can usually be relied upon to supply the special foot-joint necessary to give this extra note, although some make a stand against having to do this, on the grounds that it puts the rest of the instrument out of tune.

The low B is actually to be found in scores as early as Mendelssohn (Intermezzo from *A Midsummer Night's Dream*, see p. 159), while in the late romantics it is so common that when none of the flautists in a section can get the note it becomes a considerable embarrassment. Even low B♭ is sometimes written although very much more rarely; Balakirev's First Symphony in C and Mahler's Fifth Symphony both have outstanding examples. But this note is not on present-day instruments and the only way for it to be played is for one of the section to carry a bass flute for the purpose.

This latter instrument has no such worries at the lower end of its compass. Its bottom note is ♭ sounding ♭ and no extension to low B is ever called for in the repertoire. At the top end it too can theoretically reach its ♭ (which would sound ♭) though it might seem perverse to seek for extremes of altitude in an instrument whose chief *raison d'être* lies in its lower compass. However, Boulez, in *Le Marteau sans Maître*, writes throughout for *flûte en sol*, taking it across an extremely wide range:

Ex. 147

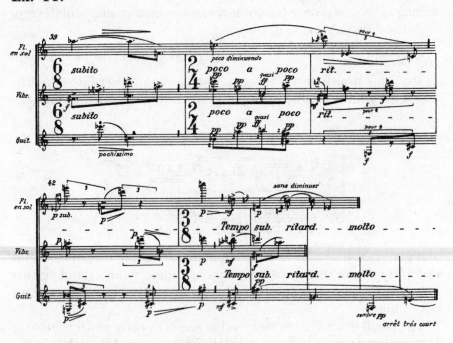

The lowest note of the piccolo presents a similar problem to that of the flute. Strangely enough it is not C but ♭ sounding ♭ though continental repertoire abounds with instances of the low C whether in Verdi's Requiem, Mahler's *Lieder eines fahrenden Gesellen* (a

156

hotbed also of flute B♮'s) or numerous Strauss works *(Rosenkavalier, Bourgeois Gentilhomme* etc.). In one way the problem would seem greater than that of the flute since the analogous extension would be to the flute B♭—i.e. a whole tone below the standard lowest note—and piccolos with the low C are hardly ever found today. On the other hand the subterfuge of arranging for the missing note(s) to be covered is relatively simple since any unoccupied flute can do this imperceptibly, whereas to cue the flute's low B's onto a clarinet (as was common practice until comparatively recently) gives an entirely different colour and is patently a very second-best expedient.

A word should perhaps be added here about methods in common use to overcome the problem of extensions where alternative instruments are not available. The head-joint can be pulled out to some extent from the main body of the flute in order to produce isolated low notes, though the problems of intonation and the danger of the flute falling apart make this practice distinctly unpopular with players. Their other method is sometimes to improvise little cardboard cylinders which, fixed to the end of the foot-joint, will extend the length of the instrument sufficiently to provide a tolerable B♮. This expedient has, however, the disadvantage that the B is produced instead of—not as well as—the C and thus a passage like the following still remains impossible:

Ex. 148   Busoni, Violin Concerto, Op 35

as for that matter does the quotation from the Dvořák Cello Concerto given as Ex. 146 on p. 155.

Returning to the piccolo, this cannot really reach its topmost D like the other flutes. Examples up to C can, however, be easily found in orchestral literature, as in Mahler's Third Symphony:

Ex. 149

At this extreme top the piccolo becomes very hard to control at anything less than an earsplitting fortissimo, and also develops serious problems of intonation. Composers have nevertheless been merciless at times, as is shown by the crucial passage from Schoenberg's *Gurrelieder* at the beginning of the section entitled 'Des Sommerwindes wilde Jagd'. Here four piccolos alternate in sustaining the upper B's in octaves *pp* over a period of no less than 24 bars. So excruciating was this when I was rehearsing the London Symphony Orchestra for the performance in the Festival Hall in London that one of the players ingeniously contrived to substitute a small whistle that produced exactly the right sound and pitch in, moreover, a true effortless pianissimo.

OBOES

It is so taken for granted that the bottom note of the oboe is as given in orchestration books that it comes as a surprise to learn that this is by no means universal and that instruments exist, especially on the Continent, that go no lower than B♮. Whilst admittedly the B♭ is not vastly common in orchestral parts it is certainly frequent enough to be regarded as essential. The same Mendelssohn example from *A Midsummer Night's Dream* music that was referred to on p. 155 in connection with the low B of the flute also shows an early example of the oboe B♭ (see Ex. 150, opposite).

Curiously enough, the bottom register of the cor anglais produces an opposite situation. Here the lowest note is normally sounding but continental instruments exist with an extension to the low B♭, sounding E♭. As a result, several parts requiring this note are to be found in the repertoire and create problems, as in Schoenberg's *Gurrelieder* where a footnote to the score says that it must *not* be taken up the octave, thus revealing Schoenberg's awareness that the note cannot be relied upon as a matter of course. Below a passage in *Das Lied von der Erde* Mahler wrote, again in a footnote, that he was prepared to accept B♮ as an emergency substitute, even though this produces different harmony—and a very interesting one (see pp. 27–8 of the full score). Dvořák, in the *Scherzo Capriccioso*, even writes low A's for the cor anglais. It seems unlikely that this further extension

Ex. 150

ever existed and the Artia edition takes the high-handed step of transposing all the low A's up the octave, thus distorting the phrases. It would be better, rather than this, to leave them out entirely (like Strauss's advice to the violins, see p. 104), and the problem should have been presented to the performer to solve in whatever way he may wish, as was done in the original Bote & Bock material.

As for the oboe d'amore and the bass oboe (or heckelphone), it is often stated baldly in orchestration books that neither goes below B but this is in fact only a half-truth. Debussy (or Caplet, who carried out the completion of the score) wrote a low B♭ for the oboe d'amore in *Gigues*, and although the bass oboe only reaches B♮, the heckelphone has extension keys down to the low A, and Strauss not only requires this note in *Elektra* but actually goes as low as an impossible F in the *Alpensinfonie* (three bars after Fig. 102).

At the upper end of the compass only the oboe itself has been taken to the extreme limits of practicability. Top F's and G's are not uncommon in the repertoire, although the G in Stravinsky's *Jeu de Cartes* remains a notorious hurdle:

Ex. 151

Stravinsky actually writes a top A in *Pulcinella*, though this is well covered by doublings in the woodwind ensemble; whereas Peter Maxwell Davies makes no bones about top G's and A's in his *Second Fantasia on John Taverner's In Nomine*, sustaining them unmercifully across long bars.

For the other members of the family, top E is normally regarded as the upper limit, and it is on this note that the cor anglais solo of Britten's *Nocturne* dies away:

Ex. 152

Yet these high cor anglais notes are often thought to be unmanageable and better given over to the oboe. Beecham, when preparing his edition of Delius's *The Walk to the Paradise Garden*, transcribed the opening cor anglais solo for oboe (even though it goes no higher than D), but the poignance of the original, which is awkward but by no means exorbitantly difficult, is unforgettable:

Ex. 153

CLARINETS

While the written E ![notation] is the standard bottom note of all clarinets (with the exception of the basset horn), this is actually only the starting point of a somewhat complex situation. As long ago as 1948 George Dazeley showed conclusively in an article in *The Music Review* that Mozart's A clarinet had an extended range to low C (sounding A) and that the surviving versions of the Concerto, K. 622, and the Quintet, K. 581, are mere bowdlerizations. This is further proved by the clarinet obbligato in *La Clemenza di Tito* that takes this extra range for granted causing problems on the rare occasions when the opera is revived. (In recent years a few players have had extended-range instruments built; these have come to be termed 'basset clarinets', but they remain rare and qualify as solo visitors rather than regular members of the woodwind group.)

For purposes of orchestral practice then, the standard instruments are indeed those going down to E sounding D or C$\sharp$ in the case of the B$\flat$ and A clarinets respectively. However, composers have been wayward enough to write the low E$\flat$, though fortunately mostly for the B$\flat$ or C instruments (even so traditionally minded a composer as Brahms wrote a low E$\flat$ for the C clarinet in the revised edition of the Fourth Symphony), but in fact B$\flat$ clarinets do also exist today with an extra key in order to provide this extension. The ability to produce the low concert C$\sharp$ is, of course, essential for those players (see p. 146 above) who prefer to dispense with the A instrument.

Similarly one might have thought that before long the A clarinet too would have come to be fitted with an extra key, thus providing composers with the bottom C$\natural$. But so far this has not happened, nor have composers optimistically written this note.

Where the smaller clarinets (E$\flat$ and D) are concerned, the standard low E has remained the bottom note, but with the larger instruments this is not so at all. The basset horn in particular has

always gone down to the low C (sounding) and having had no

developing history over the last centuries has remained unaltered with this extended range to the present day. On the other hand, the bass clarinet produces the opposite situation. Although it began life with the E as its bottom note for the B$\flat$ and A instruments alike, the extension key on the B$\flat$ became absolutely necessary since perversely enough the A instrument—despite its regular preferential use by composers—really did become extinct many decades ago. But this is not to say that even the low concert C$\sharp$ is the standard bottom note of the bass clarinet in the orchestral repertoire. Rimsky-Korsakov, in his *Principles of Instrumentation*, written in 1905, lists the bass clarinet as going down to its bottom C like the basset horn; Russian composers such as Khachaturian and Shostakovich have come to take these bottom notes for granted. The fact is that an enlarged, differently shaped bass clarinet had already in earlier years become quite common in Russia and had spread gradually westwards reaching Germany, making its more regular appearance in England only since the Second World War, though it still cannot be assumed as a matter of course. Thus works like the Khachaturian Piano Concerto or the Sixth Symphony and First Violin Concerto of Shostakovich continue to present a problem if the bass clarinettist does not happen to possess the extended instrument.

It should be added that Schoenberg already wrote down to the low concert C♮ for bass clarinet in his Serenade, Op. 24, of 1923, but this is less indicative of his awareness of the existence of larger instruments than part of his growing hobby-horse of writing all transposing instruments at concert pitch with increasing disregard for their specific limitations of range. This viewpoint led to his later practice of abandoning in many of his works the very layout of a full score in favour of an all-purpose *Particell*—i.e. short score. In such a score (as for example the Violin Concerto or *Moses und Aron*) the woodwind is written on three staves in all, of high, medium and low pitch, so that the bass clarinet part would be included in a line together with bassoons or any other wind instrument of comparable range, with only rough indications of what each instrument plays. It is hard to understand such a haphazard approach and tortured logic in the man who had concocted miracles of orchestral colour, calculated to such a fine degree, as abound in *Erwartung* or the *5 Orchesterstücke*, Op. 16.

At the upper end of the compass the clarinet is to some extent flexible in potential range, although the sound becomes so penetrating and raucous, and the intonation so hard to control, that composers are disinclined to write above ♪ or ♪ , though top A's can be found in the repertoire and Ginastera in his *Variaciones Concertantes* continues a solo scale right up to the top B for the B♭ clarinet; Elgar in *Falstaff* goes even further, taking the instrument to the very top C, though admittedly in a tutti passage. In actual fact the famous death squeal in Strauss's *Till Eulenspiegel* in which the D clarinet rushes up to seemingly alarming heights, only goes up to its top A♭, which becomes no more than a top G when played, as so often, on the E♭ clarinet.

The basset horn and bass clarinet are rarely taken very high, partly because this is against the purpose of their existence, but also because they become very unwieldy in the upper register with grave risk of squawks from even the most experienced player. However, Strauss writes:

Ex. 154

in *Also sprach Zarathustra*, though admittedly the passage is well covered by the rest of the orchestra.

BASSOONS

Although the bottom note of the bassoon is now firmly standardized as there was a time when the instrument lacked two crucial low notes above this fundamental, namely C♯ and B♮. This explains the odd makeshifts to be found in some repertoire scores such as Beethoven's Choral Symphony:

Ex. 155

Forsyth quotes a similar avoidance of the low B♮ in Weber's *Freischütz* Overture. At the same time it should be observed that by the time Beethoven reached the Scherzo of the Choral Symphony he had already forgotten to make corresponding allowances for the missing notes and was now writing low bassoon B♮'s and C♯'s with impunity.

   Wagner actually takes the bassoon a semitone lower than the bottom B♭ in *The Ring*, explaining in a footnote that if the low A is not available a contrabassoon should be used. (The latter instrument unexpectedly finds no other place in the mammoth orchestration to the great cycle.) On the basis of this instruction the printed score has changed the bassoon lines at the beginning of *Siegfried* Act I, which in the autograph are given entirely to the 1st and 2nd bassoons:

Ex. 156

so that the last phrase reads for 3rd bassoon and contra, which is nonsense as no more than three players are scored for in the entire work.

Where, unlike the above example, the low bassoon A is required but is not followed by the B♭ it is common practice for the player (amidst a certain amount of hilarity) to extend his bell by sticking in at the top a roll of cardboard whose origin is only too obvious. Like the flute extensions of the same kind (see p. 155 above) this works perfectly and can be quickly and easily inserted and removed.

The topmost notes of the bassoon are 🎵 or 🎵 . Anthony Baines[1] writes that 'mercifully nothing above E has been written in an orchestral part', but the *Sérénade* for small orchestra by Jean Françaix does reach the F:

Ex. 157

though an *ossia* is added for muted violins (!) in case of difficulty.

But these extreme high notes are very rarely found in exposed solos. Even the famous solo that opens Stravinsky's *Le Sacre du Printemps* is less extravagantly high than it sounds:

---

[1] *Woodwind Instruments and their History*, Faber, London, 1967, p. 150.

Ex. 158

The contra, which used to look simply like an oversize bassoon, originally only went down to 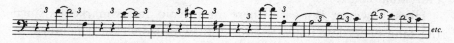 (sounding, of course, an octave lower). But this limited instrument is rapidly becoming extinct and the larger, serpentine German contra commonly in use today supplies the extra two semitones down to the bottom B♭, the standard range required by the orchestral repertoire and with the distinction of being the lowest note obtainable in the entire orchestra.[1]

The contra does occasionally find itself taken into quite high regions by even so conservative a composer as Brahms:

Ex. 159   Brahms, Symphony No. 1

though the purpose here is, of course, to continue the colourful doubling of the bass line rather than to be academically practical in leaving out a few high notes and thereby leave the player to fit in fragments of a distorted passage. Exposed high notes on the other hand are—even more than the bassoon—rare in orchestral writing.

4 FAMILY CHARACTERISTICS

FLUTES

Being the only woodwind instruments without reeds, flutes have a gentle purity of sound which, especially in the lower register, can err

---

[1] This is not to say that contras have never in earlier times possessed the extended range. Beethoven wrote repeatedly the bottom B♭ for contra both in the Choral Symphony (the ⁶⁄₈ march variation of the choral last movement specifies the bottom octave in the autograph) and the Missa Solemnis, where in the Gloria the contra takes a spectacular leap from the topmost G to the bottom B♭.

on the side of breathiness. There are strongly opposed schools of thought on the 'right' quality of flute sound, ranging from a firm but slender tone to a warm, rich—even fat—sonority. The slender style of flute tone is often thought of as belonging to the French school of playing and one recalls the kind of lithe quality inherent in the extended solo from the Second Suite of Ravel's *Daphnis et Chloé*. Yet even so essentially French a passage as the opening of Debussy's *Prélude à l'après-midi d'un faune* is far from unsuitable for the rich tone at one time characteristic of flute playing in Britain, a sound derived from the opposing German school.

In the lower register the rich variety of flute tone is shown to particularly good advantage and can actually come surprisingly close to the timbre of the trumpet, though of course lacking the power of the brass instrument. The Russian school reveals a penchant for this orchestral colour and Tchaikovsky, for example, has a predilection for two or even three flutes in unison at their low register, as in the 'Valse Mélancolique' from the Suite No. 3, Op. 55, which has a long solo passage for the three flutes treated in this way with remarkable and individual effect.

Here, however, is a case where the piccolo differs markedly, since the tone of its low notes is faint and, whilst delicate if handled in transparent ensemble-work, the instrument lacks penetration in any but its highest compass, a fact that composers sometimes fail to take into account. This is possibly because of the sound being an octave higher than written, suggesting a greater brilliance than is actually possible. Players accordingly often play an octave higher still passages like the following from Weber's Overture *Abu Hassan*:

Ex. 160

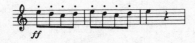

ff

or from Smetana's *Vltava*:

Ex. 161

in both of which the piccolo is intended to add brilliance to a fully scored woodwind ensemble, but as written is barely audible; or especially the final flourish of Borodin's Second Symphony:

Ex. 162

On the other hand, it has a sparkling glitter at the top that has been widely exploited in the depiction of flames (Wagner's 'Fire Music' from *Die Walküre* or Strauss's *Feuersnot*) as well as lightning flashes —which are always the essential responsibility of the piccolo (Berlioz, 'Royal Hunt and Storm'; Verdi, *Rigoletto* Act 3, etc.). By comparison, flutes are far less pointed at their highest register and the very high writing in, for example, Prokofiev's *Classical Symphony* is relatively fussy rather than truly brilliant.

One outstanding characteristic of the flute family is its tremendous agility. The repertoire is full of dazzling cascades of scales and arabesques that exploit this virtue such as the many in Strauss's *Till Eulenspiegel* or the following breathtaking passage from Janáček's *Sinfonietta*:

Ex. 163

The great solo in Ravel's *Daphnis et Chloé* also culminates in a vivid exhibition of flute virtuosity taking in the whole gamut of flute range and instruments from piccolo to the *flûte en sol*.

Again, like the bottom octave of the piccolo, the degree of penetration by the alto flute is disappointing, especially in the low notes which are—after all—its especial prerogative. Yet it has its own distinctive quality that has caused it to be chosen in circumstances in no way emphasizing the low notes, such as Boulez's *Le Marteau sans Maître* (an example from which is quoted on p. 156) and it is perhaps surprising to discover that it can rival the flute in agility and firmness of tone at quite high registers.

OBOES

The quality of the oboe family affords the greatest possible contrast to the flutes, possessing as it does the highest degree of sheer cutting power of the whole woodwind department. This, a particularly strong fundamental in its harmonic structure, and its vibrant expressiveness, are certainly amongst the qualities that have led to the oboe being adopted as the standard arbiter of pitch for the orchestra as a body. 'Giving the A' is one of the principal oboist's most important responsibilities, whether at the beginning of a rehearsal or concert, or to a soloist on his or her appearance on the platform. When there is no oboe in the score, as in Mozart's Eb Symphony No. 39, K. 543, shift has to be made with the clarinet, and so equally in other smaller combinations with flute, horn, etc.; but none are really satisfactory.

The oboist may occasionally find himself challenged over the A he has given and it is customary for principal oboists to carry a tuning fork as part of their equipment and to listen to it before venturing to pose the A, and to resort to it by way of corroboration. The installation of an electrical pitch machine guaranteed to give off A = 440 at all times is sometimes thought by well-meaning orchestral managements to be the obvious solution to the whole question, but in practice this proves to be not only far less effective but actually irritating to the players, who find it too characterless an authority to accept or to match with confidence or reliability, and thus less efficient than a human agent.

Pitch is, moreover, to a large extent a matter not of mechanical accuracy but of agreement and compromise. In the first place even after the most careful adjustment few instruments retain precisely a given pitch for more than five minutes at a stretch in concert halls of fluctuating temperatures. As instruments warm up during playing, the wind are theoretically supposed to rise while the strings drop in pitch, though anyone well acquainted with orchestral circumstances knows that in fact the wind generally complain that as the hours pass the strings tend to play too sharp for the wind's comfort. 'We can't get up to you' is the common complaint from the wind, and when the oboe is called upon to give a new A after the orchestra has warmed up, this is frequently proved to be the truth of the matter, for whatever reason and however unscientific this may seem.

Then the fact must be taken into account that the wind instruments are rarely if ever perfectly built with every note in tune over the whole compass. Hence it is one of the first prerequisites of a wind player that he learn constantly to adjust and adapt each and every note to the pitch of his colleagues as he plays. Such displays of individual tuning, therefore, player by player, section by section, to a tuning fork before the beginning of rehearsals with which some well-known conductors have built reputations for insistence on perfect intonation, are hardly more than exhibitions of lifemanship or at best a device for the establishing of discipline.

On very cold or damp days it may even be a mistake to expect the 1st oboe to go through the ordeal of trying to produce a satisfactory A on a cold instrument for an orchestra that is bound to change pitch within minutes of playing, and the wise conductor will always be prepared to let the orchestra play for a while before stopping to call for the first general tuning of the day.

Although it might be going too far to call the 1st oboe the leader of the woodwind, he nevertheless remains the key figure. Apart from his prerogative as arbiter of pitch, this is due both to his inherent virtues and limitations—his maximum expressive power and on the other hand his relative lack of flexibility. This causes the other members of the section to pay him the courtesy of working to him in matters of ensemble as well as intonation—i.e. in chord placing, or unison passage-work, etc.

For with its double reed the oboe is harder to control than either flute or clarinet and is also relatively clumsy in rapid passage-work as well as ultra-quick tonguing. The familiar hurdle of Rossini's Overture *La Scala di Seta* would have presented no difficulty to either of the other instruments. Kodály's *Dances of Galanta* contains a notorious challenge for the tongue of any but the most virtuoso of oboists:

Ex. 164

This passage (which occurs several times in different keys)is also given to flute and clarinets without presenting anything like the same difficulty. Britten also created diabolical problems of the kind in the Tarantella of his *Sinfonietta*.

The oboe's very quality of penetrating expressiveness can also be a mixed blessing, as especially, for instance, in the low register which is very hard to control in soft dynamics. This causes difficulties when trying to match the soft ensemble of the other woodwind and the Czech school have been notably demanding on 2nd oboes in this respect, Dvořák setting one problem after another of the kind:

Ex. 165   Dvořák, Symphony in D minor, Op. 70

II.

In such cases a conductor of experience and understanding may suggest that the other wind gauge sympathetically how softly they should play in order not to present the 2nd oboe with an unnerving or unrealistic demand upon his technique. There is also a much feared low 2nd oboe entry in Smetana's *Vltava* (see Ex. 166 overleaf). That doyen of Czech conductors, Vaclav Talich, used to obviate the risk of a gawky disturbance at this magical moment by replacing the unfortunate oboe with a clarinet and this expedient is still current practice in Czechoslovakia, though surely going too far, the character of the passage being unduly sacrificed in the interests of safety.

In problems such as these much depends on the nature and therefore upon the choice of reed, with the result that the very making—as well as the adjustment—of the oboe's complicated double-reed is all the province and concern of the player who is for ever scraping, testing, binding etc., in the pursuit of the right kind of reed for a given solo. This is a skill in its own right and one which has to be mastered by every aspiring artist alongside his studies in the playing of the instrument.

The oboe has again greater problems than the flute and clarinet

Ex. 166

Mondschein; Nymphenreigen. (Lůna; rej rusálek.)

where breathing is concerned, not indeed because more breath is needed, but, on the contrary, because so terribly little is released at a time through the tiny aperture between the reeds, thus requiring tremendous stamina and control. Long solos as at the beginning of Ravel's *Tombeau de Couperin* are as much tests of endurance as they are technical challenges. Some of the greatest virtuosi such as Leon Goossens and Heinz Holliger solve this by acquiring a curious skill whereby the cheek is used as a kind of bagpipe sack which can continue to supply air during an extended solo while the player relieves the pressure on his lungs. This is, however, a highly specialized accomplishment and by no means standard practice.

Whereas the character and problems of the subsidiary oboes largely resemble those of the oboe itself, there is certainly a marked variation in the degree of stridency, the oboe d'amore and bass oboe in particular being considerably gentler and mellower. This is to some extent true also of the cor anglais, as Wagner discovered to his cost when he wanted his melancholy piper in the Third Act of *Tristan* to play a jubilant fanfare when Isolde's ship is at last sighted. It was of course of the utmost importance that it should be clearly heard and in this emergency he inserted a long footnote into the score describing his attempts to invent a new instrument for the purpose. This has, however, failed to reach the universal acceptance of his other inventions (the bass trumpet and the 'Wagner tubas', q.v.) and on such occasions when the cor anglais itself has not been used, the Hungarian hybrid *tarogato* (a kind of conical wooden clarinet) has been pressed into service, or occasionally —worst of all—a trumpet.

CLARINETS

Although far less angular in tone than the oboe, the clarinet can achieve a far greater degree of sheer volume, especially in the upper register where its *fff* becomes incredibly shrill and piercing. At the same time its *ppp* has the potential of achieving a sound at the very edge of audibility, and it can therefore boast the widest contrast of volume in the woodwind section. The extremely soft effect is often known as 'ghosting', although it is not so designated in orchestral scores but rather as 'Echo-tone'. Mahler calls for this in an exquisite passage in the first movement of his Second Symphony:

173

Ex. 167

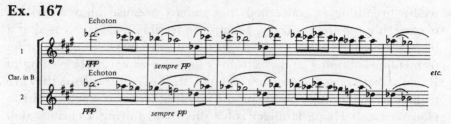

Clarinets can also match the flutes in agility, though this is markedly less true of the larger varieties. The solo in the last movement of Sibelius's Fourth Symphony springs readily to mind:

Ex. 168

and Stravinsky allocated a spendidly virtuoso *arpeggiando* obbligato to two clarinets in Jocasta's aria 'Ne probentur oracula' from *Oedipus Rex.* Tippett also very cleverly exploited the slinky liquid flexibility of clarinets in the second of his Ritual Dances from *The Midsummer Marriage*, 'The Otter chases the Fish', the darting movements of the fish illustrated thus:

Ex. 169

The bottom register of the clarinet has a character all its own which is even graced by a special term 'chalumeau', actually the name of an old forerunner of the family, now long deceased. The chalumeau register is not only particularly beautiful in quality but is also the easiest to control in the handling of very soft effects. This is so much beloved of composers that they often write long passages for two clarinets playing in unison at this register as at the opening of Dvořák's Cello Concerto or the entire slow introduction to Tchaikovsky's Fifth Symphony.

The strident upper octave has the opposite characteristic, being hard to control with reliable intonation and dynamics; the flutes and oboes, sitting immediately in front, find the upper notes of their clarinet colleagues, especially those of the E♭, a hazard in the pursuit of perfect blend of tone and pitch.

Another problem indigenous to clarinets is the phenomenon of the 'break' half-way up their compass—i.e. between  and (written notes), where the tone tends to be weak and watery as well as sharp in pitch. It is also hard to alternate notes rapidly on either side of the break. From this point of view the unknown bowdlerizer of Mozart's Clarinet Concerto committed a gaffe when, with the disappearance of the instrument with extended range, he changed Mozart's now impossible:

Ex. 170

which was both easy and effective, to the gawky and ill-sounding:

Ex. 171

Lying across the break as it does, this latter example is often held to be impossible though it is in fact not so in the hands of expert virtuosi.

The subsidiary clarinets, in keeping with the wide contrast shown by the extremes of register of the clarinet as such, also exhibit an enviable variety of characteristics. The bass clarinet can be melancholy or even sinister, as in its atmospheric evocation of witches (Dvořák's *The Noonday Witch* and Liadov's *Kikimora* are obvious examples) while at the other extreme the E♭ clarinet has also been used to depict a witch, but in no such spine-chilling way; rather, splendidly grotesque:

Ex. 172   Berlioz, *Symphonie Fantastique*

Mahler regularly used the E♭ clarinet to suggest parody, for which its cheeky tone (*keck*—one of the composer's favourite instructions) makes it eminently suitable; while Strauss's selection of the D clarinet, which in all essentials has much the same character as that of the E♭, to impersonate the jocular Till Eulenspiegel, has already been singled out (p. 162) as the outstanding example of exploitation of these little clarinets' particular quality. They have equal potential as humorists and as caricaturists, though the clowns of the orchestra *par excellence* will probably always remain, much to the fury of their executants, . . .

BASSOONS

Though admittedly no more than one facet—and by no means necessarily the more important—of the bassoons' exceptionally contrasted two-fold character, it has to be acknowledged that the inherent humour of the instrument's very tone-quality makes it the obvious choice for comic effects. There is always a hilarious atmosphere of farce or parody in a bevy of bassoons playing *fortissimo*, that no other instrument can rival:

Ex. 173   Chabrier, *España*

—while in solo bassoon passages some element of comedy or the grotesque is rarely far away: the broomsticks coming to life in Dukas' *L'Apprenti Sorcier*, the absurdly pompous Grandfather strutting around in Prokofiev's *Peter and the Wolf*, the Kraken in Britten's *Nocturne* or the porpoises in Milhaud's *Protée* are all memorable exploitations of this aspect of the bassoon.

Yet sustained lines on the bassoon can exhibit an entirely different character—subtle and plaintive. The lower register is marvellously lugubrious (one need only recall the opening of Tchaikovsky's *Symphonie Pathétique*) whereas the upper octaves have a touchingly poetic colour, used with great effect by Respighi to depict the Adoration of the Magi in his *Trittico Botticelliana*:

Ex. 174

Indeed, Stravinsky's choice of the high bassoon for the opening of *Le Sacre du Printemps* (see Ex. 158 above), causing many a raised eyebrow at the time, was a highly original use of a hitherto unfamiliar colour.

Although the bassoon is the standard bass instrument of the woodwind ensemble it is in many ways unsuitable for this role. The suggestion has already been considered (on p. 153 above) that the lowest clarinets could more successfully take over this function, though in the event they have failed to establish themselves as such and instead it is the horns who are so often co-opted to smooth the blend in the lower regions. In ensemble work horns and bassoons can produce such a perfect match as to be almost indistinguishable, while the horn has the advantage of greater weight coupled with roundness of tone. Bassoons are, however, able to reciprocate and are often added as extra members of the horn quartet to become, as it were, 3rd and 4th horns in, for example, the third movement of Mendelssohn's *Italian* Symphony, or even 5th and 6th horns—as in the Introduction to Act 3 of Wagner's *Die Meistersinger* or the Overture to Humperdinck's *Hänsel und Gretel*.

This association, it must be admitted, can have the effect of stirring up the latent resentment sometimes felt by bassoonists at their colleagues in the horn department. For the question of how much sheer tone the bassoons can muster is a thorny one and close to the heart of every player. Many a time they will turn malevolently to the enviably rifting horns who can rid themselves of all their spleen and inhibitions, a luxury denied to bassoonists for all eternity.

Yet this was not always so to the same extent as now. The purist conductor who today restores in unadulterated form Beethoven's bassoon return of the fanfare in the first movement of the Fifth Symphony:

Ex. 175

may find himself rubbing salt into the wound, for our noble if over-refined instruments are not the strong raucous bassoons of Beethoven's day and can nowadays make the passage sound no more than a feeble wheezy imitation of the horns' heroic gesture.

Yet Tchaikovsky was another who clearly expected his bassoons to sound heroic:

Ex. 176

Manfred Symphony

and here, strangely enough, the many reorchestrations for horns *et alia* by well-meaning conductors (including even Toscanini) sound positively crude.

In fact, Coleridge's 'loud bassoon' is not entirely unknown today, though very rare in the more highly sophisticated woodwind schools of Europe and North America. The bassoons of the National Orchestra of Mexico produce a roar such as I would not have believed possible had I not witnessed their performance in person.

The bassoon family has in fact the narrowest dynamic range of the woodwind department. If it is normally uncompetitive in matters of extreme loudness, so the ultimate refinements of *pianissimo* are extremely difficult or even impossible for it, especially in the lower register. In this, of course, bassoons are similar to their corresponding double-reed colleagues the oboes (see p.171), but since they lie at the bottom of the ensemble, this failing provides one of the main reasons for the bassoons' unsuitability as all-purpose bass instruments for the woodwind group. Tchaikovsky provided an unrealistic challenge to the bassoon in the famous breathless descending phrase at the end of the second subject of the *Symphonie Pathétique* where the bassoon takes over from a clarinet already marked *ppppp*. The wistful addition of yet another *p* (making six in all) cannot solve an impossible technical problem and in practice the passage is generally taken over by a bass clarinet who, on the contrary, specializes in such extremes of soft playing.

The contra naturally accentuates the lugubrious side of the bassoon in the lower register, the bottom notes, however, degenerating into hardly more than an effect. Nevertheless even in these cavernous depths the contra may be required to make a musical contribution. The beginning of Ravel's Left Hand Piano Concerto is a particularly famous instance, presenting a long, tortuous melody that requires an alert and well-trained ear to discern and check the accuracy of its rumblings.

The upper regions of the contra are too feeble and lacking in character to have been used by composers other than to continue a unison line with other instruments as shown in Ex. 159 on p. 165.

Being a double-reed instrument like the oboe, the bassoon shares many of its occupational hazards, from the question of reed-production and titivation (bassoon, and especially contra, reeds are elaborate and expensive affairs and the selection of a good reed from among the many indifferent ones can be a ruinous business) to that of stamina and breath control; though in respect of the latter the sheer physical strain is somewhat less acute. Endurance tests for bassoonists are however not unknown, such as the '2ème Variation' of the Gavotte from Stravinsky's *Pulcinella*:

Ex. 177

*) 1st time only; 2nd time Fag.II tacet.

Again like the oboe, very quick tonguing is less fluent on the bassoon, though an accomplishment which good players pride themselves on acquiring and exhibiting in solos such as the following from the last movement of Beethoven's Fourth Symphony:

Ex. 178

P dolce

Curious, perhaps improbable instrument as the bassoon may seem, its primary role as part of the continuo in classical and baroque music has led to its inviolate position in the orchestras of all periods. Indeed in seventeenth-century orchestras it was taken so much for granted that composers often failed to specify where, or even if, the bassoons should play or not. It would be assumed automatically that a pair would double the cellos and basses unless they should have something better to do in the form of an individual contribution. Hence the ballet music to Mozart's *Idomeneo* makes no mention of bassoons in the full-bodied opening Chaconne, though they appear in the Larghetto that follows; when the Chaconne resumes there are again at first no bassoons, but at bar 20 they reappear abruptly, playing to the end of that movement but never again for the rest of the ballet. Moreover, the bassoon parts are printed in this patently incomplete way in the Breitkopf & Härtel orchestral material.

By contrast, the slow movement of Mozart's Symphony No. 34 in C, K. 338, is scored for strings only, but both bassoon copies were printed in the Breitkopf edition with the cello/bass part of this movement included in its entirety. Similar anomalies can be found in many other works of Mozart and his contemporaries and the case is often far from clear even once it is assumed that the nineteenth century editions have obviously run amok. For example, the Robbins Landon edition of the complete Haydn Symphonies cites a single doubling bassoon in every one of the first half of the entire gamut of symphonies, but it is purely conjectural that bassoons, whether one or two, were ever expected to pump away non-stop alongside the basses in work after work in which they were neither specified in the list of instruments nor carried any individual line whatsoever. The spectre of pedantry soon looms in such circumstances, yet it is undoubtedly known that they did indeed contribute to some extent. There are even strange phenomena in scores as late as Beethoven which suggest the continuing tradition, such as the isolated bassoon D's in the first movement of the Pastoral Symphony which could be taken to suggest

that Beethoven was merely indicating the end of a period of doubling
so automatic as not to be worth the trouble of writing down:

Ex. 179

5 CONSTITUTIONS OF WOODWIND SECTIONS

Unlike the constitution of the strings, whose flexibility is essentially a numerical matter, that of the woodwind can be very much a question of composer's choice. The basic group may perhaps best be regarded as 'double wind', i.e. two each of flutes, oboes, clarinets and bassoons. This is the body commonly engaged as the nucleus of orchestras that are of modest but not necessarily chamber proportions. Such a section can cover the broad classical and early romantic repertoire without either leaving players idle for too many items in a programme or needing extra players time after time for this work or that.

Yet even so fundamental a formation as this cannot be thought of in terms of standardization where the repertoire is concerned. Early nineteenth-century composers to whom the double-wind group may have represented the basic norm thought nothing of varying it from work to work as the character of each seemed to dictate. Thus Beethoven, whose symphonies are all essentially conceived on the standard double woodwind pattern, used only a single flute in No. 4, but added a third player in the person of the piccolo in Nos. 5, 6 and 9 as well as a contra in Nos. 5 and 9. Brahms, who also thought in terms of the double wind, added a contra to the first, third and fourth of his symphonies, but not No. 2; used a piccolo but no contra in the *Tragic Overture* and both in the *Academic Festival*, and so on.

In actual practice it is the 3rd flute who has seemed to be the commonest extra across the broad repertoire and some double-wind orchestras find it worthwhile to engage just this one extra player on a permanent basis. At the same time, conversely, the flutes are also the family most often reduced to a single player against two each of all the other woodwind instruments, as in Beethoven Fourth Symphony (as already mentioned) as well as in some of Beethoven's concertos, Schubert's Fifth symphony, and a host of Mozart and Haydn works. The latter composers also show that where complete families are concerned it is the clarinets who are the most often absent altogether, though this is on historical grounds, as the clarinet was the newcomer to the orchestral scene, having only recently been invented. (The other instruments could claim not to have been 'invented' at all but had evolved over the centuries.)

Variations of the double-wind pattern are, then, infinite. Even Berlioz, for all his gargantuan orchestral concepts, thought in terms of

184

double wind, though taking four bassoons for granted like most French composers since their opera houses normally carried these players on the strength. Balakirev was prone to add a third clarinet though only using a single oboe in conjunction with cor anglais; Dvořák on the contrary tended to use a three-oboe section, and so on. Subtractions can naturally also be found other than the 2nd flute and/or the clarinets, but are mostly associated with the chamber-orchestral single wind group which will be discussed in due course.

Already in such basic double-wind formations one of the two players is commonly required to 'double' on the more standard accessory instrument of his family, i.e. piccolo, cor anglais, bass clarinet—or occasionally E flat clarinet—and contrabassoon. It is usually the second player who will be called upon to undertake such doubling (rewarded professionally by an extra payment) but composers do sometimes allocate the change of instrument to the first player. Dvořák, for example, in his G Major and New World Symphonies marks the cor anglais and piccolo solos respectively to be played by the 1st oboe and 1st flute. This is by no means always carried out today (even though as a result some switching of the part becomes necessary) as the principal wind soloists of major orchestras prefer not to unsettle their embouchures by such changing.

However, both players may be instructed to double, most often in the case of the flutes changing to two piccolos (e.g. in Sibelius's *The Return of Lemminkäinen*, Britten's *Peter Grimes*, etc., etc.). In larger wind formations three flutes are sometimes required to play piccolos, such as in Kodály's *Háry János*, or even all four as in Mahler's Fifth Symphony and Berg's *3 Orchesterstücke*. Yet I have known principal flautists who do not (or perhaps choose to say they do not) play the piccolo, thus necessitating the engagement of an extra player. I have even encountered one first flute who absolutely does not play the piccolo but willingly performs on the alto flute, the instrument that normally enters the province not of the second, but of the third flute in large orchestras. Certainly for a solo or chamber player not to play the piccolo at all is both unusual and enormously inconvenient. Britten, for example, in his chamber operas (*Lucretia, Albert Herring*, etc.) takes it as a matter of course that the single flute player in his 12-piece orchestra will alternate on all three instruments, and he similarly expects the single oboe player to double on cor anglais.

It is admittedly rare for a principal oboe to double on cor anglais but very far from unknown and apart from these instances and those such as the Dvořák examples mentioned above, early Haydn symphonies such as No 22 ('The Philosopher') may be cited. Here the first oboist as well as the second plays cor anglais, an example emulated in recent times by Gordon Crosse in his *Ceremony* for cello and orchestra.

For principal clarinettists to play the bass clarinet or the E♭ is even more uncommon, though again it does occur (bass clarinet also in Britten's chamber operas: E♭ clarinet in Janáček's *Taras Bulba*). It is, however, safe to say that principal bassoonists do not double on the contra.

With respect to the last named, one tends to think of the contrabassoon as primarily a modern adjunct to the post-romantic super-woodwind sections, and it may come as something of a surprise to meet it in such classical works as Mozart's *Masonic Funeral Music*, where it is even the sole member of the bassoon family. Furthermore, as a result of Beethoven's importing of the contra from the theatre for his Fifth and Ninth symphonies, in which he was followed by Brahms, it entered the standard full orchestral strength ahead of both the cor and the bass clarinet. Yet conversely, its highly individual rumble is not as ubiquitous in romantic scores as this might suggest. The French composers in particular, for all their habitual use of four bassoons as already mentioned, more frequently omit the contra (that is, until the later Debussy-Ravel era is reached). Berlioz used it only in *Les Francs Juges* amongst his overtures and it makes no appearance in the *Symphonie Fantastique*, for all the presence there of two ophicleides.

Where fees and salaries are concerned, there is no parallel in the wind departments to the string 'rank and file' status. All players are graded as 'principal' or 'sub-principal', and where sub-principal (i.e. second) players are regularly required to double on piccolo, cor anglais, bass clarinet and contra (still the most usual), their contracts make provision for this dual role. Third players however, are frequently principals since their chief occupation in life may be the accessory instrument itself.

In full-scale symphony orchestras the standard section is triple woodwind. This covers the broad mainstream of the orchestral repertoire with only small variations involving either inactivity of personnel or the occasional engagement of extra players.

Of the rarer subsidiary instruments, bass flute (= alto) and E♭ clarinet are only carried on the orchestral strength of the very largest international prestige orchestras boasting four-fold woodwind, in which they will naturally come within the orbit of the fourth players, though the second and third players will need to be prepared to cooperate where composers such as Mahler and Strauss lay their scores out with complicated woodwind doublings, or where (as in the case of the multiple piccolos mentioned above) the score calls for more than one cor anglais, E♭ or bass clarinet, basset horn, or even contra. Such cases, though admittedly the exception, are by no means unknown: Busoni used a section of one oboe combined with two cors anglais in the Sarabande from *Doktor Faust*; two E♭ clarinets are to be found in Mahler's Second Symphony, two basset horns in Strauss's *Elektra*; Webern scored for two bass clarinets in the splendid original version of his *6 Orchesterstücke*, Op. 6; and Stravinsky provides a spectacular example of two contras in the 'Death of Kastchei' from the ballet score of *The Firebird*.

The rarest instruments of all the woodwind, such as the oboe d'amore, bass oboe (or heckelphone) and pedal clarinet, are used too infrequently to be specifically engaged on a permanent basis, though if it transpires that a prospective member actually possesses one it naturally enhances his market value enormously.

There are certainly a number of scores in the repertoire of a full symphony orchestra that demand quadruple wind, but nevertheless these must always remain only a relatively small proportion of the works covered within the monthly schedule. Larger formations still can readily be cited (Schoenberg's *Gurrelieder*, Stravinsky's *Le Sacre du Printemps* and Mahler's Eighth Symphony are obvious examples) but the mammoth extra forces required for these isolated giants are always engaged by even the largest international prestige orchestras on an *ad hoc* basis.

At the other extreme end of the numerical scale there remains to be discussed the woodwind formation consisting of only a single representative of each member of its respective family. This chamber orchestral formation is of comparatively recent origin, appearing in such works as Stravinsky's *Danses Concertantes*, Britten's *Sinfonietta*, Honegger's *Pastorale d'Eté*, etc. Earlier examples of such chamber ensembles generally include a pair of one or other of the families, such as Wagner's *Siegfried Idyll* which has one each of flute, oboe and bassoon, but a pair of clarinets.

A large number of classical works (and also several twentieth century pieces written with an eye to inclusion by orchestras specializing in a classical repertoire) reduce the wind group by using just two pairs, or sometimes even only one, of woodwind instruments. A pair of oboes is probably the most frequently used of these, though bassoons may also be added on account of their role as part of the continuo (see above p. 182). More rarely, Mozart's Symphony No. 27 in G uses only flutes, and in his G major concertos for violin (K. 216) and flute (K. 313) they actually alternate with oboes for the slow movement. In Mozart's day both flutes and oboes would have been played by the same artists but this is wholly unknown now. Another curiosity is Mozart's use of only clarinets and bassoons in his Third Horn Concerto, K. 417.

Into this analysis of the smaller woodwind ensembles a visitor from the following section must here be introduced, since in works such as those last referred to, containing a wind section of perhaps only three or four players—indeed maybe no more than just a pair of oboes or flutes—a pair of horns is usually combined. In such cases the horns are treated as co-woodwind rather than as isolated members of the brass family, for this inclusion of horns in the woodwind group is integral to the character of the instrument (as will be discussed later, see below p. 189). The use of a single horn is relatively rare—horns usually hunt in pairs—but not unknown, especially together with the single-wind formation of which the Britten and Honegger works just mentioned provide typical examples.

6 LAYOUT IN THE SCORE

The woodwind normally occupies the head of a page of full score, with the flute department at the top followed in descending order by the oboe, clarinet and bassoon families, each as a rule kept together in blocks.

There are, however, all kinds of exceptions, as the result of composers' different idiosyncrasies. Tchaikovsky, for example, sometimes puts the cor anglais not amongst the oboes but below the clarinets. Though this is admittedly not his invariable practice, many of his most familiar works are laid out in this way, such as *Romeo and Juliet*, *Overture '1812'*, etc.

His reason for this change from the usual pattern must have been in order to maintain the regularly descending pitch range down the score rather than meticulously segregating the instruments by family. In the same way the bass clarinet is sometimes placed below the bassoons as by Wagner in *Tristan und Isolde* or even, oddly enough, above the other clarinets as in the original Bote & Bock edition of Dvořák's *Scherzo Capriccioso*.

On the whole such redistributions are exceptional, but one major difference in score layout must be mentioned here (though there will be more to say about it in the following section, see p. 232). This was the practice initiated by Berlioz of placing the horns amongst the woodwind—i.e. between the clarinets and the lower wind (bassoons, bass clarinet, etc.)—as part of his use of horns less as brass than co-woodwind for much of the time. This of course links up with the view of horns within the woodwind ensemble just outlined above, but was nevertheless not widely adopted by other composers.

Within each of the woodwind families themselves the instruments are usually ranged in the score in descending order of pitch. On this basis of the highest instrument being at the top, the piccolo would naturally find its proper place at the head of the page. Yet even this is not always the case, as the logical layout by pitch conflicts with another consideration: that of the top line being given to the principal player of the group, here the first flute. Hence there are two quite distinct practices: when a player plays only piccolo throughout a work, that is to say without changing to 3rd (or 2nd) flute, his line will indeed appear at the top of the score. But when the 2nd flute doubles on piccolo, his role as subsidiary flute takes priority and the piccolo line comes beneath that of the 1st flute. Ravel's *La Valse*, however, provides an exception and very muddling it is too. The melodic flute passage at the top of the page is actually for the 3rd player (who also doubles on piccolo) while the chromatic scales below it are played by the 1st and 2nd, creating a splendid trap for the conductor (see Ex. 180, overleaf).

As a result of complicated doublings with two piccolos and perhaps an alto flute the lines in some scores can get horribly mixed up, with the 2nd piccolo (played maybe by the 1st flute) placed above the 1st piccolo and the alto flute somewhere in between: it is not unknown for the composer himself to become confused over how the distribution should work out. Accordingly the players' lines may be obliged to change staves from one page to another, creating havoc.

Similar problems may arise in the clarinet department with the E♭ normally placed above the 1st and 2nd players unless doubling occurs. But the situation with oboes and bassoons is trouble-free as

Ex. 180

the subsidiary instruments are all pitched lower than the parent instrument.

Although scores can be found in which each player's line is individually laid out, it is more usual for the first and second of each instrument to be combined on a single stave. When they sometimes play in unison, they may then be shown with only single stems to the notes and marked 'a 2', this indication having the exact opposite meaning to its use in the string department (see p. 36, footnote).

7 PLATFORM PLANNING

The woodwind occupy the first rises on the platform directly facing the conductor and as near to him as the string disposition will allow. They will generally be placed in two tiers with the principals bunched together in the centre, the remainder fanning outwards in either direction:

Ex. 181

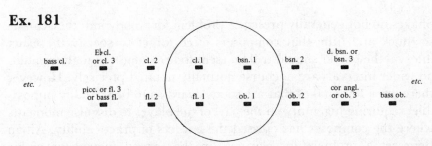

There are very few exceptions to this, although of course the position within the instrumental sections of piccolo, cor anglais, E♭ clarinet, etc. will depend on their function in each and every score. But it is not every hall or concert platform that enables the woodwind to be placed exactly centrally to the conductor.

One completely different formation has already been mentioned on p. 62 above. This was Stokowski's experimental layout with all the strings to his left and all the woodwind to his right, but he has had no followers except that in the opera pit this is indeed one of the recognized formations. Even there, however, the more usual plan places them centrally, as in the above diagram, with the one reservation that the lack of depth of many pits makes it necessary for the woodwind group to be displaced to the side, usually behind the violins to the *left* of the conductor.

The woodwind are never ranged in more than two tiers and never, if they can help it, in a single long line. If the group is large this can safely be considered out of the question, but in relatively smaller ensembles the necessity can arise in small halls or for reasons of balance, with all the attendant problems of ensemble and intonation caused by thus spreading out the lines of communication.

One important variant of the formation given in Ex. 181 remains to be considered. When the strings are disposed according to the old classical and continental practice as shown Ex. 23 on p. 50, in which the cellos and basses are placed to the conductor's left, the positions of the clarinets and bassoons are often reversed, the former sitting behind the oboes and the latter behind the flutes. The clear advantage of this arrangement is that the bassoons are brought nearer to the cellos and basses with whom their lines have often much in common.

8 TECHNICAL EFFECTS

TRILLS AND TREMOLOS

Shakes do not generally present a problem for woodwind; they can be so quick and lithe that composers often forget to specify the exact interval the player should trill on (semitone or tone), though tremolos on wider intervals are of course normally notated precisely. However there are a few shakes that are so awkward as to be virtually impossible, requiring ingenuity on the part of the player to disguise moments where the composer has crossed the borders of practicability. Alban Berg set a problem for clarinets in the second movement of his *Kammerkonzert:*

Ex. 182

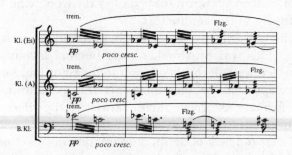

The lines in Ex. 182 are given in concert pitch according to Schoenberg's theories of score presentation, but if transposed into real clarinet terms it will be seen that some of the tremolos are quite awkward, lying as they do across the break.

For the guidance of composers Forsyth typically lists woodwind shakes and trills which he deems to be possible, barely possible or impossible, just as he does with string chords; but, unlike strings, wind technique and instruments are constantly improving and evolving, so that theoretical precepts such as he offers are too hard and fast. In general, however, shakes on oboes and bassoons tend to be clumsier and sound more ungainly than on flutes and clarinets, and are therefore used more sparingly across the repertoire.

DOUBLE TONGUING, FLUTTER-TONGUING, ETC

Rapid tonguing techniques fall properly into the province of the flutes who in this respect far outstrip their colleagues among the other woodwind. Double tonguing ('t-k-') or even triple tonguing ('t-d-k-') is frequently introduced into flute passage-work, whereas it is a rarity in clarinet writing and even more so for oboes and bassoons, though there is a notorious passage of double tonguing for all the woodwind in the third movement of Hindemith's *Mathis der Maler* Symphony. Moreover the ultra-quick oboe tonguing in Kodály's *Dances of Galanta* quoted as Ex. 164 on p. 170 is actually taken in double tonguing by some players but it is by no means every executant who can boast this as part of his or her technical equipment. On the flute, however, examples abound such as the prescribed triple tonguing in Stravinsky's 'Dance of the Firebird', the superimposed consonants showing a different method from the normal one indicated above:

Ex. 183

Rimsky-Korsakov's *Scheherazade* includes a more extended example where double tonguing makes possible an otherwise unrealistic passage at the speed required:

Ex. 184

Flutter-tonguing is again a speciality of flautists (except for some players who, distinguished artists among them, happen not to be able to roll their Rs), so that it has become one of the more common colouristic effects written for the instrument. Although theoretically possible for the other woodwind, flutter-tonguing is very much less practical on account of the reeds, and is therefore rarely prescribed. An instance for clarinets, however, is shown in the fragment from Berg's *Kammerkonzert* quoted as Ex. 182 on p. 192.

Although the normal German translation is the straightforward *Flatterzunge* (abbreviated to *Flz.*), Mahler in the finale of his Second Symphony makes the upper woodwind perform what he describes as 'Zungenstoss'—literally 'tongue-thrust'. But in the circumstances and as notated, (𝄏 in very quick tempo) this is indistinguishable from the *Flatterzunge* in Mahler's other works. A parallel term is also used by Strauss for the sheep imitations in Variation II of *Don Quixote*. Here, in a footnote, he directs that the wind tremolos must be executed by the means of 'Zungenschlag' ('tongue-beat'). Elsewhere in the work, however, he too used the conventional *Flatterzunge* (see the flutes in Variation VII), as does Mahler in, for example, the opening of *Das Lied von der Erde*:

Ex. 185

Yet, whereas it does not seem likely that either Strauss or Mahler seriously intended a differentiation of technique by the use of these various terms, the Romanian composer Vieru has in his Cello Concerto written both flutter-tonguing and tremolo for the flutes as separate and contrasting effects. It remains doubtful, however, exactly what he had in mind:

Ex. 186

(the same passage recurs shortly afterwards, marked *frullato*). *Frullato* is of course, the Italian equivalent of 'flutter-tongue', while the French is usually *tremolo dental*, though Ravel describes it as 'vibrato' in the Prelude to the ballet version of *Ma mère l'Oye*:

Ex. 187

Tippett indicates 'flatterzunge' for the flute at the beginning of the Adagio of his Second Symphony:

Ex. 188

But at the tempo given at the head of the movement ($\flat$ = 80) this is actually too slow for a true flutter-tongue and the subsequent return of the figure shows by its handling in imitation in different sections of the orchestra that the repeated notes are intended to be measured.

GLISSANDI

Here it is the clarinet's turn to shine. With a soft reed and dexterous manipulation of the keys a true glissando can be achieved over the whole compass of the clarinet, and this was unforgettably exploited by

Gershwin in the opening bars of the *Rhapsody in Blue*. Such an effect
simply does not come into question with the other woodwind, the flute
in particular—having no reed—being hardly able to simulate a true
glissando at all, though some degree of pitch variation can be
contrived with the lip. In the 'Songe d'une Nuit du Sabbat' from
Berlioz's *Symphonie Fantastique* one of the eerie effects is produced by a
glissando for piccolo, flute and oboe:

Ex. 189

in practice none of these instruments can properly be made to press
the note down more than a tone at most before the sound drops to the
lower C. Yet such glissandi are not infrequently sought, as by Mahler
in 'Um Mitternacht', one of the Rückert Lieder:

Ex. 190

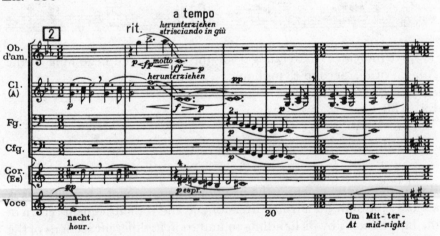

Players sometimes try to solve the difficulty by sliding with the use of
the keys, much as in the Gershwin, but unless this is very skilfully
executed the result can come close to a quick scale, patently quite
contrary to the desired effect. Indeed just how near to the composer's
intention it is possible to come can vary from one instance to another.
The bassoon can be surprisingly successful as Schoenberg showed in
the last movement of his *5 Orchesterstücke*, Op. 16; in the hands of a
good player this can make a splendid smear:

Ex. 191

HARMONICS

Although theoretically all woodwind instruments can be said to obtain harmonics by 'overblowing', in practice only the flute ones are used orchestrally and even these are a specific series overblown at the 12th: that is to say, while they are written at pitch with an 'o' placed over them—just like string natural harmonics—they are actually fingered a 12th below. Hence ♮ obtained by fingering ♮ is the lowest of these harmonics prescribed in the orchestral repertoire. The following example from Ravel's *Daphnis et Chloé* is a particularly well-known instance of their use.

Ex. 192

197

The sound is hollower and can be very telling, though it is not always reliable especially with regard to intonation. Nor is it in every instance immediately recognizable that one of these harmonics is being played. One clear characteristic is the absence of vibrato in the tone, but it is still sometimes argued that if any difference can be detected it is simply that the result is inferior to a note obtained normally, though to a specialist this is no doubt heresy and unwarrantable cynicism. However, composers do call for these flute harmonics and Stravinsky in *Pulcinella* goes so far as to give in the score itself an illustrative diagram of the keys and holes showing exactly the fingering he has in mind.

The reason why none of the other scientifically recognizable harmonics on the flute, or indeed any at all on the other woodwind instruments, are written for by composers, is veiled in technicalities and specialized knowledge. Walter Piston's excellent book on orchestration[1] goes some way towards discussing the details but even he fails to pursue the issue to the point of a comprehensive explanation relating to all the woodwind.

MUTING

Mutes, in the form of actual objects such as the horns and brass use, do not really exist for the woodwind. Nevertheless the necessity to mute does occasionally arise in orchestral practice, especially for the oboes. Stravinsky marks these instruments 'con sord' in the choral piece *Zvezdoliki* (*Le Roi des Étoiles*) although it is far from obvious what he expected to happen; similarly Britten writes for a saxophone 'con sord.' in *The Prince of the Pagodas*. When Strauss, in his 'Souffleur' (prompter) scene of *Capriccio*, instructs all the woodwind to mute he adds a footnote leaving the manner of execution to the players' ingenuity. Berlioz, in his *Treatise of Instrumentation*, talks of leather bags; but these have never become standard equipment although the comparable use of a handkerchief held between the knees is a method often deployed by experts not only for these specified occasions but also for such passages as the last fading phrase of the Berceuse from Stravinsky's *Firebird*:

---

[1] *Orchestration*, pp. 118-9 and 136-7.

Ex. 193

Clearly, however, these devices offer no remedy to either the flute or bassoon families and it is a moment of high entertainment to orchestra and spectators alike when, in Ligeti's *Lontano*, the 3rd bassoon is instructed to reach over to his neighbour, the contra and insert a *horn* mute into the inverted bell of the wretched player's instrument.

EXTREMES OF VOLUME

In the pursuit of exaggerated dynamics at the upper end of the decibel scale composers not only use verbal incitements to the players to use a rough or harsh tone—Strauss's directive in *Salome* 'hässlich kriesch-end' ('screeching hideously') is worthy of special mention—but also require any woodwind able to do so to raise their instruments and play with them stretched out at angles of up to 90° to the mouth. It is extraordinary how much increase of sheer volume this method produces though it can be difficult to induce the players to cooperate fully. No doubt it makes them feel foolish; certainly it is uncomfortable (even verging on the impossible if the stands are too near as in some halls) and robs the tone of the refinement they normally strive so hard to cultivate. As a result they tend to make fun of it at rehearsals and often conveniently forget it at the performance. But Mahler typically prescribes the effect on many an occasion, with exclamation marks after the indication *Schalltrichter in die Höhe!* printed against the relevant lines or even sideways up across the group of woodwind staves in the score. This term (= *pavillons en l'air* or 'bells up', though the English term is more colloquial) will be met again with particular relevance to horns.

UNCONVENTIONAL EXTENSIONS OF SOUND PRODUCTION

All woodwind instruments are built with the individual parts detachable—whether head-joint (flute), double reed (oboe), mouth-piece (clarinet), or crook (bassoon), not to mention the various bells or barrels, the latter generally made to pull apart in the middle. Many avant-garde composers taking advantage of this, have in recent years aimed to increase the sound resources by prescribing the use of limbs or joints divorced from the remainder of the instruments. The resultant squeaks and gurgles have thus entered the vernacular of contemporary composition though notation has not as yet reached any uniformity; noteless stems, crosses, wavy lines and other diagrammatic symbols can all be found and conventional notation has often to be supplemented by extensive verbal directions.

As a further extension to this line of pursuit, the clicking noise which the complicated key systems of modern instruments give off has also been exploited, though its dynamic range is severely limited. Heinz Holliger, the Swiss virtuoso oboist and composer, has written works using all these devices including, moreover, double-stopping which he has developed with more or less agreeable effect, and Bruno Bartolozzi's manual *New Sounds for Woodwind*[1] takes these already extreme measures still further.

VIBRATO

The use of vibrato in woodwind playing is to a large degree linked with fashion and with national schools and their traditions of style. French clarinets and bassoons use far more vibrato than their German or English counterparts, and orchestras of mixed nationalities often run into difficulties of blend. On the other hand vibrato in flutes and oboes is far more customary today, irrespective of national style, than it was forty or fifty years ago.

The subtle use of vibrato, apart from lending the tone a more ingratiating quality and greater flexibility in phrasing, can often assist in matters of intonation by softening the blend of sharply differentiated colours. Moreover, flute and oboe solos, if played with too dry and unyielding production, can sound flat, especially in the lower register. Yet paradoxically, this same vibrato can create problems of intonation in chordal passages since it is based to some extent on pitch fluctuation.

Vibrato remains essentially a personal approach to style and taste and is not normally decreed in scores or even mentioned at all by

---

[1] Oxford University Press, London, 1967.

composers. Yet its use or non-use can be crucial in interpretative matters as well as those of intonation. For example, two extended cantabile solos by the same composer may require a totally different degree and quality of vibrato. The famous Donna Anna episode from Strauss's *Don Juan*, an expression of deepest love:

Ex. 194

p sehr getragen und ausdrucksvoll

needs an entirely different texture from the remote Dulcinea melody that occurs near the beginning of *Don Quixote*. This, depicting the intangible ideal of some imaginary beauty, could perhaps be played with hardly any vibrato, as can be heard in Strauss's own recording:

Ex. 195

pp

There is, however, patently no hard and fast rule and a player will be judged—and accepted into a woodwind section—as much on the use and quality of his vibrato as on technical brilliance or musicianship.

9 PHRASING

Slurs have a far more precise application in respect of woodwind notation than in corresponding string writing, where they are so often taken to indicate phrasing rather than bowing (see p. 75 *et seq.*). In wind parts a change of slur will always presuppose the use of the tongue to mark the start of a new phrase. Moreover, as long as the slur lasts, the player will aim to refrain from taking a breath (though in the case of over-long phrases or of passages containing very wide leaps, a break in the line may be very hard to avoid). There is here a clear difference in the approach of a wind player to that of the strings who often regard slurs as having only limited compulsion and will freely alter them to suit bowing requirements, whereas a wind player will respect the slur as a positive direction in the interpretation of the music. In some long solos such as the *Prélude à l'après-midi d'un faune* the flautist's personal pride may be involved over his capacity to manage the whole phrase in a single breath. At others the conductor's preference or opinion may be sought about where the phrase may be best, or perhaps least harmfully, broken.

Where solos are doubled it is of course obvious that breathing can be staggered and some composers, such as Britten, actually indicate by means of the symbols V and Λ above or below the stave how this should be done.

The analogy between string bowing techniques and woodwind tonguing or breath control can be pursued to a certain extent. But although there are naturally the widest variations between soft and sharp tonguing and other such refinements of phrasing, the corresponding range of terminology is less rich than that of the strings and composers all too rarely indicate with any degree of precision the required style of playing in wind music.

The softest 'half-tonguing' can simulate a *portato* effect comparable with the *louré* string style (see pp. 86–7) and this may also be produced by the pressure of the lip alone. At the other end of the tonal scale, *sforzandi* can either be given weight, in order to give projection to an accent, or sharply tongued to create an explosive effect.

The end of a note or phrase normally floats naturally away on the breath, and it is unusual as well as bad style to clip a note with the tongue unless it is specifically required as a special effect.

Another feature of bad style phrasing is what is known colloquially as 'push-stroke', by which a player tongues the note below the required dynamic level which is subsequently reached by pressure of the breath, giving a bulge to the sound. Though generally regarded as disagreeable, this kind of execution is in fact deliberately prescribed by some composers, especially Schumann, by means of 'hairpins' (< >) placed above single notes.

10 SOLO PASSAGE WORK

Although the lion's share of the solo woodwind lines naturally falls to the principal player of each family, the sub-principals still come in for a considerable amount of individual responsibility, quite apart from the 3rd player's province of the subsidiary instruments. Dvořák, for example, gives more than one of the main themes in the first

movement of his New World Symphony to the 2nd flute, and the later
Romantic repertoire, in particular, abounds with important solos for
2nd and 3rd (even 4th) players. Hence the skill and resourcefulness of
the other members of the section need to be hardly less than those of
the soloistic and virtuoso first players, whose artistry and extrovert
personality may nevertheless characterize the whole orchestra itself.
Yet their interdependence is so great that it has often been said, and
with justice, that a first player is only as good as his second.

Solo passages are also (as has been suggested on p. 202) often given
to two or more of the same instrument in unison. Dvořák was very
fond of the lovely rich effect of two clarinets playing together in
pianissimo, and Tchaikovsky used the same colour for the whole of the
long statement of the motto theme in the introduction to the first
movement of his Fifth Symphony. Tchaikovsky was also especially
addicted to low unison flutes, sometimes using them three at a time as
in long stretches of the 'Valse Mélancolique' from his Suite No. 3,
Op. 55. Mahler, typically takes this to the limit in the second
(Ländler) movement of his Ninth Symphony, where large groups of
each instrument wail out in unison successive phrases of a wide-
spanned melody with calculatedly grotesque effect:

Ex. 196

(*Example continues overleaf*)

Ex. 196 *continued*

The word 'solo' against woodwind passages can have something of the same double meaning that it has in the strings (see p. 69). For although here too it can signify that the passage should be played by a single instrumentalist, it is often used to encourage the player to project the passage more prominently than he would normally do. This corresponds with another term used by composers: *hervortretend*, (*En dehors, in rilievo*) which has the similar effect of the dynamic marks themselves having to be interpreted quite liberally.

11 AFFILIATED INSTRUMENTS

RECORDERS

This instrument, also designated *Blockflöte* (Ger.), *flauto dolce* (It.) or *flûte-a-bec* (Fr.), is mostly known in this country as the 'recorder', a more favourable term than the once official name 'fipple-flute'. Until comparatively recently the word 'flute' has been used to mean the transverse flute, any other species being considered archaic and of purely historical interest. Hence it had long ceased to be necessary to specify in scores, as Bach did, exactly which kind of flute was intended. In the last decades, however, as part of the widespread revival of authentic interpretations of baroque and pre-baroque music, the recorder has made a strong come-back. Thus Bach's Brandenburg Concertos Nos. 2 and 4, which are known to have been intended for recorders (unlike No. 5), are now frequently played on these instruments, though players and scholars are by no means agreed over which size should be chosen or at which octave the lines should be played.

The recorder has a distinct educational virtue in providing a readily available introduction to the joys of co-operative musical activities with a minimum requirement of skill or preparation. But as Britten has cleverly shown in *Noye's Fludde*, this aspect of the instrument can be exploited whilst at the same time revealing the degree to which the recorder may have a pronounced character of its own if expertly handled by composer and performer. It has to be admitted that the recorder—and there is a considerable range of different members in what is strictly called a 'chest of recorders'—cannot compete with the rich characterful quality of tone which enabled the transverse flute to oust it in the first place, and in particular the sounds produced by the attractive-looking deeper members (resembling some exotic and ancient bassoon) remain sadly disappointing. However, it is important to stress that the recorder group does not *need* to have that desperate penny-whistle quality with which it is often all too reasonably associated.

The recorder's relationship with the orchestral world remains, however, essentially a specialized occupation so that, when one is required, an expert is engaged who may arrive with a Gladstone bag full of bits and pieces which he will juxtapose as he sees fit without anyone—least of all the majority of conductors—knowing what he is about, let alone able to challenge him on his view of the requirements presented by the music. It is, however, useful to know that the family members most likely to appear are the treble recorder—generally believed to be the instrument used by Bach and Handel—which sounds as written; and the descant which sounds an octave higher (together perhaps with the very tiny sopranino, which also sounds an octave above the written note). It is in fact for the treble and descant recorders that Britten writes in *Noye's Fludde*, though in the score he notates the descant recorders at actual pitch.

If the recorder then remains predominantly a solo —even concertante—instrument, it can have an orchestral function where it is used in such ensemble writing as is found in, for example, the Monteverdi *Vespers*. This work calls for a group of three or four players who must have a thorough understanding of the possible doublings and alternations with strings and cornetti, few of which are, or can be, fixedly prescribed as in a modern score.

SAXOPHONES

Few developments in the history of instrumentation are stranger than the fate of the saxophone. As logical an invention as the clarinet, it somehow failed to establish itself as anything but a special purpose instrument, as in Bizet's *L'Arlésienne*, until it came to be adopted as one of the mainstays, both as a solo instrument and in group work, of dance bands and jazz. This in turn gave it such strong prejudicial associations that it could never again compete orchestrally with the other woodwind on an equal basis. Strauss experimentally used a quartet of saxophones in his *Symphonia Domestica*, taking the precaution, however, of marking them *ad lib*. Unfortunately he chose for his purpose the German military band instruments which were pitched in C and F alternately, instead of the standard instruments of today in E♭ and B♭. Opinions have been aired that he muddled them with saxhorns but, apart from the imputation of ignorance against one of the most knowledgeable and forward-thinking masters of the orchestra, this suggestion is wholly belied by the woodwind-style flexibility of the parts given to the ill-fated foursome. It should be added that Strauss himself never insisted upon them in his own performances of the work.

Josef Holbrooke frequently incorporated the entire saxophone family into his woodwind, especially for his larger-scale works such as the post-Wagnerian Celtic trilogy *The Children of Don, Dylan* and *Bronwen*. But perhaps because of the heavy glutinous effect his precedent has remained unfollowed.

Hence the saxophone remains no more than an occasional visitor, whether the E♭ alto, as in Berg (*Der Wein, Lulu*), Britten (*Sinfonia da Requiem, Prince of the Pagodas*) and Mussorgsky-Ravel (*Pictures from an Exhibition*) or the B♭ tenor as in Prokofiev (*Romeo and Juliet, Lieutenant Kijé*, etc.). Moreover it is very rare for more than one saxophone to be introduced into the woodwind group. Ravel's *Bolero* is one exception with its sopranino and soprano as well as tenor, and Gershwin uses a family of three (alto, tenor and baritone) in his *An American in Paris*, although their status as visitors is emphasized not only by his treatment of them exclusively as an inseparable group at isolated moments during the course of the work, but in his placing them much like soloists between the percussion and the strings on the printed page. There is however, no uniformity at all in this matter, Strauss putting his saxophones logically between the clarinets and bassoons, and Ravel most oddly below the brass but above the percussion. Prokofiev places the saxophone stave between the clarinets and the bassoons, Britten between the bassoons and horns, while different editions of Bizet's *L'Arlésienne* give it in each of the above positions. Berg, however, placed his saxophone between the oboes and clarinets; while Milhaud in *La Création du Monde* conceived the highly original and unconventional idea of using the saxophones as a substitute for the violas in the string group, even placing it there in his score layout:

Ex. 197

207

The general rule is for an extra player to be engaged whenever a saxophone is required, but it can be taken as a doubling instrument in the clarinet department on account of the similarity of its single-reed mouthpiece. Oddly enough, Ravel organized his orchestral version of Mussorgsky's *Pictures* so that the saxophone should be doubled by the 2nd oboe, but this is never done in practice.

SARRUSOPHONES

The French have long had a predilection for a metal, in place of a wooden, contrabassoon. This is, in fact, the lowest and only surviving member of the sarrusophone family (the name, like that of the saxophone, being derived from its inventor). Described in the different scores in which it appears merely as 'sarrusophone' it is actually intended to be (and is to all intents and purposes) a simple and direct *alter ego* of the contra. In recent years, however, it has become increasingly rare despite the claims once made on its behalf in respect of both power and tone quality. Parts for the sarrusophone where the contra would normally stand can be found in composers such as Ravel (*Rapsodie Espagnole*, and on one page only of *Daphnis et Chloé*, where it looks as if the composer had either momentarily forgotten which he was using or regarded it as literally synonymous with contra) or Delius (*Eventyr*). But once again Josef Holbrooke made a bid, as with saxophones, to exploit a wider range of the family in his larger orchestral canvasses. In *Apollo and the Seaman* he added the alto as well as the bass instrument, presenting Sir Thomas Beecham with the opportunity for one of the best narrations in his riotous autobiography *A Mingled Chime*.[1]

But the sarrusophone has become a lost cause. The oddest revival (still of the double bass member, which is, incidentally, in C and is notated like the contra an octave higher than it sounds) has been in Stravinsky's *Threni* of 1958, but here too it is hard to find anything in the tiny part for the instrument for which the contra would not serve at least as well.

---

[1] Hutchinson, London, 1944, pp. 75*ff*

BAGPIPES

Cecil Forsyth[1] wrote very amusingly of the consequences of his omission of the bagpipes from the first edition of his great treatise on orchestration. But when, stung by those taunts 'from the sterner side of the Tweed', he tried to disprove that he had been swayed either by 'ignorance or prejudice' by inserting some account of that controversial instrument into later editions he failed fully to make clear the very real objections to its orchestral use.

That there are such objections can perhaps be most obviously deduced from the fact that they play no part in the orchestration of the one work in which they might most be expected—Weinberger's *Schwanda the Bagpiper*. There is another Czech opera of much the same period as it happens, in which the bagpipes do appear: Janáček's *The Excursions of Mr Brouček*. They come in the Second Act where Mr Brouček visits the fifteenth century, Janáček writing for them like a kind of weird oboe with a strong folky flavour. But they constitute a special effect and are played on stage following to some degree Verdi's incorporation of the 'cornamuse' in *Otello* as part of the stage group of musicians forming Desdemona's retinue in Act 2. In *Otello* however, this is rarely carried out in practice, a likelihood which Verdi recognized by suggesting that his *cornamuse* may be replaced by two oboes. In neither of these examples are the bagpipes really integrated into the orchestra, and the reasons for the instrument's non-admission to the orchestral world remain inviolate despite these examples of special pleading.

In the first place the bagpipes must be played standing, or better still striding to and fro—which in terms of the concert platform would mean in front of the orchestra if not in the very body of the auditorium, this introducing an element of star performance into the proceedings. In this country, moreover, they are so bound up with a military nationalistic tradition that they are always played in the colourful Scottish uniform with kilt, sporran, etc., and so occupy the centre of all attention—both visually and aurally, for the bagpipes are unable to make the slightest variation in dynamics which remain a relentless fortissimo. Indeed the all-pervading penetration of sheer volume given by the addition of the drones to the repeater, which

---

[1] *Orchestration*, pp. 486–7.

latter supplies the melodic part, is so great that it dominates the entire orchestra from the moment it starts to play. And when the instrument stops there is no way of avoiding the formidable glissando dip of the drones as the air collapses in the bag.

But perhaps equally crucial is the fact that the bagpipes are limited to a seven-note scale whose intonation does not conform to that of the symphony orchestra. Hence any attempt to integrate it with orchestral textures could only be made on its own terms, with devastating and confusing results.

However, Scottish composers have been known to introduce the 'pipes' into symphonic works, though always as a high-lighted soloist featured in apposition to the main body of the orchestra, as in Ian Whyte's *Donald of the Burthens* or, more recently, Edward McGuire's symphonic poem *Calgacus*.

12 CONCLUSIONS

Soloistic to a fundamental extent that can never be the case with the strings, less exclusive than the horns, more aristocratic than the brass, the woodwind department consists of a group of highly individual but interdependent artists whose work in the orchestra alternates between solo and ensemble playing. Hence arises the status, and accordingly payment, of the woodwind, amongst whom the 'rank and file' of the strings simply does not exist. One consequence of this is that works for wind alone are only very rarely included in orchestral programmes. For with the exception of music for military band (which is a different proposition) all purely wind compositions come outside the sphere of orchestral music, since all the players have solo lines and however much these may be combined in ensemble work they remain a matter of strong individual responsibility. This is so to quite as great a degree as in, for example, Mendelssohn's String Octet which, though a comparatively large ensemble, never crosses the dividing line between chamber and orchestral music in the way that Strauss's *Metamorphosen* undoubtedly does for much of the time. Thus, even when a conductor becomes more a convenience than a necessity, as in Mozart's Serenade in B♭, K. 361, the musicians will still normally be paid at a higher, 'obbligato' rate, thus putting such works outside the regular scheme of orchestral concert or broadcasting programme. This is by no means to say that, for example, Gounod's *Petite Symphonie*, Strauss's Serenade, Suite Op. 4 and Wind Sonatinas, or Stravinsky's *Symphonies of Wind Instruments* (though the latter also includes some brass on equal terms) are never played. But they can only be programmed as the result of some special contractual arrangement, and thus are far more infrequently heard than works for strings alone.

Such a state of affairs is, needless to say, much deplored by string players since it has the side effect of depriving them of periods of free time corresponding with those enjoyed by the wind during the rehearsal of string works.

Wind players need considerable resources of patience and adaptability. Their solos may occur in the midst of gruelling stretches of tutti playing or after long periods of inactivity. In the one case there is the eternal spectre of the tired lip or worn reed, in the other the necessity to play a difficult and exposed passage on a cold instrument and when they themselves have, as it were, 'gone off the boil'.

Nor are these hazards confined to the specific responsibilities of playing solo phrases, but may also haunt the frequently occurring harmonic passages for the woodwind group. The manifold characters, let alone the imperfections of so many different instruments and variations of instruments give rise to tortuous problems of intonation as well as precision of ensemble attack. The combining of woodwind into blocks of sound is not at all the exact science that Rimsky-Korsakov formulated in his beautifully logical *Principles of Instrumentation*. All his carefully contrived dovetailing of timbres gives a sound as personal and as acoustically fallible as that of other composers whose individuality is revealed as much by their distribution of woodwind chording or ensemble work as by their very style of composition. Berlioz once said in bitter irony, but with—perhaps unintended—truth, that he had only to write down a chord of D major for the critics to shout 'Impossible!'. For his orchestration is often so idiosyncratic as to be unmistakable even in a simple woodwind chord.

The varied styles of different composers may present quite unexpected problems. Many a chord which looks harmless enough on paper presents unforeseeable clashes of overtones requiring the utmost skill as the players jockey for pitch position. Even highly accomplished artists may be unsure at times who is at fault or even whether they should personally adjust up or down, sharp or flat, in circumstances where the word 'truth' has no unequivocal meaning. The problem may also arise through the acoustical flaw in our use of the tempered scale. The notorious $^6_4$ chord gives perennial trouble, as in Strauss's *Till Eulenspiegel*:

Ex. 198.

Here one of the notes in the flutes and clarinets—often enough the tonic F, strange to say—may have to be flattened with regard to the prevailing pitch before the chord will be tolerable and free of 'beats'. Sometimes the use of a certain degree of vibrato in, for example, the flutes may help. For the innate purity of the flute sound in itself can make it appear to be actually below pitch when combined with other members of the wind ensemble. The same can be true of the lowest register of the oboe, though for different acoustical reasons. These are matters which experienced and well matched players will aim to correct as a matter of course. Such a wind section will often prefer to organize their differences and make any necessary adjustments amongst themselves, especially in the case of the well-known *bêtes noires* (Mendelssohn's Overture *A Midsummer Night's Dream*, Rimsky-Korsakov's *Scheherazade*, the last chords of Wagner's *Faust* Overture, Balakirev's *Thamar* and Strauss's *Don Quixote*, etc., etc.) but the conductor's help may be sought or, despite what has been said on pp. 169–70, could be indispensable. It must also be conceded that chords and passages do occur in the repertoire which hardly ever sound really satisfactory. There are even ghost notes, played by nobody and even inaudible to the wind group though perfectly clear to the conductor and the delighted strings. The conductor, therefore, if he is to be able to arbitrate successfully, needs a specific understanding of wind problems, but it would be naïve to believe that his skill in perfecting wind intonation will be due to his possessing an impeccable ear. Such an asset, enviable as it is, has been known to lead to a tiresome misuse of valuable rehearsal time and the consequent irritation of the players, who have long learnt how to adjust momentarily to each other as occasion may warrant, while the wretched conductor embroils himself ever deeper in a fluctuating tonal quicksand.

Woodwind ensemble of attack is again an art and not a science. Orchestral leaders, sitting fretfully at their violin desks, have been known to express scorn and impatience at what they regard as the patent incompetence of wind players who appear to be unable to tongue precisely on the conductor's beat. Yet this view merely reveals a lack of sympathy with the inherent difficulties and techniques in wind playing, which are not only as specialized in every way as the numerous problems of precision with which the strings are constantly involved, but also concerned to a far greater extent with the interplay of personal styles and the close collaboration of a few interdependent soloists. However much it may be desirable for the leaders of the string group to like and admire each other as people, as well as for their artistry, in the wind ensemble it is crucial.

HORNS

1 ORCHESTRAL FUNCTION AND NOMENCLATURE

The role of the horns lies midway between the woodwind and the brass, so that although logically they seem to belong to the latter—and some composers as well as conductors positively identify them as such—they really have a foot in each camp, and take pride in a status quite apart from the main brass ensemble. Indeed, if a conductor merely calls for the brass in rehearsal, the horns will most probably remain obstinately silent. There is something more than just snobbery here—although an element of this can perhaps be conceded, there being a consciously aristocratic side to an orchestra's horn section. Much of their time is spent in having specifically to play alongside the woodwind and blend with them, and this requires refinement of a special order that is quite as important as the more robust facet of the horns' ambivalent character.

Where the printed page is concerned the colloquial English term 'French horn' only really survives in tutors and instrumental books. This may be partly due to the superseding of the old narrow-bore French or French-type instrument with its upright pistons by the wider-bore German horn with the more convenient rotary-valve action. Certainly not all 'French horns' were made in France any more than all 'German horns' are made in Germany, but the fading of the term 'French horn' amongst players themselves roughly corresponds with the arrival during the 1920s and 30s of the more reliable and consistent German instruments.

Some German scores reflect an earlier development in the history of the horn. Schumann scores, for instance, as well as early Wagner (see *Tannhäuser*, whose opening presents an outstanding example) specify the simultaneous use of both *Waldhörner* and *Ventilhörner*, the former

215

being the old hand-horns without any valves or pistons (= *Ventile*) and thus limited to the open notes of the harmonic series.

A few French scores also reflect this evolution; Berlioz presents obvious instances, and scores as late as Chabrier's *España* of 1883 describe the horns alternately as 'cors ordinaires' and 'cors chromatiques'. But the Italians have always referred uniformly to *corni*, the term also used in international Italian.

The only really confusing name for the horn is the Spanish which, oddly enough, is *trompa*. This is found in works such as Turina's *Danzas Fantasticas*, published only in the relatively rare Madrid edition, where the 'trompas en Fa' look confusingly like trumpets.

2 NOTATION

Horn parts have long been written in a variety of different transpositions, relating to the comprehensive collection of crooks once in use with the older instruments (see p. 239 below). However, horn playing and notation came during the course of the nineteenth century to be orientated around the single transposition of the increasingly standardized Horn in F, chosen possibly because of the relative simplicity of its transposition and its midway standing in the range of crooks.

Thus horn notation is normally spoken of in terms of the F horn and players will speak of the 'bad top A♭' or of 'pedal F' or 'top C' always meaning these notes for Horn in F and representing in concert pitch respectively: 🎼 , 🎼 and 🎼 .

This vernacular remains constant no matter what transposition the part is in. Thus, for example, these notes could just as well be written as 🎼 , 🎼 and 🎼 for the Horn in B♭ alto, but the player automatically transposes mentally back to the F horn, i.e. a fourth higher in this instance. Similarly, Horn in D always represents the transposition of a minor third down, Horn in G a tone up, and so on. Most worrying to the horn fraternity is Horn in H (= B♮, met particularly in Brahms), which involves the awkward transposition of a tritone.

The following table of these transpositions relative to the F horn will give an over-all picture of the situation:

216

B♭	alto[1]	4th higher	(both alto and basso were commonly used in the classical period; Haydn and Mozart sometimes neglected to specify which, with consequential uncertainty and differences of opinion. See p. 239 below.)
A	(always alto	major 3rd higher	
A♭	unless otherwise specified)	minor 3rd higher	(rare, but see Schubert's 'Tragic' Symphony.)
G		a tone higher	
F♯		a semitone higher	(rare; the most famous example is Haydn's 'Farewell' Symphony.)
E		a semitone lower	
E♭		a tone lower	
D		minor 3rd lower	
D♭		major 3rd lower	(extremely rare, though instances are to be found in Strauss.)
C		4th lower	
H	(= B♮)	tritone lower	
B♭	basso	5th lower	
A	basso	minor 6th lower	(both rare, but used by Italian composers including Rossini and Verdi.)
A♭	basso	major 6th lower	

---

[1] This was the smallest crook in normal use. H. C. Robbins Landon has argued the case for a C alto horn (playing at concert pitch, i.e. transposing up a 5th for F horn) bringing the horn parts in many Haydn symphonies into unison with trumpets and oboes; and admittedly the mark 'in C alto' can be found added to the horn line in all editions of the concluding chorus of Haydn's *The Seasons*. Moreover an even more extreme case can be found in Mozart's Symphony No. 19, K. 132 which calls for four horns in E♭, the first two of which are marked 'alto'. But while such crooks may have

217

Naturally, the further transposition to concert pitch is effected by the simple drop of a fifth.

In the bass clef, however, the matter is by no means so straightforward: indeed bass clef horn notation presents considerable complexity amid a never-ending controversy. By tradition the notes in the bass clef are transcribed an octave down, so that the transposition to concert pitch becomes a fourth upwards. This corresponds to some extent with the old-style cello writing in which passages in the treble clef were notated an octave higher than actual pitch in order to evoke an instinctive technical response, though in their case this device soon lapsed in favour of the tenor clef which more logically serves the same purpose (see p. 111). But no such alternative solution in the form of an extra clef evolved for the horns, whose lowest notes are played with a different 'embouchure' (or mouth formation) and have a strong vibrant resonance. These are the 'pedal notes', and so deep do they feel to the player that their notation, viz:

is of positive psychological and technical aid to performance.

Most orchestration manuals condemn this notation out of hand and the situation has to be faced that, however popular 'old notation' (as it is called) may continue to be amongst players, 'new notation', whereby the anomaly is corrected, has gradually come to be favoured by composers so that bass clef notes are made to transpose in the same way as those in the treble clef.

But in the end the fact remains that both notations exist side by side in scores and it is not always by any means obvious which octave is intended without pre-knowledge of the relevant composer's normal practice, even (in some extreme examples) from internal evidence of the music.

Generally, however, 'old notation' reveals itself sooner or later in the course of a work since notes are usually encountered which would lie too low to be practical if transposed down instead of up. By deduction, therefore, one may infer that doubt only arises in the player's or conductor's mind when 'new notation' is used, which is another strong and valid argument against it, especially from the player's

existed exceptionally —although this is hotly disputed by some horn specialists—the artistic evidence within the works themselves can often seem extremely doubtful (see, for example, bars 49–50 of the Finale to Haydn's Symphony No. 33).

point of view, where the least trace of uncertainty can lead to unreliability in performance.

One weakness in the argument for 'old notation' does however arise in occasional border-line instances where the bass clef is used for relatively high notes:

Ex. 199   Berg, *3 Orchesterstücke*, Op. 6

This both belies its purpose and can lead to confusion in cases such as bars 318-30 in the last movement of Beethoven's Symphony No. 7 where the horns, notated on the same stave in the score, play in the bass clef two octaves apart, viz:

Ex. 200

But in the individual parts, also written in the same clefs in the older Breitkopf material, the passage emerged as follows:

Ex. 201

which is demonstrably absurd since the note played remains identical throughout.

Broadly speaking, it could be said that traditionally-minded composers such as Mahler, Strauss, Ravel, etc. continued to use 'old notation' even after progressives such as Debussy had changed to 'new'. But this is by no means a rule-of-thumb guide. Stravinsky used 'old', while Elgar changed to 'new' though actually using both in the course of one single work, the 'Enigma' Variations, which presumably was being written at the very time that he was deciding to adopt the new style (though he temporarily reverted to 'old' in the *Cockaigne* Overture). Vaughan Williams, who kept to 'old', unfortunately muddled the issue by adding 8va signs in his Sixth Symphony, thereby introducing ambiguity where there would otherwise have been none.

An oddity of horn notation is that key signatures are not normally used. This obviously derives from the time when horn parts were always written in C—the crook (or transposition) changing if necessary, rather than the key signature—and when the horn became chromatic the custom of writing horn (and trumpet) parts without key signatures survived by means of extensive use of accidentals. Some composers (primarily those who also decided to rationalize bass clef notation) have sought to be logical here too and have written with the same freedom of key signature in these parts as with other orchestral instruments, but it cannot be entirely disregarded that horn players are less accustomed to working with key signatures and that their use can accordingly lead to unnecessary slips. Prokofiev in his Fifth Piano Concerto even stipulates that, although in the score the horn and trumpet lines are written with key signatures, in the parts the sharps and flats must be added before each note.

3 RANGE

The compass of the horn is basically from [♩] to [♩] though a few more notes at each end have been written—and can be obtained by good players—extending the range from as deep as [♩] or even [♩] to [♩] or conceivably [♩] and [♩] . Strauss is usually credited with the initiative of having widened the range, having already in *Symphonia Domestica* taken his first horn up to top E:

Ex. 202

but in point of fact he had been forestalled by none other than Schumann, who—admittedly in a concertante work—had written several top E's as long ago as 1849 in his *Konzertstück* for four horns and orchestra, Op. 86.

Moreover such altitudes, though they later fell into disuse, were quite normal to Haydn who took a written top E in his stride in the minuet of his Symphony No. 99 (written for horns in E♭—so this note is in practice no more than a top D for the horn in F, though still however above the regular compass). In earlier years, on the other hand, he had clearly known the extreme upper register to be practicable, for a most famous example occurs in the Symphony No. 51, of the early 1770s:

---

[1] All these and subsequent examples are set out for Horn in F and in standard 'old notation'.

Ex. 203

(Note also the extreme low notes of the 2nd horn which Forsyth quotes in the form of an elaborate conundrum, see also p. 239 below.)[1]
Here the transposition works against the player, as the passage being

for Horn in B♭ alto, the written top C becomes an F *in alt* (i.e.)

a very high note indeed and unobtainable by many players. Such passages are usually executed today by players specializing in high-crook instruments such as B♭ alto or even little F alto horns (see also p. 241).

Mozart, who was generally much more conservative in his treatment of horn compass, wrote up to top G (above the stave) in the horn duos, K. 487, though without stating the crook he had in mind. He may have assumed that the players would choose a crook correspond-

---

[1] *Orchestration,* pp. 79–80.

ing to the limits of their technique. Be this as it may, the omission misled the editors of the Breitkopf *Gesamtausgabe* into allocating the duets to basset horns despite the palpably hornistic style of the writing (see also p. 150).

At the bottom end of the compass it is again Strauss who quietly and unobtrusively takes the horn lower than is usually thought to be wise or safe, writing a bottom D♭ in *Die Schweigsame Frau*, though this is notated as a pedal F: for Horn in D♭, itself an unusual transposition. Some players can obtain the very bottom C: the fundamental of the F horn, but it is somewhat unreliable and in any case appears nowhere in the orchestral repertoire.

4 SEATING POSITION IN THE ORCHESTRA

The traditional place for the horns on the concert platform is on the left (as viewed by conductor and audience). This sets them apart from the heavy brass ensemble which is usually placed on the right.

Recently, however, and especially on the continent, the custom has arisen of moving the horns across to the right together with the trumpets and trombones. But apart from the unfortunate effect, both musically and psychologically, of identifying them positively as brass instruments (see also p. 232 below) this has the additional practical disadvantage of dulling their tone, since their bells are directed into the bodies and clothes of their colleagues seated centrally in the orchestra, instead of allowing the sound to project freely with ringing tone into the hall.

Of the two main seating possibilities:

$$\text{(a)} \quad 1. \quad 2. \quad 3. \quad 4.^{1}$$
$$\text{or (b)} \quad 4. \quad 3. \quad 2. \quad 1.$$

---

[1] For the sake of simplicity—for the time being—the standard 4-horn group is assumed. But see pp. 225*ff* below.

once a matter of sharply differentiated schools of thought, (b) has for many years now utterly routed (a) which was the seating firmly championed by Aubrey Brain and continued into the 1950s by his son Dennis.

The virtue of (a) lay in the 1st horn's bell being free and exposed, allowing maximum resonance and expression in solo passages; there was also the added advantage that the other members of the section were able to balance their tone with the true reflected sound of their leader, instead of receiving his tone in crude form direct from the bell. The difference is far greater than anyone would believe who has not had the personal experience of sitting in a section.

The advantage of (b) which proved so decisive is that the 1st horn is nearer the focal centre of the orchestra and in particular the principals of the woodwind. The value of this in delicate ensemble work is self-evident. But nowadays horn players have become so completely accustomed to (b) that they continue to adopt it even when moved to the opposite side of the orchestra, though here its *raison d'être* is entirely lost.

Of course platforms vary to an infinite degree and it is sometimes difficult to line up the horns satisfactorily either to the left or right of the woodwind. In this case one variant which has come to be adopted is of placing the horns centrally *behind* the woodwind. But this too has its disadvantages, for with their bells pointing backwards any increasingly remote position is detrimental to both tone and precision, while this formation once again results in pushing the 1st horn over to the right and into the territory of the brass.

On some platforms a square formation is a better proposition, viz:

$$4. \quad 3.$$
$$2. \quad 1.$$

and horn players sometimes favour this block seating for ease of ensemble; but the magnificent effect of a row of horns is too great to be sacrificed lightly, being not merely a splendid sight but also producing a livelier and more ringing quality.

Horns must always be placed in such a way as to give plenty of lateral space between them, to allow their tone to 'get away'. For they are unique in respect of the true beauty of their tone being heard by reflection, the bells pointing half sideways, half backwards, in consequence of which they are also particularly sensitive to the acoustical properties of the back or side walls of a hall or theatre, a characteristic that should never be overlooked, or even underestimated, when the orchestral seating is being planned. At the same time it must be conceded that in some broadcasting studios or in recordings for films the sound engineers deliberately place the long-suffering horns against a resonating back wall or baffle to create a special effect.

Another consideration (to be discussed again later in the Timpani Section) is that horn players will go to any lengths to avoid being placed immediately alongside or in front of the timps and heavy percussion. They are, of course, not unique in this, but have a special case to plead since the effect of sudden and violent reverberation travelling up the bell and on to the players' lips can have a serious detrimental effect on their reliability.

5 CONSTITUTIONS OF THE HORN SECTION

The seating formations discussed above are based on the 4-horn group that is the standard ensemble of the symphony orchestra. But this is by no means completely uniform throughout the repertoire, although by far the greatest number of works do use horns in multiples of two or four. This duple tendency can be traced back to baroque times, Bach writing for a pair of horns in the First Brandenburg Concerto and the Christmas Oratorio for example, whilst Handel (typically more prodigal) sometimes uses four horns, still however treated as two pairs. It is true that a single horn can also sometimes be found in Bach, in the cantatas and above all in the famous 'Quoniam' of the B minor Mass. But these examples of solo horn writing are all concertante in character and are today regarded as virtuoso engagements commanding a soloist's fee. In fact the use of a single horn treated as an integral member of the wind group is a new instrumental colour introduced only during the present century. This is partly because one horn sounds strangely lonely and unsupported, but is also to some extent bound up with the fact of the bassoon providing a less than satisfactory foundation of the wind group (see p. 153) so that the 2nd horn of, for example, Wagner's *Siegfried Idyll* fulfils a dual purpose, having links both with his partner and the woodwind ensemble. Another example of this can be seen in Strauss's *Bourgeois Gentilhomme* music:

Ex. 204

Orchestral music is thus orientated around a horn section built in pair-units, a single pair sufficing for the standard eighteenth-century orchestra with the occasional addition of a second pair, often pitched in a different crook. It is sometimes not even very important from the point of view of the scoring (as contrasted with that of the players) which of the two pairs takes priority, a situation that extends into the romantic era. In Beethoven's Overture *Leonora* No. 3, for example, all the meat is given to the 3rd and 4th horns, while even in as late a work as Brahms's Second Piano Concerto the organization of the section is quite misleading. Indeed it is only by working out from movement to movement which players change crook that one discovers that in the second movement the D horns, who are enjoying all the solo work and are printed in the score on the upper of the two horn staves, are in fact the 3rd and 4th players and are so printed in the orchestral parts.

This use of the horn pairs in different crooks had the purpose of adding melodic notes to the instrument in the days when only the 'open' notes of the hand horn were pure and round in tone (see p. 237 below). This principle was also sometimes exploited by Haydn and Mozart when using only two horns in all. Haydn's Symphony No. 44 in E minor (the 'Trauer') and Mozart's G minor Symphony, K. 550, provide examples of this kind of differentiation handled with splendid resourcefulness and skill in specific movements, though strangely never for a whole work.

French composers took this a step further and passages can be found, as for example in Berlioz's 'Queen Mab' Scherzo from the *Romeo and Juliet* Symphony in which each of four horns is pitched in a different crook, presenting a marvellous teaser to the wretched score reader:

Ex. 205

Such examples as the above cannot, however, be taken to suggest that in Berlioz's day four horns were the regular norm in composers' scores. Schubert, for instance, who had indeed used two pairs in the outer movements of his 'Tragic' Symphony No. 4—following perhaps, the example of some of the earlier Mozart symphonies—wrote for only two horns in his B minor and Great C major symphonies although both of these newly introduced a section of three trombones. Indeed this combination of two horns together with three trombones was taken over by Mendelssohn and Schumann in their *Reformation* and C major (No. 2) symphonies respectively and by Liszt in his two piano concertos; it is thereafter occasionally to be found in other composers such as Saint-Saëns. Broadly speaking it is only by the mid- to late-nineteenth century that the 4-horn group became standardized, until Brahms, Dvořák, Tchaikovsky and of course Wagner—to cite only a few key romantic composers—all used four horns as a matter of course in their large scale symphonic works.

Sometimes the employment of two pairs of horns allowed for interesting experimentation in combining the old hand horn with the recently developed chromatic piston instruments. Wagner's use of this contrasted pairing in *Tannhäuser* has already been mentioned above (p. 215), and Schumann's D minor Symphony is another instance, though it has to be admitted that in neither is there any real exploitation of contrast between the two kinds of instrument.

Examples of more than four horns are rare until the advent of Wagner. Mozart's *Serenata Notturna* (No. 8, K. 286) hardly counts as it is for four orchestras, each with a pair of horns specializing in repeated and receding echo effects. Berlioz, whom one might very well have expected to use multiple horns, in the event only does so as part of the greatly inflated wind, brass and percussion sections he introduced into works designed either for outdoor performance (*Symphonie Funèbre et Triomphale*) or for some specialized large scale auditorium such as a cathedral (*Grande Messe des Morts*). Even Wagner allowed himself the self-indulgence of eight horns only when he came to *The Ring*, where he handled the huge ensemble not only as four pairs in the accepted traditional manner, but sometimes as two quartets. Still larger groups are of course to be found in the off-stage bodies of twelve horns heard in *Tannhäuser* and *Tristan* but these again are a special effect used exclusively for fanfares, and are never integrated into the orchestral ensemble.

However isolated an instance they may have been, the eight horns of *The Ring* opened the door not only to the use of a double quartet by Strauss, Mahler and others (Stravinsky's *Le Sacre du Printemps*, Prokofiev's *Ala and Lolly*, Scriabin's *Prometheus*, etc.) but to the intermediate group of six horns which, tried out by Strauss in *Also sprach Zarathustra* and *Don Quixote* as well as by Mahler in the Second and Fifth Symphonies, was especially beloved by Delius (*Mass of Life, Paris, Brigg Fair, Dance Rhapsody No. 1*).

Furthermore the offstage bevy of horns in the Wagner operas also paved the way for similar importations for dramatic purposes in the concert hall. The six horns in Mahler's Second Symphony are supplemented by a further four in the Finale for the apocalyptic Resurrection vision, in which again they are primarily introduced in order to play offstage fanfares, although Mahler does also bring them on to the platform to join the others as a 10-horn unit. But the all-time record is the offstage twelve additional horns to the eight in Strauss's *Alpensinfonie*, making up a total of no less than twenty.

In all these composite groupings built up from 2-horn units each first player (i.e. 1, 3, 5, and 7) is a principal in the structure of the orchestra and each second (2, 4, 6 and 8) a sub-principal. This is to some extent linked to composers' practices, the leaders of each pair being eligible for solos as occasion warrants. This is not to say that solos are lacking for the 2nd and 4th horns as experience of Beethoven's orchestral works soon reveals (*Fidelio* overture, Ninth Symphony, etc.) but in the main these either lie in the lower register or make special use of it. Indeed players tend to specialize in either the upper or the lower part of the compass. Gordon Jacob[1] even recommended the student orchestrator not to write for the 1st horn below ♮ or the 2nd above ♮ , though this is quite unrealistic in terms of what these players may actually meet in the course of their working life. The most that can be said is that high exposed passages for the sub-principal players do carry a greater degree of risk.

Yet many players, not only 1st horns but others normally engaged as 2nd or 3rd, often readily take on assignments, especially of contemporary music, where the parts take for granted a reliable technique over the whole range of the instrument. Gone too in these days of cut-throat competition is the custom whereby the 4th horn solo in the slow movement of the Choral Symphony was taken over

---

[1] *Orchestral Technique*, Oxford University Press, London, 1931. p. 33.

and divided between two players, generally the 1st and 2nd; the implication is one that no 4th horn of the present day will wish to accept.

The position of 3rd horn is often felt to be the most interesting and enjoyable. Much 1st horn work will probably come his way (in a heavy programme, for instance, when the 1st player will elect to sit out the first half if this consists of classical works requiring only two horns), and his own 3rd part boasts some gorgeous solos which can be indulged in without incurring the nervous and physical strain of what is described as the 'hot seat'.

For by the romantic era it is largely the composer's whim whether a solo is given to the 1st or 3rd horn (or 2nd/4th in the lower register)—unless, that is to say, there is some reason such as suitability of crook in the decades before all four players were in F. The composer may think it a good idea to give the 1st horn a rest, or the 3rd a bit of jam, particularly if he has a real feeling for the horn and understanding of players' psychology and thus delights in keeping all the players occupied and entertained with fascinating and rewarding solos.

The situation is, however, a little more complicated on the rare occasions when the scoring is for an odd number of horns. There are various instances of this but surely the outstanding exception to the duple character of the horn section was that initiated by Beethoven in his 3-horn group of the Eroica Symphony, his choice dictated no doubt in preparation for his pre-planned triple solo-work in the Trio of the Scherzo. This pioneer section gave rise to all kinds of new possibilities whereby Beethoven, and Dvořák after him in the Serenade, Op. 44 and the Cello Concerto, used the 3rd horn in a dual role, partly as an extra 2nd horn to make up triadic harmonies, partly as an alternative 1st. In this capacity he could either relieve the 1st horn in conventional two-horn writing to enable that player to prepare for some important or difficult solo (in the Eroica even allowing him plenty of time to change crook for the purpose), or occasionally to share the solos themselves.

Amongst later composers who embraced the 3-horn group should be cited Prokofiev in *Peter and the Wolf* (the three horns representing the wolf) and Hindemith's *Schwanendreher*, both of which treat the 3rd horn in a subordinate role; whereas in Strauss's opera *Intermezzo*, on the contrary, it does enjoy something of its identity as alternate principal.

Both 5-horn and 7-horn groups do exist but are so rare that only a single instance of each comes to mind, the First Symphonies of Wolfgang Fortner and Mahler respectively. In the latter, a well-known and unique example of the use of seven horns, the 7th, normally a high-range principal, is treated as if he were in reality no. 8, providing extra weight to the lower line of horns.

Another curiosity that changes the normal function and specialities of the horn ensemble is Bantock's *Fifine at the Fair* where the six horns are disposed in two sets of three horns each, the 4th horn—traditionally the low player *par excellence*—suddenly finding himself leader of the second group, the equivalent (for example) of the 5th horn in an 8-horn section.

From the viewpoint of the layman observer much of the foregoing is confused by the prevalent figure of a supernumerary horn player, seated alongside the 1st player. This extra first horn is known as the 'bumper' (the term coined from the verb 'to bump up', meaning to 'support' and nothing worse). The function of the bumper is to share the burden of the heavier passage-work so as to relieve the strain on the 1st horn and keep his lip fresh for solos. To this end he will play either instead of, or even sometimes together with, his principal as the nature of the music may allow. Such doubling is left entirely to the discretion of the players and does not properly enter the jurisdiction of the conductor at all.

Comparatively rare until some 25 to 30 years ago, the custom of agreeing to the engagement of a bumper for the 1st horn (and incidentally even more recently for the 1st trumpet as well) has gradually grown into something of a status symbol, although it is true that many programmes are undeniably heavy for the first players of these sections.

A form of doubling, however, which devolves upon the conductor in detail, is that involving more powerful symphonic works like Beethoven's Seventh Symphony which are nevertheless scored for only two horns. It had for many years become conventional to use four horns for many such scores, especially where the two horns are combined with trombones as well as trumpets, as for example, the last movements of Beethoven's Fifth and Pastoral Symphonies or Schubert's Great C Major.

The purpose of such reinforcements is patently in the interests of better balance with the increased weight of today's larger string sections, the extra sheer power of four horns being beyond dispute. However, there is a corresponding sacrifice of refinement as well as,

231

curiously enough, brilliance—four horns blazing away have a thicker, tubbier quality than two—and many horn pairs have more recently expressed their preference for handling such parts without this gratuitous doubling.

By analogy, 4-horn works on a very large scale are sometimes played with eight. Mahler himself used eight horns for Beethoven's Choral Symphony, and conceived the *ben trovato* device of creating an overwhelming crescendo of the 'an die Freude' melody by requiring the first four players to enunciate their parts *ff* whilst the second quartet played *crescendo molto poco a poco*. Such doublings still survive in gala performances in which the Eroica, Bruckner's Fifth or Walton's First Symphonies, all scored for suprisingly modest forces, are played by gargantuan wind and brass groups either for some special occasion, in concerts forming part of some international festival, or possibly merely to underline the prestige of a star (or would-be star) conductor.

6 LAYOUT IN THE SCORE

The standard place for the horn staves is at the head of the brass, i.e. immediately below the bassoons and above the trumpets, but bracketed with the latter. There are, however, two other alternative layouts: the first, initiated by Berlioz, is based on the philosophy that since the horns work in closest conjunction with the woodwind they should therefore be placed in the score within that section and they appear therefore, in order of pitch, between the clarinets and bassoons. Weingartner so strongly believed in the wisdom of this line of reasoning that in his editing of the Berlioz *Gesamtausgabe* for Breitkopf & Härtel he took the step of incorporating this practice into the edition even though it was a departure from Breitkopf's house style.

The other is a diametrically opposite school of thought. Wagner, who otherwise habitually followed Berlioz's precendent, writes the trumpet(s) above the horns in the *Siegfried Idyll* and in only one or two isolated pages of the *Ring*, and some composers follow this procedure as their invariable practice. Prokofiev, for example, wrote for the horns as self-evident members of the brass and therefore logically placed them, again in order of pitch, between the trumpets and trombones, but thereby relegating them to a role which, however important, by no means displays their manifold possibilities to best advantage. Other composers have at various times toyed with this layout but fortunately it has never seriously rivalled the standard format. Curiously enough Reger adopted it with a different stylistic aim: that is to say, with his predominantly contrapuntal technique in which drama and colour play a comparatively subsidiary part, his brass section is treated much more like woodwind—so that the logic of pitch which placed the horns below the trumpets became relevant, if for the opposite reason from that of Prokofiev and his followers. Hindemith, in his first full orchestral score, the *Concerto for Orchestra* Op. 38, seems to have been undecided which system to adopt as he changed the order around in the middle of the work. In his subsequent scores, however, he adopted the conventional layout.

Bearing in mind what has been said above on the pair-formation as well as the register specialization of horn players, it follows naturally that the principal (odd numbered) parts will normally correspond as will—beneath them—those of the sub-principals (even numbered). If chordal work is involved the descending order of the players' notes will generally be 1.3.2.4.; if—as often occurs—the horns are playing a melodic line in octaves, the upper line is usually given to the 1st and 3rd in unison, the lower to the 2nd and 4th. These are naturally tendencies, rather than inflexible rules, orchestration being an art and not a science, and it would be folly not to concede that many examples can be found in the repertoire where composers have either forgotten to follow the usual practices or preferred to ignore them. However composers so consistently lay out their horn parts in this manner that they sometimes come to find the technically correct notation (with the 1st and 2nd players on the upper line and the 3rd and 4th on the lower) tiresome to write and pedantic in appearance. Hence scores abound in many pages of which the horn lines are re-aligned, the 2nd and 3rd parts changing staves so that 1 and 3 appear together, as do 2 and 4. While obviously expedient, this can sometimes be found to reflect a little too mechanically on the layout of the parts, and thus lead to oversight, such as when Strauss—in the Introduction to Act 1 of *Rosenkavalier*—forgot how he was organizing his section and absently-minded wrote:

Ex. 206

a passage in which the players should obviously be sitting side by side, as indeed they are a few bars later:

Ex. 207

This kind of shorthand also robs the horn quartet of the stylistic character derived from its origin in independent pairs. Moreover the 2nd and 4th can easily find themselves endlessly rumbling about in the depths simply because they have been put together on a single stave in the bass clef:

Ex. 208   Bartók, *Dance Suite*

234

An extension of the problem arising from this kind of segregation occurs in the fire music from the Third Act of *Siegfried* where Wagner had intended his first quartet of horns to unite sonorously in playing Siegfried's horn call in unison while the second quartet played the fire motif in full four-part harmony. But, realizing that this entailed taking the low-orientated 2nd and 4th horns up to their top C, he added a footnote advising a redistribution of the parts as a result of which they were printed with the disparate elements inextricably intertwined. The resulting loss of cohesion in the ensemble is admittedly in practice less damaging to Wagner's initial concept than one might fear but is nonetheless regrettable since ideally the two elements should remain sharply differentiated.

Horns are rarely written out in open score (i.e. a stave to a part) unless either they are all pitched in different crooks, as in the Berlioz example quoted as Ex. 205 on p. 227, or where the lines would otherwise present too confusing an appearance:

Ex. 209   Prokofiev, Symphony No. 5

By far the most usual score layout is for two horns at a time to occupy a stave, and this may persist even when they have different

clefs, viz: . But of course every kind of variant can be found

ranging from the simplest chords or unison passage, notated on a single stave, to the many staves required by immensely complicated horn polyphony. Exigencies of space can also create some weird layouts or even faulty readings: the Eulenburg miniature score of Strauss's

Heldenleben attempted to reduce the eight parts from the four staves of the original Leuckart printing to two, but at the sacrifice, alas, of textual accuracy:

Ex. 210

standing for:

Ex. 211

7 OPEN AND STOPPED NOTES

As the strings are linked technically to the 'harmonics' of their open strings, so the horns—in common with the other brass families—are rooted on the open notes which correspond to the harmonic series listed on p. 113 of Section I and repeated here for the sake of convenience:

236

Ex. 212

This row, then, gives in fact the range of open notes available to the horn without the use of the valves, irrespective of crook except for two practical considerations: on the one hand the fundamental no. 1, shown in brackets, is hardly available to horns other than those in the higher crooks (see p. 222); and conversely those above no. 12 become more and more inaccessible to horns other than those in lower crooks.

These notes were, of course, the only ones properly available before the introduction of valves during the course of the nineteenth century: the only ones, that is to say, other than those obtained by altering the pitch through the manipulation of the hand in the bell. This, however, affected the quality of tone of each note to a different degree, and only a limited number of such notes were therefore tolerated and written by classical composers. Nevertheless several such 'stopped' notes (see also p. 244) can be found in the eighteenth-century repertoire including notes in the lower register which lie close to an open note and are not unduly exposed in the orchestral texture. Beethoven, though still writing essentially for the open harmonics, can be found to use all sorts of stopped notes for tutti passages. In the 'Eroica' Symphony, for example, the 1st horn plays the whole of the big tune of the finale including:

Ex. 213

clearly [music] and [music] or [music] must have been sufficiently reliable notes, lying very near the out-of-tune 7th and 11th harmonics (marked with a '×' in Ex. 212). On the other hand, for the sake of a solo he sacrificed the 1st horn for some 57 bars in the first movement to give the player plenty of time to change to the F crook so as to play the principal theme on the best open notes, knowing that it would have given the most beautiful ringing tone:

237

Ex. 214[1]

However, when he found no opportunity to allow time for the change of crook he took quite startling steps to avoid stopped notes in the famous would-be entry of the Fifth Symphony:

Ex. 215

(see p. 178 for a discussion of this same passage in its application to the bassoons to whom he gave it instead.) Yet only a very few years later Schubert used these stopped notes with impunity, though admittedly in *piano* for the famous and totally solo opening (again for two horns in unison) of the Great C Major Symphony:

Ex. 216

Finally reference must be made to the notorious and controversial 4th horn solo of the Choral Symphony:

Ex. 217

[1] The last A♭ is to this day often played by using the hand in old hand-horn manner to raise the pitch from the G without touching the valves.

Even Tovey's conjecture of a pioneer two-valve instrument belonging to the 4th horn player is now widely discredited. Certainly if hand-horn technique had reached such heights of refinement the step to the Brahms Horn Trio—written forty years later with extraordinary freedom for the natural instrument—becomes more credible, and might even make Brahms appear less ridiculous in his antipathy to the ever more prevalent valve instrument with its surely obvious advantages and liberating possibilities.

8 CROOKS AND VALVES

One way for the eighteenth- and early nineteenth-century composer to obtain different notes was, of course, to change the horns' crooks or to use a number of differently crooked horns together. Generally, but by no means invariably, the horns would be crooked in the prevailing key of the music, but although this would provide the greater number of open notes to match the harmonies of the moment, some very interesting results could be conjured up by choosing other crooks. The classic (Haydn and Mozart) use of horns in differing crooks has already been cited (p. 227 above) as has Berlioz's device of obtaining almost any note by juxtapositions of four horns each with a different crook (Ex. 205). It needs however to be added here that crooks really were detachable objects, ringed appendages of tubing available to the player in different sizes; as long as these were in regular use the purpose of the instruction 'in G', 'in B♭ alto' etc., was specifically to tell the player which to attach to his instrument, whereas today it merely tells him (and the conductor or score-reader) in which way the part will need to be transposed; a list of the crooks at one time in use is, in fact given on p. 217 in connection with transposition.

Sometimes there remains doubt over the choice of crooks where there is an 'alto' or a 'basso' of the same pitch, especially the B♭ crook since composers did not always bother to specify. Ex. 203 on p. 222 above gives the famous instance which Forsyth cited as an insoluble conundrum. Contrary to nineteenth- and early twentieth-century custom, it has gradually come to be believed that when Haydn did not say which he wanted, he always meant 'alto' and certainly in the same instance of the Symphony No. 51 the high passages for the 1st horn have been shown in recent years to be perfectly playable on the B♭ alto crook. Nevertheless, there is no question but that by Beethoven's time an unqualified B♭ positively always meant 'basso'; this is a curious anomaly which has created a highly controversial state of affairs, and in the case of eighteenth-century music is still by no means the open and shut case that many scholars believe it to be. Certainly the use of the high crook often lightened the texture to great advantage, but if too inflexibly adopted on every occasion it can sound hardly short of grotesque, the horns straining for long spells at uncharacteristic and ungainly altitudes. As so often each case should be decided on its own artistic merits, the decision being based on internal evidence such as chordal layout or the style and register of the parts.

Quite a new situation arises when the scores of early Wagner are reached. In *Lohengrin*, for instance, he writes the following:

Ex. 218

For Wagner, unlike Brahms, was a progressive—however much he remained a traditionalist at heart. Hence although he was in fact writing for valved instruments, he nevertheless retained the characteristic style of horn writing based on the open notes by the use of this method of notation, grotesquely acrobatic though it appears. For taken literally such *instantaneous* crook changing is completely, ludicrously, beyond the realms of possibility and it is self-evident that the instructions must mean something quite different; i.e. Wagner reckoned that the depressing of the relevant piston in effect transposed the instrument in the same way as by a change of crook. (This was not by any means improbable reasoning, except that his to-and-fro alternation of horns in G, E, D and A♭ make a riddle of which crook he thought the players were actually pitched in.)

The effect of the three main valves of the horn, like those of the trumpet, is to introduce extra lengths of tubing and thus to lower the pitch of the selected open note by in turn:

a tone	(1st valve)
a semitone	(2nd valve)
and a tone plus a semitone	(3rd valve)
(i.e. a minor third)	

Since the combined total equals three whole tones, the use of the three valves simultaneously gives the desired result of bridging the gap between the second and third harmonics shown in Ex. 212, as well as taking the horn three tones below the second harmonic itself. Thus the chromatic potential of the horn is for all intents and purposes complete, only excepting some very low notes—and on many horns these are supplied by means of additional fourth and even fifth valves connected with the relatively recent 'double' or alternatively 'compensating' horns as they are called. For, with the introduction during the present century of wide-bore rotary-valve German horns in which the crook is no longer detachable at all, the double horn (i.e. with double sets of tubing for the whole central portion of the instrument including the valves) soon became a standard feature. Such horns have two sets of harmonics built in. At first the new standardization lay in favour of F and high B♭ but, in view of the never-ending need for reliability in high solo playing, high B♭ and A became a frequent pair of keys for a double horn, with a myriad other variations[1] shortening the tube length even up to an instrument in F alto. This is not really a

---

[1] Even a triple horn has been marketed in—who would doubt it?—Chicago.

241

recognized member of the family but occasionally appears as a convenience for exceptionally high parts, even though it is admitted by players that recourse to such short-tubed horns carries with it an inescapable sacrifice in tone quality. In fact the F alto horn more or less corresponds to a once much derided so-called Koenig horn that was suitable for playing on horseback. It was pitched an octave above the normal F horn and had a trumpet-type mouthpiece. It also had the peculiarity that its bell faced the opposite way to the normal horn, i.e. to the left of the player.

The standardization of the F crook referred to on p. 216 takes no account of these modern refinements. It had become the crook most readily taken for granted already by Tchaikovsky (the F horn having become standard particularly early in Russia), and was gradually accepted by most other composers. (The C crook—which might have led to the horn ceasing to be a transposing instrument—lay too low to become a viable standard.) Mahler already wrote automatically for the horn in F, and only Strauss continued all his life to use other transpositions—purely out of a love of the old tradition, and in the confidence that the knack of transposition was a stock-in-trade of the hornist who likes to see the part written in the crook corresponding with the prevailing tonality.

While Strauss actually went too far in this belief (some of his parts are horribly complicated to transpose even for the expert and thus introduce wholly unnecessary extra difficulties) the principle is correct enough.

Transposition undoubtedly is a basic part of any horn player's equipment, for despite the introduction of valves the orchestral horn parts of the classical repertoire are mostly printed exactly as written by the different composers for Horn in D, Horn in E♭, etc., and accordingly need to be transposed at sight by the player of the now standard F horn. As a result conductors usually refer to the written note in discussing a player's part, though it is also usual to avoid misunderstanding by saying so. On the other hand, where the score is unfortunately written entirely in concert pitch, this may lead him to use the actual sound to describe a note to the player, and this can cause confusion and altercation. Customs vary over the years and in different countries, but the fact remains that it is easier to think in terms of the transposed parts where, as in classical or early romantic music, the tonality sense is strong and the notes used by the composer—often limited in scope and carefully selected—are related to the key of the music. Hence it was a misguided idea that led Boosey & Hawkes to publish the Mozart Symphonies in Sir Thomas Beecham's edition with the parts re-transposed for the F horn; similarly the American reprints of Breitkopf & Härtel materials of the standard repertoire—including many works by Beethoven, Brahms etc.—include horn parts transcribed for Horn in F throughout, often in the most exotic looking keys and bristling with accidentals, in the vain hope of being helpful, especially to the inexpert player or student.

One of the worst examples of retransposition has recurred in the otherwise beautiful authoritative edition of Bizet's *Carmen* published in 1964 by Alkor of Kassel. Here throughout the opera the four horn parts have been uniformly transcribed for horns in F. This makes Bizet's choice of player for the individual passage-work, as well as the actual writing itself, seem mere artless whimsy, and it quite obscures the logic and skill of Bizet's genius in his original selection of crooks and transpositions and in his fascinating choice of open and stopped notes. This is a melancholy instance of theoretical musicology taking precedence over practical musicianship in the pursuit of seeming common-sense, when faced with the changed circumstances of present-day instrumental and technical developments.

9 MUTING

In the 'Marche au Supplice' from the *Symphonie Fantastique* composed in 1830, Berlioz adds an elaborate technical instruction to his horn players:

Ex. 219

This outstanding early example of valve-horn technique (though admittedly here concerned with *not* using the pistons) refers to one of the muting effects of which the horn is capable. Although in the days of hand horns the manoeuvring of the player's hand in the bell was directed towards obtaining otherwise impossible notes, and accepting *faute de mieux* the distortions which resulted (see p. 237 above), once the valves had made the complete chromatic range possible the same technique was now available precisely for the purpose of exploiting the sound of the stopped notes. But since their tone-quality, however diverse, is nevertheless always less strong and ringing than the open notes, they now come into the category of muting. These 'hand-stopped' notes are best known by their French term *bouché* (oddly marked 'plugged' by Stravinsky in the closing bars of his *Symphonies of Wind Instruments*) which corresponds to the German *gestopft*, the Italian *chiuso* and the internationally used symbol of a cross '+' over the note or notes (contradicted by 'o' to represent *naturale* or 'open'). A good example of the effect with its contradiction, used in the rapid alternation of which it is capable, can be seen in Borodin's Dances from *Prince Igor*:

Ex. 220

The strange technical fact about this manner of playing is that as the hand is inserted into the bell the pitch at first becomes muffled as it gradually *drops* and it is only when the hand is firmly pressed in to the utmost that quite suddenly the sound rises and, as the tone is—and has to be—produced with an abrupt tongued accent, the pitch becomes edged and buzzy as well as a semitone *higher*, the F horn player (for example) having to transpose for Horn in E.

This *bouché* technique becomes exceedingly difficult in lower notes until below a certain point (roughly ♭) it becomes less and less possible and in any case begins to lose the snarling quality which is its strongest characteristic and often its very *raison d'être*.

It may, however, be the woolly hushed sound that the composer requires. In this case the player need not strive to reach that degree of pressure with the hand in the bell since, it will be remembered, the tone with less pressure of the hand has more of a muffled—even an echo—quality. But in this case the player needs of course to transpose the other way—i.e. a semitone *higher* to compensate for the initial lowering of pitch. Composers do not normally prescribe this second style of muting but Dukas made a speciality of it, marking in his scores exactly how (and, in *Ariane et Barbe-Bleue,* which notes) the player should finger:

Ex. 221   Dukas, *L'Apprenti Sorcier*

The reason for these opposite styles of muting is extremely compli-cated and elusive; as a result commentators are apt either to mistake which way the transposition is made (such as Widor), or confuse the two methods (as did Gevaert), or—like specialists of the horn world—get bogged down in mathematical acoustics and technicalities of what is happening to the column of air in the tube, a matter best forgotten by the practical man of the orchestra.

Lastly, and superficially the simplest form of muting: with actual mutes a muffled tone can be obtained without difficulty over the entire compass and even including, if required, a degree of edginess in the tone—though no mute can quite emulate the savage bite of the best hand-stopped notes. Moreover, unlike handstopping, the insertion of the mute does not affect the pitch at all and hence no transposition is necessary in either direction.

Muting by means of an actual mute is prescribed by *sourdines Dämpfer, sordini* etc., exactly as in string writing and not by the symbols '+' and 'O' which are specifically reserved for handstopping. But composers are not always precise in their instructions and Walton, for instance, will often write *chiuso* and *aperto* without regard to the method of obtaining the sound. Moreover mutes ideally need a moment or two to insert or remove, and many instances exist when the composer has marked *con sordini* or *senza sordini* without even allowing so much as a semiquaver rest to enable the player to carry out the instruction. Where the part lies high enough he will then usually simply handstop and as a result the different forms of muting are frequently interchanged according to convenience. It is, however, a mistake to regard instantaneous manipulation of a mute as quite impossible. A player can physically carry on even if the hand in the bell is inconveniently holding a mute in readiness or has not found time to dipose of it. (The crook of the knee is often found to be a practical make-shift lodging-place.) Beethoven set the 2nd horn this problem in his popular *Rondino* for wind:

Ex. 222

Here the passage is too low to be played *bouché*, but if the mute is used it involves just this manipulation between the muted and unmuted bars.

Ravel amused himself in the *Rapsodie Espagnole* by making play with the different effects of *sourdine* and *bouché* used in immediate alternation:

Ex. 223

247

Again as in string writing, composers are not always alert in specifying the end of muted sections; problems constantly arise where after a muted solo a tutti passage follows that seems to demand the open sound though no new instruction appears. Or alternatively a little later the instruction *avec sourdine* may recur although no unmuted passage has intervened. Hence a question arises whether the composer has simply repeated the instructions, either overlooking the fact that the instrument is already muted or perhaps because other horns or brass are unmuted elsewhere in the vicinity, or even—as players often suggest in rehearsal—because an interim instruction *sans sourdine* has been left out somewhere along the line, as indeed is often enough the case. The scores of Debussy are notoriously full of this particular problem, but one outstanding instance might be cited which always perplexes players and conductors alike: in the following example from Schoenberg's *Kammersymphonie*, Op. 9, the 1st horn mutes while the 2nd remains open:

Ex. 224

But as can be seen, the two horns come together again immediately and pursue their lines in thirds making it improbable in the extreme that Schoenberg intended such a contrast in tone quality as now exists between them. It seems likely that some oversight must have occurred though the solution is by no means obvious.

Mutes come these days in all shapes and sizes, and may be either of metal or fibre[1] but composers do not specify any particular variety as they do in trumpet writing (see p. 313).

Some indications are often taken to be associated with muting that do not actually refer to it at all. The term 'echo' for example, seems to imply a muted effect and is often wrongly played so. On the contrary a true echo is far better produced open, a good player being able to achieve miracles of pianissimo without muting:

---

[1] An excellent description of the various kinds in current use can be found in R. Morley Pegge's *The French Horn*, Benn, London, 1960, pp. 141–3.

Ex. 225   Delius, *Summer Night on the River*

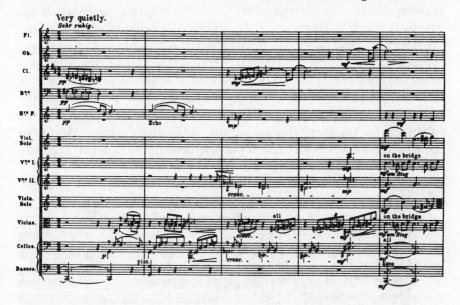

10 VERY STRONG EFFECTS

At the other end of the dynamic scale the term *cuivré* ('brassy') is all
too often taken to mean stopped or muted. But the word signifies the
exaggerated over-blown quality of the horn, which, although admittedly a feature of the strong muted or *bouché* sound, is also a real effect
in the open horn, and which Debussy exploits in, for example *Fêtes*; or
in *L'après-midi*, where he writes the one followed immediately by the
other:

Ex. 226

The German equivalent, much used by Mahler is *schmetternd* (='blar-
ing', 'blazing') but this is never confused with muting in any form.
   The next degree of this kind of 'rifting', as it is colloquially called, is
for the player to take the hand completely out of the bell which is then
turned upward as far as possible. This technique, known as 'bells up'

249

(*Schalltrichter hoch, pavillons en l'air* etc.) is unpopular with players—as with oboes and clarinets, see p. 199—but this time rather for practical reasons. Not only is the embouchure disturbed, increasing the risk of cracked notes (see p. 261 below), but intonation is no longer controllable and there is a resultant tendency to play sharp. Nevertheless, players have to come to terms with it however much they may seek to compromise with half measures through pressurizing the conductor against his judgement or conscience. For there is no substitute for the sheer riotous hilarity of Chabrier's *Joyeuse Marche* or the true furore of a horn section playing bells up as in Stravinsky's *Le Sacre du Printemps*:

Ex. 227

Ultimately, the most famous instance occurs in the eagerly awaited climax to Mahler's First Symphony where he enjoins the players to stand up as well as raising the bells. The effect—visual as well as aural—is unforgettable.

11 TECHNICAL DEVICES AND OTHER MISCELLANEA

TRILLS

Though trills and shakes are naturally written for horns as they are for woodwind, wider intervals than a tone are seldom found, as they are somewhat cumbersome. Horn trills can be achieved either with the valves or, where the two trilling notes consist of adjacent harmonics not more than a tone apart, purely by lip flexibility. All trills in classical music for hand horns were obviously lip trills, but as these are a virtuoso accomplishment they are found largely in solo work such as the Mozart concertos. Today even such instances are not always taken in this way because valve trills, though much less smooth, are considerably easier and therefore often substituted, though at some sacrifice of style.

The most hilarious example of lip trills occurs in Mozart's *Musikalischer Spass*:

Ex. 228

The upper trill for the 1st horn presents no problem as the next adjacent harmonic is very close, but the lower one entailing a to-and-fro of a fourth is hardly possible and the player's efforts cannot fail to sound comical in the extreme, as Mozart well knew.

More recent instances of horn trills presuppose the use of the valve, such as the very beautiful solo in Mahler's *Das Lied von der Erde*:

Ex. 229

In the Third Act of Verdi's *Falstaff* the horns participate in the universal trills, some of which could very well be taken as lip trills and some not, the players having the choice how to execute each in turn (see Ex. 230, opposite).

GLISSANDI

Horns produce a tolerable glissando effect, that consists of pushing the sound with the lip across the harmonics; it works better upwards

Ex. 230

than downwards and is hardly viable at anything less than full speed. Typical examples occur in Stravinsky, as in *The Firebird*:

Ex. 231

An interesting earlier instance of the same effect exists in Gabriel Pierné's *Les Enfants à Bethléem*, published in 1907. Here it is notated thus:

Ex. 232

and one wonders whether perhaps Pierné suggested it to Stravinsky, or perhaps showed the younger composer his own work at the time he, Pierné was conducting the first performance of *The Firebird* in 1910.

Roussel's Third Symphony gives another later (1931) instance in which his notation shows that he is reckoning on more than just open notes:

Ex. 233

Admittedly by skilful cheating—a combination of a free half-juggling with the valves and flexibility of the hand in the bell—horn glissandi can be simulated to a far greater extent than the strictly theoretical account of their technique suggests, though they remain of necessity clumsy and inaccurate. Nevertheless by such means even slow and soft glissandi can be contrived to cover such requirements as that of Berlioz's *Symphonie Fantastique* where the 3rd horn should imitate the already 'quasi-impossible' downward woodwind glissando (see p. 196). The fact is that the horn can get nearer to the idea of a continuous smear than the woodwind ever manage. But this is still not a device normally to be found in the repertoire.

LONG BREATHS

Horns share with oboes the peculiarity that very long breaths carry the problem of pressure on the lungs, since the rate of release through the very small aperture in the mouthpiece is extremely gradual in soft playing.

Nevertheless, long held notes do abound in the horn repertoire and players acquire the art of holding notes for longer than is normally believed possible—sometimes for more than two minutes at a time. A famous test of endurance is the link between the second and third movements of Beethoven's 'Emperor' Concerto, some soloists indulging themselves in the creation of atmospheric anticipation without regard or mercy for, in particular, the suffering 2nd horn—for the lower notes are harder to control and require more air than those in the middle of the compass. Wagner presents two similarly severe tests upon the 2nd horn's sang-froid as well as his lip and breath control in the *Siegfried Idyll*, as, for example, the totally exposed horn duet in the middle of the work:

Ex. 234

An even more exacting passage occurs in the concluding bars of the Idyll, as it is here a pedal B (i.e. pedal C for E horn) which has to be sustained *pp* for no less than eleven very slow bars. Moreover, the problem is paradoxically aggravated by the fact that pedal notes expend considerably *more* breath while requiring the maximum of lip and lung control.

Mercifully however, the first horn, who is otherwise resting, can in this instance come to his partner's rescue if necessary. Nor need this first-aid be heard as the note is to some extent covered by the (very soft) string texture, especially after the entry of the cellos with the principal melody at the sixth of the eleven bars.

For the most part, however, exaggeratedly sustained notes are sufficiently blanketed for the player to snatch breaths unheard. But even in these circumstances Strauss thought it worthwhile trying to avoid such breaks in the continuity of the sound and, having encountered a splendid new invention, prescribed its use in both his *Festliches Praeludium* and *Alpensinfonie*. The contraption, described as 'Samuels Aerophon' has sadly long since vanished without a trace—the vision is irresistible of the wind players sitting in rows, the long tubes hanging from the corner of their mouths like some weird hookahs, their feet pumping away to maintain air in their systems artificially, while effortlessly blowing the interminably long notes which Strauss had eagerly seized the opportunity to write, thanks to the ingenuity of Herr Samuel.

RAPID TONGUING TECHNIQUES

Horns, in common with other wind and brass instruments, find themselves faced with some extremely fast tonguing. Often enough this forms part of tuttis which are heavily enough scored, and the rapid notes given to other instruments as well, that even if the players should find themselves in trouble no-one need be aware of it; Strauss's *Don Juan* is full of such passages.

But should repeated notes be totally exposed and, worst still, continue for several bars, the danger of one's tongue seizing up can turn into a real nightmare. The Scherzo of Borodin's Second Symphony is a familiar hurdle in this respect, especially as it cannot be successfully double-tongued for reasons of tempo and accentuation:

Ex. 235

Generally speaking, however, the remarks given above in relation to woodwind—especially flutes—on double and triple tonguing (see p. 193) apply equally to horns. On the other hand, these techniques cannot be found actually prescribed in scores for horns as they are for woodwind, players normally adopting them or not as the speed or style of a specific passage may dictate. Ravel's *Alborada del Gracioso* shows a good illustration of a passage in which the composer will clearly have assumed that it will be triple tongued:

Ex. 236

Flutter-tonguing is also common practice and freely demanded in the repertoire. It is normally specified by the German *Flatterzunge* and translated equivalents but Stravinsky writes 'tremolo' in *Oedipus Rex* and many other composers (Britten, Honegger, etc.) merely add tremolo strokes (𝄇) to the tails of the notes.

CHORDS

One of the more amusing tricks of which the horn is capable, though
not by any means in the hands of every player, is the execution of
chords. Weber wrote a whole assortment in the middle section of his
Konzertstück but by and large they are pure fantasy and it is a mystery
how he was led to believe they could ever be played. The chords
which *are* possible are a series such as: and so
on downwards, for which either the top *or* the middle note is sung
while the bottom one is played. The third note (the middle or top
one, as the case may be) emerges as a kind of buzz—but still a
recognizable note through the scientific effect known as 'differential'
or 'summation' tones.

   Although occasionally brought out of the hat for a solo *tour de force*
(one of the better practical examples is the cadenza of Ethel Smyth's
Concerto for Violin and Horn) the use of chords has mercifully never
been used within the orchestra.

VIBRATO, TONE AND STYLE

The accepted tone quality of the horn varies enormously from country
to country, possibly more so than that of any other orchestral
instrument, ranging for example from the tremulous vibrato (not
unlike a saxophone at times) of many French, Russian and East
European players, to the thick mellifluous horns of the Vienna
Philharmonic. It seems a far cry from the days when Brahms
resolutely championed the hand horn, complaining that the introduction of valves muffled the fine ringing quality which characterized the
true horn tone. For this ideal has receded more and more over the last

decades with the universal adoption of wide-bore instruments until a true horn tone has even come to be discredited in some countries. Many an Italian player, for example, so far from holding the bell aloft to aim at resonance and vitality, will turn the instrument over so that the sound goes directly towards his thigh, and when begged to raise the bell in an attempt to lighten his thick tubby sound will protest that to comply would be as much as his position in the orchestra is worth.

Even in Britain and America where the tradition of a slender tone—more graceful yet entirely free from vibrato, firm but round and warm—had long continued to fight a rearguard action, the tendency towards a thicker sound has been growing steadily in the pursuit of a more homogenous blend both within the section and together with the other wind and brass groups. This has been achieved not only by the use of wide-bore instruments but also of instruments with shorter lengths of tube—that is to say, pitched in higher crooks.

Both these factors are also believed to lessen the risk of cracked notes (that bane of horn playing) and, in the present day pursuit of flawless reliability, are a prime reason for the sacrifice, much deplored by purists, of the characteristically vivid and hauntingly beautiful tone of the older instruments.

The constant bogey of cracked (or split) notes—more an occupational hazard for the horn than any other brass instrument, even the trumpet—is an age-long subject of controversy and cause of distress, no less within the orchestras themselves than to audiences curious to understand the cause. It is important to recognize that fluffing need not be the result of faulty technique, but may afflict even the greatest virtuoso on account of atmospheric or acoustic circumstances or the slightest untoward distraction. This is simply because virtually every note is produced in exactly the same way (horn playing is very much like singing in this respect); and it remains an inherent difficulty in many a horn solo merely to come in on the right note, let alone with a clean attack. Naturally the risk of mispitching becomes the more acute where the harmonics lie closest together—i.e. from the middle to the upper register, though even lower down the horn player should not be thought free from anxiety; the 8th horn solo that sets in motion the vast span of Wagner's *Ring* is one of the cruellest tests of reliability and requires an iron nerve, simple as it looks on paper:

Ex. 237

Nor is it a matter of taking extra care (although the capacity for unswerving concentration is a first prerequisite for a reliable player), indeed an over-careful hornist is an anathema to his section and his orchestra. The very psychology that aims to steer clear of trouble through caution will rob him of his bravura, the sense of musical line and the extrovert spirit, which has ever marked the greatest players, as well as landing him sooner or later into the very fallibility he so assiduously aims to avoid.

OUT-OF-TUNE HARMONICS

The fact that the 'natural' notes of the harmonic series marked '×' in the table on p. 237 are out of tune in terms of the Western scale has occasionally been exploited by composers as a special effect. A notable example occurs in Vaughan Williams's *Pastoral Symphony*:

Ex. 238

*)It is essential that this passage be played on a real F Horn and that only natural notes be used, to secure the true intonation of the Bb (7th partial) and the D (9th partial)

Verdi, at the beginning of the last scene of *Falstaff*, writes a solo for an off-stage horn (pitched in A♭ basso) stipulating that it should be played 'senza chiavi'—without the use of the keys or valves—even though all the notes used are open ones anyway:

Ex. 239

The suggestion is that as in the Vaughan Williams example all the partials should be played with true and untempered intonation, hence sounding out-of-tune to modern ears. Needless to say this is never carried out in practice although the idea is interesting and could surely be hauntingly beautiful.

The device remains, however, primarily soloistic and is never used for two or more horns in unison, presumably because the degree of 'out-of-tune-ness' may be an individual matter with dire consequences in ensemble work. Hence the best examples are actually in solo or concertante pieces such as the Dukas *Villanelle* or Britten's *Serenade*, Op. 31, for tenor, horn and strings. Yet it remains a cause for anxiety that even the most eminent performers of these works have been accused of faulty intonation by ignorant commentators and as a result they have occasionally been played with the offending harmonics 'corrected'.

WATER EMPTYING

The sight of horns emptying the water out of their instruments by turning them over, taking the slides out one by one and blowing through them, continues to be a favourite audience attraction. Horns are not equipped with spring escape valves like all other brass instruments because the water (largely condensation rather than pure spit, it may be disappointing to learn) collects in too many obscure bends of the endlessly curved tube. In many atmospheric conditions, the accumulations of water in the bowels of the instrument can be a real hazard causing distortion of tone and even contributing to the odd split note. Nor is the player always able to locate the trouble instantaneously, and if it lies in one of the least accessible places there may simply not be time to take the horn to pieces until, say, the end of a movement. The conductor will thus often be seen to wait for his horn players to reassemble their plumbing before restarting.

12 WAGNER TUBAS

Despite their name these instruments fall wholly within the province of the horn department; indeed even the same mouthpiece is used. They are played by the 5th-8th horn players either exclusively, as in Bruckner's Seventh Symphony (where they are added in the slow movement and finale only) or more generally as alternate doubling instruments to the horn itself. Wagner tubas are usually treated as a quartet and consist of a pair of tenor tubas, played mostly by the 5th and 6th horns, and a pair of bass tubas, played by the 7th and 8th. So much are Wagner tubas a matched quartet that players do not even possess their own instruments, which are acquired as a set of four by orchestras, opera houses, broadcasting stations or occasionally conservatoires.

The tenor Wagner tubas, not to be confused with the true tenor tuba (see p. 281), are pitched in B♭, while the bass Wagner tubas, once more by no means to be taken as proper bass tubas (see again p. 279), are pitched in F. The tenor and bass Wagner tubas correspond in length of tubing and manner of execution with B♭ alto and F horns respectively, though they have fourth valves which work the opposite way to the fourth valve of a double horn, i.e. taking them a fourth lower, the B♭ tubas down to F, and the F tubas down to C.

The danger of confusion with the tuba family proper is not to be taken lightly. In the first place although universally known as 'Wagner tubas' and constructed entirely individually as a genus in their own right, they are nowhere so designated in scores, where they are indeed listed simply as 'tubas'. The question will inevitably arise at once: how are the uninitiated to know when it is 'Wagner tubas' that the composer has written for and when not? Undoubtedly to the layman the best guide would be a list of relevant works—and it is surprising in view of the importance of the Wagner tubas in the orchestral scene how few there are: Wagner's *Ring*, Bruckner's Symphonies 7–9, Strauss's *Elektra, Die Frau ohne Schatten* and the *Alpensinfonie*, Schoenberg's *Gurrelieder* and the list is already practically complete.[1] In *Elektra* Strauss describes all four Wagner tubas, tenor and bass alike, simply as '4 Tuben' but in the later works he calls all four 'Tenortuben'.[2] Stravinsky's *Sacre* and Bartók's *Miraculous Mandarin* are both unusually scored for only two tenor tubas (used in each case briefly in alternation with horns). Stravinsky, as he already has two bass tubas in his brass section, reasonably reckons that he has no need for the lower pair of Wagner tubas, the two tenors joining the ordinary bass tubas to form an *ad hoc* quartet. In 1960 Elisabeth Lutyens took what has become the rare step of reviving the quartet of Wagner tubas for her *Quincunx*, although at no time do the players double on horns.

It might have been expected that the Wagner tubas would be notated like horns in the transpositions in which they are crooked, that is to say B♭ and F. Unfortunately their very inventor, Wagner himself, complicated the issue early on during the composition of *The Ring*, the work for which he caused them to be specially constructed. In *Rheingold* all goes smoothly, although oddly enough Wagner still retained the same octave (i.e. 'new notation') when writing in the bass clef for the F bass tubas (whereas he was still writing conventionally

---

[1] Other works often wrongly thought to contain Wagner tubas are the Janáček *Sinfonietta, Don Quixote, The Planets* etc., all of which are scored for the real tenor tuba in B♭.

[2] Strauss had by then abandoned the Wagner/Bruckner method of describing the normal bass tuba as 'Kontrabass Tuba' (see p. 280).

in 'old notation' (see p. 218 above) when using the bass clef for horns). But the scores of the other three music dramas contain a footnote which reads:

'In this, as well as the $\left\{\begin{matrix}\text{following}\\ \text{preceding}\end{matrix}\right\}$ scores, the tenor tubas are

written in *E flat*, the bass tubas in *B flat*, because the composer believed this way easier to read; when copying out the parts, however, the keys of B flat and F should be retained according to the nature of these instruments, and the notes must therefore be transposed.'

This is complete confusion; especially as it is not entirely true and is moreover only half the problem. Certainly in *Walküre* and *Siegfried* the tuba parts are given (as stated in a footnote) in E♭ and B♭ , the tenor tubas in the treble clef sounding a 6th lower than written, the bass tubas in the bass clef a tone lower. In the *Vorspiel of Götterdämmerung*, however, the tubas revert to the B♭/F notation as in *Rheingold*, but alas with a difference. This time Wagner experimented with notating them an octave higher so that the tenor tubas sound a ninth lower and the bass tubas an octave and a fifth lower than written, and now all uniformly in the treble clef, this possibly being the purpose of the experiment. At all events, he clearly came to the conclusion that it was a failure because by Act 1 (see pp. 314ff. of the Schott miniature score) he changed back yet again to his 'easier-to-read'(!) double transposition of E♭ and B♭ where they remain to the end.

Mercifully, orchestral parts exist which in deference to the wishes of the players—such as those at the Royal Opera House, Covent Garden—have been totally retranscribed, retaining the standard F horn transposition throughout. Certainly this contrivance removes once and for all the morass of uncertainty that resulted from such experimentation. For, strange to say, the E♭/B♭ double transposition was adopted by Schoenberg when he used the Wagner tubas in his *Gurrelieder* (where they are played by the 7th-10th horns). Bruckner, on the other hand, retained the B♭ and F notation, in which he was followed by Strauss. Unfortunately however, Bruckner got caught up in Wagner's muddle with respect to the octave in which the tubas should appear. In the Seventh Symphony he unwisely adopted Wagner's *Vorspiel*-to-*Götterdämmerung* notation so that superficially the tubas all appear to be squeezing away at the very limits of possibility:

Ex. 240

No doubt when he came to the Eighth Symphony Bruckner saw the absurdity of this just as Wagner had done before him. But what he did was to continue with the same notation, though usually adding the indication '8va bassa' at each of the tubas' entries. And in the Adagio of the Ninth Symphony the situation worsens, for the tenor tubas are notated a tone above the sounding pitch until letter Q where without warning or comment of any kind they are—in the score, though not in the parts—suddenly written an octave higher (i.e. a ninth above pitch). Moreover the bass tubas are written a fourth below pitch, instead of a fifth above as in the Seventh and Eighth Symphonies, though mercifully they are at least consistent during the Adagio.

Strauss followed Bruckner's example of the Seventh and Eighth Symphonies and the Wagner tubas appear in his scores an octave too high (though without comment, as may be seen in Ex. 241). In the parts they are, however, correctly printed an octave lower throughout.

One consequence of all this is that it is hardly ever obvious at which octave the Wagner tubas should play. In the *Sacre du Printemps* either octave is at least feasible for his B♭ tenor tubas and it is primarily from internal evidence that the right decision is reached that they should sound a tone and not a ninth lower than written. Elisabeth Lutyens ultimately wrote for all four Wagner tubas in F on the practical advice of players and librarians, though this gives her score at any rate a unique appearance—suggesting that she was writing for some different member of the clan, since in no other scores at all are the *tenor* tubas actually described as being F instruments.

The use of the 5th–8th horn players to double on these instruments presents seating problems as they always need to join the bass tuba at some point in a 5-tuba ensemble. This means that either the bass tuba could sit near the horns and away from his normal position near the trombones, or vice versa the horns might move across to the heavy brass, which is not only undesirable in itself but may be impracticable.

The position of the Wagner tubas in the score is another case where no uniformity exists. Wagner himself placed them together with the biggest tuba, i.e. below the trumpets and trombones, not unreasonably since he was scoring for a 5-tuba ensemble. This is also their position in Bruckner's Seventh Symphony where, as has been said, they at no time double on horns. But in the Eighth and Ninth Symphonies, Bruckner changed his mind since he was now thinking of· them as part of the horn group, and they are placed above the trumpets, even bracketed with the horns. Strauss also had second thoughts on this matter, for in *Elektra* the tubas are grouped below the trombones but thereafter (in the *Alpensinfonie* and *Die Frau ohne Schatten*) they are to be found above the trumpets as in Bruckner 8 and 9.

In range the Wagner tubas correspond broadly with the horns (see p. 221 above) despite their extra weight, though the bass tubas are naturally less flexible than the tenors. But the upper notes are rarely found in the repertoire and this passage from *Elektra* can be considered exceptional:

Ex. 241

Though neither Wagner nor Bruckner ever prescribed mutes for the
Wagner tubas, Strauss introduced them for *Elektra* and Schoenberg

wrote a splendid veiled solo passage for muted Wagner tubas at the beginning of Part 3 of *Gurrelieder:*

Ex. 242

Nevertheless, undeniably effective, even magical, as this passage is, the use of mutes for Wagner tubas remains a side-issue. It was perhaps inevitable that mutes would be supplied for them as for all other brass instruments, yet their use to some extent negates Wagner's very purpose in inventing these tubas in the first place—that is to give to his beloved horn section the possibility of greater weight and breadth of tone, and thereby provide them with a bridge to the nobler aspects of the heavy brass and to their fundamental as personified by the deep bass tuba. For all their problems and difficulties, and these are many, the Wagner tubas continue to be regarded by horn players as an adventure and a challenge.

Section IV

THE HEAVY BRASS

1 DEFINITIONS

The brass section proper consists of members of the trumpet, trombone and tuba families, though—like the woodwind—some rarer or more exotic visitors may also be co-opted as required.

The word 'brass' translates directly as *les cuivres* (Fr.) or *Blech* (Ger.), while the Italian *ottoni* is to be found in scores such as Puccini's *Turandot* to denote a brass band analogous to Verdi's use of 'Banda' for military band (see p. 29).

Many orchestral works are scored without the full complement of heavy brass, but trumpets are for the greater part included even in smaller combinations. In fact, after Beethoven had set the precedent in his Ninth Symphony, the term *grosses Orchester* came to be quite specifically applied to indicate the additional use of, at least, trombones—although in one isolated instance Brahms used the term exceptionally for a work with no more brass than a pair of trumpets together with a horn quartet. This was in his very first orchestral work, the Serenade in D, Op. 11, and his purpose may have been to point the contrast with his 'kleines Orchester' of the Second Serenade in A, Op. 16, which is scored for no brass at all other than a single pair of horns.

By the time of the late romantics the term *grosses Orchester*—which corresponds with 'full orchestra' or the French *grande orchestre*—seems to presuppose the complete formation of trumpets, trombones and tuba, as in Tchaikovsky and Strauss; but strictly speaking it merely requires the addition of trombones for the term to qualify, as the symphonies of Schumann, Brahms and Dvořák show.

As towards the end of the nineteenth century very large orchestras came to be more frequently used, the omission of heavy brass became rarer in works of symphonic stature. But one *locus classicus* stands out, the Fourth Symphony of Mahler, whose only brass (other than horns) to balance the large woodwind section is the group of three trumpets. In this connexion it was therefore incorrect of Erwin Ratz's latest edition of this symphony—unlike earlier editions—to give it too the heading 'für grosses Orchester' in uniformity with its far more extravagantly scored companion symphonies. Perhaps, however, the point might be stretched in view of the use not only of a large wood-wind section but also an elaborate percussion group.

Wind bands of any size which include no brass at all are unusual, but there are certainly brass bands which are composed purely of brass instruments, particularly in the North of England where they abound. Theirs is, however, a highly expert specialized outlook in many respects, their exclusively amateur status being jealously pre-served. Another strange difference is the extraordinary layout of brass band scores, which are written entirely in the treble clef (including the deepest bombardon) with the single exception of the bass trombone; the appearance of such scores is entirely unfamiliar and perplexing to even the most adept orchestral score reader.

Brass bands are, therefore, a world of their own and hardly impinge upon the orchestral scene except for special importations in such scores as Walton's *Belshazzar's Feast* or Respighi's *Pines of Rome* (where the notation used is, mercifully, conventional.)

2 NOMENCLATURE AND SPECIES

TRUMPETS

The standard valve trumpet of the present day is the B$\flat$ instrument. At one time this was equipped with a switch converting it into A, but as the notes obtained with the valves were thrown out of tune the switch became obsolete, though it was sometimes replaced by long slides for the sake primarily of range extension (see p. 289). But the pre-eminence of the B$\flat$/A instrument in the decades between 1920 and 1950 caused a very large number of works and arrangements to be published in which these two crooks were taken for granted in a way exactly parallel with the B$\flat$ and A clarinets. Furthermore, many popular editions, including the American reprint of many Breitkopf & Härtel materials, give transposed parts for trumpets in B$\flat$ or A alongside the original notations, just as they do with the standardized horns in F.

There are, of course, numerous other trumpets in various different pitches. Of these the smaller D is perhaps the most regularly carried for use as an accessory instrument in the higher register. Dukas had already used this smaller trumpet in his *Symphonie en Ut* and D'Indy scored for a 'petite trompette en Mi♭ aigu' in his Second Symphony in B♭, Op. 57. It was Rimsky-Korsakov, however, who claimed the credit for the whole idea of a little trumpet. The instrument is not without its problems, especially in respect of intonation, but has come sufficiently into its own for composers to call regularly for it in parts lying high for much of the time. Britten tends to pitch his 3rd trumpet in D habitually, his 1st and 2nd being in C, this therefore placed above the other two in chordal passages as well as often having the solos (see *Peter Grimes, The Prince of the Pagodas*, etc.).

For the lower end of the compass two larger instruments will be found listed in scores, both actually invented by composers. First, the ever resourceful Rimsky-Korsakov contrived an instrument which he called a 'Tromba Contralta in F'. This can be seen not only in his own music (such as *Coq d'Or*) but also in that of the Russian school who followed him, from the earliest Stravinsky (*Scherzo Fantastique*) to Shostakovich (Symphony No. 1) and Rachmaninov (Symphony No. 3), generally listed, perhaps confusingly, as 'C-alta tromba—in F'. It has, however, never established itself (for reasons that will emerge later in the section dealing with range—see p. 290) and does not even exist today outside Russia.

The bass trumpet, on the other hand, is still very much a part of the large orchestra. Invented by Wagner for the *Ring* (like the Wagner tubas) it can be found in many scores, for which purpose it is imported as a doubling instrument, sometimes by one of the trumpeters but equally often by a trombone—even a bass trombone—player, as the larger mouthpiece is often found more suitable for its weight and character. Despite the many crooks in which it is written (and this is a part of an elaborate subject also to be dealt with in due course, see p. 284 below), the bass trumpet in C is the one most commonly used by the players.

Other trumpets regularly carried are the C trumpet and the little one in high F. This is again irrespective of the appearance of the relevant transpositions in scores, and the instruments are used purely in accordance with the whim or needs of individual players and the range of the parts with which they find themselves confronted. The C trumpet has many advantages of intonation and tone quality, especially in the upper register, that caused it for a time to present a serious challenge to the supremacy of the B♭. (Trumpeters, it should be added, unlike horn players, tend to think in terms of concert pitch.) The tiny F instrument is often known as the Bach trumpet, not because it corresponds with the trumpet of Bach's own time, but because it is the more reliable instrument on which to tackle the extremely high and exacting parts encountered in, for example, the Second Brandenburg Concerto, the Third and Fourth Suites, and the B minor Mass. Nor is this the end of the story because in recent years an even more minute trumpet in high B♭ has come into favour for use in 'clarino' parts (see p. 295). This touching little instrument (known amongst trumpeters as the pea-shooter) also has the virtue of a detachable shank with replacements putting it into other keys like the old horn crooks, the A shank, for instance, being suitable for very high parts written in D.

One further doubling instrument of outstanding importance remains to be mentioned. This is the *cornet-à-pistons*, regularly to be found in scores between the early 1880s and the first decade of the present century, though rarely since, for its overriding advantage of a complete chromatic range has long ago been matched by the introduction of pistons or valves to all other members of the trumpet family. The cornet is, however, still used in orchestras—mostly played by the 3rd (and 4th) trumpets—though the striking squat individual shape is no longer invariably to be seen in modern cornets. This may lead to the discomfiture of meticulous conductors on the alert for players using trumpets for cornet parts, since the smooth mellower tone quality of the cornet has also come to have less significance in the present refinement of orchestral brass playing; and it now has to be faced that few people can honestly tell the difference. It is hard, nevertheless, to justify the substitution of trumpets for a composer's specification of *cornets-à-pistons* as in the recent 'scholarly' Alkor edition of Bizet's *Carmen*.

There are not many problems of nomenclature in the trumpet family, although the Italian *tromba* can lead to confusion with the trombone when used in abbreviated form. In old scores the archaic *clarini* can frequently be found: Mozart's autographs show that he habitually wrote *clarini* rather than *trombe*, and another example is the Schott first edition of Beethoven's Choral Symphony—where, however, the *clarini* change to *trombe* just for the Adagio(!). But strictly speaking the term *clarino* referred to the higher register of the trumpet rather than to the instrument itself. As for the cornet, it is particularly disconcerting that there should be another and quite different instrument of the same name—the *cornetti* of Monteverdi's day, also called *Zinke*, which are the treble members of the serpent family (see below p. 336).

In French scores, cornets are often simply called *pistons*; the Italians generally use *cornetti*, though *pistoni* is not unknown, and whereas the Germans also primarily use the Italian *cornetti*, Mahler in his Seventh Symphony asks for one high solo actually scored for the F *trumpet* to be played instead 'auf einem kleinen Piston', presumably in the light of experience that the passage could be more effectively executed on a cornet with its (at that time) shorter tubing.

TROMBONES

The trombones are exceptional throughout the orchestral wind in having two members of the family that are equally standard; the tenor trombone, pitched in B$\flat$, and the bass trombone. The latter used to be built in G in Britain and in F on the continent, causing problems when composers wrote passages for the one that lie badly or even impossibly for the other. The difference in the open harmonics actually render unplayable passages such as Bartók's famous raspberries[1] in the Concerto for Orchestra, where he derides a theme from Shostakovich's 'Leningrad' Symphony in protest against the subjugation of his beloved Hungary:

Ex. 243

---

[1] Lest this term be thought to be an unwarrantable colloquialism, it may be noted here *en passant* that Lambert in *Summer's Last Will and Testament* really does use it in a passage marked 'come lampone'.

Here the bass trombone's glissando is from B, played with the slide fully extended, to the open F, the slide being brought right back to the first position. Clearly if the instrument is built in G the whole scheme goes wrong, and it is the increasing prevalence of parts in contemporary scores that assume the continental bass trombone in F which has contributed materially to the gradual disappearance of the old G instrument. However, this is not the end of such problems. Schoenberg in *Gurrelieder* writes a glissando passage absolutely requiring yet another bass trombone, a still deeper one pitched in E♭. The disappearance of this purely German nineteenth-century military instrument has made it impossible to obey Schoenberg's implicit instructions to the letter.

Although there are exceptions, as will be discussed below (p. 306), the standard orchestral section trombone ensemble is a trio of two tenors and a bass. To these may be added, as less frequent additions or alternatives, the alto and contrabass trombones; the former usually instead of a first tenor, but the latter always requiring a fourth member to be added to the group. The little alto, pitched in E♭, is regularly to be found in classical and early romantic scores. Even a composer as late as Rimsky-Korsakov can be found giving all the trombone solos to the second of the three players in his *Scheherazade* and the *Russian Easter Festival* Overture in order to specify that they should be played on a tenor and not an alto trombone. The latter then briefly became archaic but has recently made a strong come-back, partly because composers such as Alban Berg sought to make use of its potential in the upper register, and partly because trombonists came to relish its advantages in parts written for it such as Beethoven's Fifth or Schumann's Third Symphonies (see p. 299 below). Walter Piston in his book *Orchestration* (p. 270) asserts that high trombone solos are generally taken over by a trumpet, but this is absolutely not the case anywhere in Europe.

The contrabass trombone in deep B♭ is less commonly found in orchestras; it was another of Wagner's importations although other composers, including d'Indy, sought to profit by the seeming virtues of such an instrument.

A soprano trombone is to be found in Alois Schmitt's edition of Mozart's C minor Mass, but it is unlikely to have had any reality in fact; nor is it substantiated in later more scholarly editions of the work. It might perhaps have corresponded with Bach's 'Tromba da Tirarsi'[1] but it seems highly dubious that Mozart could have known it. Nevertheless a soprano trombone is cited as one of the instruments in Gluck's *Orfeo* though curiously enough as an *ossia* for the *cornetto* (see p. 336). Schmitt's inclusion of a soprano trombone together with the alto, tenor and bass instruments was based on his appreciation of the classical tradition of doubling all voice parts in sacred works with trombones throughout. This custom is to be found reflected in Schubert's masses, during which the trombones are playing with the vocal parts for pages on end. In practice this is not only unthinkable on grounds of sheer endurance but musically intolerable, and it is hardly credible that the trombonists of Schubert's day actually played all the notes as they appear in the score.

One further instrument needs to be included here, which is increasingly prevalent in orchestras even though it is not often specifically prescribed in scores (Wagner specifies it in *The Ring*, and Berg's *Kammerkonzert* provides another example). This is a so-called tenor bass trombone, built as a composite double instrument in B♭ and F and therefore ideal for the wide-ranged parts found in so many late-romantic and contemporary works.

Where terminology is concerned, 'trombone' persists in Latin countries as in English, but the Germans use *Posaune* which is of inestimable value for ready identification in scores especially where abbreviations are to be found, 'Pos.' being unmistakable, unlike 'Tromb.'. On the other hand Scandinavian *Basun*, a low German corruption of *Posaune*, creates the comical confusion already mentioned earlier (see p. 153).

TUBAS

The tuba family is actually quite large in orchestral terms—that is to say from the point of view of the composer and his score—but they boil down essentially to only two, or perhaps three: the tenor, the bass and the contrabass, though the last is another of Wagner's special ideas. And of the remaining two the first-named is not a member of the regular orchestra but is imported as required for special occasions such as Strauss's *Don Quixote* or Holst's *Planets*. Mahler, perhaps curiously, never included a tenor tuba in his brass ensemble, although

---

[1] See Charles Sanford Terry's exhaustive book *Bach's Orchestra* (pp. 30–32) for a detailed description of this very unusual and rare instrument.

there is an example of a close relation in the *Tenorhorn* of the Seventh Symphony (see p. 333 below).

This then leaves only the bass tuba, which is in fact the instrument meant when in the broad mass of the repertoire the orchestration simply stipulates a 'tuba' (the word is consistent in all languages). The bass tuba is most often coupled with the trombones, to whom it is added to provide a heavier fundamental line than is given by one of the deepest members of the trombone family.

The standard unit is therefore the mixed group of three trombones and tuba, which implies that there is only one orchestral tuba and that since the situation is so simple, composers have no need even to specify exactly which instrument they mean.

To believe this, however, is to live in a fool's paradise. It may not have gone unnoticed that no mention has yet been made of what key the instrument is pitched in. There are, in fact, no fewer than four 'bass tubas' in common use, of varying size and weight. They are:

1) The tuba in F: this relatively light-weight instrument was for a long time recognized as specifically the orchestral bass tuba and was not normally used in the other formations such as military or brass bands, the corresponding instrument for which is:

2) The tuba in E♭: a slightly larger version and the higher of the two regular band instruments, though it has not infrequently been used by players in orchestral work because of its extra sonority and range in the lower compass.

3) The tuba in C: a comparative newcomer that, at the time of writing, has ousted the F tuba and become the favourite orchestral instrument for the overall working repertoire.

4) The great double B♭ tuba: the lowest of the tubas used in bands and also known in band vernacular as the bombardon. It is an oversize instrument such as this that is indicated by Wagner's 'Kontrabass Tuba' (since he had already used the term 'Bass Tuba' for the lower pair of the quartet of so-called 'Wagner tubas'—see above in the Horns Section, p. 265) or equally by the slenderer but no less massive *cimbasso* of Italian opera scores, although both these instruments were actually built in C. (The Italian *bombardone* is also to be found, as in Ponchielli's *La Gioconda* and the orchestral material —though not the score(!)—of Rossini's Overture to *Semiramide*.)

The confusion arises primarily because, unlike most orchestral wind instruments, development has failed to run parallel in different countries. This resulted in many composers writing for the local instruments they knew, with consequent dissimilarity in requirements of range and weight. Hence often enough, neither the F tuba of yesterday nor the C tuba of today can serve the player across the spectrum of even a single programme, and it is not unusual for tuba players—like trumpeters—to bring more than one instrument to the concert hall.

The tenor tuba is quite apart from any of the above and corresponds essentially to that homely and much-loved member of the military band, the euphonium,[1] also—like that instrument—being pitched in B*b*, an octave above the bombardon.

3 NOTATION

TRUMPETS

Trumpets are really written exclusively in the treble clef. The word 'really' has to be added, however, because very occasionally the bass clef is actually to be found, as in Strauss's *Till Eulenspiegel*:

Ex. 244

---

[1] In the Chappell reprint of the *Tintagel* full score, where Bax's instrumentation has been anglicized, 'tuba' has been changed throughout to 'euphonium' in the misguided belief that the one was the simple translation of the other.

as also for the pedal notes which, when used in classical works such as Mozart's *Don Giovanni* or 'Jupiter' Symphony, were written in 'old notation' like horns (see p. 218):

Ex. 245   Mozart, Overture to *Don Giovanni*

Also like horns, trumpets are found notated in the whole gamut of different transpositions. Confusingly, however, these do not always work in the same direction as horns when in the same crook. Moreover—unlike horns—there is no single trumpet to which all the others relate, although the strongest claimant might seem to be the B♭ trumpet since this is the standard instrument and so occupies the nearest analogous position to the F horn. Nevertheless, since trumpeters do not instinctively transpose back to B♭ but to concert pitch when confronted with awkward intervals, the following table of transpositions, corresponding with that of the horns given on p. 217, is given in relationship to C.

G	5th higher	(Used by Berlioz in, for example, *Benvenuto Cellini* Overture but avoided by classical composers—see any Haydn or Mozart symphony in G.)
G♭	tritone higher	(Excessively rare)
*⌈F	4th higher	The F was the standard natural trumpet of the classical and early romantic era while the E, E♭, D, C and B♭ crooks were also the most commonly used in accordance with the crooks of the horns and the prevailing tonality of the music. This is not to say that the D♭ crook cannot be found: Berlioz thought especially highly of it and Strauss used it in *Guntram*. The B♮ is also rare, but two instances of its use can be found in the Brahms symphonies.
E	major 3rd higher	
E♭	minor 3rd higher	
⌊D	a tone higher	
D♭	a semitone higher	
B♮	a semitone lower	
B♭	a tone lower	
A	a minor 3rd lower	
A♭	a major 3rd lower	

*N.B. Contrast with horns in the same keys

Of the last named A♭ is again particularly rare (examples can, however, be found in Schumann's *Overture, Scherzo and Finale* and in Meyerbeer's *Les Huguenots*); even A is generally avoided by classical and early romantic composers—both Beethoven and Mendelssohn, when writing in the key of A (in the Seventh and *Italian* Symphonies respectively), choosing trumpets in E for preference.

The reason for this is bound up with the nature of the instruments themselves which, though a different subject from trumpet notation as such, is obviously connected with it and therefore worth unravelling here.

As the late romantic era merged into the mid-twentieth century, the most commonly used transpositions changed completely and became instead C, B♭ and indeed A. This is because the trumpet itself changed radically, the modern instruments in these keys having half the length of tubing and thus being pitched an octave higher than their noble predecessors (still mourned by some older players). The notation, however—and this is crucial—remained unaltered, creating the apparent anomaly in printed scores that A, a rare crook in classical and early romantic scores, became particularly common towards the latter half of the nineteenth century, only to recede once again as the present day is approached. For the A trumpet has once more become virtually extinct, even the simple and convenient switch added to create a composite B♭/A instrument ceasing to be a standard attachment (as already discussed above on p. 274), composers accordingly no longer writing for A trumpet freely alongside the B♭ in circumstances when they would similarly turn from the B♭ to the A clarinet. This use of identical notation for trumpets in the same key but of different length of tubing started to apply to other transpositons when higher and higher (i.e. smaller and smaller) instruments came onto the orchestral scene. The little trumpets in D, E♭ and E♮ ('aigu', as d'Indy and other French composers termed them), though totally different from the classical trumpets in those keys, are once more notated in exactly the same way and their transpositions can still be correctly deciphered from the above table. (Equally, of course, the trumpet in C continues to sound at concert pitch and there is no vexed question of C alto or C basso as in horns.)

On the other hand there are some subsidiary members of the trumpet family that are not accounted for at all in the above table, such as Rimsky-Korsakov's contralto trumpet in F, which is notated like the F horn, i.e. sounding a fifth lower than written, and the bass trumpet which is, moreover, also notated in a variety of keys. Wagner himself wrote for bass trumpets in D, E♭ and C, in each case in the treble clef only, but again sounding an octave lower than the corresponding trumpets in those keys. Strauss in *Guntram* and *Macbeth* added to these the B♭ crooks, both alto and basso (sounding a tone and a ninth lower respectively); but this is likely to have been in line with his Wagnerian use of horn crooks to keep the appearance of the part as near to the prevailing tonality as possible since, with the minimal time allowed, he clearly did not expect them really to change crooks. Stravinsky in *Le Sacre du Printemps* wrote only in E♭, while Janáček in his *Sinfonietta* used B♭ (actually 'basso' though he does not say so explicitly, taking it—curiously one might think—for granted). Some contemporary composers such as Elisabeth Lutyens now write in A, although both the B♭ and the E♭ instrument are reputed to be still in existence, the latter possessing an extra key putting it into D (Zimmermann actually writes for a bass trumpet in D in his *Photoptosis*).

One further complication still needs to be documented. The cornets are notated in the same manner of transposition as the trumpets (in fact they correspond in length of tubing with the modern shorter instruments) though there is one notable exception. In addition to the cornets in A and B♭ which ultimately alone survived, the latter in particular becoming pre-eminent, Berlioz wrote for cornets in G in the *Symphonie Fantastique* and these, believe it or not, were notated not a fifth lower than they sound, like G trumpets, but a fourth higher (like G horns). And with this *coup de grâce* the subject of transposition may be abandoned.

Like the horns, the traditional notation for the trumpets is to write without key signature and to add accidentals as they occur (see p. 220).

TROMBONES

It would be convenient to be able to say that the alto, tenor and bass trombones are notated each in their corresponding clef; but although all three clefs are in fact used, so that there is indeed an element of truth in this, it is needless to say by no means the whole story.

In the first place, although pitched in various keys (as outlined on p. 277 above), of which C is, however, *not* one, the trombones are always notated at concert pitch. This means that the members of the section may frequently share staves in the layout of the orchestral score even though they may be playing different types of instrument. More will be said in detail about this later in the relevant section (see p. 311) but here the point is that as a result parts will frequently appear exactly as in the score rather than in the specific clef related to the appropriate instrument. In consequence, trombone parts can be found equally in alto, tenor or bass clefs and players need to be conversant with all three.

To be more precise it should be added that it is the tenor trombone who is the greatest sufferer in this confusing jumble, parts written for alto and bass trombones being at least more likely to be written in their corresponding clefs.

TUBAS

The notation of the bass tuba—whether described as such or simply as 'tuba', or even as 'Kontrabass Tuba'—presents no problem in the normal way. No account is taken of which of the many possible instruments the player may be using, and the part is written in the bass clef at concert pitch. It is extremely rare to find an exception to this but one does exist in the case of Bax's *Overture to a Picaresque Comedy*, where the tuba is written as a transposing instrument in B♭ (sounding a tone lower).

The tenor tuba is a different story, however, for it has no standardized notation at all. German composers treat it as a transposing instrument in B♭, sounding (like Bax's treatment of the bass tuba) a tone lower though using the treble clef as well as the bass, as for example Strauss in *Don Quixote*. Holst in *The Planets*, on the other hand, writes in the treble clef throughout and a ninth higher than actual pitch. This is strangely in contrast not only with the continental practice but also with English notation of the analogous euphonium, which is normally written in the bass clef at concert pitch.

4 RANGE

TRUMPETS

In discussing the range of the trumpet one must first be clear whether one is talking about the range of individual instruments or of trumpets as a whole.

The range of the modern trumpet is often cited as 𝄞 [to] which is more or less sound, if conservative. The notes given in such a range will of course vary in pitch according to whether the instrument to which it is related is in B♭, C or D etc. Taking the trumpet family as a whole therefore, an overall range in terms of concert pitch can be built up stretching from 𝄞 [to] . This presupposes the use of the A trumpet for the bottom note and the little Bach trumpet in F for the top, and would certainly come nearer to the actual range encountered in orchestral work.

The fact that the lowest note of any particular valve trumpet is its F♯ should perhaps be examined first. The modern trumpet is orientated around the following harmonic series:

Ex. 246

(The fundamental, harmonic no. 1, is crossed out because it cannot be obtained.) Since the effect of the valves (as described on p. 241) is to lower the pitch as far as a combined total of three whole tones, this not only links chromatically all the harmonics continuously down to no. 2, but lowers no. 2 itself by a maximum of three tones—i.e. the tritone to F♯. But notes are frequently required beyond the low F♯ of the B♭ trumpet, even down as far as the low D—i.e. the concert C ( ); the reason for this lies in the essentially different nature of the old classical trumpets for which such parts were written. These classical trumpets were not listed or discussed in the relevant sections above (pp. 274–7) dealing with the different species of trumpets, because they are no longer used at all in orchestras. But before they finally disappeared they had left their mark on composers' scores until well into the twentieth century, their different range characteristics presenting an important problematic situation.

In the first place, as already briefly mentioned on p. 283 above, the classical trumpets had twice the length of tubing of their modern supplanters. The effect of this was that their harmonic series was an octave lower than the series illustrated above, i.e.:

Ex. 247

Comparisons between the two series show that while the fundamental of the old trumpets was even less obtainable than that of the new, the

2nd Harmonic of the old was none other than the note 𝄞 . Hence

this, the out-of-reach fundamental of the modern short-tubed trumpet, was not only very much obtainable on the old instrument, but was a noble pedal note and thus everywhere to be found in scores, although

of course sounding at different pitches from 𝄞 (for example) to

𝄞 according to the crook used.

Another important factor which arises from this is that the introduction of valves bridged the entire chromatic compass of that lower

octave from 𝄞 via to and hence created the possibility of such

passages as the following from Dvořák's Slavonic Dance No. 7:

Ex. 248

When all this is said and done, the problem still remains of how these low notes are to be obtained today. The answer, as often in such matters, lies in compromise; down to concert E there is no difficulty as this corresponds with the bottom note (F♯) on the B♭ trumpet. But in Schumann's *Manfred* Overture:

Ex. 249

or in the closing bars of Strauss's *Ein Heldenleben*:

Ex. 250

the bottom E♭'s (concert) are already a hazard now that the A trumpet
has become a rarity and the A switch on the B♭ instrument obsolete
(see p. 274). Gevaert states that Ex. 249 is commonly taken over by a
trombone, and Piston says that Ex. 250 is given best to a bass
trumpet, but as in the parallel instance mentioned on p. 278 above,
neither is true of present day practice. The bass trumpet, in particular, whether played by a trombonist or by a trumpeter as a doubling
instrument, is too rare a visitor to the standard orchestral strength to
be used freely as a substitute on such occasions. Most commonly the
player will use a B♭ instrument with the slides, extra long for the
purpose, well pulled out. The low D and the C's in Mozart's *Don
Giovanni* and 'Jupiter'[1] Symphony respectively (already mentioned on

---

[1] The Eulenburg miniature score of the 'Jupiter' Symphony, edited by Theodor
Kroyer, actually bowdlerizes the text of the *Menuetto* so as to lose the problematic
pedal C in the 8th bar.

289

p. 282 in connexion with their notation), aggravate the problem that can be, and usually is, solved by trumpeters in various ways through faking with a relaxed embouchure, pulling out the slides still further, or by other ingenious uses of the instrument or mouthpiece at his disposal.

It was of course the troubles of this bottom octave that led Rimsky-Korsakov and Wagner to invent their 'contralto' and 'bass' trumpets respectively. But Rimsky-Korsakov's instrument, being in F, was simply putting the clock back, since it was only marginally different from the old F trumpet with which, indeed, it corresponded exactly in length of tubing and hence in the distribution of its harmonics. Moreover the composer himself wrote a footnote in his *Principles of Instrumentation* stating that 'in order to avoid the difficulties of finding a contralto trumpet in ordinary opera houses or concert halls I have refrained from using the bottom notes. The parts can therefore be taken by the normal trumpets in Bb and A.' This self-defeating policy was then followed dutifully by all other Russian composers using the great master's splendid 'new invention', whose usefulness accordingly became confined purely to the doubtful purpose of providing a slightly fuller tone quality for the 3rd player to support the trumpet timbre in three-part writing. It is hardly surprising therefore that it failed to establish itself and, as discussed on p. 275, quickly became obsolete outside Russia.

The bass trumpet is however, a different proposition, and Wagner as well as subsequent composers (Stravinsky, Schoenberg, Janáček etc.) utilized this to the full for its rich vibrant tone, though without, curiously, exploiting its range potential any more than did Rimsky-Korsakov. Wagner wrote no lower than ♪ and even Strauss goes only a semitone lower still. At the upper end, the bass trumpet is rarely used far above the stave, Wagner limiting it to ♪ though Strauss did extend this to ♪ (for the bass trumpet in C) in *Guntram*.

Although as mentioned on p. 286 the written top C, i.e. the 8th harmonic, is still normally listed in instrumentation manuals as the upper limit of the trumpet's compass, this is not at all the highest note to be found in trumpet parts. Strauss, as adventurously as in his horn writing, took the trumpets two whole tones beyond this in the *Alpensinfonie*:

Ex. 251

and in contemporary scores the top D has tended to become almost a commonplace. Hans Werner Henze, however, after writing several top D's for the D trumpet (i.e. sounding), thought it as well to give the E for the same instrument as no more than an *ossia* in his Cantata *Novae de Infinito Laudes*:

Ex. 252

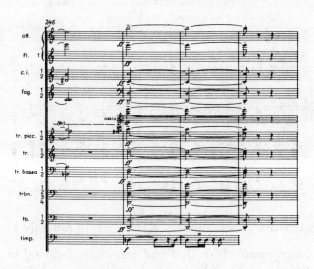

It is thus the more remarkable that Schubert, in his early overture *Des Teufels Lustschloss* composed in 1811, wrote up to top C for the F trumpet in passages such as:

Ex. 253

These top C's sound, of course, , an impossibly high note for the large instrument of his day and especially bearing in mind that 'clarino' playing had not been in use for well over half a century. It seems more likely that the boy Schubert wrote such parts through lack of knowledge and experience. Certainly Beethoven, writing at this same period, refrained from writing even as far as  for the

large trumpets of the day, a sense of propriety that accounts for the
disappointing trumpet entries in the Eroica Symphony, long since
amended by most conductors:

Ex. 254

Over-cautious as one may consider Beethoven to have been, it nevertheless tends to come as a surprise to find, when just over a hundred years later Mahler made no bones about writing the upper G for the trumpet in F in *Das Lied von der Erde*, that this still remains a significantly high and hazardous note:

Ex. 255

Yet this apparent use of the once shunned upper register of the old F trumpet may have already become to some extent a matter of notation, since already in earlier symphonies Mahler had alternated between the F and B♭ instruments in a way that looks very much as if the two had become interchangeable.

With the frequent reappearance of baroque music in orchestral life, 'clarino' playing, as in Bach's day, has again become a required accomplishment for trumpeters. It is, however, by no means positively known just what instruments Bach and his contemporaries expected to be used for 'clarino' parts, such as the familiar solo of the Second Brandenburg Concerto:

Ex. 256

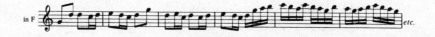

The great Arturo Toscanini threw the musical world into confusion when he performed the work using an E♭ clarinet. Yet he had more historical justification for so doing, whatever the artistic merits, than was generally recognized at the time, justification which is indeed linked to the very choice of the original Italian name for the newly invented 'clarinetto', which is patently the diminutive of 'clarino'.

At all events the range of clarino writing was characterized not only by its extreme altitude but by the narrow limits within which it was confined, since its purpose lay in using the octave at which the harmonics lay close together so that melodic or motivic passages could be played as readily by horns and trumpets as by woodwind and strings. The avoidance of the low compass (Bach wrote no lower

than) then favoured a specialized mouthpiece and technique

that could be thought enviable by present-day players.

TROMBONES

Taken corporately the trombone family can command a comprehensive chromatic range from 𝄢 to 𝄡 . The low notes from 𝄢 downwards are the pedal notes, with characteristic rumbling quality like those of the horns. The obvious instance of the full splendour of this lower range can be found in Wagner's *Ring*, for which purpose indeed the deepest instrument, the contrabass trombone, was introduced by Wagner into the orchestra:

Ex. 257   (from *Das Rheingold*)

Berlioz was especially fond of the effect of the trombone pedal notes, using them for many a grotesque effect such as in the macabre 'Marche au Supplice' from the *Symphonie Fantastique*; though the editors of the Breitkopf Gesamtausgabe so little understood his intentions that they reorchestrated the relevant passages switching the trombone lines with those of the tuba. Consequently it became necessary to re-engrave several pages when in a more enlightened decade the true originality of the music was at last recognized.

Nor is this the only passage of its kind in which Berlioz has been repeatedly misunderstood until recent years. Undoubtedly the famous exposed trombone pedal notes in the *Grande Messe des Morts* are an extreme example of idiosyncratic instrumentation, but this daring stroke of genius was written off not only by Forsyth, saying that 'it probably sounds very nasty', but by Gordon Jacob who, unlike Forsyth, had heard the work and was thus able to give his confirming opinion that 'it does':

Ex. 258

Berlioz was so proud of this passage with its extraordinary sonorities that he described it in detail and quoted Ex. 258 in his *Treatise of Instrumentation*.

It is, nevertheless, obviously more usual to find these rumbles cloaked in some kind of orchestral texture even if it is specifically the trombone group as a whole which is being exploited. Examples of pedal notes introduced in this connection can be found frequently in Janáček, as for instance in the *Sinfonietta* or the *Glagolitic Mass*.

Alban Berg made splendid use of the trombones' pedal notes in his *3 Orchesterstücke*, Op. 6, although he landed himself in difficulties, since in the original version he overlooked that the 1st trombone part was marked for an alto trombone, which put some of the notes in question out of reach. When in 1924 he revised the work he cancelled this use of the smaller instrument, but thereby made the lot of the wretched first player distinctly perilous at the very outset of his part:

Ex. 259

The fact is that the work cries out for the original alto trombone in many passages and the player of today will, as also in many similarly demanding works, use either the alto or tenor instrument according to range. Moreover, taking into account that rests in the part allow time for change, the instrument not in use will reside on a specially built stand at the player's side, much like those for the contrabassoon or other large doubling instruments.

Now that the alto trombone is no longer obsolete, it is often used for the very high passages in, for example, Beethoven's Fifth Symphony and especially the cruel entry in Schumann's Third ('Rhenish') Symphony, where the very opening passage soars quickly to the uppermost E♭ after the player has been fretfully *tacet* for the whole of the first three movements:

Ex. 260

Even these E's and E♭'s do not quite represent the extreme upper range of written trombone parts, as  can be found in the 'Chorus of Furies' from Gluck's *Iphigénie en Tauride.*

Where the upper range of specifically the tenor trombone is concerned, there is surprisingly little difference from that of the alto, this being clearly a strong factor in the latter's disuse for so many years. Strauss, for instance, writing for the normal trombone section consisting of tenor and bass instruments only, thought nothing of taking the first player up to top D in *Also sprach Zarathustra*:

Ex. 261

The bass trombone, on the other hand, cannot be found taken above G: , this being already a very high region for what is essentially a heavy, even cumbersome instrument. Where the 3rd trombone is taken to such exalted altitudes, it is generally because the composer is thinking in more general terms of the trombones as a group rather than of the 3rd player necessarily playing a bass instrument—as in the following example from Shostakovich's Third Symphony, where the instrumentation only stipulates 'three trombones' even though the 3rd is written in the bass clef:

Ex. 262

Such a passage (and others occur frequently, as in the 1911 version of Stravinsky's *Petrouchka*) will either be played on a tenor-bass trombone or occasionally, if as in these instances the line is for the three trombones in unison, left for safety to the first two players alone.

Equally it is perhaps hardly profitable to consider in detail the upper possibilities of the contrabass trombone whose chief virtue lies in its magnificent bottom notes (see p. 296).

Verdi exploits the lower notes of the trombone to comic effect in *Falstaff*:

Ex. 263

This passage illustrates the problem posed by the very low legato notes, and is quoted by Piston[1] as being written for a valved contrabass trombone (although the score only says 'trombone basso'). Piston also asserts that the passage is usually played on a tuba, but, like the other such expedients he mentions, this is by no means general practice today.

TUBAS

Even without making allowance for parts written specifically for either the tenor tuba or the contrabass tuba, the range covered by tubas is also very wide. The reason for this is (as already discussed on p. 280) bound up with the wide variety of tubas that composers have written for under the name of either 'tuba' (plain and simple) or 'bass tuba'. The high solo in 'Bydlo' from the Mussorgsky-Ravel *Pictures from an Exhibition*:

Ex. 264

though written for a small French six-valve tuba in C, is perfectly possible on the normal larger orchestral instrument, but is in the event often played on a tenor tuba; Wagner, who usually wrote for the deepest and heaviest tuba, sent it up into a dangerously high register in the 'Venusberg' music from the Paris version of *Tannhäuser*:

---

[1] *Orchestration*, pp. 280–1.

Ex. 265

It is perhaps surprising that composers have called so rarely for the
tenor tuba which can of course go a little higher than its larger
brethren, although the hippopotamus-like character of the instrument
tells against its use in any very exalted region. Strauss in *Don Quixote*
takes the tenor tuba up to top B when it is impersonating Sancho
Panza, and Holst goes even higher in *The Planets*:

Ex. 266

302

At the lower end of the compass most larger tubas are equipped with a fourth and even a fifth valve to extend the range by letting in extra tubing, but even so it is rare to find very low notes in orchestral tuba parts. Even Wagner, when writing for the contrabass tuba to support his mammoth brass ensemble, actually takes it no lower than

E♭:  , its purpose being purely in respect of extra weight and

power.

The Russians often take a very large tuba for granted, Glazunov beginning his Fifth Symphony with the following:

Ex. 267

Theoretically these largest tubas can actually go even further down,

and examples can be found of, for example, C's, i.e. —Berg

asks for this note in his Violin Concerto though adding wistfully 'if possible'.

5 SEATING POSITIONS IN THE ORCHESTRA

The heavy brass is usually placed to the rear right of the orchestra, where they may either be in block formation:

Pos. 1. 2. 3. Tuba

Tr. 1. 2. 3.

or, if there is plenty of space on the platform, in a line, in which case the trumpets will reverse their positions so that the 1st trumpet is next to the 1st trombone:

Tr.   Pos.

3. 2. 1.   1. 2. 3. Tuba

One advantage of this layout is that the trumpets do not suffer through the formidable blast of the trombones coming from straight behind them. In some studios, and even occasionally in concert halls

303

where they are so close that they find the movement of the slides disturbing, the trumpets are even seated behind the trombones.

The brass can also be arranged so as to extend across to the rear left of the orchestra, especially when the horns are moved to the centre. In such cases they may all be reversed so that the tuba, instead of being at the extreme right, is now at the left end of the row; but this again is an exceptional layout.

When there are two tubas, the second player sits on the far right—unless he is a tenor tuba, when he will more usually sit between the bass trombone and the bass tuba. But in Strauss's *Don Quixote* the tenor tuba often elects to sit away from the brass department and near to the bass clarinet, with whom he has many difficult ensemble passages. Understandable as this may be, it also has disadvantages and is condoned unwillingly by conductors.

Another variation of seating occurs when the Wagner tubas are in operation, for the bass tuba is then to a large extent scored for in conjunction with these rather than with the trombones; and it may therefore be better to seat the tubas together, which means putting the bass tuba on the other side of the platform and away from the trombones, in order that he should be at the end of the line of horns (horns 5–8 doubling the Wagner tubas as described above, see p. 265).

6 CONSTITUTIONS OF THE HEAVY BRASS

The basic brass section is based on the formula to be found in catalogues of orchestral works: 4.2.3.1., in which the '4' refers to the horn quartet, and the '2' to the trumpets, leaving the '3.1.' to represent the trombones and tuba. In fact, Bach habitually used a 3-trumpet section for his larger choral movements, as did Handel in for example, the Fireworks Music. But thereafter, a pair of trumpets for long became the standard section, lasting for the classical and romantic eras with only a few exceptions. For special purposes a 3rd trumpet was sometimes added, as by Berlioz in his overture to *Les Francs Juges*, Mendelssohn in the coda only (!) to the overture *Calm Sea and Prosperous Voyage*, Schumann in the *Manfred* overture and Liszt in several of the symphonic poems. Berlioz was quick to add to his pair of trumpets a companion pair of the newly invented cornets, taking advantage of their pistons; and French operatic composers made a habitual practice of enlarging the brass section to include four players, with two each of trumpets and cornets, the latter being played by the 3rd and 4th trumpet players even though they tend to have much the more interesting and important parts and may be placed in the score above the first and second (see the passage from Stravinsky's *Petrouchka* quoted in Ex. 270, p. 311 below).

As a result, the 3rd trumpet, like the 3rd horn, is rated as a principal player with, moreover, the added perquisite of a doubling fee when he plays the 1st cornet.

This 2-pair formation was later adopted by composers in other countries such as, for example, Vaughan Williams in his *London Symphony* and Sibelius in *Pohjola's Daughter*. This is not to say that 4-trumpet sections invariably consist of two trumpets and two cornets. Strauss wrote for four trumpets in *Also sprach Zarathustra,* Bartók in his *2 Images,* Op. 10, and numerous other instances abound.

Larger sections can naturally also be found, though they continue to remain somewhat exceptional. Berlioz's six players in the overture *Benvenuto Cellini,* with four trumpets in addition to the two cornets, would seem to be pioneer; but their only purpose is to provide all the notes of the big tune when this is declaimed *en masse* at the climax of the piece, since Berlioz was writing for the natural instruments without valves, which he pitched in all sorts of different crooks for the purpose. The overture is now always played by a total of four with the melodic notes more practically reallocated.

Debussy uses a group of five in *La Mer,* three trumpets plus two cornets, an adaptation of the French tradition which he inherited from César Franck and his followers. Strauss calls for five trumpets in *Heldenleben,* three B♭ trumpets plus two in E♭, the first E♭ trumpet being hardly less a principal player than his corresponding colleague, the first B♭ trumpet; Kodály has six trumpets in B♭ in *Háry János*. But the record is surely held by Janáček with his nine extra trumpets for the *Sinfonietta* (making a total of twelve including the three in the orchestra proper.) This, however, may be thought a case apart, as the relevant movements (which also include two bass trumpets and two tenor tubas) were originally written for a youth brass band.

Opera, too, provides numerous instances of extra trumpets being required off-stage for fanfares as in the Third Act of Verdi's *Otello,* or

Britten's *Gloriana* where no limit to their number is specified—merely that they must be 'in multiples of three'.

A single trumpet in the wind ensemble of an orchestra—other that is to say than its solo appearances, as in Bach's Second Brandenburg Concerto—hardly exists until the mid-twentieth century, the short appearance in Wagner's *Siegfried Idyll* being an isolated and very special instance. But as soon as the Schreker *Kammersymphonie* and Stravinsky's Suite No. 1 for small orchestra had blazed the trail, further instances of writing for a single trumpet were quickly added by Milhaud, Respighi, Tippett and others.

Where the brass ensemble carries two or three trumpets it is more usually balanced by the 3-trombone section, consisting in the normal way (as already said) of two tenors and a bass. Yet Berlioz wrote in the *Symphonie Fantastique* for an alto and two tenors, and the classical combination—to be found well into the romantic era—was a trio consisting of one each of alto, tenor and bass. Beethoven, however, in the Pastoral Symphony and in *Fidelio*, used only two (an alto and tenor in the one and a tenor and bass in the other) but the fact that such combinations are unsatisfactory is shown by their subsequent disuse.

In classical times, from well before Gluck's day, the trombones were largely confined to sacred and ceremonial music; but a century before their symphonic appearance they played an important role in opera, being used predominantly for special occasions such as supernatural, *deus ex machina*, or religious manifestations. Here they are already found used as a trio:

Ex. 268   Mozart, *Idomeneo*

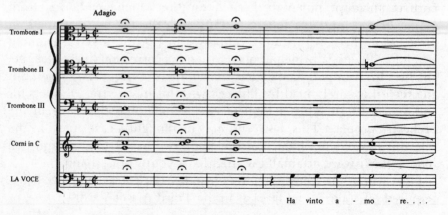

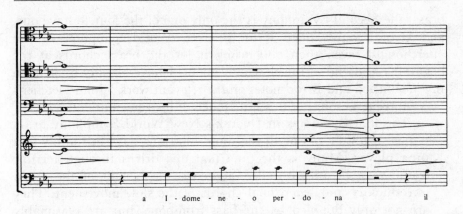

a   I - dome - ne - o   per - do - na   il

The use of a single trombone by itself is rare but has a classical tradition, especially in *opéra comique*. Hence Rossini, for example, reckoned to use three trombones for *opera seria* but knew that he could only count on a single instrument for *opera buffa*. This accounts for the different scorings of the two main versions of the overture originally written for the comedy *Aureliana in Palmira*, but which we associate with *The Barber of Seville*. (A case could be made for regarding the use of the 3-trombone version—re-composed for the *opera seria Elisabetta d'Inghilterra*—as fundamentally incorrect for *Barbiere* which is again *opera buffa*.)

From this tradition may well come such symphonic uses in the full orchestra of a single bass trombone such as in Weber's *Konzertstück*, the two Chopin piano concertos, and Glinka's little *Kamarinskaya*.

The single trombone, though no longer specifically a bass instrument, then reappears in the twentieth century as a feature of the chamber orchestra like the single horn and single trumpet, in works such as the numerous Stravinsky pieces for small orchestra: the two Suites (the first of which has one each of horn, trumpet, trombone and tuba), *Pulcinella* and the *Danses Concertantes*, these to be followed by later works for small orchestra like Berkeley's *Divertimento*.

The most normal and basic brass ensemble on contract with present day symphony orchestras has already been defined above (p. 304) as using the (bass) tuba to support the 3-trombone group, as this is the requirement of most full orchestral works in the mid-nineteenth to mid-twentieth century era.

There are, however, two main exceptions to this. First, works exist—and considerable pieces at that—in which the tuba is not scored for at all. Brahms by no means always added the tuba to his brass; the Second Symphony is the only one of the four to have one, and Dvořák only added it to the New World Symphony as an afterthought, even then only using it for the brass chords at the beginning and end of the slow movement. I have already quoted (in my 'Confusion and Error' notes on the relevant work[1]) John Fletcher's very amusing account of this little touch of instrumentation:[2]

'The fourteen notes in Dvorak's New World Symphony are a typical example of one of the more hilarious days in the life of a tuba player. Many is the time that one drives through terrible traffic to give an enthralled audience the benefit of the seven introductory and seven final chords of the slow movement. They are not only doubled by the bass trombone, but are reasonably low—sheer agony! Obviously Dvorak, for just those chords, wanted the richer sonority of the tuba (it is certainly not needed in the rest of the symphony).'

Perhaps, however, the most surprising reticence in this direction is that of Richard Strauss, who found no need for a tuba in his large-scale symphonic fantasy *Aus Italien*; while a striking contemporary instance of the same economy can be found in Tippett's *Midsummer Marriage*.

The other exception is the substitution of a 4th trombone for the tuba. Wagner was certainly not alone in considering the ponderous and round-toned tuba an unsatisfactory fundamental timbre to the trombone group. Its establishment in this capacity came about for no other reason than that it was the nearest available equivalent to the ophicleide, which it automatically superseded as this became obsolete during the second and third decades of the nineteenth century (see p. 335 below). Among the many composers who sought some other replacement was Verdi, who in his maturity chose to abandon the *cimbasso* (the Italian bombardon—see p. 280) in favour of a quartet of trombones, i.e. three tenors and a bass; and d'Indy was another of the curiously few composers who followed Wagner in writing for the contrabass trombone, using it as a substitute for the tuba in his Second Symphony in B♭.

The use of more than one tuba in the brass section remains exceptional, and a second tuba is never carried on the strength. Indeed, apart from the quartet of Wagner tubas, which belongs

---

[1] *Orchestral Variations*, Eulenburg books, London, 1981
[2] *Composer*, No. 44, Summer 1962, p. 8

properly to the horn ensemble, no more than two tubas are found in any score, with the sole exception of the Te Deum from Havergal Brian's *Gothic Symphony* (even the mammoth orchestras of Mahler's Eighth Symphony or Schoenberg's *Gurrelieder* only have one apiece). Where two are to be found they may be either a pair of bass tubas—as in Berlioz's *Symphonie Fantastique* (where they actually replace two ophicleides pitched in different keys, see p. 335 below) and Strauss's *Zarathustra*—or one tenor tuba and one bass tuba as in both Strauss's *Don Quixote* and *Heldenleben* as well as Holst's *Planets*.

There seems, perhaps curiously, no instance of a score containing a tenor tuba but no bass. On the other hand there are occasional instances of a bass tuba being used without trombones, such as Prokofiev's Violin Concerto in D, Op. 19; but of these the most famous example is undoubtedly Mendelssohn's Overture *A Midsummer Night's Dream*, although it has once more to be borne in mind that the instrument Mendelssohn actually called for was the rougher and more grotesque bass ophicleide. Shostakovich's First Violin Concerto goes still further in that it has a tuba but no other heavy brass at all, not even trumpets, the tuba acting as fundamental to the four horns alone.

7 LAYOUT IN THE SCORE

The standard place for the brass in the orchestral score is below the horns and above the percussion. They are also reasonably placed in descending order of pitch though keeping the family members together, i.e. trumpets, including bass trumpet; trombones, including bass and contrabass trombone; and tuba(s), headed by the tenor tuba if there is one.

There are, however, exceptions to this traditional format, beginning with the arrangement already discussed in the Horns Section (p. 232) whereby the trumpets are placed above the horns, as by Reger and Prokofiev and, though curiously only in certain works, by Lalo and Shostakovich. The logic in this scheme is the unification of the horns and the brass which, when accomplished, then keeps *all* the brass instruments of the orchestra together in strictly descending order of family pitch-level, the horns representing the alto and the trombones the tenor voices of the brass choir.

A further and greatly perplexing variation of brass format in orchestral scores, however, is the isolation of the trombones in many early, and especially vocal or operatic, scores. Here the trombones may be isolated below the timpani as in Mozart's *Zauberflöte* or Beethoven's *Fidelio*, this being perhaps an indication of their being imported into the orchestra as a special visitation. Yet Beethoven, and Mendelssohn after him, transferred this odd arrangement across to their symphonic works; and Mendelssohn's *Reformation* Symphony actually places the trombones above the trumpets, an extraordinary scheme in which he was followed by Berwald in his overture *Estrella di Soria*:

Ex. 269

There is little uniformity in scores over whether the brass are given independent staves or are laid out in groups. Instruments most frequently placed together on a single stave are the 1st and 2nd, and 3rd and 4th, of both trumpets and trombones. If there are only three the 3rd trumpet will normally have a stave to itself below the others (unless of course they are all playing in unison) whereas the bass trombone usually shares a stave with the tuba. This mixing of instruments on a single stave makes it the more important to add specific identification ('3°' or 'col tuba'), and when a composer fails to do this it can on occasions be none too clear if he really intends the combined sound of the tuba playing in unison with the bass trombone.

The standard 3-trombone section consisting of two tenors and a bass is by no means always specified by composers, and scores often merely state '3 trombones'. This leads to the problem discussed above, where in so writing the composer tends to forget that the 3rd player is generally playing a bass trombone and writes for him in the upper register together with the first and second. Many instances of apparently extremely high passages for the bass trombone owe their origin to this method of writing. Indeed sometimes, if the trombones are all playing in unison, they too will find themselves put together on a single stave as in Stravinsky's *Petrouchka*:

Ex. 270

This ignores the fact that the bass trombone has a more restricted range than the other two.

Such score notation, written without regard to the actual instruments playing the lines, dates back to Schumann's habit, adopted by Balakirev and the group of Russian composers which formed around him, of writing for the 1st and 2nd trombones together on one stave and using the <u>alto</u> clef—thus producing the anomaly that the instruments actually used whilst reading in this clef will be not at all two altos but at least one and most probably two <u>tenor</u> trombones.

The situation of the tuba or tubas in the orchestral score is to some extent confused by the Wagner tubas, as already outlined in the Horns Section above. At the cost of possible repetition a few words should perhaps be added here, because nowhere in scores are the Wagner tubas so called, but merely designated as tenor and bass-tubas. Where they interchange with horns as doubling instruments they are generally placed in the score with the horns and above the trumpets. This at least preserves their identity, though it appears strange for the deepest genus of the brass family to be placed so high on the page, and also to be so widely separated from the true bass tuba which continues to be placed in its conventional position below the trombones (though in these circumstances now called the contrabass tuba). In view of the oddity of splitting up the tuba group in this way, the Wagner tubas are to be found in some scores moved down to their logical position between the trombones and the (contra-) bass tuba, though this in turn tends to obscure the true identity of their executants as horn players.

8 MUTING

Mutes are prescribed for trumpets in scores as early as Haydn's Symphony No. 102 in B♭, the Andante of which provides a strange and characteristic effect, since the horns are not muted to match. There is nothing to tell us what kind of trumpet mutes Haydn would have expected but, unlike horn mutes which continue to be unidentified in scores up to the present time despite the many varieties now in use, the particular trumpet and trombone mutes required are quite often specified in twentieth century scores. This to a large extent results from the influence of jazz or other forms of popular or dance music; but the lack of standardized terminology either amongst players or even in makers' catalogues causes a highly complex situation, especially since many of the mutes stipulated by Bartók, Stravinsky, Milhaud, Gershwin etc, and which were everyday objects at the time they wrote, have either changed out of all recognition or at worst no longer exist at all.

Different types of mutes actually to be found in printed scores include:

(a) Cardboard mute	(Bartók, Violin Concerto 1938)
(b) Metal mute	(Villa-Lobos, *Chórós* No. 8)
(c) Straight mute (= fibre mute)	(Bartók/Serly, Viola Concerto)
(d) Double mute	(Bartók, Violin Concerto 1938)
(e) Harmon—which is similar to, but not identical with:	
(f) Wa-wa mute	(Walton, *Façade*)
(g) Hat (this really is made to look like a small bowler hat)	(Gershwin, Piano Concerto)
(h) Felt crown	(Gershwin, Piano Concerto)
(i) Cup mute	⎰ (Copland, as in Piano Con-
(j) Hush mute	⎱ certo and other jazz-orientated
(k) Jazz mute	works)

A decision often has to be taken with regard to the quality of sound best suited—in the opinion of player and conductor—for different styles and periods, especially as with changing fashions players tend to favour quite different mutes, and made of totally varying materials. This reflects equally on the interpretation of classical or romantic works where no more than the simple *con sordino* (*mit Dämpfer, avec sourdine*) is indicated. Metal or fibre mutes are the most frequent alternatives: the latter usually have a sharper, thinner quality, and it is therefore particularly important that in recent years they have strangely fallen into disuse.

Trumpet and trombone mutes can be put on or off in a trice, though many players are loath to acknowledge the fact. Ravel tends to exploit this potential, often giving the trumpets very little time for muting and unmuting, while in Stravinsky's Violin Concerto the 1st trombone is given hardly any time at all to get the mute in between phrases. This is a particular instance often regarded as quite impossible, although in actual fact it can be done if the player is sufficiently resourceful and willing.

Ex. 271

The whole question of trombone mutes is similar to that outlined above for trumpets, though the variety and complexities are less if only because, on the whole, composers have been less demanding or have concentrated less on different effects with muted trombones than with muted trumpets.

Tuba mutes are a different proposition altogether. All tubas, bass and tenor alike, do have mutes but composers do not at any time specify different types. The reason all kinds are to be seen is not because there is any intentionally marked difference in their sound but, on the contrary, because there have never been any standard tuba mutes. The various different ones to be seen in use include some very picturesque pagoda-like contraptions and many of these are actually constructed by the players themselves, since commercial mutes are often clumsy affairs and may well be out of tune.

The tuba is usually marked *con sordino* with the rest of the brass simply as a matter of course; but occasionally muted tubas really are used in the pursuit of a new and individual tone colour, as in Strauss's *Don Quixote*:

Ex. 272

As with horns (see p. 244) trumpets are also called upon to play *bouché*; but in their case this has no practical reality and the indication causes endless trouble and uncertainty whenever it occurs. Rimsky-Korsakov lists it as a valid technique in his *Principles of Instrumentation* and French composers in particular frequently call for it:

Ex. 273   Milhaud, *Sérénade*

Even Mahler wrote for trumpets *gestopft* (the German word for the same effect) in, for example, his *Lieder eines fahrenden Gesellen*, though the fact that the indication is not to be found in later reprints of the score (unlike the parts where it still appears) suggests that he came to realize its impracticability.

The truth is that no one seems to know how the required sounds differ from those produced by mutes or, more important, just what the player is supposed to do. The very shape of the instrument impedes him from successfully putting his hand into the bell to shut off the sound by a manipulation of the wrist as in horn hand-stopping. Even though he may just be able to reach the end of the trumpet, the angle of approach could hardly be more awkward, and moreover the bell is too small for the hand and wrist to be inserted. The best efforts of good and conscientious players sound dismally woolly and out of tune; believing therefore that this cannot possibly be the intention of the composer, they usually fall back on mutes, and a 'stopped' sound on the trumpet thus remains in practice an unattainable ideal.

One instance of the word *bouché* applied to the trombone should perhaps be documented. This is to be seen in Debussy's *Fantaisie* for piano and orchestra, a very early work published posthumously. It is hard to know whether to regard this as a genuine piece of experimentation or a mistake on the part of the very young and inexperienced Debussy; but in the event it is even more impracticable than on the trumpet since, apart from the trombone's equally unsuitable bell, the player has no hand free for the purpose.

9 SPECIAL EFFECTS

EXTREMES OF DYNAMICS

One of the salient features of the heavy brass is its sheer volume (one recalls Strauss's 'Golden Rules for the Album of a Young Conductor': 'Never look encouragingly at the brass . . . if you think [it] is not blowing hard enough, tone it down another shade or two'). Hence encouraging indications are much rarer in brass parts than for the horns, with their frequent *schmetternd* or *cuivré* indications. It is true that brass 'bells up' is much less visually spectacular than with the woodwind or—above all—the horns, since trumpets and trombones are, by their very nature, normally played with the bells pointing more or less towards the audience; nevertheless the instruction 'bells up' does still have a real effect in terms of sheer decibels, and it is often used, especially by Mahler, with striking success. One instance worthy of especial mention is for the trombones in Strauss's *Tod und Verklärung*: in depicting the death struggles of the sufferer who is the subject of the tone poem, Strauss adds a footnote: 'Here . . . the trombone passages must be presented in a horrifyingly biting manner, maybe by blowing with the bells pointed straight at the audience!' The overwhelmingly blatant effect of this—as indeed of the whole heavy brass section playing at full blast—can hardly be exaggerated.

At the other end of the dynamic range, it is surprising how softly the brass can play and with what refined beauty. The *ppppp* for trombones and tuba near the end of Tchaikovsky's *Symphonie Pathétique* is an extreme example, but the *ppp* chord sequence for full brass ensemble that opens the Adagio of Dvořák's New World Symphony is only one of many to reflect a composer's appreciation of this aspect of the brass choir.

GLISSANDI

Whereas the glissando hardly exists on trumpets and tuba, it is a built-in special effect of the trombone family, with their freely movable slides, and composers accordingly exploit it to the full. The most spectacular instance is probably the 'glissez fantastico' in Elgar's overture *Cockaigne*:

Ex. 274

Bartók's famous glissando raspberries have already been quoted as Ex. 243 on p. 277 and, like the Elgar example, show ascending glissandi. Nielsen provides the best instances of descending ones in the hardly less notorious 'contemptuous yawns' (so described in a footnote) of the Sixth Symphony;

Ex. 275

It should perhaps be pointed out that, as examples 243 and 275 show, the distance of the glissando in either direction is limited to the length of the slide, which in fact gives the interval of a diminished fifth—thus corresponding with the use of all three valves of the other brass: Ex. 274 has to be carried off by spectacular faking, as suggested perhaps by the 'fantastico'.

The glissando of the trombone is, curiously enough, a two-edged weapon. So easy to exploit and to accomplish, it on the contrary presents a problem difficult to surmount in very legato solos where the notes are adjacent, or in passages such as the following from Schoenberg's *5 Orchesterstücke*, Op. 16 where glissandi were not intended but are hardly avoidable:

Ex. 276

Where Schoenberg really did want the trombones to play glissando he made it absolutely clear, as in the *Gurrelieder* passage for alto and bass trombone referred to on p. 278, where he even added a footnote detailing the method of execution, the two instruments sliding to and fro in octaves.

319

RAPID TONGUING TECHNIQUES

Double and triple tonguing is particularly brilliant on trumpets and the remarks and examples given on the subject in the Horns Section above (pp. 257–9) are here again relevant with perhaps even greater effectiveness and virtuosity. Stravinsky writes a particularly quick example of virtuoso trumpet double-tonguing in *Le Sacre du Printemps* (at the second bar of Fig. 134), but perhaps the outstanding instance occurs in the last movement of Rimsky-Korsakov's *Scheherazade*; this, taken at maximum tempo, never fails to sound dazzling:

Ex. 277

It will be seen that in this last example the trumpets are combined with horns rather than trombones, and the same is true of the cadenza of triple tonguing in the same composer's *Capriccio Espagnol*. This is not to say the trombones cannot produce the techniques, rather that with the heavier instruments and larger mouthpieces they are proportionately less agile and thus less spectacular even when they achieve it. Similar examples of both rapid double-tonguing and triple-tonguing can be found in *Scheherazade*; but the exceptional example of the latter in Ravel's *Alborada del Gracioso* shown as Ex. 236 on p. 259, though given extensively to the trumpets, never goes to the trombones at all. Nor does the tuba tackle these techniques anywhere in the repertoire.

Flutter-tonguing on the other hand, can be accomplished with total success by all the heavy brass. The second movement of Janáček's *Taras Bulba* gives a striking instance of trumpets flutter-tonguing over a sustained period:

Ex. 278

Strauss used four trombones flutter-tonguing to horrific effect at the moment Barak's wife sells her shadow in *Die Frau ohne Schatten*, and Milhaud gives a rare example of a solo tuba flutter-tonguing ('enroulant la langue' he writes) in his formidable *La Mort d'un Tyran*.

USE OF NATURAL HARMONICS

The 'out-of-tune' open notes of the modern trumpet lie too high for effective featuring and have thus not been exploited by composers. On the other hand those of the old range of trumpets are more suitable since, it may be remembered, their harmonic series was an octave lower (see p. 287). Yet even so, examples are rare, perhaps the outstanding instance occurring for the old big E♭ natural trumpet in the same movement of Vaughan Williams's *Pastoral Symphony* and a little earlier than the passage for natural horn quoted as Ex. 238 on p. 263, with which it closely corresponds.

There seems no logical reason why this effect should not be emulated equally well on the trombone, but examples are lacking except for the passage in Ravel's *Daphnis et Chloé*:

Ex. 279

At the same time it must be admitted that although this was clearly intended to be played across the open notes (i.e. without the use of the slide) Ravel does not actually stipulate that it must sound 'naturally' out of tune, as Vaughan Williams does in a footnote to his solos.

OFF-STAGE EFFECTS

Like horns, perhaps even more so with their exceptional power of penetration, trumpets are used in splendid off-stage effects; at the same time it is always necessary to remember that they are also particularly subject to pitch variation at a distance, sounding markedly flat to the orchestra and so having to tune artificially high for such passages as, for example, the opening fanfares in Mahler's First Symphony.

Distant calls, like those of the three trumpets here, as well as the battle scene in Strauss's *Ein Heldenleben*, (but unlike the fanfares in

Verdi's *Otello* or the Requiem) have, however, the sometimes slightly ridiculous side-effect of the players' embarrassed reappearance on the platform after their off-stage work is over, since they also form part of the main orchestra. Even in this more enlightened day and age members of the public have been overheard complaining of the orchestra's poor discipline ('fancy the trumpeters arriving late' or 'do you know, they actually went off for a quick smoke during the performance' etc.); while the popular anecdote of the trumpeter being marched off by a policeman while trying to play the *Leonora No. 3* off-stage fanfare (''ere, you can't do that, sir. Don't you know there's a concert going on inside?"), although an old chestnut, is still fact and a real hazard that must be taken into account. One of our most eminent players recently managed heroically to achieve the famous solo whilst in the process of being dragged away by an irate attendant.

Conductors have, perhaps for these reasons, been known to instruct the players of—for example—the *Heldenleben* fanfare to remain in the orchestra, perhaps even playing the passages muted, thus totally sacrificing Strauss's intentions. But this work is particularly vulnerable to such bowdlerization, as correct synchronization requires either the services of an off-stage conductor or, ideally these days, closed-circuit television.

Off-stage trombones and tuba are rare except as part of a larger body of brass as in Berlioz's *La Prise de Troie* or the separately placed ('Isoliert postiert') brass of Mahler's Eighth Symphony. Stravinsky wrote for Wagner tubas 'Dans la coulisse' (in the corridor—i.e. the wings) in the ballet score of *Firebird*, and Strauss featured six trombones 'Auf dem Theater' in *Die Frau ohne Schatten*. The most effective off-stage solo tuba is certainly the fog-horn in the Third Act of Britten's *Peter Grimes*.

10 FAMILY CHARACTERISTICS

Apart from its enormous power, one of the principal qualities of the brass is rhythmic incisiveness, which can have the edge on the entire orchestra. At the same time, this very virtue can be a problem in itself; in many halls (especially radio or recording studios) the brass may tend to sound behind the beat—and this often leads to acrimony since, whilst the weight of the brass can hold back the tempo beyond recovery, nothing is more upsetting for players than to be asked to anticipate, especially in syncopated passage-work.

The ability of the brass to complement its extreme reserves of volume with a magical *pianissimo* has already been discussed above (p. 317), but it is worth commenting here that the brass can more easily produce a sudden dramatic drop to a hushed echo quality, as well as a background of velvety softness, than the woodwind as a body can ever achieve.

The upper end of the trumpet's register is so immensely striking that it imposes as a direct consequence the severest strain on human nerves and psychology in the entire orchestra; indeed the casualty rate during the past years gives a certain cause for concern. The bright shining tone of the upper notes soars out with so dominating an effect that even moderately high passages such as the moving solo in the coda of Walton's First Symphony:

Ex. 280

need a strong and confident personality with nerves in prime condition, while Strauss's famous fanfare in *Also sprach Zarathustra*:

Ex. 281

actually remains a tour-de-force, though by present day standards it too by no means takes the player to the extreme end of his compass. The same applies to Stravinsky's duet for two trumpets, one in D, the other in B♭, descriptive of the mocking spectre of the furious Petrouchka:

Ex. 282

In his 1947 revised version Stravinsky rewrote this for C trumpets, redistributing the parts in the interest of increased reliability and ease of execution, viz:

Ex. 283

but despite the apparent logic which lay behind the revision, the passage remains more effective and even easier in its original form.

Where extended individual solo work is concerned, both the trumpet and trombone carry in-built associations with other walks of musical life that need to be taken into account in respect of style. Long *cantabile* solos inevitably evoke military and brass bands, the Salvation Army, etc., unless executed in impeccable taste. The solo at the beginning of the Second Act of Donizetti's *Don Pasquale* (written indeed for trumpet and not, as the idiom leads one to expect, for cornet) or the out-and-out trumpet tune in Stravinsky's *Scènes de Ballet* can fall into vulgarity far more readily than corresponding solos on the horn or on any string or woodwind instrument. Britten even caricatures the effect in Thisbe's solo in the Third Act of *A Midsummer Night's Dream*. Here the question of vibrato, specifically marked in the score, is a salient factor since this is a manner of tone-production very rarely demanded symphonically, even in those countries where horn players indulge in it, but belonging rather to the world of military, brass and dance-band soloists.

Trombone solos have a further problem already hinted at on p. 319 above. The slide, whilst always—even from periods of antiquity—the chief characteristic of the trombone and its ancestor the sackbut, makes a sentimental portamento (or worse still, glissando) very hard to avoid in legato phrases. No doubt it was on this account that the

valve trombone made its brief appearance,[1] although it never established itself and is now orchestrally obsolete. *Cantabile* solos are thus a
rarity in symphonic literature and become a major feature where they
do occur, as in the slow movement of Berlioz's *Symphonie Funèbre et
Triomphale*:

Ex. 284

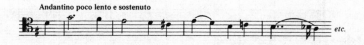

Generally trombone solos avoid the inherently bad style of the
slide-executed legato by using a declamatory phrasing, as Mahler so
cleverly did in the long solo in his Third Symphony, even though it is
specifically marked 'sentimental':

Ex. 285

The trombone (not, of course, tuba) solo that characterizes the
'Tuba Mirum' of Mozart's Requiem thus becomes a curiosity, not
merely for its own time but for any period at all, and it is understandable that in other less purist days than our own it was always, after the
first declamatory phrase, split up between various other instruments
(horn, cello, etc.) in the belief that Mozart would surely not have
written it this way had he lived to complete the score:

---

[1] There is a part for a 'trombone-à-pistons' in Enesco's Third Symphony (first
performed in Bucharest in 1919).

Ex. 286

Yet it can be executed with considerable beauty, as the unprecedented refinement of present-day trombonists has proved.

The tuba, despite its cumbersome nature, is capable of surprising agility. It is, however, rather indistinct in quick solo passage work and as a result composers tend to double it with other instruments, who are better able to supply the edge to the tone while the tuba concentrates on supplying the weight. Moreover, an element of comedy is inescapable in acrobatic solos such as the Scherzo of Vaughan Williams's F minor Symphony, which was really intended to sound grotesque rather than comical:

Ex. 287

It is, no doubt, the intrusive element of comedy that prejudices composers against extensive use of *cantabile* tuba solos in symphonic work. As a soloist the tuba remains a 'character', and true solo status remains the province of the euphonium player in the military band where he is, conversely, hardly less than a star performer. Probably the most famous solo is the ponderous if wide-spanned melody that Ravel transcribed for the tuba in his orchestration of 'Bydlo' from Mussorgsky's *Pictures from an Exhibition* (already quoted on p. 301).

11 UNUSUAL VISITORS

FLÜGELHORN

This is a kind of super-cornet, also pitched in B flat and with a still mellower tone. Forsyth lists it amongst the saxhorns, but whether or not it originated from this family it has only a limited relationship with them today. The Italian equivalent for the flügelhorn is *flicorno*, while the French, rather confusingly, call it a contralto bugle; indeed Stravinsky uses this name (only adding 'flügelhorn' in brackets) when scoring for it in *Threni*.[1] D'Indy writes for two so-called 'bugles' in his opera *Fervaal*, though these are certainly small members of the saxhorn family (see p. 333). The English use of the word 'bugle' conjures up quite different associations, as will be discussed later.

In Britain the flügelhorn is primarily a brass-band instrument, where the player is a soloist; on the continent, however, it is a standard military band instrument corresponding to our band use of cornets. The flügelhorn has nevertheless made a few striking guest appearances in the symphonic field: in Vaughan Williams's Ninth, Tippett's Third and in particular Mahler's Third, even though the revised score changes it to 'Posthorn' (but see p. 330).

Stravinsky, in a footnote to *Threni*, cites the range of the flügelhorn as [musical notation] (written notes) although in the event he only uses

[musical notation]

---

[1] The original orchestral version of *Les Noces* calls for '2 bugles'. Presumably Stravinsky intended flügelhorns here as well.

Actually it covers much the same compass as the cornet. Vaughan Williams uses most of this although he is cautious enough only to use the upper notes in fully orchestrated passages. The totally exposed Mahler 3 solo is easily the most elaborate of symphonic flügelhorn solos and takes the very exacting and extended passages up to top B, which for this instrument, much more than for either cornet or trumpet, is—and sounds—a very high note.

The flügelhorn is not used muted, nor are rapid figurations written for it; it is essentially a melodic instrument and is brought into the orchestra purely on account of its mellow singing tone.

POSTHORN

This rare visitor to the orchestra occurs twice in Mozart: in the Serenade No. 9, K. 320 (which is indeed known as the 'Posthorn Serenade') and in the last of the *Deutsche Tänze*, K. 605, subtitled 'Die Schlittenfahrt' ('The Sleighride'). Mozart writes in various pitches: the Serenade is for 'corno di posta' in A while the *Deutsche Tanz* uses two instruments in B♭ and F. The range is from ♪ to ♪ (written) although the two posthorns in the 'Schlittenfahrt' only play the notes ♪ and ♪ .

The posthorns are of the trumpet species and are not horns at all, so that they transpose upwards. Like the flügelhorn, therefore, the posthorns are played by trumpeters, though using various substitutes for the old instruments which were played by the post, i.e. mail coaches of earlier centuries; indeed sometimes quite realistic-looking long straight natural instruments are actually to be seen in the orchestra.

The long and elaborate off-stage solo in the third movement of Mahler's Symphony No. 3 is another orchestral appearance of the posthorn, at least as far as the revised score is concerned. Yet this is entirely different in character from the Mozart posthorn examples, and is perfectly suited to the flügelhorn to which instrument it was originally ascribed and on which it is still always played. It is difficult to understand what Mahler's intention could have been in changing the part to 'Posthorn', other than perhaps some pictorial programmatic idea.

BUGLE

Of all the sub-species of the trumpet family perhaps the bugle is the best-known, even though it never appears in the brass section of the orchestra; for mention of bugles inescapably calls to mind images of either the military or boy scouts, in whose provinces the instrument properly belongs.

The name itself is not free of confusion; although no one has the least doubt over what a bugle is in normal British usage, text-books refer to different species (including so-called 'keyed bugles'), which apply the word 'bugle' in an altogether wider sense. Moreover the continental terms are incredibly muddling: the French do possess the word 'bugle' but transfer it to flügelhorns and saxhorns (as already mentioned above). The military bugle is called a *clairon* in French, and in German, *Signalhorn*; this latter might also seem confusing bearing in mind Haydn's Symphony No. 31, subtitled 'Mit dem Hornsignal' but certainly written for horns.

The bugle is a natural instrument without valves, pitched in B♭ and possessing only a severely limited compass—indeed only five or, at the most, six notes can be obtained on it; the sixth, the flattened seventh, being even more unreliable in intonation than the others:

Ex. 288

Another limitation, making the bugle unsuitable for normal orchestral use, is its potential dynamic range which is also very restricted, since, although it can be played very loudly indeed, at the soft end of the range can hardly be made to speak at less than a *mezzo forte*; yet this is of course consistent with its primary purpose as an open air instrument.

Bugles generally play together in bands, and Britten writes for a boys' bugle band in *Noye's Fludde*, a work that specializes in the co-opting of non-professional groups. He uses all six notes, writing unusually in concert pitch—the familiar military bugle calls being conventionally notated in C, that is to say, a tone higher than they sound. Britten allows the leading bugler some solo notes, which is in accordance with the best traditions, and he also writes for mutes, which is not. There are in fact no such things as authentic bugle mutes and these have to be improvised or specifically hired from the publishers, who have prepared suitable objects especially for Britten's purposes.

LITUI, ETC.

Buccine and *litui* were both essentially Ancient Roman band instruments, their exact physiological details being to some extent conjectural. Their intrusion into the orchestral scene is purely on account of their isolated appearance in scores. The *lituus* is to be found in some Baroque works, and especially in Bach's Cantata No. 118, *O Jesu Christ, mein's Lebens Licht*. It seems unlikely, however, that in such a context the antique band instrument will have been used, musicologists being unable even to decide whether the two *litui* in Bach's work approximated more nearly to high horns (they are pitched in B♭, sounding a tone lower than written) or trumpets.

Buccine appear in Respighi's *Pines of Rome* where he calls for no fewer than six, though of different kinds. Moreover Respighi specifies his modern replacements, which are listed as soprano, tenor and bass 'flicorni'. This produces a further complication owing to the national variations in the development of brass instruments; but the closest instruments corresponding to Respighi's stated requirements would be flügelhorns and saxhorns, even though the tone-quality would surely be too mellow and tubby for the brilliant brass of the Roman Consular Army that Respighi is trying to conjure up from the mists of antiquity.

SAXHORNS, TENORHORN, ETC.

Saxhorns are such very rare visitors to the orchestral scene that when they do appear in scores the problem is not so much just exactly what they are, but rather to what other more familiar instrument they most nearly approximate.

Forsyth gives a fairly comprehensive list (pp. 163–5) although he does not relate them to their actual use by composers. Of the seven varieties he enumerates, the two uppermost are used by d'Indy in *Fervaal* under the name of 'petit bugle en Mi♭' and the 'bugle en

Si*b*'. This identifies these smaller saxhorns as corresponding with flügelhorns (see above p. 329). Berlioz in the march which concludes his *Te Deum* wrote for a 'petit saxhorn en Si*b* alto', adding a footnote to the effect that it sounds a seventh higher than written. This seems to establish it as a smaller and higher instrument than any in Forsyth's list. In *La Prise de Troie* he also uses two smaller members of the family although he describes these as soprano and contralto saxhorns (again in E*b* and B*b*). They transpose respectively a minor third higher and a tone lower than written. It is these B*b* instruments that correspond with Respighi's 'flicorni soprani in Si*b*' in his *Pines of Rome*.

The next saxhorn in descending order is the alto in E*b* also used in both Berlioz's and d'Indy's ensembles, although unlike d'Indy (who does call it 'saxhorn alto') Berlioz actually names it a 'saxhorn ténor en Mi*b*'. This is otherwise unknown in orchestral literature, but corresponds closely with the *althorn*, an instrument known in military or brass band circles—where it often replaces the French horn—as an 'upright grand'. It transposes a major sixth down.

Then comes a tenor in B*b*, which is much like our so-called baritone of military bands, an instrument similar to the euphonium and with the same range but lighter in character and tone quality. It is the tenor saxhorn which, described on the continent simply as *Tenorhorn*, is used by Mahler in the first movement of his Seventh Symphony; perhaps the strangest feature of this isolated appearance is that at no time does the tenorhorn take part in the brass ensemble, but appears purely as a solo voice with its own particular theme. It is heard in the introduction and at the basic joins of the traditional sonata form, the entry before the recapitulation being its last, not only in the movement but in the whole vast 80-minute symphony. In this country it is generally taken by a tuba player, but wrongly on a euphonium or a tenor tuba, both of which are too heavy and clumsy for Mahler's intention.

Mahler writes for the tenorhorn conventionally in the treble clef a ninth higher than it sounds, as does Respighi, with whose 'flicorni tenori in Si*b*' in his *Pines of Rome* this instrument corresponds; but the analogous 'baritone' is normally written like the euphonium at concert pitch in the bass clef (see for example, Schoenberg's *Theme and Variations,* Op. 43a or Hindemith's Symphony in B*b* for Concert Band).

The most bewildering of the saxhorns is the fifth in the list, for it is also in B♭ with a similar range but differing in character, weight and constitution. This really does correspond with our euphonium, and is given the bass supporting role by d'Indy to his quartet of saxhorns in *Fervaal* (though maddeningly under the name of 'saxhorn baryton en Si♭') and by Respighi as the deepest of his 'buccini' again in his *Pines of Rome* where, however, as already has been said, he describes his analogous instruments as 'flicorni bassi'. Moreover the two composers differ in their notation, for d'Indy writes a ninth higher in the treble clef as for the tenorhorn (indeed one cannot be absolutely sure that he was not confusing the two instruments) whereas Respighi writes a tone higher in the bass clef.

The sixth of the saxhorns is a bass saxhorn in E♭, cited by Forsyth as first used by Meyerbeer in *La Prophète* and also incorporated by Berlioz into his saxhorn group in *La Prise de Troie*. Here it is notated in the bass clef but, perhaps unexpectedly, a minor third lower than it sounds, and under the description of 'saxhorn contrebasse en Mi♭'. This was not an accurate name, however, as a true *saxhorn contrebasse* does exist as the seventh of Forsyth's collection, a very low B♭ instrument and corresponding with our bombardon or Wagner's 'Kontrabass Tuba'. This can be found in Massenet's oratorio *La Terre Promise*, where it is notated in the treble clef two octaves and a tone higher than it sounds. It has also been written for in recent years by Messiaen in *Et Exspecto Resurrectionem Mortuorum* (notating it at concert pitch in a score written entirely 'en sons réels'). He describes it as 'saxhorn basse en si bemol' and cites its range in his 'Nomenclature des Instruments' as: . In the event, however, he uses it primarily in its lower register (taking it lower than he does the tuba).

The overall range of these saxhorns, which is in each case essentially the same as those instruments they most nearly resemble, is hardly exploited in their very few orchestral appearances: neither are virtuoso techniques, extremes of range or effects such as muting. Their purpose, when all is said and done, lies essentially in their weight and mellifluous homogeneity of tone.

OPHICLEIDE, SERPENT, ETC.

Mention has already been made briefly above (p. 309) of Mendelssohn's use of the bass ophicleide in his overture to *A Midsummer Night's Dream*. Whilst only one of numerous instances of the ophicleide in orchestral scores, it is unusual in that the tuba is not automatically substituted in modern printings of the score as it is in other relevant works. For the two instruments are not at all similar in character, even though Berlioz, an ardent writer for the ophicleide, can already be found anticipating the usurping power of the tuba, then a newcomer, by giving it as an alternative in his *Symphonie Fantastique*.

Where Mendelssohn was concerned, such a substitute—now invariable practice since the ophicleide has long ago become an archaic rarity—would certainly not have been desirable, as he was caricaturing the comic figure of Bottom, and the smooth fat tone of the tuba is far less suitable for this purpose than the rough and somewhat raucous ophicleide.

Only the bass ophicleides were used orchestrally, although others did also exist. Berlioz wrote in detail about alto ophicleides in E$\flat$ and F, though he never used them. In orchestration manuals the smaller members of the family are generally described as 'keyed bugles', these being however primarily military or band instruments.

Until a few years ago the appearance of the ophicleide survived on the weekly front cover of *Punch*, played by an angel in flight, but now even that historical design has been relegated to limbo. But typically in these days of passionate authenticity a few specialist players are attempting to resurrect the long forgotten monstrosity with its undeniably humorous qualities.

Two bass ophicleides were used in the orchestra, in B$\flat$ and C, although the C was by far the more common. Berlioz wrote for both, the B$\flat$ being notated as a transposing instrument. They were always written in the bass clef, especially as they were not taken very high. Berlioz, though listing the range in his *Treatise of Instrumentation* to be

from 𝄢 to and regretting that 'perhaps sufficient advantage has not yet been taken of the very high notes', himself hardly writes above

𝄢 .

The ophicleide survived long enough to be used as the bass to the trombone ensemble in the seat now occupied regularly by the tuba (see pp. 307–8). Late examples of this can be found in both Wagner—in *Rienzi*—and Verdi who, as late as 1874, specified 'officleide' in his Requiem.

Another, though even rarer, bass to the brass group was the serpent (Italian *serpente* or *serpentone*) to be found for example in Mendelssohn's overture *Calm Sea and Prosperous Voyage* or in operatic scores by composers such as Spontini and Bellini. Although named identically to the ophicleide (which is simply the Greek for 'keyed serpent') the serpent itself—of course also keyed—is an entirely different instrument with a much stronger claim to the name since, unlike the ophicleide, it does at least look like a serpent.

It is, however, not a brass instrument at all but the bass of another family which is also archaic today, although once again specialists have revived its members especially for performances of old music. These are the *Zinke* or *cornetti*, wooden instruments covered with leather, but blown with a mouthpiece, so that they are to a great extent hybrid, with links both to woodwind and brass—though probably with stronger leanings towards the latter. *Cornetti* are much used by composers from Monteverdi to Bach and are not to be confused with cornets, though they had a similar range and therefore many of Monteverdi's *cornetto* parts are still sometimes played, however anachronistically, on cornets or small trumpets (*faute de mieux*) for practical reasons. It has been said, however, that of present day instruments clarinets and oboes played in unison give the nearest approximation to the quality of *cornetti*.

No modern use of the *Zinke/cornetto* is known, but the serpent has occasionally made isolated reappearances. I myself had occasion to conduct an ensemble including a serpent, which was played by Mr Eric Halfpenny, for Franz Reizenstein's incidental music to a radio version of Kafka's *Metamorphosis*. It was specially imported on this occasion for its grotesque, uncouth quality (for which Berlioz berates it), not unlike a kind of draconian contrabassoon though of course without the real buzz of that unmistakable woodwind instrument. The serpent has the same range as the ophicleide and is notated at concert pitch in the bass clef.

COWHORN, ALPHORN, ETC.

The last visitors to the brass deserving consideration perhaps belong in the category of 'effects'. Wagner's 'Stierhörner' in *Die Walküre*, *Götterdämmerung* and for the night watchman in *Die Meistersinger*, were specially made instruments each playing only a single note (its fundamental). These are respectively: 𝄢 (*Walküre*) 𝄞 and (*Götterdämmerung*) and 𝄢 (*Meistersinger*). They are written as shown here (including clefs) and the notes represent the sounding pitch—that is to say the *Walküre* C *Stierhorn* really does sound an octave lower than the one in *Götterdämmerung*. Usually they are played by trombonists.

Britten also called for a cowhorn in C in his *Spring Symphony* and again this had to be made to order for his purpose. He wrote the two calls 𝄢 and 𝄢 which meant that his instrument had to have two keys added to make the extra notes possible.

Elgar wrote for the Jewish Ram's Horn, called the 'shofar', in *The Apostles*, giving it the two notes: 𝄞 and Strauss went so far as to write for an alphorn in *Daphne*, an instrument at least eight feet long. But he wrote passages such as:

Ex. 289

clearly expecting the effect which would be obtained on some heavy brass instrument. In fact the true alphorn is made of wood, and can get only a few natural harmonics. The part is today played on two trombones doubling with a Wagner tuba.

It is amusing to note that the famous horn theme from the beginning of the finale of Brahms's First Symphony was inspired by a phrase which the composer heard actually played on an alphorn.

Section V

TIMPANI AND PERCUSSION

Part I—Timpani

1 STATUS AND NOMENCLATURE

While it stands to reason that the timpani are technically speaking part of the percussion, nevertheless the two are not entirely synonymous within the hierarchy of the orchestra. The timpanist is very much king in his own province, and in larger orchestras it is only in exceptional circumstances that he is called upon to play any other percussion instrument whatsoever.

He will not even participate when (as does sometimes occur) an odd triangle or perhaps cymbal stroke is printed in his part, or touch isolated works as Sibelius's tone poem *En Saga* which is scored for no less than three percussion players but wholly without timpani. Only, as a rule, in smaller orchestras with limited percussion sections is a timpanist sometimes engaged with the agreement that he will 'double' other instruments if required. The same may apply in chamber orchestras playing works containing a single percussion line of which the timpani forms only a small part, such as Prokofiev's unconventionally scored Overture, Op. 42.

Visually, the timpanist appears to be enthroned, presiding as it were over the orchestra. Nor is this empty pomp, or altogether illusion; a good timpanist really does set the standard of the whole orchestra, electrifying the other players as well as the audience, for his role is far more an integrated musical part of the whole than any of the other percussion, however important or elaborate may be the special effects they provide.

Timpani is, of course, the Italian name though widely used internationally. The spelling sometimes varies, Dvořák and a few other composers or editions giving 'tympani'. (The singular form, less often seen since these drums are so rarely used singly, is *un timpano*.) However, the French do use *timbales*—not to be confused with Latin-American *timbales* (see p. 418)—and the Germans also have their own word *Pauken*. Our own homely 'kettle-drums' should also not be forgotten, though the name now sounds either old-fashioned or military and is no longer used orchestrally despite the championship of Delius, Percy Grainger and a few other composers who aimed at using English names and directions as far as possible.

2 POSITION IN THE ORCHESTRA AND ARRANGEMENT OF THE DRUMS

The timpanist is the most inflexibly positioned member of the whole orchestra; he sits surrounded by his drums which require a great deal of space and consideration when the orchestral layout is being planned. In the purely classical repertoire no more than two drums are necessary, but the majority of symphonic programmes call for at least three and possibly four or even five. Six drums or more require extra players and are laid out in appropriate clusters around the executants.

The conventional place for the 'timps' (as they are colloquially abbreviated) is centrally at the back, but in some halls they may be positioned more or less to one side (see also p. 364 below). One determining factor should always be the well-being of the horns who are the chief sufferers when finding themselves placed too near the timps, for the shock reverberation travels up their backward turned bells and vibrates most disagreeably on the lips.

It has become the most general custom in Britain for the timpanist to arrange the drums with the biggest (and lowest) on his left. But this is not entirely universal, Germany in particular being a stronghold of the opposite layout. In *Salome*, however, Strauss requires a timpani layout that is unconventional by either school of thought, adding in a footnote exactly how a certain virtuoso passage is to be played:

Ex. 290

3 PITCH AND RANGE

The timpani are the only orchestral drums with definite pitch. They come in various sizes and between them command an overall compass of some two octaves from 𝄢 to 𝄢 . This is covered by the overlapping ranges of timpani measuring from 30 inches to 22 inches, with the addition of an even smaller one of 19 inches (and touchingly little it looks) when a *piccolo timpano* (*kleine Pauke*, *petite timbale*) is called for, as in Strauss's *Salome* or Stravinsky's *Sacre du Printemps*. Janáček tends to feature high timpani, and there is even a D♮ in Ravel's *L'Enfant et les Sortilèges*.

Broadly speaking each drum has a practical range of roughly a fifth, subject to weather conditions (and players complain bitterly of extremes either of humidity or temperature, even with the new plastic heads now increasingly in evidence to replace the traditional calfskin which, always unreliable, has become hard to obtain).

By way of extension to the range given above, notes higher than those supplied by the *piccolo timpano* (♩ to ♩) are sometimes called for by the most recent avant-garde, and these are simulated by means of various exotic drums, such as the so called Rototoms[1] which even take the range as high as ♩ .

Finally mention should perhaps be made of the *Piccoli timpani orientali* which Ippolitov-Ivanov introduced into his *Caucasian Sketches*. These he writes in the treble clef on C and F:

Ex. 291

In the event however, these can hardly be rated as timpani, for all Ippolitov-Ivanov's use of the word. As Tom Wotton wrote entertainingly in *The Musical Times* of July/Sept 1930:[2]

'Possibly the instruments are well-known to Russian musicians, but there is no description given of them, despite the prominent part they play in no. 2 of the Suite.

'These drums, of which the Russian name is apparently *timplipito* may be described as a couple of ginger jars of different sizes, bound together by a strip of rawhide, which also serves to secure the two membranes. The pair are played with a couple of little drumsticks, and cannot be tuned, remaining at the pitch decreed by Providence and the vagaries of the drying hide. The choice of jars of appropriate size may ensure the notes being approximately a fifth apart.'

---

[1] James Holland describes these in detail on p. 111 of his admirable book *Percussion*, Macdonald and Janes, London, 1978.
[2] Quoted in Jacques Barzun: *Pleasures of Music*, Michael Joseph, London, 1952. pp. 386–7.

A single and surely quite exceptional use of conventional timpani as instruments without definite pitch is worthy of mention. This occurs in Gabriel Pierné's *Les Enfants à Bethléem*, (the work that also contains the pioneer example of horn glissandi quoted above on p. 254), and is notated as follows:

Ex. 292

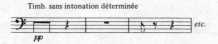

Presumably the intention was for the timpanist to over-slacken the head of one drum. Inevitably tone quality would be crucially affected and it is perhaps significant that Pierné only uses the effect in *pp* and that his example did not lead to its subsequent imitation.

4 METHODS AND PROBLEMS OF TUNING

At one time taps were the sole method of tuning, these being placed at intervals around the circumference of the timps and used both at the beginning of a piece or movement and for minor adjustment of intonation. Since their operation could be cumbersome and time-consuming, composers had to make a point of leaving suitable bars rest for the purpose; hence, if a composer did want an instantaneous pitch change for a special effect, some artificial expedient was contrived such as Mahler's instruction in his First Symphony for a second timpanist to tune down the F while the first player is actually playing on that very drum:

Ex. 293

Mechanically tuned drums began, however, to transform the orchestral scene already around the turn of the century. Experimentation was made with various methods of rapid chromatic tuning until finally pedal timpani swept the field and are now universally taken for granted. This has not only enormously increased the speed and flexibility of tuning but all kinds of new effects have become possible including, for example, glissandi (see p. 368 below).

Pedal timpani or other forms of 'machine drums' (as they are collectively known by the percussion fraternity) are seldom mentioned specifically in scores, although the French, in particular, do sometimes list *timbales chromatiques* at the beginning of certain scores and/or in the list of instruments, as in Florent Schmitt's *La Tragédie de Salomé*.

Since pedal, or 'chromatic' timpani make practically any note available at a moment's notice, there no longer devolves upon the composer the responsibility, hitherto largely accepted, of organizing how the drums should be tuned and retuned. Hence in Bartók's Concerto for Orchestra we find him writing whichever note suits him without working out how each is to be obtained and on which drum—the very antithesis of the Mahler example above. Smith Brindle in his book on the later developments and use of percussion quotes a particularly thorny passage from Bartók's fourth movement with details of the complicated pedal manoeuvres it calls for.[1]

The pedals also give players the opportunity to amend older composers' timpani parts where these may seem inadequate or even downright incorrect. It is actually surprising how both classical and romantic composers would often write notes quite foreign to the harmony rather than forfeit the colour of a drum stroke, confident —not without reason—that the pitch clash would pass unnoticed by all except the actual player:

---

[1] Reginald Smith Brindle: *Contemporary Percussion,* Oxford University Press, London, 1970, p. 141.

Ex. 294   Schumann, Symphony No. 4

Strauss already in his *Burleske* for piano and orchestra of 1886, a
work featuring the timpani, anticipates the practice of such casual
emendation by himself specifying notes which should only be played
when chromatic timps are available, and in this he was followed by

other composers including, for example, Vaughan Williams, who gives alternative notes in his *Five Tudor Portraits*. Yet in Sibelius's Second Symphony a timpani roll is actually omitted altogether in a parallel return passage solely because the drums happen to be inappropriately tuned, a matter now easily enough restored by the use of the pedal if this is thought to be artistically justified. But textual revision is not always the simple ethical matter is may seem. Toscanini, often cited as a stern upholder of the sanctity of the printed text, used to add a timpani part of his own invention to the climax of the finale of Brahms's First Symphony, a most doubtful procedure and one rarely condoned or followed today.

Despite modern technical aids, tuning the timps is still a highly skilled accomplishment. Players show a remarkable expertise in the sheer manner and speed with which they tune their drums. It can be done unbelievably silently during quiet passages and this is of particular importance, of course, when the timps have to be re-tuned while the orchestra is playing. Strange to say a timpanist is still able to hear what he is doing when the orchestra is at full tilt: a flick of the finger-nail may tell all that needs to be known, or for more careful and accurate adjustment the player will lean over the drum with his ear to the skin as he taps it in different places to make sure that the tuning is true. Sometimes he can even be seen pressing the skin all over to stretch it into the required condition: or he may hum softly into it, his mouth close to the head, to obtain a sympathetic vibration back in return. Skins may give off all kinds of harmonics in addition to—and more prominent than—the actual tuned note, misleading non-experts and to the possible discomfiture of conductors (a point generously acknowledged by my dear friend Jimmy Blades in his splendid and exhaustive book on the whole field of percussion[1]). Drums can even be in tune when played *forte* and out of tune when *piano*, a real hazard in a solo such as the famous passage in Shostakovich's First Symphony:

Ex. 295

---

[1] James Blades: *Percussion Instruments and their History*, Faber, London, 1970. p. 355.

Timpanists often have to be very resourceful over tuning during rehearsals when thoughtless conductors go back and forth over a passage where the drums' tuning has to be changed; and conductors conversely also need to be aware when time is essential for complete retuning before starting a new movement.

5 NOTATION

Strange to say it was not always thought necessary to indicate the timpanist's part in the score at all. In Mozart's 'Haffner' Serenade, K. 250, no timpani are to be seen although the scoring for trumpets presupposes their use, a fact not always realized and taken into account today. Actually a timpani part in Mozart's hand does exist, and is printed in the Eulenburg miniature score though in an appendix. In the case of the Symphony No. 32 in G, K. 318, however, the situation is more complicated. The Breitkopf score includes a line for timpani—and a very curious one it is[1]—but with a footnote to the effect that the autograph contained no timpani. This is a half-truth: the autograph showed neither trumpets nor timpani, but trumpet parts in Mozart's own handwriting have survived whereas the surviving timpani part is in another hand. In keeping with custom the timpanist will however have been expected to invent a part for himself, which might to some extent explain the origin of the part subsequently included in Breitkopf.

Timpani are normally notated in the bass clef at concert pitch, but although this might seem self-evident, it was by no means always so. In classical times when a single pair of timps was the standard complement, and traditionally tuned to the tonic and dominant of the prevailing tonality, the timpani were often notated as transposing instruments, the tuning of the drums being in this case stated at the beginning of the piece or movement and the notes written as C and G. This can be seen in many scores of the period, but curiously it was not a universal custom. Bach wrote his timpani in this way but Handel

---

[1] Apart from some most unlikely notes the part is improbable in that the G drum is tuned to the upper octave 𝄢, a pitch not obtainable at that time.

did not; Mozart did, but not Haydn; Beethoven did not—indeed by his day the practice was dying out—yet Schubert did in just his Second Symphony(!). These anomalies can be seen reflected in printed scores including many nineteenth and twentieth century editions, in which moreover still further anomalies can be found: the Breitkopf Gesamtausgabe of Mozart's works gives transposed timpani in some symphonies (e.g. the 'Haffner' and the 'Paris') and not others (the 'Prague' and the E flat, K. 543), in which it is duly followed by the corresponding Eulenburg miniature scores.

In his *Treatise of Instrumentation,* Berlioz complained indignantly of so illogical a custom that could, as a result of limited availability of timpani pitches at that time, represent the sounds 𝄢 ♩ ♪ ♩ by the notation: in A.E. 𝄢 ♩ ♪ ♩

Nevertheless a most bizarre survival of the custom can be seen in Berwald's overture *Estrella de Soria* (this is shown as Ex. 269 on p. 310) and in some sections (only) of his *Sinfonie Singulière*, where he oddly enough wrote his tonic and dominant timpani notes on C and G in their treble clef positions though preceded by the bass clef, viz:

Ex. 296

349

A further archaism that survived for some decades in the scores of many composers was the omission of accidentals which can be found in music as late as Dvořák, so that timps in E♭ and A♭ would be

written: (in Es, As)

This misleading notation has been known to cause even very experienced and world famous conductors to misread a timpani entry, such as the startling B♭ in the 'Dona Nobis Pacem' of Beethoven's *Missa Solemnis*, the timpanist finding himself in a most awkward situation on being sternly requested to produce a B♮.

6 LARGER TIMPANI FORMATIONS

The use of a third timp as standard equipment impinged only gradually on the symphonic scene. Brahms introduced it as no more than a special augmentation for one movement only (the Scherzo) of his Fourth Symphony, and Dvořák added it for just the very last of his symphonies, the New World. Moreover the addition of a third timp did not by any means necessarily presuppose the abandoning of tonic-dominant tuning for the other two. The choice of 3-drum tuning by composers such as Tchaikovsky in his different orchestral works makes a most interesting study, and there is clearly an analogy between the traditions of timpani tuning and of horn writing based on the harmonic series: for as with horns the old style of writing dominated the treatment of the instruments long after the greater freedom of possibilities had meant that strict adherence to those traditions was no longer necessary.

Furthermore, the greater range of tuning possibilities quickly became irresistible and before the end of the century a fourth and even a fifth was added. Strauss's *Burleske* has already been mentioned above in another connexion but is of particular interest here, since the four timpani are so tuned as to present the principal theme in the opening bars of the work:

Ex. 297

and in *Till Eulenspiegel* Strauss extended still further the motivic use of multiple timpani:

Ex. 298

Of course a fourth timp might become the responsibility of a second player, should the four drums be written as two pairs; or for special effects the use of multiple timps could require a different player for each drum. Berlioz, whose passion for the timpani (which he played himself) led him to make every kind of experiment, used already both procedures in the *Symphonie Fantastique*, the two pairs being employed in the last two movements: but in his thunder imitation at the end of the 'Scène aux Champs' he requires four players:

Ex. 299

351

In the overture *Benvenuto Cellini* Berlioz also rides his hobby-horse of using his timpani to build up harmonies, stipulating one player per drum, even though there are only three drums; moreover occasionally two players are expected to play on a single drum, a demand seemingly so unlikely that the Breitkopf material evades the issue by bowdlerizing the text.

The use of two timpanists in works using basically normal orchestral forces is more common than might be supposed. Walton's First Symphony, for example, scored with remarkable economy in other respects, introduces this enlarged timpani section at the climax of the finale with riveting effect (see Ex. 313 below). Mahler of course, with his inflated forces, regularly takes such a double timpani section for granted, although in most instances the second timpanist will—unlike the principal—be co-opted from the percussion section.

For sheer multiplicity of timps however, one still has to return to Berlioz, the famous 'Tuba Mirum' from whose *Grande Messe des Morts* still ranks supreme with its eight pairs of timpani specifically directed to be controlled by ten instrumentalists.

7 POSITION AND LAYOUT IN THE SCORE

The traditional score presentation of the timpani line, irrespective of the different notations just discussed, is for the pitch of the drums to be indicated by the names of the notes at the beginning of a work or movement; it will then be mentioned again only at each change of tuning, this being given (again like horns' and trumpets' crooks) with the words *muta in* ('change to'—sometimes *cambia in* especially with Italian composers) or the equivalent in the different languages: *umstimmen nach* . . . , *changez en* . . .

In view of the timpanist's limited range the name of the note would often suffice, since there is little likelihood of mistake such as the wrong octave. Timps in C and G would, for example, be unlikely to be tuned 𝄢 *and* or 𝄢 *and* unless especially marked: ('Timp in D tief', 'in G hoch' etc.) as can sometimes be seen in Mahler. This has nevertheless led to the nice style, adopted by some composers, of giving the pitch for the drums' initial tuning in actual notation on the first page of score, viz:

Ex. 300   Elgar, Symphony No. 2

Many of the late romantics, however, no longer bother to indicate timpani tuning at all. Strauss abandons it after *Tod und Verklärung*, Debussy and Ravel in most of their mature and later works, Mahler altogether, and so on. Much would depend on the nature of the writing: Sibelius, for instance, continued to indicate tuning until his last orchestral work, *Tapiola*, but omitted it where the use of different timpani pitches was very free, as in the Seventh Symphony written in the previous year, 1924.

The standard place for the timpani stave is immediately below the brass and above the other percussion: the harp(s), celesta, etc. then come below these. There are, however, exceptions to this format. Schoenberg puts the harps, etc., above the percussion group, and in a few works (e.g. the *Variations for Orchestra*, Op. 31) the timpani line is placed below that of the other percussion. Berg usually keeps to the standard layout but in the *3 Orchesterstücke* Op. 6, which has an immense number of percussion parts, the timpani appear in various positions in the score, beginning below the mass of other percussion staves but shifting their relative placings as the work progresses —sometimes to the middle, sometimes even to their conventional position at the top. Reorientating of the timpani occurs to a considerable degree in contemporary works, especially where there is an elaborate percussion department such as Zimmermann's *Canto di Speranza*, and this can be quite confusing.

353

8 TIMPANI ROLLS

The roll is the drums' equivalent to the strings' tremolo and shares many of the notation troubles of that device. It is designated equally

by 🎼 (which unlike strings or wind notation does not mean a

trill with a different note); or by any of the following, often used

indiscriminately: 🎼

Strangely the word 'tremolo' (or its abbreviated 'trem.') is not often found in timpani parts, though Glazunov provides a few examples. As for the number of strokes added to the notes, this can be immensely variable. Haydn normally writes ♪ , and until recently timpanists have been strongly in favour of playing measured semiquavers, especially in slower tempi. Modern scholarship, however, holds that

Haydn always intended the roll (even when he wrote ♪) and

certainly the famous drumrolls that give the name to the E♭ Symphony No. 103 are notated ♪ in the autograph, the third stroke in many modern scores being mere editorial addition.

Mozart normally used 'tr', in which he was followed by Beethoven, so that when Beethoven wrote ♪ , even in an Allegro movement, he certainly intended demisemiquavers (see Ex. 305 below).

However, when in the final fermata of the Fifth Symphony, at the

end of the *prestissimo* coda, he wrote: 🎼 it is not at all clear

what he could possibly have meant.

Broadly speaking ♪ is the most usual alternative to ♪ when

composers intend an unmeasured roll, but caution is always necessary. Tchaikovsky habitually wrote his timpani rolls as ♪ in quicker and ♪ in slower tempi; nevertheless passages such as the following from the *Symphonie Pathétique* show that on the contrary he sometimes thought of ♪ as being measured:

Ex. 301

355

It is frequently unclear how composers mean a roll to end—that is to say with the final note marked or not. In Mendelssohn's *Scotch* Symphony for example, the timpani part by itself suggests that the quaver (or crotchet) which ends the rolls should be separated, whereas the appearance of the score as a whole, revealing the wind ties, indicates that after all this is unlikely to have been Mendelssohn's intention:

Ex. 302

In the following example the score again shows from the horn line that the ringed timpani notes are only the endings of rolls, but in the player's part they are in no way different from the quavers that follow and which on the contrary mark the horns' melodic line:

Ex. 303   Rawsthorne, Symphony No. 3

Even Mahler, normally a tyrant for precision in his scores, writes:

Ex. 304   Mahler, Symphony No. 7

against tied notes on the woodwind, horns and strings; whereas the timpani should surely also start each new phrase at the semiquavers.

Another confusion of timpani notation lies in composers' different indications for extended rolls, many of which are equivocal over whether the roll should be restarted in each new bar or not. Dvořák will often write: ♫ when he intends a continuous roll, and he is by no means unique. On the other hand in the Choral Symphony we find Beethoven writing: ♫ in circumstances where a continuous roll is the more probable intention. Moreover in the first movement of the same work Beethoven, generally scrupulous about his timpani notation, fails to indicate the surely necessary accentuation of the motivic A in the following passage (which also proves that his demisemiquavers are measured):

357

Ex. 305   Beethoven, Symphony No. 9

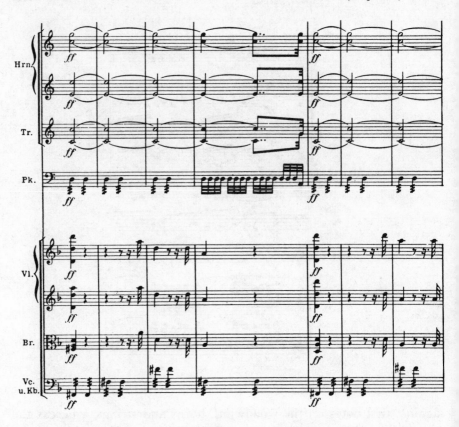

Perhaps the most carefully organized timpani notation appears in the finale of Brahms's First Symphony:

Ex. 306

and timpanists watch conductors with eagle eyes to see if they are conscious of the rhythmic relationships involved, and especially if the group of twelve ♪'s is enabled to equal two new groups of six ♪'s in the Più Andante.

It is of course apparent that timpani rolls are equally valid on two drums as on one. A rhythmic figure such as the following:

358

Ex. 307   Glinka, Overture to *Russlan and Ludmila*

may easily turn into a roll:

While this is a positive device in its own right, it is not actually

synonymous with ⟨notation⟩ although so near that the one is some-

times substituted for the other, an economy (since the latter needs two players) that can be indefensible where the composer's dramatic intention is thereby weakened.

9 VARIETIES OF TONE QUALITY AND OTHER EFFECTS

USE OF DIFFERENT STICKS OR OTHER IMPLEMENTS

Amongst his other innovations for the instrument, Berlioz was the first composer to indicate in his scores a differentiation in the sticks he wanted used. He made a great point of the three types of sticks he recognized to be the outstanding alternatives: sponge-headed, leather-covered, and wooden. Of these, however, he deplored as rough and crude the currently excessive use of leather, and hence only actually prescribes the first and last, in which he was followed by other composers such as Strauss. His French terms—'baguettes d'éponge', 'baguettes de bois'—are realized in German as *Schwammschlägel* and *Holzschägel* and in Italian (though these are curiously rare) *bacchette di spugna* and *bacchette di legno*. Needless to say, over the years customs have changed and the instructions to use specifically sponge-headed sticks are ignored, sponge being regarded as altogether unsuitable because it damps the quality. Instead, players use felt-covered sticks of various degrees of softness which they choose as they themselves consider the style of the part may require. It is quite normal to see a player select different pairs of sticks during the course of a work although there is no indication in the score or the part. The conductor too may often express a preference for 'hard' or 'soft' sticks in respect of a particular passage, hard sticks giving greater clarity for a rhythmic figure but soft ones producing a more beautiful resonance.

The heads of the sticks also vary enormously in size and shape, from those with straight sides and flat circular ends to woolly-looking spherical heads not unlike young tennis balls, and timpanists have their own preferences within a surprisingly wide range.

The one variation that remains linked unquestionably to the composer's special instructions is wood. When this is prescribed players commonly change to light sticks with wooden knobs on the end, although to facilitate very quick changing felt-headed sticks are often fitted with wooden heads at the other end. The switch can then be made in a split second when the composer has allowed minimal time for the purpose. Elgar actually stipulates the handle in *The Dream of Gerontius*, marking it 'With the stick. Mit dem Griff'.

The sound of wooden sticks is highly characteristic, and a very high proportion of the repertoire absolutely requires their use. Nevertheless timpanists sometimes try to avoid using them on the grounds of damage to the heads. There is some truth in this as a result of the introduction of plastic heads, which unlike the old skins, can show alarming indentations after strong use with wooden sticks.[1]

It is generally on account of their extra stridency that wooden sticks are indicated, but they are also sometimes used *pp*. In this case a further variant is the indication for side drum sticks (which are also wooden though with slenderer heads) for the shallow rattling they produce. Elgar in Variation XIII of the 'Enigma' Variations wrote this requirement in the score, but it is well known that what he really wanted for so atmospheric a passage was two pennies (that is to say, our old large pennies) and it is coins of the realm of one sort or another that are to this day used by all who know the tradition. The way this and the instantaneous change back to normal sticks (here marked 'naturale') is accomplished can be found described in detail by James Blades on pp. 331–2 of his previously mentioned book.[2]

---

[1] There is a serious conflict here and I am indebted to Eric Pritchard for the advice that sticks made of the softer balsa wood produce the correct sound without inflicting damage.

[2] Bax in *Tintagel* calls for a similar effect through the use of the player's fingernails.

The contradiction to *Holzschlägel* may in later scores (actually already by Mahler writing in 1904) be *gewöhnliche Schlägel* which is accordingly interpreted by players as they see fit and appropriate. But composers often forget to make it clear whether wooden sticks are indicated only for a specific passage or whether their use should continue for longer periods. Liszt's *Faust Symphony* gives one such example, for if printed instructions are followed to the letter, one finds that the greater part of the long first movement is played on wooden sticks, not at all an impossible but at times a surprising state of affairs.

Various composite uses of these colours are also to be found from time to time. Holst in *The Perfect Fool* instructs the player to hold a wooden stick in one hand and a felt stick in the other. Contemporary composers have also written for timpani to be played with some foreign body—a cymbal, tambourine, etc.—placed on the drum head.

STRIKING VARIOUS PLACES ON THE HEAD

It is widely believed that the nearer the edge of the drum one strikes the skin the drier and less resonant the tone becomes, and there is certainly some truth in this although opinions are divided over composers' use of the different methods. This is because the opposite is also true—that is to say, if the drum is hit in the very centre a dull thud ensues. Hence it is not at all obvious what Kodály intended, or believed would be the effect, in the passage from the *Galanta Dances:*

Ex. 308

x) a Mitte b. Rand

For if, as is probable, he meant by 'Rand' the very rim, then by 'Mitte' he only intended the normal striking place and this would put the hard dry sound logically enough on the staccato quaver. But timpanists taking his instructions at face value will sometimes argue the precise opposite.

Bartók, however, who was something of a specialist in percussion effects, certainly meant precisely what he wrote when he specified 'to be played at the edge of the head' in his Violin Concerto (1938), a dry effect which he further intensifies by the use of wooden sticks.

Ex. 309

USE OF TWO STICKS, OR TWO DRUMS, SIMULTANEOUSLY

Mention has already been made above (p. 352) of Berlioz's unusual demand for a second player to strike the same drum as one already in use by the timpanist. This is, of course, only the beginning of a larger subject in respect of the pursuit of greater resonance and dynamism from the timpani. One obvious method is by the use of both sticks on each drum, indicated by tails both up and down as in Mahler's Fourth Symphony:

Ex. 310

or by the simple mark over the line 'a 2'. Where there are two timpanists in the orchestra, however, the use of this indication may make it ambiguous whether two sticks by one player or the two players are required. The timpani lines of Stravinsky's *Le Sacre du Printemps*, a work that specializes in the galvanizing effects obtainable by two timpanists, is often very unclear in this respect and the parts produce interpretations of Stravinsky's instructions quite unforeseeable from the layout in the score.

The two sticks are frequently used together though on different drums. A particular example of this occurs in Busoni's music to Gozzi's *Turandot* where, with four drums tuned in octaves, the player has to use two sticks in each hand in order to produce four-note chords:

Ex. 311

Bartók, who in his Violin Concerto (1938) wants extra timpani notes although the single timpanist is already fully occupied with a roll, marks in a footnote (on p. 101 of the score) that these should be supplied by one of the other percussion players. However his meaning is sometimes misunderstood and the crotchets can occasionally be heard played not only, for example, by the bass drummer but actually on the bass drum itself.

More than one drum tuned to the same notes are used with remarkably dramatic effect by Nielsen in his Fourth Symphony, *The Inextinguishable*:

Ex. 312

Here, for programmatic reasons, as well as clarity and contrast, he additionally demands that two timpanists should be placed on the extreme opposite sides of the orchestra. Walton, in the climax to the finale of his First Symphony already mentioned on p. 352 above, also

364

makes great and spectacular play of two timpanists handling six drums where, of each player's three drums, two are tuned the same as those of his colleague, thus providing both chords and reinforcements:

Ex. 313

365

MUTING

For an extremely dry quality the standard method of robbing the drums of their resonance is by placing pads on the heads. This is certainly one form of muting, but alternatively the timpani may be wholly covered with cloth, as for example in a military funeral procession. It is this which is clearly expected also when composers (whether as early as Mozart in *Idomeneo* or as recently as Walton's Violin Concerto) use the term *coperti*. Other indications are 'muffled' or words used for muting other instruments (*gedämpft, con sord*, etc.). Whichever term may appear in the score and part, however, players today more usually revert to the pad because of its quicker and conveniently simple application and removal—although the effect is not the same and Berlioz, in particular, comments on the notably lugubrious effect of the covering cloth.[1]

Dusters are also placed on the heads when not especially asked for in the score in order to control tone quality or length of reverberance; they are also placed on drums not actually in use to prevent sympathetic vibration.

DAMPING, RAPID OR DELAYED

Short as is the sustaining power of the timpani, there is enough range in the duration of a well-placed stroke to make the difference of resonance into a real variation of tone quality. Composers often specify this by the use of quite large note-values such as ♩ or even 𝅝 , as opposed to ♩ or ♪ although each of these latter can be carefully differentiated by skilful use of the hand or fingers after striking. It is often believed that when Beethoven, for example, writes a simple semibreve for the timps whilst the orchestra is sustaining, a roll must surely have been intended, but this is not necessarily the case:

---

[1] The notoriously fallible Breitkopf edition of the *Symphonie Fantastique* marks the timpani to be muted throughout the 'Marche au Supplice' (i.e. in the *fortissimo* as well as the *piano* sections).

Ex. 314   Beethoven, Piano Concerto No. 3

The words *laissez vibrer,* though normally applied to long vibrating
percussion effects such as cymbals or gong (see p. 386) can sometimes
be found marked for a timpani stroke.

Conversely, the extreme speed possible in damping the sound has been widely exploited, even on occasions when two drums need to be damped in rapid succession as in the third movement of Mahler's Second Symphony:

Ex. 315

and Stravinsky gives an especially taxing and extended instance during a complicated passage of cross-rhythms in the 'Jeu du Rapt' from *Le Sacre du Printemps*.

Composers occasionally call for analogous extreme special effects such as *hart* (hard) or *weich*, which latter means soft but by no means necessarily *piano*. Mahler uses the word equally in *forte* to signify a soft quality of tone even when the dynamic is strong. These measures are of necessity interpreted by each player for himself whether in respect of choice of sticks or the striking position on the head.

GLISSANDI

The combination of a roll with the manoeuvring of the pedal in modern mechanical drums gives rise to the splendid effect of timpani glissandi. Nielsen was amongst the first to exploit this, again in his Fourth Symphony, *The Inextinguishable*, composed in 1916:

Ex. 316

Bartók, in the *Music for Strings, Percussion and Celesta*, shows further that the duration of a single ringing timpani note is long enough to allow for a glissando without restriking. This is similar in effect to the pizzicato glissando on the strings (see p. 99) which in fact he introduces immediately afterwards:

Ex. 317

Such glissandi work equally well upwards or downwards, and can even go up and down on a single stroke, though this is more rarely asked for. They can of course be halted at a given note so that Bartók in his Violin Concerto (1938) was able to write:

Ex. 318

369

10 CONCLUSION

Although in theory there is virtually no limit to the possible experimental devices to which timpani could be put, further adventures hardly come within their specialized province to the extent of the other percussion, whose métier is—on the contrary—primarily concerned with colouristic effects of every kind. In practice the timpanist continues for the most part to be held in especial respect by composers as an aristocrat in his own field; this role can however be double-edged, since a composer such as Messiaen regards it as so restrictive, that within the wide spectrum of colouristic effects which is the essence of the particularly lavish percussion section found in the majority of his works, he can find no place for the pure classicism of the timpani, which are thus conspicuously absent. This move away from the timpani, which has been pursued by a number of avant-garde composers, can be traced back (apart from isolated instances such as Sibelius's *En Saga* already cited) to Schoenberg's *5 Orchesterstücke*, Op. 16, composed in 1909, where only a few timpani notes occur in the first movement, the instruments thereafter being totally ignored in favour of the other members of a large and varied percussion group. Yet the timpanist's days are very far from numbered, and his position as king-figure remains firmly secure in symphony orchestras all over the world.

Part II—Percussion

GENERAL MATTERS

1 TERMINOLOGY

The collective term for this department, often referred to colloquially in English-speaking countries as the 'kitchen', is the French *batterie* or German *Schlagzeug*; these terms appear in orchestra lists as well as in titles of works. The Italian word corresponds with the French—i.e. *batteria*, though both, if more rarely, do also use the term analogous to our own (*percussion* or *percussione*).

2 PLATFORM ORGANIZATION

Although the general area allocated to the kitchen department may be chosen by the orchestral management perhaps in consultation with the conductor, having regard to the shape or acoustics of the hall or platform, the arrangement of the individual instruments is entirely the responsibility of the players. They will need to plan together with the orchestral attendants how much space they need, bearing in mind their movement to and fro between instruments of widely differing character and technique such as xylophone, cymbals and tubular bells, all of which may very well have to be handled in turn by a single player. Composers very occasionally plan ahead for a particularly complicated percussion layout with very large assortments of instruments distributed amongst many players: Henze's *Antifone* for example, actually gives a map on the front page of the score.

For obvious reasons the percussion is normally arranged along the back of the platform, whether centrally or to one side, and sometimes also in two tiers, the heavy, noisier instruments behind, and the pitched agile instruments such as vibraphone, marimba, etc. in front. An outstanding exception, however, exists in the case of Roberto Gerhard's *Epithalamion* where the composer expressly desired that the all-important kitchen department be spread out in front of the strings and hence nearest to the audience. Though by no means without its problems, this layout proved less intransigent than at first appeared.

3 INSTRUMENTAL ARRANGEMENT IN THE SCORE AND NOTATION

The standard position for the percussion in the score is immediately below the timpani, although as has already been said in the Timpani Section of this chapter it may occasionally stray above, to confusing effect.

But where the different instruments in a multiple percussion group are concerned, there is virtually no uniformity of order. It might be thought that on the whole the higher, lighter instruments such as triangle, side drum, tambourine etc., would be at or near the top, with bass drum and tam-tam at the bottom, but although this is a principle often followed it is no more than that. In the first place there is a unique dichotomy in the percussion between the number of instruments used in a work and the number of players required to operate them. In nineteenth and early twentieth-century scores it is rare to find in the orchestration lists any indication of how many percussion players the composer had in mind. Ravel's *Daphnis et Chloé*, for instance, lists twelve instruments in addition to timpani (not including celesta, which is also a part of the list—a confusion that will be discussed later) requiring eight players to cover the situation.

Moeran's Serenade in G is laid out with six percussion lines for seven instruments on the first page of score, but scrutiny will reveal that, surprisingly enough, two players (always in addition to timpani) can cope with all they have to contribute.

Sometimes the composer reckons to have worked out the problem and lists the number of players at the head of the score; but it is a mistake for the orchestral manager to receive this list from the librarian and to order the forces accordingly. In any case it is the specialized province of the principal percussionist to report on the minimum number of players he regards as necessary for a given programme; and it is he who will study the parts (or a little note-book with a compendium of works built up over years of experience) and decide how many extra musicians need to be engaged. This may depend on a number of factors including the location or importance of the performance. For there are numerous ways of getting round the difficulties, and it is astonishing how much of an apparently extravagant percussion ensemble can if necessary be fitted in by a smaller group of willing and resourceful musicians, however much the practice may be understandably resisted on ethical grounds by the highly organized percussion freemasonry of the larger symphony orchestras.

Nor can one turn to even the most efficient composer fc: guidance: the full score of Strauss's *Rosenkavalier*[1] stipulates '3 Spieler' against the ten percussion instruments listed, but a glance at the heavier moments of the opera (Ochs's Waltz scene in Act 2 or, above all, his exit in Act 3) show that five or even six players are necessary. Nor are the composers' lists of instruments always reliable: Stravinsky's *Le Sacre du Printemps* contains a careful list of the vast orchestra which nevertheless forgets to mention, of all instruments, the cymbals (reserved with stunning effect for the passage between figures 138 and 140).

Their entry in that particular section is notated below the bass drum, but this is unusual. Moreover, because of their close association, bass drum and cymbals are often written on a single stave, in which case the very universality of the phrase 'bass drum and cymbals' rather than 'cymbals and bass drum' causes a lack of clarity in scores such as Elgar's Second Symphony:

---

[1] Not the study score, which, however, in translating Strauss's *Orchesterbesetzung* into Italian also commits woeful sins of condensation in Strauss's explicit requirements.

Ex. 319

Here the layout suggests that the bass drum is notated on the upper
line and the cymbals on the lower, whereas the opposite is intended.

It will be noticed that in the above example all the instruments are specified by name (and hence on each page of score) and that they are notated on conventional staves headed by clefs. Yet none of this can be taken to be standard practice. Where the listing is concerned it is not at all uncommon to find a set of six or more lines of percussion without a single indication of which instrument is playing, and it is necessary to check back to (or memorize) the first page of the music, as for example Balakirev's *Thamar* or Shostakovich's First Symphony. Indeed, where the latter work is concerned, the lack of indication on p. 51 of the original score has led to a possible misreading, since a later printing hazards 'piatti' where 'tam-tam' is surely more likely to have been the composer's intention in such a context.

Composers will also, especially in more modern scores, mark the percussion lines with the number of the percussionist instead of the instrument he plays. But in the heat of rehearsal, the sign 'Perc. 3' is little help to a conductor who may address the right player but without knowing instinctively what to expect from him.

The use of staves with conventional clefs for percussion instruments of indefinite as well as definite pitch (see the Elgar example above) is quite common, although there is also a standard layout in which non-pitched instruments are placed on single lines, either headed by some neutral symbol such as +——— or even without anything at all.[1] But where instruments such as drums or tom-toms (even maybe combined with cymbals, etc.) are used to suggest higher or lower sonic relationships, several such symbols are often placed together on staves, viz:

Ex. 320   Britten, *The Rape of Lucretia*

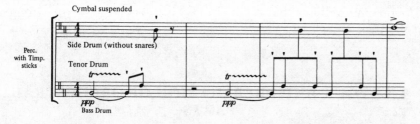

---

[1] A recent fashion has come into being in which composers use pictorial signs to illustrate the required instruments, but in the absence of standardization such a practice can be most confusing. Moreover, although Smith Brindle embraces it in his *Contemporary Percussion*, it is in deep disfavour amongst percussionists.

or with crosses instead of note heads as in Walton's *Scapino* and *Façade*:

Ex. 321

Walton, Overture, *Scapino*

Walton, *Façade*

or

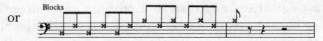

or even token staves with no more lines than the number of instruments portrayed.

If clefs are used to symbolize instruments of indefinite pitch it is normal to find only treble or bass, the former to suggest high sounding instruments such as triangle, tambourine, side drum etc., the latter for deep sounds—bass drum, tam-tam. So much is obvious, as also that borderline cases can be found, the composer making his own *ad hoc* decisions. Of these the outstanding example is that of the cymbals, which are surprisingly often notated in the bass clef, even when given a separate stave from the bass drum to which they surely supply the contrasting high sounds. Exceptions to this can, however, be found such as Delius's *Eventyr* (but not *Paris*), Strauss's *Heldenleben* (but not *Till Eulenspiegel*) and especially the Adagio of Bruckner's Eighth Symphony in which Bruckner actually ascribes to them two different notes, a B♭ and an E♭, as if he imagined the clashes harmonizing with the climaxes they decorate. Also, though they are both in a dynamic of *fff*, one may well feel that the higher E♭ is intended to be the stronger of the two.

4 LAYOUT AND PREPARATION OF ORCHESTRAL PARTS

There is no standard procedure for dividing the percussion parts between the players. Often the publishers will concoct some kind of division with, say, bass drum and cymbals on one part, triangle, tambourine and tam-tam on another, xylophone on a third and so on;

but errors of judgement are frequent, causing much inconvenience and confusion. It is all too easily forgotten, for instance, that the bells as well as all the glockenspiel, vibraphone, xylophone group of instruments must by the nature of their execution have plenty of time for manoeuvre.

Many composers try to avoid complaints by providing a multiple part containing all the percussion, a copy being supplied for each player who can then select his own line as it best works out. But theoretically ingenious, even fool-proof, as this may seem, the result in a work with a great deal of complicated percussion can not only look horrifically complex, but may take up so much space on each page that the players find themselves endlessly struggling with impossible and frequent page-turns.

Occasionally composers and/or publishers also show themselves unaware of the orchestral hierarchy by putting some stray percussion notes on the timpani part, or by putting the celesta among the percussion (it is hardly ever played by a percussionist, but by a pianist; nor is it placed near the kitchen department but with the harp and piano).

5 RANGE OF DYNAMICS AND COLOUR

Whereas percussion other than timpani was initially introduced into the orchestra in the pursuit of local colour (such as the Turkish music of Haydn's 'Military' Symphony, Mozart's *Entführung,* Beethoven's Choral Symphony, etc.), during the romantic era it can be found to be increasingly used for extra sonority or brilliance in climaxes on the one hand, and to enlarge the spectrum of orchestral colours on the other. It is as interesting to observe composers' economy as well as their extravagance in the use of percussion. The total abstinence on Tchaikovsky's part in his Fifth Symphony as well as his careful economy in the *Pathétique,* the surprisingly few percussion instruments and players required for the enormous orchestra of Wagner's *Ring* (it is an instructive occupation to count the tam-tam strokes of the entire epic)—these are as positive hallmarks of instrumental resourcefulness as the self-indulgent batteries of percussion effects to be found in so many twentieth-century scores.

At the same time it has to be recognized that in the latter part of this century the percussion department, with its myriad techniques and evocation of exotic cultures from all over the globe, has blossomed into arguably the most important section of the entire orchestra. The range of effects has become virtually infinite, and so too has the potential range of dynamics, from the cataclysmic to the most delicate. In the latter respect Bartók gives the unusual instruction in the second of his *Two Portraits,* Op. 5 for the cymbals, triangle and side drum all to play 'con sord'. As these are all instruments capable of the most refined pianissimo without having recourse to special muting devices it is not obvious what this instruction signifies. However, in the parts, though not the score, the solution is to be found by way of footnotes. It is indeed further varieties of colour which Bartók explores here: in the case of the cymbals these are to be struck 'with the hand', the side drum is to be played 'with a hand placed on the skin while striking', and the triangle too is 'to be clutched whilst being stirred (*gerührt*) by a larger or smaller stick'.

These are therefore not conventional muting devices such as apply to the other sections of the orchestra, but further imaginative sonic effects which the multifold resources of the percussion department have aroused in the creative minds of so many composers. Many of these will be outlined in the list of percussion instruments that follows, though naturally any attempt at a complete compilation would be a hopeless task.

INSTRUMENTS

BASS DRUM AND CYMBALS

After the timpani the percussion instruments most commonly found in orchestral scores are the bass drum and cymbals, which, while often used separately, may belong together. Indeed, in many Italian operas it is extremely difficult to know when or if the cymbals should play, as scores may merely cite *gran cassa* which by tradition includes *piatti*, the player being expected to know where to add cymbal strokes. It can be as much a howler to leave the cymbals out, on the purist grounds that they are not mentioned in the score, as to put them in on every bass drum note, as one sometimes hears. In Grand Opera such as Verdi's *Aida,* or *opera seria* (e.g. Rossini's *Semiramide*), they have to be added with knowledge and taste; and in *opera buffa* it is even more unsure whether they are required, as composers like Rossini would

have had a smaller orchestra with perhaps only a single percussion
player. It should not be assumed, however, that the bass drum and
cymbals in, for example, *The Barber of Seville* must be played by a one-
man band, and it seems likely that on the contrary he reserved the use
of cymbals for his more lavishly scored operas.

Indeed the very fact that bass drum and cymbals can technically be
played by one person produces a controversial orchestral situation.
For either a single suspended cymbal can be struck, thus sacrificing
the proper sonority of the clash, as in many small and pit orchestras,
or one of the two clashed cymbals can be attached to the head of the
bass drum, as is normal today only in military or jazz bands. The loss
of tone resulting from screwing one of the cymbals down in this way is
only half the question, as the sound has a particularly characteristic
tubby quality that immediately evokes associations with army bands,
popular circus music, Salvation Army meetings and so forth; and it is
specifically for these associations that, ever since Mahler established
the precedent in his First Symphony, the composite unit of bass drum
and cymbals played by a single player has been scored for by
numerous composers as a special effect in addition to a separate bass
drum and pair of cymbals played by two other musicians. Occasionally borderline cases do arise, such as Stravinsky's *Petrouchka*, but here
too percussionists claim with justification not only that the music is
imitating a circus band but also that the passages are much harder to
divide between two players:

Ex. 322

However, unless specially scored for, the combined one-man bass drum and cymbals should never in any circumstances be resorted to, even in cases where finance restricts the employment of all the desired percussionists, so evocative are its cruder associations.

Orchestrally speaking, the term 'bass drum' has become accepted rather than the circus or army 'big drum'. Translations include *gran cassa* (It.),[1] *grosse-caisse* (Fr.) and *grosse Trommel* (Ger.) but I have a special affection for the Spanish *bombo*.

Bass drums are of various shapes and sizes. Toscanini used to insist on a very large one for his performances of the Verdi Requiem, the instrument being laid flat on its side in the manner prescribed also by Berlioz in, amongst other places, the *Symphonie Fantastique* (where it is played by two drummers). The late Gerard Hoffnung produced a vast bass drum for his first Festival in 1956, so large that the doors of the Royal Festival Hall in London had to be dismantled to admit it. Alas, it was only visually effective, its tone being puny (as it was never intended for use, being no more than a manufacturer's advertising stunt). For sheer size has curiously little to do with the matter and even relatively small bass drums can produce a very good quality of sound. It is therefore wrong to assume too readily that a bass drum which looks as if it is only suitable for a boy scout band must, apart from its disappointing visual impact, necessarily be inadequate.

Bass drums also differ in being double or single-headed. The single-headed 'gong drum' (as it is called) is often superior in tone quality. The score is no guide to choice as particular types or sizes of bass drum are not usually specified (nor is the term 'gong drum' found in scores; Peter Maxwell Davies's opera *Taverner* is an exception). Nevertheless the double-headed bass drum is the standard orchestral one, having specific advantages of versatility over the gong drum. Moreover, it allows for various kinds of sticks or implements to be held in either hand, in the manner of older traditional practices. The most important of these was the use of the birch (German: *Ruthe*, or nowadays *Rute*), to be held in one hand and the stick in the other. This is what is intended in bass drum parts written with tails both up and down, such as the Turkish music in Haydn's 'Military' Symphony:

---

[1] As will be seen in Ex. 323 the international Italian term 'tamburo grande' (Or 'gran tamburo') is also widely used in classical scores.

Ex. 323

Until recently this custom had lapsed, however, and the birch, which should be played on the actual skin, wholly forgotten. Even today performances are rare in which a double-headed bass drum is correctly played in classical works of the kind, although the birch itself can be found prescribed by Mahler for use in his symphonies, whether to be rustled on the wooden rim of the drum as in the scherzo of his Second Symphony (marked 'auf dem Holz') or in the conventional manner as in the Seventh Symphony in which he already found it necessary to go into details in a footnote:

Ex. 324

This is nevertheless not the only bass drum usage notated with tails up and down. Another important effect is the alternate striking of the two sides of the double-headed bass drum, often with sticks of different weight as in Balakirev's *Thamar*. Here the Russian inscription signifies 'hit on each side alternately':

Ex. 325

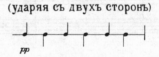

The bass drum is sometimes scored for motivically as a kind of super contra-bass timp, but it is always without definite pitch even though some variation in depth can be effected by tightening or slackening the surrounding cords. Moreover its sound in *p* or *pp* has a hollowness that is far from the world of timpani and can be exploited to magical advantage, as Verdi does in the 'Mors stupebit' from the Requiem.

At the other end of the dynamic scale the bass drum has far greater weight than the timps, to which it can accordingly add an additional sense of climax even when the timps are already fully occupied:

Ex. 326   Tchaikovsky, Symphony No. 6.

Players are often loath to give the full treatment to the bass drum and need great encouragement. Nor is the true heavy bass drum stick (Fr. *mailloche*; It. *mazza*) always automatically used. The two-headed stick is the authentic implement for a bass drum roll, but is clumsy and hard to control and therefore rarely seen these days, players generally using the one heavy stick or resorting to a pair of timpani sticks. Nevertheless the latter should really only be used as a special colour when specified.

Apart from this, however, it is very rare to find any particular stick called for, and the player will decide whether in rhythmic passages requiring greater clarity, for example, the *mailloche* may prove unsuitable.

Cymbals also come in a large range of sizes, which again are not normally specified except where particularly small ones are required. In this case German composers may call for a *Zymbal* as opposed to the usual word *Becken*. The little *Zymbal* is primarily a dance band variety and rarely clashed, hence the word being in the singular (*Becken* is a plural term for the pair of cymbals). Thus when Tibor Serly, attempting to realize the sketches of that master of percussion, Bartók, wrote for both large and small cymbals in the posthumous Viola Concerto, he left an area of doubt over whether a single small cymbal should not be conventionally suspended and contrasted with a pair of the large.

Normal orchestral cymbals vary between 14 inches and the oversize 22 inch. Naturally the biggest make a splendid sound but are inclined to be unwieldy and are therefore mostly reserved for tremendous isolated clashes in big romantic works.

The French term *cymbales* is similar to the English, but the Italian is either *cinelli* (used, for instance by Breitkopf in the Berlioz Gesamtausgabe, and by Bartók) or, more usually, *piatti*, i.e. plates,[1] corresponding with the German *Teller* although this latter is reserved exclusively for the instruction to clash the pair: *mit Teller(n)*. The English equivalent to this is 'clashed' (as opposed to 'struck' which implies 'with a stick'); other languages seem to lack a simple equivalent, the most usual being 'a 2' though this can be ambiguous when more than one pair is used. The Russians sometimes give:

---

[1] The Spanish *platillos* is perhaps self-evident, but less so the Portuguese *pratos* found in Villa-Lobos.

Ex. 327   Shostakovich, Symphony No. 1

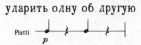

signifying 'strike the one against the other', but Prokofiev, who interchanges the effects of clashing and striking very frequently, uses the two symbols 'o' and '+' to indicate the pair and the stick respectively.

When there is no indication at all, the pair is generally intended, and one term for a clash with the two cymbals is *gewöhnlich* (i.e. in the usual manner) or *ordinairement, naturale,* etc. But some doubt arises from time to time especially with strokes such as the isolated cymbal entry in the last movement of Dvořák's New World Symphony:

Ex.328

Until recently this used always to be played with the stick, but custom is changing and the more normally accepted effect has become the gentle clash. This can be produced by using the whole of both plates, or players will often merely sweep the one half way up with the tip of the other. The latter method is usually employed in very delicate strokes such as the ending of Debussy's *Fêtes*:

Ex. 329

while the former may be thought more suitable for the pianissimo clashes in the 'Saraband of the Sons of God' from Vaughan Williams's *Job*.

As so often, the choice of execution is a matter for personal style on the part of the player. Exceptionally, however, Strauss marks the cymbal stokes 'pp zischend' (an onomatopoeic word denoting the use of the whole plates) in the 'critics' section of *Ein Heldenleben*.

Few orchestral effects are so dramatic—visually as well as sonic-ally—as the sustained clash ('allow to vibrate', *laisser vibrer, klingen lassen, lasciare vibrare*) the cymbals often held flamboyantly aloft after striking. Yet it is not by any means always shown in the score when this is intended, and indeed the very duration of a clash can be a matter of individual interpretation. Composers' notation can be curiously lax, and a short value note ($\downarrow$ or $\rangle$) should not necessarily be taken to mean that the sound must be damped at the end of its precise value. The clashes at the climaxes of Wagner's *Meistersinger* Prelude, or the crest of the music at Octavian's entrance for the presentation of the silver rose in Strauss's *Rosenkavalier*, would be greatly reduced in their splendid effect if the cold printed text were to be followed pedantically.

All the above applies not only to the clashed pair (which may be damped very quickly against the body) but equally to the suspended cymbal (which is controlled by the hand). The cymbal can be hung from a stand or lifted by its leather thong in one hand and struck with the other. A roll can also be effected in this way by repeated strokes of one stick, although a two-stick roll is often specified to obtain a smooth shimmer. At the same time a roll produced with a single stick has the advantage that it can, if so required, be instantly silenced with the other hand as in Webern's Passacaglia, Op. 1:

Ex. 330

Another kind of cymbal roll consists of rubbing the two plates together. The climax of the *Tannhäuser* 'Venusberg' music gives a prolonged two-cymbal roll, this being Wagner's intention even though it has to be deduced negatively, i.e. through the absence of any indication that a change should be made to the stick. Indeed all too often this is the case with the two-plate roll (Liszt's *Christus* and Janáček's *Glagolitic Mass* both provide examples), but it is a mistaken assumption that a single cymbal rolled with a stick must be the answer. Moreover, unless especially instructed to the contrary, players will more generally adopt the standard method of producing the cymbal roll with the stick because they regard the two-plate roll as crude and unsatisfactory, although it is very dramatic. Indeed, many instances can be found where it really is specifically called for, especially in Bartók's scores, in which he uses the marking 'a 2'. Roussel's *Suite en Fa* has the unusual term *roulée*, but this is more open to ambiguity than Ravel's particularly explicit *2 cymbales frottées*.

When, from amongst the numerous sticks that can be used to strike a cymbal, composers merely indicate 'hard' or 'soft', it is usually taken to mean one of the grades of timpani stick; and where, for example in Vaughan Williams's *Pastoral Symphony*, no more specific demand than the single word 'struck' is shown, a hard felt stick is normally understood. Wooden sticks are only used when specially prescribed and are not synonymous with side drum sticks even though these are also wooden. Being light in character they give a much shallower, more clattery effect and are generally asked for in a soft roll.

A light metal stick such as a triangle beater (*Stab* is an alternative word used in German) provides another cymbal colour; and Walton in *Façade* goes still further by requiring the cymbal to be struck by the triangle itself, thus getting the best of both worlds.

Elgar further prescribes a heavy metal beater in the 'Enigma' Variations at the climax of the finale, but in practice this is not always obeyed as there is some risk of damage to the cymbal.

The wire brush, though borrowed from the dance-band world, can occasionally be found in symphonic literature, especially in American or English scores where the name gives no problem. But there is as yet no standard translation and cases occur where it could be that a wire brush is incorrectly used:

Ex. 331   Prokofiev, *Peter and the Wolf*

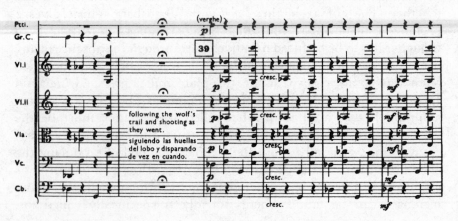

Strictly speaking the word *verghe* signifies a switch, and Varèse in *Intégrales* co-relates it with the French *verges = Rute* (German), on the strength of which Read's *Thesaurus of Orchestral Devices* identifies it too blithely with Mahler's *Ruthe* (= birch, see p. 380). But on the contrary where a cymbal (as opposed to a bass drum) beater is concerned, percussionists generally believe that the *verghe* should not be wooden and hence that the wire brush is intended, though the effect of this might seem too gentle for the huntsmen's music in the above example.

The striking of more than one cymbal is a real effect in its own right. Janáček provides examples of this in the repeated alternations of tails up and down in *Taras Bulba*, taken to be illustrative of clashing swords:

Ex. 332

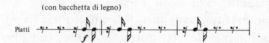

Moreover different cymbal effects are sometimes dramatically combined, i.e. one with stick simultaneously with the pair played by another percussionist, or of course several pairs may be clashed simultaneously. Mahler in his Third Symphony reinforces the already magnificent effect near the beginning of the work by asking for no less than three pairs for the return of the passage at the reprise. Extravagant as it may seem in theory, in performance it proves to be marvellously calculated.

The shimmer of a softly struck cymbal contains within it a bell-like resonance which, although always of indefinite pitch, can vary in height and depth to a certain extent, nor will a larger cymbal always give off a deeper ring. Passages such as the opening of Nono's *Y su sangre*, in which high, medium and low cymbal strokes are set in apposition, require much experimentation with different cymbals to get the effect he asks.

A curious quality can be produced if the cymbal is struck on the dome, the shimmer in this case being largely excluded. Bartók, ever the pioneer, was among the first to exploit this new colour, and in his Violin Concerto (1938) he also experimented with all kinds of unlikely beaters such as knitting needles and pen-knives. His example was later followed by Roberto Gerhard who even contrived a set of screw-rods (metal rods screw-threaded along their length) which he used extensively in his *Concerto for Orchestra*. However this does the cymbals no good at all and players are prone to bring out their most inferior equipment for such harsh treatment.

Another effect dear to Gerhard's heart is the use of a cello bow drawn across the edge of the cymbal. This device is found first in Schoenberg, both in the fourth of his *5 Orchesterstücke,* op. 16 and in *Erwartung*, although in the latter Schoenberg oddly enough changes to a double-bass bow. Well-rosined, the bows will conjure up a penetrating ring, but it is hard to keep the cymbal in position for long. Schoenberg only used the effect in isolated single places in each work whereas Gerhard, on the other hand, exploits it over long periods with several players dove-tailing their strokes to ensure its continuity.

It has been said with much wisdom that the effect of the cymbal clash is in inverse proportion to its frequency. Although undoubtedly the single climactic explosion, such as marks the high moment of intensity in the first movement of Sibelius's First Symphony, creates tremendous poignance by its unique position, this effect is only one side of the cymbals' role and is of comparatively recent and romantic origin. Tiresome as the rhythmic pattern of clashed cymbals may become, especially in loud passages such as the last pages of the finale of Tchaikovsky's Second Symphony, it is this which was the original function of the cymbals in Turkish music (used invariably together with triangle and bass drum) and is thus historically authentic. The interpreter may, however, feel that the conventional lack of dynamic marks will need some attention to add to the shape of the music in passages such as the coda of Dvořák's *Scherzo Capriccioso* if its eighty odd cymbal strokes are not merely to sound relentless, or at worst mechanical.

Cymbals are primarily Turkish (although a branch of the famous Zildjian family now operates from other countries) but there is also an important variant that comes from China and which is occasionally specified. Chinese cymbals, instead of slanting evenly after the central dome, viz:

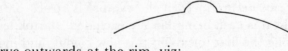

curve outwards at the rim, viz:

with very pronounced quality and limitations on use and technique. They are therefore never employed unless specifically asked for as in works by Messiaen and Gerhard, and are always simply clashed —usually fairly strongly—with far cruder and less controlled effect than is possible with the Turkish variety.

Contemporary composers have occasionally used other more specialized forms of cymbal such as the sizzle-cymbal (always suspended); this has holes punched at intervals round its surface with inset jingle-like bits of metal that vibrate when the cymbal is struck. 'High hats'—also imported from the jazz world—have also been written for, as in *Pastorals* by Alexander Goehr. These are cymbals with damping pads added, an upper cymbal being brought down on to a fixed lower one by a pedal mechanism.

TRIANGLE

The third indispensable member of the Turkish group found in classical scores, such as Mozart's *Entführung* or Beethoven's *Ruins of Athens*, is the triangle; again a treble instrument of indefinite pitch (at least, it should be, although triangles of really indefinite pitch are often difficult to find).

Again triangles come in different sizes, but this has little relation to the height or depth of the sound, and composers writing for a number of triangles with this purpose in mind create more problems than they cater for. Boieldieu, for example, in *The Caliph of Bagdad* calls for alto and bass triangles.

The range of dynamic power in a triangle is necessarily limited, but if held up high above the stand it is surprising how well the sound will carry against an orchestral *forte* tutti, especially in a roll. It is worth emphasizing this necessity for the triangle to be raised, as it is generally slung from a stand and in many halls or orchestral formations its sound is lost amidst the mass of music and bodies. Yet it may be quite inconvenient to hold it aloft for each entry, especially in a work with complicated to-ing and fro-ing for the percussionists.

The triangle is usually played with a thin metal beater and if no other stipulation appears in the score this is taken for granted. In fact other implements are only rarely used, such as wooden sticks for a more jangling sound.

Although seemingly a mild and delicate instrument the triangle can add an excellent splash of colour, and it is not at all uncommon to find it the only percussion instrument in a symphony other than the timpani. Following Brahms's example in the Fourth Symphony, Dvořák frequently used it in this way, as in the last movement of his early E♭ Symphony, Op. 10, and for the scherzos of both his Symphony in F, Op. 76, and the New World. But for sheer genius in economy one of the most famous triangle solos in the repertoire is Richard Strauss's favourite: the single stroke in the entire second act of *Siegfried*, occurring very near the end.

TAMBOURINE

The question of size hardly arises with the tambourine. They do exist in all sizes—in Sicily I once saw a real monster, giving a reminder both in appearance and use of its origin in the drum (*tambour*) family—but orchestrally this has little reality. The same is true of the hoop tambourine without parchment, i.e. nothing but frame with jingles, or its opposite—hoop with parchment but no jingles—both of which exist but are no more than occasional visitors to the orchestral scene; Falla uses the latter in *El Retablo de Maese Pedro* (see also p. 427).

One awkward feature of the tambourine is the similarity of its name to the *tambourin*, i.e. the Provençal long drum. The French get out of the difficulty by calling the tambourine the *tambour de basque* as do the Germans with one of their words for it, *Schellentrommel*; this is, however, rarely used and the standard German name is in fact none other than *Tambourin*, completing the confusion and leading to the famous howler of using a tambourine for Bizet's *L'Arlésienne*. The Italians use both *tamburino* and *tamburo basco* but the Breitkopf Berlioz edition uses 'tamburi piccoli' in, for example, *Le Carnaval Romain*, which is fortunately as unusual as it is dangerously ambiguous.

It is rare to find technical methods prescribed for the tambourine as it is mostly either struck, usually with the fingers as in the 'Brigand's Orgy' of Berlioz's Symphony *Harold in Italy*, or shaken; it is never played with a stick. Nevertheless in point of fact a number of important variants make up the player's technique, of which the most usually found in the printed score is *Mit den Daumen* or *avec la pouce* (with the thumb), referring to the method of producing a trill or rapid figure by wetting the thumb to increase the friction and juddering it over the surface of the skin. Poulenc's *Concert Champêtre* and the 'Danse Arabe' from Tchaikovsky's *Casse Noisette* both call for this method, though the latter being slow and measured is an instance where it is particularly difficult and players rarely obey the instruction:

Ex. 333

This thumb technique is in fact standard practice for a soft and shortish unmeasured roll, but for anything longer or louder it is more usual to shake the whole thing, especially if the roll ends in a dramatic tap, for which the tambourine can even be raised above the head with great panache. Moreover, in complicated sections players will also use the knee, either to rest it on, or to strike it against, or both. One of the hardest technical problems is to play the tambourine really softly. The jingles will ring out at the slightest vibration and the catastrophe of a dropped tambourine is not infrequent and in every way as disastrous as a cymbal. Stravinsky actually asks for a tambourine to be held above the floor and then dropped in the last scene of *Petrouchka* at the moment when the puppet's neck is broken by the Moor.

Single taps or rhythmic passages can be played either on the skin of the instrument or, turning it over, on the frame. The quality is, of course, different and it is odd that composers do not show awareness by specifying one or the other. Elgar in his *Falstaff* wrote:

Ex. 334

which is often taken to mean a short roll and is therefore played with the thumb or even by shaking the tambourine briefly, whereas there is an authentic tradition that Elgar himself asked that it be played 'struck lightly on the parchment'. This is typical of the doubt which pervades tambourine notation. More precise is Khachaturian who, in the ballet *Gayaneh*, specifies a composite technique:

Ex. 335

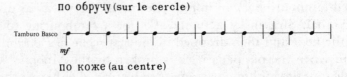

The use of more than one tambourine is rare, but Berlioz writes for two (in unison throughout) in the Overture *Le Carnaval Romain* as well as in *Harold in Italy*, a splendidly imaginative stroke.

SNARE DRUMS

The side drum is not only by far the most commonly found of the snare drum family but is also orchestrally the highest, the others being, in order of pitch, the military drum and the tenor drum.

It is necessary to add the word 'orchestrally', because in the drum world, whether military, civilian or dance band, it is easy to get caught up in a morass of specialist detail, admittedly both important and highly interesting but without immediate relevance to the orchestral scene. So interlocked indeed is the situation that the different drums become entangled in their very nomenclature, and one often has only the most general idea of what instrument the composer really meant, coupled with the suspicion that he may himself have had no very positive views.

First as to the names: the term 'snare drum' is sometimes, as in Copland, used to mean the side drum specifically, but in view of the other snared drums this is clearly a dangerously ambiguous practice. The French call the side drum either *caisse claire* (its real unequivocal name) or *tambour militaire*. Yet this latter produces another ambiguity, for *tambour militaire* might also really mean 'military drum', though for this they may just as likely merely say *tambour*. Delius uses a 'military tambour' in *Eventyr* and a 'military drum' in the *Dance Rhapsody No. 2*, which are presumably both intended for the same side drum. Even Grove's dictionary gives the one as a straight translation for the other with, it has to be admitted, an element of historical and geographical truth. Yet again, *tambour* might possibly mean 'tenor drum', for which the real name is *caisse roulante*, a term on the whole less frequently found in orchestral scores.

Turning to the German, a parallel situation exists: *kleine Trommel* is clear enough, but some composers put *Militärtrommel* when they palpably mean a simple side drum, making things difficult for others like Henze who, when he puts 'Militärtrommel', really means what he says. At the same time this kind of specialist terminology can cause confusion as when Strauss writes 'kleine Militärtrommel' in *Rosenkavalier*. To be precise, this is actually deeper both in appearance and quality than the side drum (*kleine Trommel*) which is what he calls for in, for example, *Salome*, and which it is more than likely what he meant here too.

The German for tenor drum (*Rührtrommel*) is fortunately clear enough and in common use throughout the literature. These also come in different sizes so that Wagner was able to specify a 'grosse Rührtrommel' in *The Ring* (where it totally supplants the bass drum—a curious touch).

Italian terminology corresponds more or less with a combination of the French and German. Side drum is *tamburo piccolo* and tenor drum *cassa rullante*, though again the latter is less often found and may be what the composer means by *tamburo*, which in its turn may also signify the military drum (otherwise *tamburo militare*). Rimsky-Korsakov, for instance, plainly regards *tamburo, tamburo piccolo, caisse claire* and *tambour militaire* as all synonymous and corresponding with the side drum. One has only to consult his book on instrumentation to confirm this, let alone his scores in which the terms may be mixed up in a quite random manner. (In *Scheherazade*, the 'tamburo' of the third movement becomes the 'tamburo piccolo' in the list of instruments that heads the fourth, though thereafter the word *piccolo* vanishes once more.) For Balakirev also there is no differentiation either, the 'tamburo' of the First Symphony becoming the 'tamburo militare' of *Thamar*.

The trouble arises really because the many borderline instruments only came late onto the orchestral scene and by the time the military drum, for instance, appeared with an existence of its own, its name had already been introduced by way of differentiation from the larger tenor and bass drums.

Although all these drums are of indefinite pitch, they vary in depth to sufficient extent to be used by composers as a kind of substitute for timps when scoring for small or unconventional groups. For this purpose their differences are most marked when played without snares (Ger., *Saiten*; Fr., *cordes*; It., *corde*); these are both quickly and easily fixed by a kind of clasp, and are left on for normal playing. Nevertheless it is often necessary to ask drummers to slacken the snares, when the drum is silent, to prevent them rattling in passages where the timpani or other neighbouring instruments are in loud action.

'Snares off' is occasionally stipulated (*senza corde*, etc.) but may also be regarded as an interpretation of the requirement *dumpf* (dull) or even 'muffled', as the effect is so much less strident especially with the side drum. But 'muffled' is really the same as 'muted' (*gedämpft*, *coperti*, *voilé*) which stipulates the covering of the instrument with a cloth, though in practice, as with timpani, players will more often simply place a handkerchief or pad on the skin. In the closing bars of Elgar's *Falstaff* a muffled drum marks poor Falstaff's death. But this is not to say that a muffled drum need be soft: in *Till Eulenspiegel* the terrifying *fortissimo* side drum with which Till is arraigned before the judges is marked 'dumpf' and played with snares off, sometimes on one or more deeper drums than the true *kleine Trommel*.

Again like timpani, these drums can be played in different places on the head, producing variations of pitch and quality. Bartók exploits all these colours (together with the snares on and off) as a major feature in the slow movement of his First Piano Concerto, placing his percussion section unconventionally near to the solo piano for the purpose.

The frequently met instruction 'on the rim' constitutes a problem as it presupposes that the rim is wooden, whereas in modern instruments it is generally of very thin metal giving a very different—and far less resonant—effect, so that players use their ingenuity to imitate the desired sound in other ways. A 'rim-shot' however, remains an absolute reality of the most galvanizing nature (always in *fortissimo*), the whole stick being slapped across the side drum, rim and head, creating a crack like a pistol shot—in specific imitation of which Tchaikovsky uses it in his symphonic poem *The Voyevode* and Copland for the gunfight in his ballet *Billy the Kid*.

Wooden sticks are the standard implements for this group of drums, and 'side drum sticks' the generic term establishing the conventional shape. This is not to say that other beaters are not called upon, such as timpani sticks, etc.

Snare drum rolls and figures can be produced across the widest imaginable range of dynamics. Janáček in *Taras Bulba* uses both extremes with startling effect, the murmur in the first movement being no less dramatic than the crashes in the third. Ravel, ever on the look-out for new ideas and variations of effect, hit on the riotous idea of reducing a side drum *pianissimo* even further in his Left Hand Piano Concerto by making the drummer continue the rhythm with the sticks no longer on the drum but on each other. In the overture *La Gazza Ladra* Rossini uses two side drums placed on either side of the orchestra, alternating rolls before coming together. (This is only one of the works in which an opening side drum roll suggests the beginning of our National Anthem, with disconcerting consequences.)

Many of the figures and rhythms used and practised by drummers and forming the back-bone of side drum techniques are known by names such as 'paradiddle', 'flam', etc., but these have not entered orchestral (as opposed to the specialist percussion) vernacular. They are numerous and varied enough, however, for Nielsen to instruct his side drummer in the Fifth Symphony to improvise upon them 'à toute la fantaisie de son imagination'.[1]

Side drummers need great stamina and control as well as an iron inflexibility of pulse. Hence works such as Ravel's *Bolero* or Shostakovich's 'Leningrad' Symphony (No. 7), both containing twelve minutes non-stop repetition of a rhythmic figure, are examples of the capital composers have made of this accomplishment.

Notation with tails up and down may be used to identify two different drums on the same stave, but is of course also used to signify a single drum played with two sticks.

TABOR, TAMBOURIN

Elgar's 'tabor' (an Olde Englishe instrument used in Morris dancing) presents a problem on account of its rarity in orchestral scores. In a preliminary note in *Falstaff* the composer suggests substituting a military drum (proving, incidentally, that he recognized this instrument in its own right), but the nearest equivalent is certainly the Provençal long drum or *tambourin*.

The tabor has no snares, but the *tambourin* has one only—so that the usual custom of substituting a drum without snares for both equally is not wholly correct. The *tambourin* is found in many French scores (notably Bizet but also twentieth-century composers such as Milhaud) and is generally given straightforward rhythmic patterns. Its name gives rise to the confusions already discussed above (see p. 392), and, being essentially a French instrument, no translations appear to exist. Furthermore it is very rarely to be found in any other than French scores, coming into the category of 'local colour'. However Copland unexpectedly writes for 'tabor (long drum)' (*sic*) in *Appalachian Spring*.

The French *tarole* (or *tarolle*) perhaps also belongs here, being a local variant of, this time, the side drum, though without snares. Poulenc uses it in two of his concertos and Varèse in *Ionisation*.

---

[1] *Sic* (in French) in the original Borups edition. The later publication of the score, edited by Erik Tuxen, omits this and other essential indications together with countless bowdlerizations of the text.

GONGS AND TAM-TAMS

The gong family is confused by the fact that the generic titles are also used for the quite different subspecies. In English speaking countries the word 'gong' comprises all the various gongs and tam-tams while on the continent 'gong' is only occasionally used as a term of differentiation, the all-embracing term being, on the contrary, 'tam-tam'. English dictionaries further confuse the issue by giving 'tam-tam, see tom-tom': it is maddening that there is actually a grain of truth in this thoroughly confusing and inadequate definition because the African tom-tom is sometimes known ethnically as 'tam-tam'.

Essentially, the difference between gongs and tam-tams (both exist in all sizes) lies in their very shape, though this of course crucially affects the sound they make. True gongs are flat with a broad flange, like the domestic dinner gong in fact, although most orchestral gongs are considerably larger. They will usually give off a more or less definite pitch but in any case they have a well focused boom. Since they come from the Far East they were, until recently, only introduced into the orchestra for local colour in such works as *Turandot* or Strauss's *Japanisches-Festmusik*, in both of which they are written at actual pitch. Vaughan Williams in his Eighth Symphony then deliberately borrowed the *Turandot* set of gongs and amused himself by scoring for them. But Berg, Webern and subsequent composers also called on the 'gong', whether *hoch* or *tief* (high or low) without specifying pitch and in order to add variety of colour by contrasting it with the more conventional tam-tam.

This latter is of various shapes but in particular lacks the flange of the true gong. Tam-tams can have a widely varying depth of sound according to size, but are always of indefinite pitch (although if struck in the centre, some instruments will give a recognizable bell-like note: Delius in his *Mass of Life* actually writes a deep E♭ for the tam-tam to suggest the tolling of Nietzsche's Midnight Bell). Tam-tams may be Chinese (and some of the more beautiful have dragons beaten out on their central portions), but can also be Turkish, though unlike cymbals the difference is academic and never mentioned in scores.

The real tam-tam sound is a great wash of shimmering tone which can even swell slightly after the initial impact of a single well-poised blow. It is particularly significant that the mighty stroke with which Sindbad's ship sinks at the climax of Rimsky-Korsakov's *Scheherazade* is skilfully marked only single *f*. On the other hand a violent blow sacrifices beauty of tone in favour of a metallic roar, though this naturally has its uses too.

Orchestration books mostly ignore the duality of gongs and tam-tams, and certainly many composers write simply for a tam-tam or gong as if the terms were wholly synonymous, in this case always meaning the deep tam-tam as used by Tchaikovsky in *Francesca da Rimini* or the Second and Sixth Symphonies (the *Pathétique* solo *pp* stroke being perhaps the most famous so-designated 'ad-lib' in the repertoire—see the list of instruments at the beginning of the finale. Hence the 'gong' in Delius's tone-poem *Eventyr* is precisely the same instrument as the tam-tam of the same composer's earlier scores; Bax also uses the term 'gong' in his orchestral works as does Britten, although when adding the mighty stroke to the climax of the Passa-caglia of his opera *Peter Grimes* for the concert version he forgot and marked it tam-tam. (The suggestion that he really meant two different instruments is not borne out by his practice in other works.) Even Hindemith unexpectedly calls for a 'grosse Gong' in his Violin Concerto in circumstances which make it unlikely that he really meant to differentiate.

Outside the standard orchestral world there are all sorts of different gongs such as Javanese gongs (in Orff's *Antigonae* where they are called Buckelgongs) with a pronounced nipple and accordingly a particular tone of their own, though they remain more like gongs than tam-tams; and with the contemporary passion for introducing specialized native instruments from every corner of the globe, the very similar Burmese gongs have now found their way into the orchestra in the works of Messiaen and his followers. Messiaen himself tends to write for tam-tams as the bass instruments of the gong ensemble, as for example in his *Et Exspecto*.

Gongs and tam-tams are normally struck with a heavy but soft-headed beater in order to minimize the metallic clang-tone. But Strauss in *Macbeth* and again later in *Elektra*, deliberately seeks just this crudity by instructing that the tam-tam be rubbed ('gerieben') with the triangle stick, a terrifying sound.

The resonance of even the shortest tam-tam sound can last a very long time and it is always necessary to consider where it should, however gradually, be damped, especially when the score fails to specify. One danger inherent in tam-tams, not always sufficiently allowed for either by composers or performers, is that repeated strokes can cause the sound to grow to immense proportions, the roll becoming virtually submerged in an all-enveloping mass of resonance. As a result, rhythmic patterns become difficult to discern unless the player resorts to very hard beaters.

Good tam-tams are hard to come by, and it is not unknown for quite reputable orchestras to make do with what are little more than glorified tea-trays. Hardly less than the timpani, and perhaps to a greater extent than the cymbals, the quality of the tam-tam can be said to reflect the artistic standard of an orchestra.

CASTANETS

Although one might reasonably expect castanets to have no more than a special-purpose Spanish connotation, they are in fact more widely used than that and are to be found in the scores of composers of every country and school, from Wagner (the 'Bacchanale' in the First Act of *Tannhäuser*) via Sibelius (*Festivo*) and Dohnányi (Suite in F sharp minor, Op. 19) to contemporary composers such as Stravinsky (*Agon*).

Since composers can rely on the orchestral type in which the castanets are fixed on a board or manipulated with a handle, the repertoire is full of elaborate passage-work that would be hardly practicable with the true Spanish loose castanets held in the palm of the hand.

It is normally taken for granted that castanets are wooden, but Saint-Saëns also wrote for iron ones in *Samson and Delilah* ('castagnettes de bois et de fer') and his example was followed by Milhaud (*Les Choéphores*, etc.). Since in actual fact iron castanets are unknown in the profession it has been said that *castagnettes de fer* and *crotales* (see p. 420 below) are identical, but this is an over-simplification—crotales are never made of iron in any case—even though 'untuned' crotales may sometimes be used as an expedient.

The general term for castanets is broadly the same in most languages allowing for small spelling changes; only the Italians do also say *nacchere*.

Castanets are often used to give odd clicks during the course of a passage where they act as a kind of substitute for claves or even a very light variety of wood block. For this purpose they can even be struck, not upon each other, but with an independent object, such as the 'legno' (wooden stick) prescribed by Stravinsky in the 'Bransle Gay' from *Agon*, though the purpose here is not very clear since the usual technique (also wood against wood) gives a virtually identical sound.

BELLS

Generally speaking, orchestras are equipped with a double row of not particularly large tubular bells with a chromatic range of one and a half octaves from [music: to] (actual pitch). This means that with a

phrase of, say: [music] the conductor is at once in trouble, and has to send for extra tubes which may or may not be available. Moreover, if substitutes should be obtained they always turn out to be higher, not lower, and it is unbelievably hard to find a bell with a deep note amongst the tubular variety. On one occasion, for the climax of Bliss's opera *Tobias and the Angel*, the London Symphony Orchestra procured an enormous tubular bell at considerable cost and trouble only to find, after the player had mounted a monster step ladder to reach its striking point, that impressive in tone as it undoubtedly was, the actual note it gave was no lower than before.

Bells always remain a special effect and tubular bells can never be anything but a compromise at best, though they are taken for granted in most circumstances. Moreover the 'ring of chimes' (as they are also called, particularly in American scores) is an awkward contraption making it virtually impractical to read the part from a music stand. It is therefore quite usual to see the player, who is trying to keep an eye on the conductor, take the music in one hand as he goes over to the bells and with mallet in the other hold the music up before him as he plays. As there is only one spot on each bell that gives the pure tone instead of a disagreeable metallic clang, the hazardous nature of the enterprise can well be imagined. Players have been known, even in professional orchestras, to play the bells back to front in the heat of

the moment so that the phrase: [music] from Debussy's

Ibéria came out as [music] without the harassed musician

being aware of it.

Composers are for ever prescribing deep bells in the optimism that some solution will be sought and found. But the famous knell of Berlioz's *Symphonie Fantastique* provides for the piano as an *ossia*, a device savouring of despair; it is even known that Berlioz did indeed regularly accept this woeful substitute since, as Hugh Macdonald says, 'deep bells were rarely found, then as now'. Undoubtedly the modern tubular bells (which he would not have known) are also far from Berlioz's real dramatic vision, but unlike the piano they do at least evoke bell-like associations. In any case the usual interpretation:

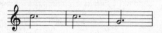

is of course too high and in the prevailing absence of a low G tubular bell I myself have had recourse to a compromise in the form of:

which does create some illusion of deeper bells, even the low G being suggested to the unprejudiced ear. But some orchestras have sets of real bells of which they are justly proud, and others use different types of resonant metal plates.[1] These last are particularly useful for Mahler's 'tief unstimmte Glocken' in his Second, Sixth, Seventh and Ninth Symphonies, where tubular bells give quite the wrong colour, and in a footnote to the finale of the Seventh Symphony he at last prescribes these 'Stahlstäbe'.

Normally, however, tubular bells serve adequately for most purposes, and one can reasonably take it that they correspond with the designated *campane, cloches, Glocken* (very occasionally *Rührenglocken*) to be found in so many scores. The range actually called for by composers can generally be made to fit available resources though trouble arises when a really large bell is needed as in 'Sunday Morning' from Britten's *Peter Grimes*:

---

[1] James Holland gives a detailed account of these 'bell plates', together with a photograph of a particularly large one (*Percussion*, pp. 59–60).

Ex. 336

It is clear here that the B♭ bell should not only be large and deep (ideally, of course, bell-shaped) but should not be played by the same player as the E♭ bell, as is generally done.

Bells have so many overtones that there are times when it might seem immaterial which octave is played—or even what note is struck as long as bell noises are going on. Yet the choice of an inept pitch can also be more destructive than some composers take into account. For example, the bell in Tchaikovsky's *Manfred* Symphony is of unprescribed pitch, the only instruction being that it should be of medium size (though a German translation in the score adds the suggestion of A as a suitable note). Certainly it would be an irresponsible conductor who left the pitch entirely to chance, as also in the case of the countless operatic clocks that strike twelve to an unprescribed note (*Rigoletto* Act 3, etc.).

The most usual notation is in the treble clef at pitch, but when composers (such as Bartók in his *2 Images*) specify deep sounds they do also write in the bass clef (though still usually at pitch). Britten in the above example can be seen writing in both. Rachmaninov writes for

4 *Campane*:  in his choral work devoted to the subject (a

modest requirement in the circumstances though he imitates the sound of bells with great orchestral virtuosity). The great tolling in Wagner's *Parsifal*:

Ex. 337

Glocken auf dem Theater

is, of course, notorious and has been contrived, even at Bayreuth, with a variety of quite different and many-coloured effects in the search for Wagner's ideal: piano strings, an elaborate hammered bell machine, gongs and even a tuba have all contributed at one time or another.

Bells hardly lend themselves to different techniques, although Britten in *The Turn of the Screw* managed with the collaboration of the great percussionist James Blades to devise, through trial and error, a very telling glissando.

GLOCKENSPIEL

There still exist two completely different species of glockenspiel: the usual standard instrument consisting of two rows of steel plates mounted so as to correspond with the black and white notes of the piano and played with hammers: and the 'keyboard glock' which is a contraption usually with rather limited range and doubtful action but which, having a keyboard just like an actual piano, is capable of a few effects not strictly practicable with hammers.

The term used for identification of the keyboard glock is basically simple enough —*avec*—or *à*—*clavier, mit Claviatur*, etc.—though others are also used as will soon be seen. A number of important instances can be found of composers stating that it is this kind of glockenspiel they require—Mahler's Seventh Symphony, Ravel's *Ma mère l'Oye*, Dukas' *L'Apprenti Sorcier*, etc.—but partly because keyboard glocks

rarely have a compass of more than ♭ to ♭ (sounding two octaves

higher) and partly because so few are reliable, percussionists will usually try to persuade the conductor to accept the normal hammer glock even if it entails calling upon two players to cover the situation. Sometimes, as in the Mahler, this works well enough, but *Ma mère l'Oye* as well as various scores by Messiaen such as *Turangalîla-Symphonie* set such problems that they are really impracticable except with the keyboard instrument.

Normal hammer glockenspiels have a compass of two and a half

octaves: ♭ to ♭ (sounding two octaves higher) but composers

such as Honegger, in his Fourth Symphony (*Deliciae Basiliensis*) or Prokofiev in his First Piano Concerto, Op. 10, write for a three-octave glockenspiel, viz:

Ex. 338

(sounding *one* octave higher)

But these instruments are rare, and many players will be found bringing the top or bottom notes of a passage up or down the octave in order to bring the part within the range of the smaller set, however much the line may be distorted in the process.

The archetype of the keyboard glock must surely be the one Mozart used in *Zauberflöte* and which we know he played himself. Details no longer survive of exactly what this was, but undoubtedly it would have been a softer-toned affair sounding more like a dulcitone (see below, p. 491) or celesta which is usually substituted for it these days.

The word *glockenspiel*, while clearly German in origin, is used in other countries, though the French also use *jeu de timbres*, a term which properly (though not invariably) applies specifically to the keyboard glock. The Italians have their own word *campanelli*[1] (which does cause occasional confusion with small bells) or 'carillon' as Respighi writes in *The Fountains of Rome*—uniquely for him in order to differentiate from his usual 'campanelli'—indicating the keyboard glock, as he here writes figuration hardly possible on the hammered variety. Puccini, having previously used 'carillon' or 'campanelli' ('campanelli a tastiera' = keyboard glock in *Butterfly*) reverted to 'glockenspiel' from *Fanciulla* onwards. Curiously Strauss, in *Don Quixote*, writes 'Glöckchen' although elsewhere he writes normally for 'Glockenspiel'; possibly he meant to specify some difference. Kurt Atterberg in his Sixth Symphony writes especially for the keyboard glock (as emphasized in a footnote) designating it, amidst the prevailing Italian terms, as 'timbre'. Debussy and Dukas can also be seen to use 'glockenspiel', and in *La Mer* Debussy wavers between this instrument and the celesta (see p. 471). Grove's dictionary baldly states that Debussy was writing for the keyboard glock (despite his choice of term), but this can only be surmised, possibly on the grounds of the alternative celesta, itself a keyboard instrument.

In writing for the *jeu de timbres* Messiaen specifically states that the sound is two octaves higher. This is by no means invariable practice; Wagner certainly writes for the glock sound to be one octave higher, and both Mahler and Strauss follow his example as well as Prokofiev in the passage quoted above as Ex. 338. But since other composers very rarely indeed state the octave sound required it can for practical purposes become academic, and passages will generally be played

---

[1] Forsyth gives *campanette*, but I have never seen this in a printed score.

simply wherever they lie most conveniently for the available instrument. For the conductor or score-reader, however, the issue remains a complicated one and not only confined to the glock as will be seen.

Dohnányi, who again does specify a transposition of two octaves, also asks in his *Variations on a Nursery Tune* for a second glockenspiel of 'exceptional purity and clarity of sound' ('besonderer Zartheit und

schlackenloser Reinheit') which he writes at actual pitch: [musical notation: *bis*]

He states that this is what he means by the term 'Glocken' in order to differentiate from the normal 'Glockenspiel' which he uses in a later variation, but unfortunately it is not very clear exactly what instrument he had in mind, and many players are quite wrongly led to substitute the tubular bells. Possibly the best solution is a vibraphone played without the vibrators.

In the last movement of Sibelius's Fourth Symphony there is another conundrum over the use of the term 'Glocken'; Sibelius is said to have told one conductor or another that it was a misprint and certainly the passages are more usually played on a glockenspiel today, but the whole context is so odd that it is quite possible Sibelius's original intention had been bells but that under pressure he later changed his mind. It might also be significant that when in the tone poem *The Oceanides*, written only three years later, he really did want glockenspiel he described this, unconventionally if accurately, as 'Stahlstäbe'.

Like Dohnányi, Orff writes for a large glockenspiel under the designation of 'metallofono' in *Catulli Carmina*, using both treble and

bass clefs, with a range of [musical notation: *to*] . Another similar instrument

is the tubaphone, which is described later, see p. 491.

Theoretically, chords (with more than one beater in the hand or hands) and glissandi (the beater swept up or down the bars) are practicable just as on xylophone or vibraphone, but are not written to anything like the same extent as with those instruments. Probably the most famous example of this effect (in which the glockenspiel is curiously called 'bells') is in the 'Can-can' of the Rossini-Respighi *Boutique Fantasque*:

Ex. 339

Trills are a commonplace, though the indication 'tr' can be equivocal. With the keyboard glock it can only mean across two notes such as   (whether ♭ or ♮) but with the hammered glock it is ambiguous as it could equally well signify

The individual steel bars of the normal glockenspiel, being only slung loosely on the frame, can easily be detached and held up for striking. In this way they are sometimes used as a very tolerable substitute for antique cymbals in, for example, *L'Après-midi*, but Hindemith in his *Kammermusik No. 1* actually calls for 'Der Stab aus einem Glockenspiel', meaning that one bar should be used on its own in this manner.

In *Enter Spring*, Frank Bridge specifies a 'Military Glockenspiel', presumably intending the upright lyre-glockenspiel as used in bands on the march (a picture of one of these is given by Blades amongst his illustrations between pp. 400–1), but this is not actually used in performance. Strauss, in *Panathenäenzug*, also uses this instrument, simply describing it as 'Lyra'.

XYLOPHONE FAMILY

The xylophone is in a way first cousin to the glockenspiel in that it has a similar arrangement of bars, with the chief and obvious difference that they are made of wood instead of metal. A further important deviation lies, however, in the way the instrument has developed from the 'Holz- und Strohinstrument' of Strauss's *Salome* (this was nothing more nor less than a primitive xylophone, the wooden bars having been literally laid over a straw-strewn base) to the modern elaborate instrument with its resonators and movable wheeled structure.

It is practically impossible to state categorically the range of the xylophone. It may vary from the two and a half octaves of the glockenspiel (see above, p. 406) as in the simplest table model, to a four-octave contraption suitable for the dazzling displays of light music solo virtuoso players. The instrument has, however, developed in the process through the impinging upon it of another and very similar instrument, the marimba.

The standard orchestral xylophone is a simple dry-to-clattery sounding instrument, with straight, non-resonating wooden bars, high in pitch though in fact an octave less high than the glockenspiel. At the same time, in determining this pitch factor the question of timbre has to be taken into account and this can be incredibly confusing. In the case of the lower register of the xylophone the overtones can even be so much stronger than the fundamental that one is totally misled over what note is actually being played.

There does exist, moreover, a bass xylophone with a range lying an octave lower than the ordinary xylo, though it has rarely been called into service in the symphony orchestra. A famous instance, however, is to be found in Puccini's *Turandot* where, unlike the xylophone, it is notated in the bass clef.

It is with this bass xylophone that the marimba corresponds, though differing in character partly in the softer material of the wood used, partly in the curved shaping of the bars, and partly also in the use of resonators fixed beneath each bar. Furthermore, unlike the bass xylo, the marimba has the full range of four octaves, thus corresponding with the large virtuoso-model xylo, though sounding an octave lower and much gentler in timbre.

Where confusion has occurred over the past decades it has been due to the adaptation of the modern xylo to include such marimba features as resonators, and even the extension of the range to a total of five octaves. The resultant hybrid has been christened a xylorimba since it can—and frequently does—serve as an all-purpose machine capable of playing parts written for either of its parent instruments. In the end it fulfils this function even though something of the more aggressive characteristics of the xylophone have inevitably been sacrificed in favour of the more ingratiating resonance of the marimba.

It is only in the most contemporary scores that the three instruments are differentiated and specified by name, and even so, composers of the avant-garde have been known to go astray in trying to master their ranges and pitch-differences, writing too low for the xylo, too high for the marimba, etc. But it does not matter: the players shrug their shoulders and play everything on their xylorimbas, and at the most convenient pitch.

Until recently the xylophone was the only member of this family recognized by symphonic composers, and although long known to be capable of virtuoso accomplishments, these were still not exploited except in such illustrative solos as Britten's *Young Person's Guide*, designed solely to show off its possibilities. Otherwise xylophone solos are generally simple in character and technical requirements, the colour of the instrument being usually the end in itself. Its first appearance in the symphony can be found in Mahler's No. 6.

With the researches of composers such as Orff in Germany and the Messiaen/Boulez school in France, however, all three members of the xylophone family have begun to be exploited from every point of view. Orff uses further additional fringe instruments in *Antigonae* such as Trogxylophones, soprano, tenor and bass no less, and following his lead, Hartmann writes fantastically elaborate parts for marimba on two staves in his later symphonies. Here (as already referred to in glockenspiels above) the use of several sticks in each hand is a clear extension of technique. Different kinds of sticks (rubber, hardwood, felt, etc.) exist for all these instruments, but are not often prescribed by composers as this comes into the province of interpretation.

In *Bluebeard's Castle* Bartók writes for a 'xilofono a tastiera' which is none other than a keyboard xylo. In practice, there being no longer any such thing, the passages in the opera are normally given to two players using conventional hammers.

It is not usual to find xylophone passages laid out so as to show how they should be distributed between the hands, though the 'Laideronette' movement from Ravel's *Ma mère l'Oye* is an exception, no doubt at the time being considered particularly exacting and even notated on two staves.

The name of the xylophone is international, only occasionally the characteristic 'x' being changed to an 's' or 'z' for some scores using Italian terminology: *silofono, zilofono*. (Percy Grainger's term 'hammer-wood' comes into the same orbit as his 'middle fiddle' for viola, etc.) Schoenberg in *Gurrelieder* calls it a 'Holzharmonika' but adds the conventional 'xylophon' in brackets.

411

The xylophone naturally comes into its own in music descriptive of wood or bones (skeletons, etc.) as in Saint-Saëns' *Danse Macabre* of 1874; so much was this a pioneer use of the xylophone that the score contains a note explaining what it is ('de bois et paille'—like Strauss's in *Salome*, see p. 409), and stating that it could be obtained from the publishers. Bartók's *Wooden Prince* and Walton's *Belshazzar's Feast* ('Praise Ye the God of Wood') give further obviously appropriate uses of the xylo, while the solo at the opening of Janáček's *Jenufa*, descriptive of the turning of the mill-wheel, is a famous atmospheric stroke of genius.

VIBRAPHONE

A relative newcomer to the symphonic scene, the vibraphone is very specialized and limited in its usage. Normally extremely soft toned, its particular quality of vibrating resonance has the side effect of blurring any passage-work of even moderate speed and as a result it is generally used precisely to add its characteristic pulsating shimmer in the form of either isolated notes or chords. These latter are an especial feature and are often of up to as many as six notes (three beaters being held in each hand). Berg features the vibraphone in *Lulu* as part of his evocation of the 1930s jazz idiom, and Walton's Cello Concerto may be cited as a more recent work making prominent and pervasive use of vibraphone chords.

In range and appearance similar to the marimba (apart from its silvery metal bars), it is also written at pitch. While the vibrating fans are so much an integral *raison d'être* of the whole instrument they are in fact a separate mechanism that has to be independently set in motion. It is, however, more usual for scores to specify when they are not required, rather than when they are, as in the Adagio of Britten's *Cello Symphony*. Another important part of the vibraphone's equipment is a sustaining pedal, again hardly ever prescribed but used by Britten in *Death in Venice*, a score which specializes in the use of the vibraphone without the fans.

Despite the confused effect of any rapid vibraphone passage work, instances are constantly to be found in contemporary scores. The following virtuoso writing from Boulez's *Le Marteau sans Maître* gives an extreme example:

412

Ex. 340

The matter of different beaters also comes into question. One inherent difficulty with the vibraphone is that a generally undesirable 'clang' tone very soon becomes evident both in loud passages and especially when hard sticks are used. These are, however, sometimes deliberately called for as in Gerhard's *The Plague*.

WOOD BLOCK, TEMPLE BLOCKS, ETC.

Sometimes called 'Chinese block', the wood block is precisely what its title says: an oblong block of wood, but so fashioned that it gives a very resonant sound when struck. The primary difference from a single bar taken from a xylophone lies in its having no definite note, although wood blocks can be of all sizes with consequent variations of pitch that are then sometimes used together—high, middle and low. The standard orchestral use, however, is of a single small block with high and acute tone, that may be found termed (perhaps rather perfunctorily) simply 'legno' as by Prokofiev in the Sixth Symphony; Blomdahl charmingly uses 'pezzo di legno' (piece of wood); the Germans also say *Holzblock*, as do the French (*bloc de bois*). In *La*

413

Création du Monde Milhaud calls for a 'bloc de bois' as well as a 'bloc de metal'. This latter is essentially an anvil (see below, p. 421). There is some doubt over what Atterberg, again in the Sixth Symphony of 1927, intended by writing 'wooden box, Trälåda, Holzkasten, boite de bois'—and then, in the list of the orchestra, 'tamburo di legno' (like Prokofiev in his Fifth Symphony!)[1] which is not necessarily the same thing (see p. 428, below). Another area of doubt surrounds the '2 Tavolette' in Respighi's *Feste Romane*; he writes a rhythmic pattern for them on a single line and they are played, at any rate in Britain, on two wood blocks; but they may well correspond with Indian tablas or with some oriental hand drums such as Bantock uses in his *Omar Khayyám* and which Respighi may have believed to have been in use amongst the Arab community in Ancient Rome.

Although it is unusual to find methods of execution, type of stick required, etc., detailed in scores, there are ample instances of the wood block used for rhythmic or colouristic effects with full range and gradations of tone: if the block is struck really viciously the resultant 'crack' can match the 'rim-shot' on a side drum, though lacking the exciting dramatic impact of that effect. Xenakis uses the wood block stridently in works such as *Pithoprakta*, and the unmotivated, spaced-out blows once produced such unnerving shocks to the members of the Philharmonia Orchestra that they were unable to restrain themselves from recoiling at each savage fortissimo stroke; nevertheless the composer expressed disappointment that a particular Japanese variety of wood block with even greater brilliance could not be obtained.

Roberto Gerhard was particularly interested in wood blocks and his works are full of their exploitation in various sizes and pitches, going on from there to temple blocks and beyond these to Korean blocks (similar but larger and deeper), all in splendidly exotic rows of graded size and depth.

Temple blocks, also confusingly called Chinese blocks in some scores[2] look rather like skulls decorated with red and gold, and give a softer, 'plopping' noise. They are usually rigged up three or more at a time, of different pitches, and are very often written for in groups of three, as in the Walton examples quoted on p. 376.

---

[1] In practice a wood block is used for Prokofiev's Fifth and Sixth Symphonies alike.
[2] Reginald Smith Brindle (*Contemporary Percussion*) rightly observes that it is often unclear whether wood or temple blocks are meant. His graphic description of temple blocks appears on his p. 94.

CLAVES

These are another effect of resonant clicking, consisting of two short pieces of wood struck together. Generally speaking they only make one sound but composers sometimes try to make more out of them. Gerhard in his *Concerto for Orchestra* suggests different pitches through striking in different places: , whilst Elisabeth Lutyens writes for no less than four sets played simultaneously in her *Essence of our Happinesses*.

Claves are not very frequently found in symphonic scores, and have only recently started to make appearances through the influence of Spanish and especially Latin American composers such as Chavez, who writes rhythmic passages for them in many serious symphonic works. A pioneering use of claves—amongst numerous other special or localized devices—is to be found with detailed description and instructions in Varèse's *Ionisation* of 1934.

RATTLE, RATCHET

A ratchet is really not quite the same as a proper rattle; both come in various sizes (some disappointingly small). Ratchets are used mostly for individual clicks not unlike those produced by castanets or claves, but sharper as well as deader—less resonant. To obtain the clicks at will, even in a prescribed rhythm, a handle is often fitted as to the 'carrara (piccolo raganello)' (*sic*) used by Falla in his *El Retablo de Maese Pedro*, the part for which is sufficiently controlled to be better played in this manner. Strauss's 'grosse Ratsche' in *Rosenkavalier* is often executed in this way on account of the precise rhythmic pattern:

Ex. 341

even though it later changes to a hilarious *ff* roll. Ravel, in *L'Enfant et les Sortilèges* goes so far as to specify a 'crécelle à manivelle', i.e. 'with a crank'.

All this is quite opposed to the rattles such as are used in Beethoven's *Battle Symphony* (where there are two, one for the French, one for the English side), Strauss's *Till Eulenspiegel*, Milhaud's 'crécelle' in *La Mort d'un Tyran* or even Respighi's 'raganella', in his riotous *Feste Romane*, all of which need rattles that can be swung round, not unlike those at football matches, to make the maximum furore. Such uses are indicated as a trill, mostly of reasonable duration as shorter trills give the player little chance to get the thing going.

The rattle also turns up in the most unlikely scores such as Nielsen's *Pan og Syrinx* where it is curiously indicated by the two words: $\begin{cases} Crotales, \\ Schnarre \end{cases}$ the one vertically above the other. Strangely *crotales* is indeed a dictionary word for rattle, though in the context of percussion vernacular *crotales* means something entirely different (see p. 420). Both *Ratsche* and *Schnarre* are found in German dictionaries although neither is the common-or-garden lay word, which is more often *Gerassel*; this, however, is never used in scores.

WHIP

The whip is another special purpose instrument. Like the English, the French and Italian terms refer to what the instrument emulates, viz: *fouet* and *frusta*, but the Germans and Americans, being realists, call it *Holzklapper* and 'slapstick' respectively, which is what it actually is, no more nor less, i.e. two pieces of thin resonant wood hinged together. Because of this, fast repeated strokes are possible in a way that could not be achieved with a real whip, and extended passages are written like the relentless whip-strokes in the Scherzo of Mahler's Fifth Symphony:

Ex. 342

Nevertheless the whip is usually associated with single electrifying slaps such as at the climax in the first movement of Milhaud's *Protée* or

417

the notorious first crack of Ravel's G Major Piano Concerto, surely the most striking of all.

Whip strokes are generally loud; just as the real whip would not crack at all unless vigorously lashed, so the imitation model flapped gingerly creates little effect, though Britten does ask for a succession of *p* and *pp* strokes in the *Cello Symphony*.

THE BONGO/TOM-TOM FAMILY

In recent years tom-toms have entered regularly into the symphonic repertoire, as have bongos which they resemble closely both in appearance and sound, though the bongos are appreciably smaller. Both tom-toms and bongos are used in sets, bongos always a pair, tom-toms either a pair or, occasionally, three. They are all played with fingers or the flat of the hands, but tom-toms in particular may also be played with sticks even though composers rarely specify this. There is never any doubt over what bongos are, but tom-toms are a major problem, the issue having been confused through the development—largely in connection with dance-band work—of another kind of tom-tom which is hardly more than a very deep snare-less side drum. A pair of these will most often form part of a drummer's 'traps' or kit—i.e. a whole grouping together of equipment that will enable the player to sit in its midst confident that he will have all he needs for an evening's 'gig'.

As a result players almost always produce a pair of dance-band tom-toms unless 'African tom-toms' are specifically ordered, even though such a definition is hardly ever given in scores. In fact the whole question of tom-toms is both controversial and specialist—far more so indeed than most composers allow for when blithely writing for them. There is, moreover, a family relationship between African tom-toms and South American timbales which are, however, shallower and a little larger in circumference. Timbales are more rarely specified in their own right except by very percussion-conscious composers such as Gerhard. The confusion with the French word *timbales* meaning timpani is, like the tambourine/tambourin muddle, a serious hazard to investigation of proper timbales. Most reference books either omit them *in toto* or manage to entangle them with kettle drums; even the index to Blades's volume puts them together most misleadingly, though the text itself makes the situation admirably clear.

There are also Chinese tom-toms, but these are different again and, on the contrary, are never produced unless composers (again like Gerhard or Copland in his Piano Concerto) particularly state that these are required. They are still smaller (even allowing for their range of different sizes) with curved sides, and are narrower from top to bottom than African tom-toms (which in turn are narrower than dance-band instruments). They are also beautifully decorated with a dragon on the head used for playing.

Congas are quite different in appearance although their sound is not very far removed from deeper tom-toms. They stand high from the ground (both bongos and tom-toms are placed on supports at a suitable height for the player) and really do look splendidly African.

None of these instruments is of definite pitch, although between them they provide a whole range of sounds from deep to quite high in the smaller bongo. But Smith Brindle, in his very thorough account, rightly states that in certain circumstances tom-toms may be tuned, and this accounts for the *ossia* for high timpani given in Stravinsky's *Agon*.

Occasionally there is—strange to say—confusion in scores between 'tom-tom' and 'tam-tam' especially as in many composers' handwriting the two words tend to be indistinguishable. Worse still is the classic dictionary reference mentioned above (p. 399) giving 'tam-tam, see tom-tom', which is based on an element of truth in that the word 'tam-tam' really is also an African variant of 'tom-tom' and locally used to mean that instrument. But orchestrally the tam-tam is always a species of gong.

Although Hindemith calls the little drums in his *Kammermusik No. 4* (Violin Concerto) 'Trommeln', they really belong here. Writing in 1925, when bongos, tom-toms and timbales were hardly known and in any case still especially jazz instruments, he describes them in a lengthy footnote that also details his bass-clef notation for the four contrasted drums.

Also belonging, perhaps, to this section are the Indian *tabla*: a pair of small drums again played with the hand. These have been scored for by Boulez, Berio (in error, according to James Holland), ApIvor and others. Khachaturian in his *Gayaneh* ballet writes for 'daira', an oriental-Russian version of the same species and played in the same way, notated 'colla dite' (with the fingers) and 'colla mano' (with the hand.) Arabian hand drums can also be found, described as 'tarbuka' in the Ballet Music from Berlioz's *Les Troyens*, and 'darboukka' in Ibert's *Suite Symphonique*.

ANTIQUE CYMBALS

The career of the antique cymbals in the symphonic repertoire was at first centred round the two isolated appearances—some fifty years apart—of these enchanting instruments: in the 'Queen Mab Scherzo' and *Prélude à l'après-midi d'un Faune* of Berlioz and Debussy respectively. Both called them 'cymbales antiques', Berlioz using two sets in B♭ and F and Debussy in E and B, Berlioz's sounding one octave and Debussy's two octaves higher than written. Ravel then used them in various pitches in *Daphnis et Chloé* and *L'Enfant et les Sortilèges* etc. but, and this is important, under the name of 'crotales'; and Stravinsky too, having written for 'cymbales antiques' in *Le Sacre du Printemps* changed to 'crotales' for *Les Noces*. There is another typical percussion confusion here in that the dictionary definition (including Larousse) of crotales, based on ancient historical evidence, is 'rattle', or the castanets of the priestesses of Cybele. Even Percy Scholes's *Oxford Companion* gives the crotales as a variety of castanets.

Orchestrally, however, crotales and antique cymbals are virtually synonymous, the only difference being that strictly speaking crotales are thicker and less finely wrought and unlike antique cymbals are not held freely in the hands.

Antique cymbals are normally played in pairs, two identical tiny cymbals being struck edge to edge, the smaller pairs usually slung together by a cord, thus obtaining the true shining ring of matchless tone. Crotales, on the other hand, are laid out in fixed rows of pitches, not unlike the bars of the glockenspiel, where they may be struck not only by other crotales but by various beaters for more complicated passages.

It is almost always as 'crotales' that these instruments are written for today, the avant-garde school using them in complete chromatic range on the one hand or, strangely enough, as instruments of indefinite pitch on the other. Certainly the high crystal-clear 'ting' can be thought of in terms of pure colour and the illusion of indefinite pitch is easy to obtain by striking together two crotales of slightly different notes. Boulez writes for two sets in this way in *Le Visage*

Nuptial, differentiating them merely as 'aigu' and 'grave'. Again this is an area in which James Holland goes into considerable detail.

ANVIL

This may reasonably be said to have started its orchestral life in 1853 when Verdi and Wagner in that very same year used anvils in *Il Trovatore* and *Das Rheingold* respectively to represent real anvils on the stage. Verdi notated his gypsies' anvils in higher and lower C's with the indication 'martelli sul incudini' (literally 'hammers on anvils'); Wagner wrote specifically for eighteen 'Ambose' divided into nine (in three groups of three sizes arranged: 3.3.3: 2.2.2: 1.1.1) notating them in the treble and bass clefs on three octaves of F's which, like those of Verdi, were in unison with the prevailing orchestral harmony. It would not have been the intention, however, that anvils would really sound C's or F's and in fact the anvil, being simply the 'clang' of a metal beater upon a metal bar, is always taken to be of indefinite pitch.

Although a rarity in the orchestra to this day, its entries are very stirring. The single anvil stroke in Bax's Third Symphony is a splendid idea, replacing the isolated cymbal clash with a new and exciting climactic sound. The anvil representing the god of iron in Walton's *Belshazzar's Feast* is as obviously apt as the numerous operatic examples, but in the closing section of Copland's Third Symphony it is used simply as part of a large percussion group to add point to claves and xylophone.

JINGLES, ETC.

These, used already by Mozart in 'Die Schlittenfahrt', a movement from one of his most famous *Deutsche Tänze*, K. 605, are sets of small spherical bells attached to a harness strap and shaken. What they really are, of course, is sleigh bells and in English and American scores this term is sometimes used instead of 'jingles'. Mozart's 'Schellen' are actually written as pitched instruments, but by the time of their more familiar symphonic or operatic appearances such as Vaughan Williams's *London Symphony*, Mahler's Fourth Symphony, Strauss's *Arabella*, Massenet's *Manon* ('grelots'), Respighi's *Feste*

421

Romane ('sonagliera') etc. it is assumed that they are of indefinite pitch though written in the treble clef.

Sleigh bells are not, however, the only jingling instruments, amongst which must also be included such effects as 'jingling johnnie', *pavillon chinois*, bell tree, *sistrum*, etc. There can be some mystery about composers' intentions when these terms crop up, as in Rossini's *Barber of Seville*, Berlioz's *Symphonie Funèbre et Triomphale* or the contemporary school (Elisabeth Lutyens and others); for these jingles mostly derive either from antiquity or from the military bands in various foreign parts. They can be built in any number of shapes and sizes, but all bearing clusters of little bells shaken with gratification by the proud owner without regard to pitch. Berlioz writes his 'pavillon chinois' (Turkish crescent) (translated into Italian for the Breitkopf score as *capello chinese*) on a single line, as does Rossini his 'sistro'.

MARACAS, GOURD, ETC.

Since the maracas are originally derived from gourds some confusion is apt to arise when a score like Copland's *El Salon Mexico* merely says 'gourd'. But in fact the maracas are treated so differently that it is sensible to assume that they are only to be used when actually so called. Basically the important distinction is that maracas are shaken so that the seeds inside the hollow heads rattle, whereas gourds are rasps scraped with a furrowed stick. Maracas are so essentially Latin-American in character that they are mostly used specifically in that context. However, while their rhythmic swishing is to be found naturally enough in composers such as Chavez, Varèse's *Ionisation* introduces them largely because this pioneer adventurer set out to use virtually everything he could think of. Maracas have also been introduced in recent years by Boulez, who exploits various pitches as well as techniques in *Une Dentelle s'Abolit*.

Copland's gourd is actually first cousin to Stravinsky's 'une rape guero' (literally, 'a gourd rasp') which makes its brief but notorious appearance in *Le Sacre du Printemps*, and the strangeness of which together with its odd notation mystified so many of us before such exotics became a relative commonplace. Villa-Lobos's 'reco-reco' is another scraper, though he notates it on a single line and without bothering about Stravinsky's up- and down-strokes, which look so confusingly like bowing marks.

WIND MACHINE AND THUNDER MACHINE

The so-called 'kitchen' department of the orchestra has already been seen to have broad enough shoulders to embrace all sorts of instruments that, not being struck, are patently not percussion in the literal sense, such as the maracas/gourd group or even the rattle. Indeed, there are even aspects of the tambourine that hardly qualify—such as when it is rubbed or shaken.

The same is true of the wind machine which is sounded by swishing a large wooden barrel-shaped structure, rotated at varying speeds, against a canvas cover; but it is always played (if this is the right word) by a percussionist, who cranks away at the unwieldy contraption with surprisingly realistic effect. In fact there is a school of thought that regards its imitative function as cheating, as much as if one imported a recording of a real flock of sheep to bleat in Variation 2 of Strauss's *Don Quixote*; and Respighi really does approach—if not actually reach—such corresponding lengths for his *Pines of Rome*, in which he scores for a real nightingale imported into the orchestra by means of a gramophone. The actual record is listed in the score, catalogue number and all, but now the old style gramophone is usually replaced by an off-stage tape recorder.

Strauss uses the wind machine in *Don Quixote* to add pictorialism to his already graphic depiction of the Don's mock flight with his wretched squire through the air on the magic horse in Variation 7. Vaughan Williams uses it much more nakedly for the spine-chilling gales in his music for the film *Scott of the Antarctic*, sections of which he afterwards re-assembled for the so-called *Sinfonia Antartica*. Here, where it essentially replaces composed music by pure imitation, the accusations of cheating have perhaps more foundation. A symphonic design should arguably be constructively integrated even to the point of stylization, whereas in a film score the straightforward naturalistic effect is obviously valid.

Ravel uses the wind machine under the name of 'éoliphone' for the manifestation of the god Pan in his ballet *Daphnis et Chloé*, but unlike the Vaughan Williams example, it serves merely as an extra colour in an already composed piece of music.

Since the only contribution the wind machine can ever make is the rise and fall of its rushing sounds, it is naturally enough notated by a trill (usually on a single line or note) with hairpins of crescendo and diminuendo. Tippett tried in his Fourth Symphony to avoid this rise and fall of pitch by replacing it with an electronic amplification of the sound of human breathing; but it has to be admitted that this ventures even further into the department of realism and is in the event somewhat embarrassing.

When Strauss returned to the wind machine in his *Alpensinfonie*, scoring liberally for it to represent the mighty mountain tempest, he also combined it with a thunder machine (*Donnermaschine*). This is now mostly a great hanging sheet of metal which the player shakes with devastating effect, though other devices and contraptions were once used in theatres and opera houses. According to Reginald Smith Brindle, Strauss's machine was operated like a wind machine (i.e. revolved with a handle) though, instead of the wooden drum being swished round against canvas, heavy balls were made to tumble about inside it.

SIREN, WHISTLE

Both the siren and the whistle are special purpose instruments with only one potential. The difference between them is confined to the fact that the siren fluctuates in pitch while the whistle remains constant. Both are equally full of extra-musical associations, whether the melancholy wailing of the ambulance or air-raid siren or the shrill penetrations of the police whistle, but composers have tried to use them musically as well as histrionically—although there is a strong satirical element in Hindemith's 'Sirene' in his *Kammermusik No. 1*, notated merely as:

Ex. 343

without suggesting the pitch rise; while Ibert's 'sifflet à roulette' in his riotous *Divertimento* derives from the work's origin as incidental music to the play *The Italian Straw Hat*, where it represents the frenzied whistle of an outraged French policeman faced with an uncontrollable mass débâcle. The part is marked *fff*—which is just as well, as this kind of whistle hardly works any other way.

COWBELLS

Mahler's 'Herdenglocken' of the Sixth and Seventh Symphonies, taken over by Webern in his *5 Orchesterstücke*, Op. 10 and by Strauss as 'Herdengeläute' in his *Alpensinfonie* are, of course, broadly naturalistic effects; but at least Webern, and certainly his successors in the Boulez/Stockhausen camp, have developed the instrument into a purely abstract concept; they are sometimes referred to as *Almglocken*, as in Henze's *Antifone*.

Although cowbells undoubtedly do have definite pitch they are normally written without pitch specification since this is supposed to be haphazard, to obtain (as Mahler put it) 'the realistic imitation of the tinkling bells of a grazing herd'. With this in mind the bells are intended to be gently and intermittently shaken, but players are sometimes tempted to strike them randomly with beaters— not only an undesirable practice as they are easily dented but also in any case giving the wrong effect. The notation is an extended trill (⸺) over long notes either in the bass clef (Mahler) or treble (Strauss). Nevertheless Delius writes a precisely rhythmical passage for the similar camel bells in the closing scene of *Hassan*, and Lambert stipulates the use of one small cowbell in *The Rio Grande* which, having had its clapper removed (as he instructs), can only be played with a beater. Messiaen, in *Et Exspecto*, uses a Mexican variety of cowbells called 'cencerros' which he writes with definite pitch in treble and bass clefs giving no less than three ranges. Unlike the cowbells of romantic masters, the cencerros are written with precise notation and thus have (like the Lambert instance) to be struck with beaters instead of shaken. Cencerros are abnormally hard to come by, and since they have until recently been usually the property of only a few individual musicians it has still to be seen whether they will become standard equipment, even though they are used in important works of the contemporary avant-garde.

HAMMER

This apparently simple term hides a multitude of possibilities. The idea originated from Mahler, who in his Sixth Symphony inserted three hammer blows of fate, the last and most important of which he later deleted out of superstition, as it was to have 'felled the hero' (i.e. himself) 'like a tree'. All he said of its execution was that it should sound like the blow of an axe.

This is, of course, all very well but unfortunately it is somewhat difficult to produce a thud that drowns an orchestra of a hundred and twenty complete with bass drum, timps, etc. It requires, moreover, much ingenuity with regard to what the hammer should strike in order to obtain a deep-toned 'whomp' rather than the high-pitched 'crack' such as any hollow platform or box would produce even if it did not split under the assault. As for the hammer itself, this is usually taken by a large sledge-hammer, since although undoubtedly imposing in appearance, a wooden mallet of whatever size is simply not heavy enough.[1]

Regardless of all these problems, Schoenberg and Berg at once took over the idea in *Die Glückliche Hand* and *3 Orchesterstücke*, Op. 6 respectively. Milhaud also uses a hammer in *Les Choéphores*, but seems to have a different effect in mind as he stipulates a plank ('coups de marteau, sur une planche') and writes a series of fairly rapid strokes in varying rhythms, adding the word 'maillets' (literally: 'mallets').

SOUTH AMERICAN INSTRUMENTS

Villa-Lobos writes for a long list of South American instruments, hard to identify precisely, and mostly unknown in Europe. The scores of his *Chórós* No. 8 and No. 10, for example, list the following, with instructions that they are to be obtained through the publishers together with the orchestral material.

(i) *Xucalhos de métal et de bois*: These are apparently species of artificial gourds, comparable perhaps with maracas. (Milhaud in *Saudades do Brazil* writes for 'choucalha avec mouvement de rotation' adding

---

[1] See also the present author's study of Mahler's Sixth Symphony, London, Eulenburg books, 1980, p. 127.

significantly in a footnote that a *tambour de basque* played *ppp* could serve as substitute.)

(ii) *Reco-reco*: a rasp instrument like the guero (see above, p. 422)

(iii) *Matráca*:⎫   These are rattle-like instruments

(iv) *Caraxá*: ⎭   of various types and sizes.

(v) *Pandero sia sonajas*: a tambourine without jingles such as Falla also uses in *El Retablo de Maese Pedro* (see above, p. 392).

CHAINS

It is only natural that chains should appear in opera to represent, for example, the chained prisoners in Janáček's *From the House of the Dead*. But the *locus classicus* for the orchestral abstract scoring for chains is in Schoenberg's *Gurrelieder* where they are described as 'einige grosse eiserne Ketten' ('some large iron chains') for which he writes rolls, viz:

Ex. 344

Typically Varèse also writes for 'chaines' in *Integrales*. Like so many of these extra-musical effects there is no hard and fast rule as to how the chains are to be manipulated, the percussionist usually amusing himself by rattling them about on a large inverted tray or gong, trying to make a convincing noise.

FLEXATONE, AND OTHER CURIOSITIES

This funny little gadget would hardly come within the scope of even the wide flung orchestral kitchen department were it not for the important repertoire works that contain parts for it—works as far apart as Schoenberg's *Variations for Orchestra*, Op. 31 and the Khachaturian Piano Concerto. It cannot be pretended that its scope or range are wide, but such as it is, it is quite irreplaceable. Its curious penetrating whine is created by rapid oscillation of the little wooden knob at the end of the thin flexible strips against the broad curving metal plate, whose curvature—and hence pitch—is controlled by the thumb. This effect cannot be emulated by any other means except possibly the Ondes Martenot (see below, p. 495) or perhaps the musical saw: but the latter is orchestrally wholly unknown, and the Ondes being electronic bring a new element into the sound pattern that is an ethic apart.

The flexatone is notated at pitch: Khachaturian's solo is melodic in style and ranges from ![notation] . Schoenberg takes it a third higher

to top B natural and also writes unrealistically, viz:

Ex. 345   Schoenberg, *Variations for Orchestra*, Op. 31

accurate bursts of widely spaced sounds being hardly obtainable with such abruptness.

Like the chains, the flexatone is only one example of the host of borderline sound effects summoned up by twentieth-century composers, whose desire for new orchestral sonorities is insatiable, instruments and effects from every part of the world being introduced in great profusion. They cannot, however, be accepted as valid members of the orchestral percussion department until, like perhaps the flexatone, they have to be taken into account through their appearance in a work of reasonable stature. Others include:

(i) *Holztrommel* (log drum); *Holzschlitztrommel* (slit drum); and *Holzplattentrommel* (woodplate drum). These native drums as used by Orff and Stockhausen are described by Reginald Smith Brindle on pp. 95–6 of his book. According to him this last is what Puccini wrote for under the name of 'tamburo di legno' in *Turandot*, and it is not inconceivable that it may also account for Respighi's 'tavolette' (see above, p. 414).

(ii) *Sandbüchse*: Hindemith writes for a metal canister filled with sand in his *Kammermusik No. 1*; Orff in *Die Kluge* asks for several under the name of 'Sandrasseln'. Sandpaper blocks rustled together are called for by Copland and others, such as Britten who uses them to imitate the shuffling feet of the Prodigal Son in his Church Parable.

(iii) *Steinspiel*: this instrument, invented by Orff and also used in *Die Kluge*, consists of a row of suspended stone slabs struck with wooden beaters. It is perhaps in its way analogous with Britten's do-it-yourself row of slung mugs struck with wooden spoons in *Noye's Fludde*.

(iv) The lion's roar (*cuica* or string drum are alternative if less graphic names) has been known to appear in the occasional score, for example Varèse's *Ionisation* (described as 'tambour à corde'). It has even been notated with a long sustained crescendo but that is virtually impossible as its horrific effect is necessarily brief, being dictated by the length of the player's arm and of the string as he tugs it through the narrow drum-like container.

The bull roarer, similar as it sounds, is a quite different affair; it appears in Ronald Stevenson's Second Piano Concerto in a passage evoking American Indian native music, this being the source of the device which is a long flexible object attached to a string. The task of playing it is, however, not readily undertaken by percussionists, since the danger to life and limb as the player whirls it about his head is considerable.

(v) Ernst Toch writes for glass balls in his Third Symphony and Haubenstock-Ramati similarly for '4 Glasses (Cristals)' (*sic*) in his *Symphonies de Timbres*.

(vi) *Bouteillophone* (tuned bottles), which speak for themselves, are used by Honegger (*Le Dit des Jeux du Monde*).

(vii) Metronomes: these are set in motion to different tempi to imitate the ticking of clocks at the beginning of Ravel's hilarious *L'Heure Espagnole*.

(viii) Motor horns, identified specifically as belonging to taxis, appear in Gershwin's *American in Paris*.

And lastly for the time being, perhaps,

(ix) Typewriters: these no doubt complete with secretaries, are scored for particularly in Satie's *Parade*.

Section VI

KEYBOARD AND OTHER INSTRUMENTS

1 GENERAL DEFINITIONS AND REMARKS

There is no simple blanket term to describe this last group of instruments which in the orchestral score is generally placed between the percussion and the strings. Indeed, as will be seen, even the word 'instrument' is misleading, since this section must cover every remaining performer or group of performers who may contribute to the interpretation of an orchestral work however wide and heterogeneous these may be.

The basis of the chapter remains, however, first the stringed instruments (harp and piano, together with the guitar, mandoline, etc.) mentioned on the very first page of the first chapter of this survey as contrasting with the 'stroked' instruments of the true string orchestral group; and then the keyboard instruments (piano again, of course, but thence to celesta, organ, etc.).

The order or placing of these instruments in the score cannot be said to be standardized. The keyboard instruments are perhaps mostly placed above the harps, as by Strauss, but there is no invariable rule and they can be found to vary even within the span of a single work. There is even less common practice in the placing of the more infrequent visitors, the organ, for instance, being sometimes found far away from the conventional overall area for such instruments, at the very bottom of the score, for example (see p. 475).

In the section that follows, where the instruments are treated individually, the harp is discussed first because it is the most widely used in the orchestra of these accessory instruments.

2 INDIVIDUAL INSTRUMENTS

HARP

1. Terminology and Personnel

There are few complexities where the terms or species of the harp are concerned. All the names in different languages are closely allied and readily recognizable—*arpa, harpe, Harfe* (to cite the Italian, French and German forms)—and the few variants of the instrument itself such as the little Irish harp make no appearance in the orchestra. There is a smaller version of the true full-sized orchestral Gothic or Concert harp which is called the Grecian harp, but in all practical details it is the same and is only unsuitable for use with full orchestras because of its relatively small sound.

The one exception to this simple state of affairs consists of an instrument written for by Falla in his *El Retablo de Maese Pedro*. Although it is always played on a harp, as cited by the very orchestral part, the score throughout specifies a so-called 'arpa-liuto' or 'arpa laud', a Spanish translation of the same word which in English would of course be 'harp-lute'.

Documentation is lacking on what this instrument could have been; there was indeed at one time a true 'harp-lute'; details of the instrument, with pictures, can be found in dictionaries such as Grove. But its range and type are quite different from anything Falla might have intended, judging from the way he wrote for the instrument; alternatively there was once a harp-like instrument called the *claviharp* which had a chromatic keyboard. Bearing in mind the participation at the first performance of Madame Henri Casadesus, whose husband was the founder and director of the *Societé des Instruments Anciens* in Paris, she might well have played on one or other of these old instruments which perhaps belonged to her husband's collection and in which he may have interested the composer.

The harp has by long-standing tradition always remained the especial stronghold of women musicians, and this raises a thorny matter, though of considerable importance. There are now many male harpists in the profession, but it has always in the past been more usual for the orchestral harpist to be a woman, and often enough moreover, the only person of her sex in the entire orchestra.

Today this question is of greater delicacy than ever before.

Although during the last decades the doors of the orchestral world have been opening ever wider to women, there are still major symphony orchestras who limit their membership to men with the sole exception of the harpist. Even in orchestras where the presence of women is fully recognized it is still considered undesirable that women should be in too great a preponderance over men and as a result this is still unofficially taken into broad account at auditions. Moreover there are orchestral positions such as leader (concert master) which are almost totally closed to women. Women thus complain, and with undeniable reason, that even in these enlightened days of equal opportunity some prejudice remains and that, all artistic considerations being equal, orchestras will very often give preference to a man.

But still none of this applies to the harpist whose position, however much it may be invaded by men, as it is today to a great extent in our British symphony orchestras, continues to remain a primarily feminine province.

2. Range and Tuning

Unlike the piano, the harp has a separate string only for each note of the diatonic scale. Experiments were once made to create and popularize a fully chromatic harp but, although Debussy's *Danse Sacre et Danse Profane* was actually written for this very purpose, the instrument proved too cumbersome to secure a foothold.

The full chromatic range is therefore achieved by means of pedals each of which control all the octave strings of any one note and which have three positions, flat, natural and sharp (see diagram on p. 439). Academically speaking, the harp is tuned in C♭, and this is certainly the instrument's dormant state with all pedals relaxed into the upper, flat position, but a less confusing way of presenting the facts is to think of the harp as being in C major with all pedals in the central, natural positions.

Since the harp has 47 strings with a range of six and a half octaves it will thus have an overall range of to although the topmost F♯ (= G♭) may have to be tuned especially as required because harps lack the mechanism for the highest and shortest string, the top F. Yet in *Das klagende Lied* Mahler actually writes not only the top G♭ as part of a series of rising arpeggios, but the B a third higher still, though this is not normally obtainable on any harp. The same problem also attaches to the two bottom strings, C and D, so that the following example from Szymanowski's *Sinfonia concertante* requires quick and skilful manipulation:

Ex. 346

Alban Berg uses the lowest notes retuned in *Wozzeck*:

Ex. 347

Unlike the pianist who invariably relies upon a highly skilled professional piano tuner, the harpist has to do it himself and is to be seen on the platform at rehearsals or performances alike, tuning the harp long before the rest of the orchestra assembles. Moreover every opportunity is taken during the session to adjust different strings which are all too apt to go out of tune in the course of a work. Occasionally the upper harp strings can break during rehearsal or even performance; annoying as it patently may be, this is by no means the total disaster it is when a piano string snaps. At the first opportunity the player will whip out a new length of string and an experienced harpist can effect the repair surprisingly quickly. The lower covered strings are more troublesome to deal with but are by their nature far less prone to unforeseeable disintegration.

3. Appearance in the Score

The introduction of the harp into orchestral literature was at first a very slow and gradual process. Gluck wrote for a harp with obvious programmatic purpose in the Second Act of his opera *Orfeo* where the hero subdues the monsters of the underworld, but this is an isolated early example. Nevertheless, even though the harp has no place whatever in the orchestras of Bach or Handel, it is known that it did sometimes serve as a continuo instrument: hence its usage by conductors such as Beecham for *Messiah* or by Albert Coates for the B minor Mass, which has come to be derided as unacceptable, does in fact have historical justification.

It was, moreover, by no means unknown as a concertante instrument. One of Handel's organ concertos (in Bb, Op. 4 no. 6) is commonly known as his Harp Concerto, suggesting that he was writing specifically for an instrument with whose technical requirements he was well acquainted; yet the score cites the harp as no more than one of many solo instruments on which it would be equally valid to perform the work.

Mozart too never scored for the harp except as a solo instrument together with the flute in the C major Concerto, K. 299; and in all Beethoven's orchestral music the harp can only be found in one brief number of the ballet music *Prometheus*.

The fact that Beethoven's unique introduction of the harp into his orchestra was for the ballet should be linked with that of Gluck for the opera, since in those early years of orchestral history harps were found only in the theatre.

Since, moreover, Paris was always in the lead where the harp was concerned, this accounts for a Frenchman, Berlioz, being the pioneer who scored for harp in his *Symphonie Fantastique* already in 1830. In keeping, moreover, with the resources he was accustomed to finding at the Paris Opéra, Berlioz calls for not one but two harps, writing for them again in other works such as the *Romeo and Juliet Symphony, Les Troyens*, his instrumentation of Weber's *Invitation to the Dance* and so on, in all of which he exploits many different and novel harp techniques.

After such examples the harp quickly took its place in the orchestral scene though it was still for some time sternly excluded from purely abstract symphonic forms. For instance the harp has no part to play in the symphonic work of that implacable classicist Brahms who, nevertheless, gave it a most poetic role in his *Deutsches Requiem* and who had in early years composed the magical *Gesänge* for women's voices, two horns and harp.

Hence César Franck's inclusion of harps in his Symphony of 1888 was long regarded as revolutionary even though by that time the instrument had gained the widest acceptance in programmatic orchestral works. In general it continued to be the French School who remained in the foreground of orchestral harp writing and it is remarkable how rarely French composers deprive themselves of the instrument, mostly indeed writing for two harps in works for larger orchestras.

In this, however, they were soon not alone. Liszt predictably features the harp in his symphonic poem *Orpheus*, though going one better than Gluck, as it were, by using two; Smetana scores for two harps in *Vyšehrad*, Balakirev in *Russia* and *Thamar*, Sibelius in *The Oceanides*, Strauss in *Ein Heldenleben* and so on. Nor is it only in large orchestras that they are to be found. Strauss's *Ariadne auf Naxos* numbers two harps amongst its 35-piece chamber orchestra.

Nevertheless the second harp can often have a curiously discouraging time. In *Otello*, Verdi reserves it for only one short passage in the Second Act (Otello's 'Ora e per sempre addio'). This is only one of several works where the second harp appears purely as a doubling instrument, such as in the Finale of Franck's Symphony, the Brahms Requiem, and many works by Shostakovich; or primarily in that capacity, as in Elgar's *Falstaff* and Second Symphony. Yet—especially in the case of Shostakovich—it would be entirely incorrect to regard the use of the second harp as optional.

The presence of more than two harps is a rare event. Stravinsky produced a curious and isolated example of three harps in the original ballet score of *The Firebird*, Schoenberg's *Gurrelieder* calls for four harps and the score of Mahler's Sixth Symphony specifies four harps though—strange to say—only in one place during the scherzo.

D'Indy's *Forêt Enchantée* is ostensibly for eight harps but like the Mahler Symphony there are actually only two different parts and both works are always played with no more than two harps. The outstanding example of multiple harps is, of course, Wagner's *Ring* which is scored for six separate parts. This involves so big and complicated a score layout in *Das Rheingold* that even the conductor's full score is printed with the harp parts most inconveniently relegated to an appendix. Mahler wrote for six harps in the original version of *Das klagende Lied*, but just as in the orchestral parts of the *Ring*, in the recently published material for the (ultimately rejected) first part, 'Waldmärchen', the six parts prove to have been redistributed by the publishers so that in practice all the important passages are fully covered when only two harps are used.

4. Notation and Layout in the Parts

Instances of harp parts can be found notated on a single line, such as Gluck's early example in *Orfeo*:

Ex. 348

but the standard layout is similar to that of piano music, that is to say across two bracketed staves with treble and bass clefs. Exactly as with the piano, however, these clefs can be used freely on either stave as either hand can play in any register even though the lower compass is properly the province of the left hand and the upper that of the right. But harp technique does differ substantially from piano playing and composers, who by and large play the latter and not the former, rarely organize harp parts to the satisfaction of the players who accordingly re-mark the music to suit their own needs.

The same applies to chromatic passage work in harp parts. The following from Delius's *Eventyr* involves the player in a mass of complicated pedal changes:

Ex. 349

As a result harp parts are generally thick with players' marks, with lists of notes, enharmonic alterations or rewritings for the sake of practicality.

Some composers try themselves to work out how the strings need to be organized, usually by listing the seven diatonic notes with the sharps, flats or naturals added to show the pedal positions to be prepared for the opening of a work or movement. Other composers, such as Ravel, may then also add the pedal changes during the course of the music:

Ex. 350   Ravel, *Le Tombeau de Couperin*

Even this method may not be entirely foolproof as harpists tackle problems in quite different ways, and continue to mark and reorganize the parts.

Yet another way to indicate harp pedal positions, which used to be purely a shorthand method of the players themselves but has recently

been turning up in composers' scores, is based on a diagram of the
pedal positions:

To decipher this it is necessary to know the arrangement of the pedals
which is:

With the failure of the chromatic harp to establish itself, the claim
of many harpists that it is possible to play any music on the harp
which is written for a keyboard instrument remains an exaggeration.
Apart from some obviously impossible types of figuration that need to
be reconstituted, some wholly chromatic passage-work may turn out
to be outrageously impracticable and the player will have to re-write
the part so as to give the illusion that justice has been done. Yet it is
surprising how many seemingly impossible passages can be made to
work; for example the very young and inexperienced Webern wrote
the following in his symphonic idyll *Im Sommerwind:*

Ex. 351

Fortunately the passage is ascribed to two harps and can be made
possible by dividing it up like this:

Some works are even scored for two harps precisely in order to use
the harp chromatically by means of division between the two, where
too many pedal changes might be required for a single player, as in

Rimsky-Korsakov's *Coq d'Or*, a work which otherwise shows little justification for such extravagance:

Ex. 352

Yet here too technique has improved out of all recognition since the days of such devices and many a work laid out in this way for two harps, such as Balakirev's *Thamar*, is now regularly played by one.

5. Placing on the Platform

Harps may be on either side of the platform according to space or the way in which they are written for by the composer. In Mahler's First Symphony, for example, the harp plays a great deal in unison with the lower strings and is therefore best placed to the right; in Tippett's Ritual Dances the harp has intricate ensemble work with the upper woodwind and is therefore best placed to the left centre, and so on. They may be near to the audience so that their relative lack of projection can be taken into account, or set amongst the body of the orchestra so as to take advantage of the stepped platform, though the height of the instruments themselves can then cause difficulties of visibility for the players behind. Harpists themselves ask not to be placed too far to one side, and on the whole express a general preference for the left rather than the right because of the risk of the instrument masking the conductor's beat.

6. Colouristic Effects

Glissandi

The device of sweeping the hands up and down the harp strings is so obviously dramatic that its overuse has been the object of deprecation by many a commentator. Harpists often use both hands for greater effect but the single line with which it is usually indicated rarely shows whether the composer would have wished for this:

441

Ex. 353   Mahler, Symphony No. 6

Sometimes one octave of a glissando is written out in full to show the tuning required:

Ex. 354

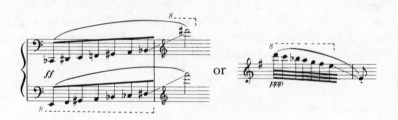

or in two sections at top and bottom as by Strauss:

Ex. 355   Strauss, *Feuersnot*

or even with just the instruction, e.g. 'up in 3 beats'—'down in 2 beats', printed between the single extreme notes of each end, as in *Neptune* from Holst's *The Planets*. In such a case, of course, the tuning of the strings is necessarily added by listing the notes, viz: A♭ B♮ C♯ D♭ E♮ F♭ G♯.

The direction of the glissando can be changed rapidly and this is sometimes featured in dramatic to-and-fro sweeps such as the famous *Scheherazade* solo which, notated by a graphic arrow design, is often over-embroidered by virtuoso players using both hands in a style evoking that great master of the instrument, Harpo Marx:

Ex. 356   Rimsky-Korsakov, *Scheherazade*

(Harpo also invented and perfected a pedal trill, but this splendid accomplishment has not been exploited by composers.) As this example also shows, one of the many ways of setting the pedals results, by dint of enharmonic duplication, in the chord of the diminished seventh and this is another very useful glissando device. Strauss so takes it for granted that he does not bother to indicate the tuning method by which it is accomplished but notates it with double strokes:

443

Ex. 357   Strauss, *Also sprach Zarathustra*

A miscalculation often made in the writing of glissandi is in the time required to travel from one end to the other. Mahler is one of the very few composers to recognize this problem which he did in the revised version of his Sixth Symphony, altering the number of beats' duration for several glissandi. For the most part the error is one of allowing too much rather than too little time, so that the glissando becomes too slow to make a striking effect. Harpists in such circumstances often double over with the other hand, or make a little change of direction in the middle in the manner of the *Scheherazade* example above to spend the excess time and yet keep the brilliant speed of the glissando, or simplest of all, add an extra octave to the limits prescribed. But this last may be artistically quite wrong inasmuch as the change is clearly audible, and furthermore, assuming that the composer has taken into account the resultant sacrifice in volume, a slow glissando may be what was meant. In such cases the actual appearance of the word glissando in the score and part is of primary importance since otherwise such passages could perhaps be fingered out, i.e. with each note separately plucked; conversely there are instances where scales are written which are too fast to finger clearly but there is still no indication to show that a glissando was intended:

Ex. 358   Elgar, Symphony No 2

Arpeggiando

A very large proportion of harp writing in orchestral work consists of chords. Sometimes these may be marked with a vertical wavy line to the left of each chord, signifying *arpeggiando*, that is to say 'spread' with the notes sounding one after the other. If there is no indication to the contrary, chords are normally played from bottom to top, the reverse being shown by an arrow pointing downwards. Occasionally they are even instructed to be played in both directions simultaneously as in Bartók's Violin Concerto (1938):

Ex. 359

All this would seem to imply that in the absence of such indications harpists will play the chords with the notes sounding together. It is not always so, however; the effect of this is so rudely terse and hard that it becomes a dramatic device in its own right, which may be indicated by marks such as *non arpegg.* or in German *nicht harpeggiert* or *nicht gebrochen*. A square bracket to the left of the chord is another method of showing that the fingers must pluck precisely together.

Failing these or other similar signs, and it is remarkable how rarely scores give guidance in this respect, most players take it upon themselves always to spread chords to a greater or lesser extent, their artistry, taste and judgement playing a large part in producing the right quality of style and sound in each context.

Different Methods of Plucking

To obtain the true ring of the harp, the player normally plucks the strings near the middle. But other methods are also called for in order to vary the quality, such as the less resonant sound that results from playing near to the sound-board, i.e. at the bottom of the strings. The French use the instruction *Près de la table* for this effect, an extreme example of which can be found in Stravinsky's *Rossignol* which is quoted as Ex. 371 on p. 454. So much is this a speciality of the French-orientated schools that it is hard to find equivalents in other languages: however Mahler's 'Resonanz' is one, and important to be mentioned as it is not always recognized and understood.

Another specifically Mahlerian harp term little understood is 'Mediator' which is to be found especially in the Sixth Symphony. The explanation for this is actually a plectrum (as for a mandoline) but in practice players use their fingernails to get the required hard and twangy sound, an effect which Copland also uses in his *Appalachian Spring*, though marking the passage explicitly 'with the nail, like a guitar'.

The usual method of plucking is with the tips of the fingers and harpists develop hard corns in the course of training. So important a protection are these against what would otherwise be quite a painful occupation that harpists are rarely able to take a holiday of any length of time away from their instruments.

Occasionally, however, instructions appear requiring the use of quite different implements other than any part of the hand. In the first movement of Bartók's Concerto for Orchestra the 2nd harp is directed to use a metal stick for a short quasi-tremolando passage:

Ex. 360

Apparently straightforward enough in principle, when it comes to practice it is impossible to change direction quickly enough unless the beater is extremely light; hence many harpists in the event use some ready-to-hand object like a pencil which works perfectly well.

Control of the Duration of Resonance

Like the harpsichord, though unlike the piano, the harp has no sustaining pedal. Nor has the harp any damping device and left to itself it has quite a long resonance which is very perceptible beyond that of the tutti orchestra unless specifically controlled. This is done by using the hands and arms to damp the strings, and since in the majority of instances there is no appropriate injunction in scores or harp parts this becomes an instinctive part of a harpist's style and technique.

However, the deliberate curtailing or extension of the harp's resonance is a positive part of orchestral colouristic technique and the terms *Laisser vibrer* (*klingen lassen*, etc.) which are so often applied to the cymbals and other percussion instruments can occasionally be found applied to the harp. The opposite, i.e. the injunction to damp the strings immediately, is often *secco* (= dry) or the German *kurz* (= short). The French sometimes use *étouffée le son*, which needs to be differentiated from the more extreme *sons étouffés*, another French speciality requiring a particular technique of damping each string immediately after it is plucked, whereas the former injunction requires the player to use the forearm to stop all the strings vibrating at once. Another Italian term for this needs to be mentioned: Bartók, following the confusing example of Verdi's *Otello*, marks the end of some harp entries in the second of his *Two Portraits*, Op. 5, 'con sord.' during a passage where several other instruments (including percussion) are similarly marked. But it is clear that this does not signify that the harp should be played with a mute but that the sound should be damped immediately. For there is in fact no method of muting the harp in the conventional sense as applied to the violin family or even the wind.

Occasionally harpists are instructed to interlace the strings with paper or other materials, as in Arbos's orchestration of 'El Albaicin' from Albeniz' *Iberia*; but these are specialized *ad hoc* devices of the kind to which the harp, like every instrument, has become increasingly the prey.

Harmonics

As for the violin family and the flutes, harmonics are also written for the harp. These are obtained by stopping the string with the base of the hand while plucking with the thumb of the same hand. Harmonics are normally played with the left hand except for the higher notes

which are more conveniently taken by the right. Above   har-

monics become increasingly impractical as the strings are too short but Ravel writes up to G in the 'Feria' of his *Rapsodie Espagnole* and Schoenberg even to B♭ in his *Variations for Orchestra*, Op. 31. Equally the bottom covered strings of the harp are quite unsuitable and the

lowest one sees harmonics written is in the region of   as in

the 'Berceuse' from Stravinsky's *The Firebird* or in Vaughan Williams's *Pastoral Symphony*, which goes a tone lower and is often regarded by harpists as unrealistic:

Ex. 361

The two hands frequently play harmonics together to provide chords and although, owing to the angle, the right hand can only play one harmonic at a time, the left hand is capable of playing two, three or four harmonics within the span of up to a fifth so that four- or even five-note chords can be found entirely made up of harmonics as, again, in Ravel's *Rapsodie Espagnole*:

Ex. 362

The standard notation for harmonics is, once more like the strings and flutes, an 'o' over each note; but the difference is that these notes are written an octave lower than they sound. This is because, being the 2nd harmonic of the series—and no other harmonics are possible on the harp—they always sound an octave higher than the string upon which they are played. Nevertheless, needless to say, many exceptions can be found which cause immense confusion. Stravinsky wrote the harmonics at pitch in the 'Ronde des princesses' from the *Firebird* but sounding an octave higher in the Berceuse of the same work. Even Berlioz wrote in his *Treatise*:

Ex. 363

but proceeded to notate the equivalent passage in his 'Queen Mab' Scherzo at pitch:

Ex. 364

Tom Wotton discussed this situation with such clarity and completeness that it can be quoted here:[1]

'For the benefit of admirers of the scherzo of the *Romeo and Juliet* Symphony I would add one more mildly technical detail. In modern practice harp harmonics are indicated by writing the notes to be plucked by the player, with a small 'o' or 'sons harmoniques' above them, the actual sounds being an octave higher. But for some years after the introduction of the effect into the orchestra by Boieldieu in *La Dame Blanche* composers were uncertain about the best mode of notation, and Berlioz was no exception. In the Ballet of the Sylphs the *plucked* notes are given; in the scherzo, the *actual sounds* are noted in all editions, with the possible exception of the original one published in 1848.[2] That is, the harpist must play his part an octave lower. *Of this there is not a shadow of doubt.* If the reader will collate the last bars of the second example in Berlioz's Treatise with the corresponding ones in the miniature score, he will see that in the latter, the harp notes are written an octave higher. In the section devoted to the harp in the Treatise the author explains how he meant the harmonics of the second example to *sound*—an octave above those in the example, but in unison with those in the miniature score'.

Works as late as Bartók's Violin Concerto (1938) can be found with the harp harmonics notated at pitch and in many instances one can only decide by internal evidence at what pitch a passage should

---

[1] Tom Wotton, *Hector Berlioz*, Oxford University Press, London, 1935. pp. 110–11.
[2] Throughout the German edition the notes to be plucked are indicated by notes with open diamond-shaped heads. As Bizet had already used these to indicate the *real* sounds, and as such notes are employed in violin practice with another signification, the method has little to commend it. (Wotton's footnote).

sound, as in Mahler's Third Symphony. In Debussy's 'Nuages' from the *Nocturnes* there is merely the indication '8ª bª. . .' (*sic*) printed over the notes, but reference to the original Froment edition (in which the passage is played in the normal manner) reveals that this is no more than economy on the part of the publishers when preparing the revised score: hence what is meant—though not stated—is that the passage should be *played* an octave lower, but should sound as written through being taken as harmonics.

Tremolos and Trills

The fact that harpists have to pluck the strings instead of merely pressing down keys as in keyboard instruments, makes rapid reiterations both clumsy and unreliable. This is reflected by the notation or demands of some composers but is ignored by others who write tremolos and trills as if for the piano and leave it to the player to work out the best or nearest approximation possible.

Dvořák writes a series of quick repetitions of a single string in his symphonic poem *Die Waldtaube* and although this is by no means impossible, Dukas' notated solution of a similar problem by means of enharmonics shows more understanding of harp technique:

Ex. 365   Dukas, *La Péri*

This points the way to very rapid rearticulations of the same pitch playing on two strings enharmonically tuned as given by Bartók in the Adagio of his *Music for Strings, Percussion and Celesta*:

Ex. 366

452

whose actual method of execution is revealed by Honegger in *Horace Victorieux*:

Ex. 367

This is equally the technique adopted for extended trills as Ibert indicated in little notes at an entry of the sort in *Escales*. Hence the notation used by Enesco in his *First Romanian Rhapsody* must be regarded as mere abbreviation:

Ex. 368

Nevertheless rapid alternations of enharmonic chords with the same pitch are also possible and are used by Holst in the atmospheric passages of Neptune from *The Planets*:

Ex. 369

Such tremolos of direct alternation between the two hands are also standard technique in *fortissimo*, as in Mahler (Second Symphony), Delius (*Appalachia*) and so on, while pianissimo tremolos are often marked *bisbigliando*, signifying 'murmuring' or 'whispering' such as, for example, the familiar passage in Strauss's *Don Juan*:

Ex. 370

One last method of *tremolando* specified by Stravinsky in his opera *Le Rossignol* as well as by Bartók in his Concerto for Orchestra (quoted above as Ex. 360) is the to-and-fro style; when applied to the string orchestra this is sometimes marked *quasi guitara*, but in these harp examples it is simply indicated by means of arrows:

Ex. 371

7. Sonority

While hardly one of the most powerful of instruments, the harp is capable of considerable penetration in even the fullest orchestral tuttis when used skilfully. Many, however, are the contexts in which the score contains elaborate harp parts no vestige of which comes across to the audience. Sometimes composers use enharmonics, so far discussed in relationship to glissandi and tremolos, for purposes of reinforcement; it is doubtful whether, even so, the following harp passage is likely to be audible:

Ex. 372   Szymanowski, *Sinfonia Concertante*

455

whereas, on the contrary, the following from Bartók's Violin Concerto (1938) is riveting in its effect:

Ex. 373

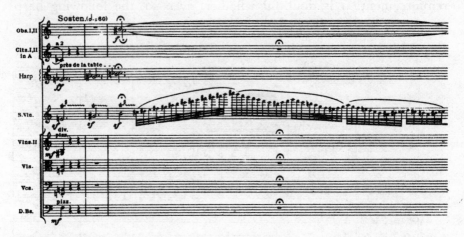

The purpose of using two harps, especially when the second is used primarily—or even wholly—as a doubling instrument as described above (p. 436), is patently for extra sonority, but beyond that it is curious how little numerous extra harps add to the total weight of tone. I once had the privilege of conducting a work for 28 harps in a concert given by the U.K. Harpists' Association and was astonished to discover that the benefit of so many of these beautiful instruments lay far more in the varieties of possible textures than in the power or sonority of their massed tone.

PIANO

1. Terminology and Personnel

The piano is known by its full name 'pianoforte' primarily in scores using Italian terminology; otherwise it usually appears in the familiar colloquial abbreviation. Strangely enough the Russians still use 'fortepiano' as the full name of the instrument, a form elsewhere reserved for the eighteenth and early nineteenth-century predecessor of our modern piano. Of other languages, only German preserves in current use an entirely independent word *Klavier* (derived from the generic term *claviatur* in both French and German—with appropriate spellings—to signify the keyboard as such) which, though it has come to mean the piano in common usage, strictly denotes not merely that instrument but any with keyboard, as in Bach's *Klavier Konzerte*, once widely accepted as piano concertos but today mostly played on the harpsichord.

Moreover, a grand piano, as opposed to an upright or even a baby grand, is known in German as *Flügel*, Strauss, for example, specifying a *Konzertflügel* in the orchestra list for the opera *Ariadne auf Naxos*.

As a rule, a grand piano is taken for granted unless otherwise stipulated, e.g. in Glazunov's ballet *The Seasons* or Berg's *Wozzeck*, where an upright piano is described as *pianino*; in the latter instance it is called for precisely because of its homespun sound, representing a pub piano on the stage. Peter Maxwell Davies similarly uses what he describes as an 'out-of-tune "honky-tonk" piano' in his *St Thomas Wake*. Upright pianos are, however, not normally used orchestrally since, apart from their greatly inferior tone-quality, the player is virtually unable to see the conductor or other players for accurate ensemble playing. Nevertheless in Rachmaninov's Third Symphony the extraordinary instruction can be found sanctioning the use of 'a small upright piano' as a substitute for the 2nd harp. It is hard to imagine Rachmaninov, the great piano virtuoso, seriously contemplating this awful possibility; perhaps it was forced upon him by his American publishing house.

Not every symphonic orchestra carries a pianist on its regular strength; but if he is a member, the player will also be responsible for other keyboard work such as celesta and sometimes, though more rarely, keyboard glockenspiel. He may also be asked to take on continuo work but on the other hand he may or may not be an organist or harpsichordist, and this work could require the engaging of a specialist for the occasion.

2. Status in the Orchestra and Character

The piano occupies a slightly curious position as an orchestral instrument. Its role is unusually composite, being sometimes featured as a semi-concertante instrument, joining the orchestra in closely integrated ensemble work as well as emerging from time to time in a soloistic capacity, (e.g. d'Indy's *Symphonie sur un Thème Montagnard* or Stravinsky's *Petrouchka*); alternatively it may be scored for as a kind of replacement for the harp (Shostakovich's Symphony No. 1, Martinů's symphonies or Falla's *El Amor Brujo*—Falla even marks it 'quasi arpa' in one place); or it may even serve as an extra colour in addition to the harps and celesta (e.g. Prokofiev's Fifth Symphony or Bartók's *Dance Suite* and *Music for Strings, Percussion and Celesta*).

This latter incorporation of the piano as part of the orchestra is a comparatively recent development, emerging gradually out of its more conventional role of continuo (as in Mozart and later Rossini and Donizetti, whose *L'Elisir d'Amore* specifies a piano for the recitatives). Berlioz gives the piano as an *ossia* for the bells in the *Symphonie Fantastique* (although this is never done), see p. 403, and Glinka writes for a piano together with the harp to imitate the Russian minstrel's *guzli* in *Russlan and Ludmila*. But in general it is either ignored or deplored by authorities on orchestration, and certainly it is surprising how unfavourably it often compares with the harp, in orchestral works that use both, or when used in apposition with harp and harpsichord in a work such as Frank Martin's *Petite Symphonie Concertante* whose object is specifically to flatter each of the three instruments equally. It is interesting in this connection that whereas there is a piano in the original ballet score of Stravinsky's *Firebird* together with the three harps and celesta there is very little for it to do, whereas the elaborate part it has to play in *Petrouchka* derives from the fact that the material for the second tableau, which features it, was at first planned as a *Konzertstück* for piano and orchestra. On the other hand in *The Firebird* Stravinsky greatly augmented its role when rescoring the music in 1919, turning it into a strident kind of celesta (which however he retained as an *ossia* in the Berceuse) in keeping with his own increasingly astringent feeling for colour.

It is indeed particularly composers with a brittle style, or who are prone to spiky textures, who tend to add the percussiveness of the piano to their scores—Copland, Britten, the later Russians (Scriabin's *Prometheus* is sometimes cited but here the Chopinesque piano arabesques are treated in a concertante manner) and many of the modernistic composers. In his *Concerto for Orchestra* Tippett partners the piano with the xylophone in a manner richly indicative of its strongest role and character.

Most important of all, however, remains the difficulty of suppressing the mental image of the piano with its partly domestic self-contained existence on the one hand, or its equally familiar appearances pitted against the orchestra as a soloist on the other, in order to accept it simply as just another orchestral instrument. Moreover, it has a further function as a key member of small salon or pit orchestras and it is with these in mind that, for example, Ibert and Strauss include the piano in their *Divertissement* and *Bourgeois Gentilhomme* respectively. In *Ariadne auf Naxos* Strauss further emphasized its latter function by specifically associating the piano with the theatrical *buffo* figures, whilst reserving the harp for the classical world of the *opera seria*.

Nevertheless there are excellent examples of purely orchestral piano writing dating back to Saint-Saëns' pioneering Third Symphony, more famous for its introduction of the organ but equally remarkable for its use not only of the piano in the scherzo, but also of a piano duet—i.e. one piano, four hands—for a beautifully colourful passage in the finale. No doubt this was the inspiration for the unconventional scoring of Debussy's early *Printemps* whose texture embodies a piano four-hands in Henri Busser's orchestration published during the composer's lifetime. Respighi and Bartók also use a piano four-hands in various works, but piano duet playing (even in the present recessional days of hi-fi and television) continues to recall music making in the home, looking a little cosy as the two players sit side by side intimately at work.

Stravinsky scores for two pianos in the unusual orchestration of the *Symphony of Psalms*, as does Villa-Lobos in his *Chórós* No. 8, whilst there are no less than four pianos in the totally unconventional instrumental forces Stravinsky finally decided upon for *Les Noces*. These are exceptional, however, partly perhaps because of the inescapable attendant problems of ensemble; few things are harder than for even two pianists to strike a chord absolutely together unless they have developed that sixth sense by constantly working as a two-piano team.

3. Range and Notation

The standard range of the piano is the seven octaves from

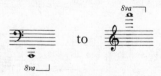

and this is to be found in all instruments whether upright or grand with the exception only of a few mini-pianos which are sometimes used in small orchestra pits for continuo or recitative work.

In addition, however, a large number of pianos have extra top notes extending the range to and these are used in orchestral works by composers such as Prokofiev—in, for example, the Fifth Symphony —making them indispensable for practical purposes. Yet a further extension of range, this time at the bottom end, was introduced by Bösendorfer for their largest concert grands, taking the range down to F: and even to the very bottom C: for their largest of all, the 9 foot 6 inch model. But these additional low notes have never been used by composers and remain mere luxury even though the full range of the piano has been regularly exploited (e.g. in Copland's *Billy the Kid*) and the extra notes might have been thought a valuable extension. Moreover the change in appearance which this wide range gives to the extent of the keyboard upsets the equilibrium of players and the manufacturers found it necessary to provide a felt or wooden cover for the bottom notes 'when not in use' or, in the case of the latest models, to paint the extra keys black.

Although extra staves are sometimes added for extremely complex passage-work, the piano is normally notated, like the harp above which it is mostly placed in the score, on two bracketed staves, the upper in treble clef for the right hand, the lower in bass for the left. However these can naturally vary as required even while the relationship of hand to stave is retained wherever possible:

Ex. 374   Falla, *Nights in the Gardens of Spain*

Where, however, the right hand is required to take notes on the lower stave, or vice versa, some indication (such as 'R.H.' or the French 'm.d.') is often added, reflecting the extent to which so many composers are especially conversant with pianistic technique.

4. Pedals

Where the simple indication 'Ped.' appears, it is always the sustaining (right) pedal that is meant. This is often given in a stylized typography: ' 𝄿 ', the cancellation of which is an equally stylized form of asterisk: ' ✳ '. Other systems can naturally also be found, of which the most interesting is that of note-heads, a method used by Prokofiev in his Suite *Ala and Lolly*:

Ex. 375

This is not to say, however, that in the absence of any such pedal marks none is to be used. On the contrary, it is taken for granted that the player will add pedalling according to his musical taste and judgement much as string players use vibrato and portamenti; a score such as Strauss's *Ariadne auf Naxos*, for example, gives extremely few indications and the pedal marks that are given occur mostly at places where the player might otherwise be misled, as, for instance, by rests:

Ex. 376

Sometimes, however, composers do positively want either a great deal of sustaining carried out, or alternatively, none at all, and then specific instructions (*mit viel Ped.*, *senza Ped.*, etc., etc.) are to be found in piano parts.

The soft (left) pedal is the piano's equivalent to muting, but neither this word nor any of its translations is used in relationship to the piano, although an exception can be found in Debussy's use of 'con sord.' in 'Claire de Lune'. This can be confusing for the odd reason that *senza sordini* was occasionally used in classical times, as by Beethoven to indicate the use of the *sustaining* pedal—i.e. without dampers. The most general term is *una corda*, even though the action of the soft pedal on the modern piano no longer causes the hammer to strike only a single string, but—over most of the compass—two out of the three strings.[1] The contradiction is also correspondingly *tre corde*, even though again this does not accurately describe the state of affairs with respect to the piano's bottom octaves.

The French term for the soft pedal (*petite pédale*) does not appear in scores, but the German *mit Verschiebung* (literally 'with shift', indicating the resultant movement of the entire keyboard) can occasionally be seen, especially in Schumann, as in the opening of the *Konzertstück*, Op. 92.

Since the piano is most often exploited either for its resonance or its percussive quality in orchestral textures, the soft pedal is rarely

---

[1] *Una corda* can also be seen applied to the violin family, but then of course it has nothing to do with muting, but is an instruction to take a higher position on a lower string.

prescribed. Prokofiev, however, uses it in *Ala and Lolly*, and Casella in the Pastorale of his *Scarlattiana*; Falla asks for 'les 2 ped' at several places in *El Amor Brujo* as does Stravinsky in the 1945 version of *Firebird*.

Some larger pianos, but only those of certain makers, are further supplied with a third pedal; this enables the player to catch and hold notes individually whilst those played subsequently are not sustained. Although useful and standard equipment on all modern Steinways, and hence available to composers and players throughout the world, this cannot be found anywhere specifically prescribed nor has it indeed any terminology other than 'third pedal'.

5. Tuning

In company only with the organ, whose tuning is an operation of the most enormous magnitude, the piano stands apart from the remainder of the orchestra in that if it is out of tune there is nothing whatever the player can do about it. This could perhaps also be argued in respect of the celesta and the whole family of glockenspiels, xylophones, bells, tuned gongs and the rest; but the difference with these is that if they are out of tune it means that they are either faulty or otherwise unsuitable for orchestral work and it is necessary to replace them. In the case of the piano, a tuner has often to be summoned, especially for concerto work, generally before rehearsal and again, for touching-up, between rehearsal and performance; but occasionally during recording sessions a tuner may be kept on hand, since if a single important string goes out of tune it is still outside the player's scope to put it right. The art of the piano tuner is a highly specialized and skilled accomplishment.

6. Placing on the Platform

The position of the piano *vis-à-vis* the orchestra presents perennial problems that can only be partially solved by means of some compromise. Concert grands vary between 7 foot 6 inches and 9 foot (the even larger instrument mentioned above is exceptional) and this constitutes a considerable bite out of the available space for the orchestra.

Furthermore it tends to place the player (who hardly ever has any say over the choice of instrument and has to make the best of what he finds at each location) at some remove from the conductor, unless he is a soloist.

Even with respect to the concerto position for the piano there was for long a divergence between this country and the practice abroad. Here the piano used to be placed between the conductor and the orchestra, a formation which, even after it had otherwise lapsed, lingered for a time in borderline concertante works such as Dohnányi's *Nursery Tune Variations* or Falla's *Nights in the Gardens of Spain*, the solo part needing to be particularly closely integrated into the orchestral texture. The established continental tradition, however, has always been to place the piano nearest to the audience with the conductor behind, viz:

Ex. 377

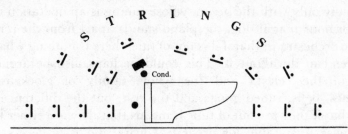

The disadvantage of the piano being placed between the conductor and orchestra is primarily that, the lid being always fully up for solo work, the players immediately in front (generally violas) are totally masked from the conductor who, moreover, receives such an amplified sound of the piano that he can hear little of the orchestra whilst the soloist is playing.

On the other hand, the now universally adopted position illustrated above is also not without its disadvantages. If the conductor stands in the conventional central position the raised lid now acts against him and he both receives a muffled sound and is out of contact with his soloist. For these reasons the conductor stands to the side as shown, where he has admirable contact with the soloist but little with the right-hand group of string players who see hardly anything but his back for much of the time.

The long stick that raises the piano lid is rarely used when the piano is only orchestral, since in this case the tone is likely to be too obtrusive and the player may find it hard to see the conductor's beat; as an alternative to the full stick, therefore, a short stick is used (and it is very short) or the lid may be taken off altogether, though this has a sharp and not always agreeable effect on the resonance.

The piano is generally placed to the side and rear (either left or right according to platform space); attempts have been made to keep the instrument in the centre of the platform with the lid off for obbligato works using the orchestral player, but the size of the instrument remains a deterrent, splitting the string group into two dissociated halves.

One more factor needs to be taken into account in placing the orchestral piano: the player is frequently required to double on celesta. For if the two instruments have to be played in rapid alternation, a suitable space must be chosen where the celesta can be placed adjacent—preferably at right angles to the piano keyboard—and yet on the one hand the celesta must not be masked from audience or conductor (see p. 471), whilst on the other hand the pianist is still able to change from one instrument to the other with a quick swivel in circumstances such as occur in the 'Cortège' from Ibert's *Divertissement* or the last of Ives's *Three Places in New England*.

7. Glissandi, Harmonics and Other Effects

Glissandi and Clusters

While hardly less effective than those on the harp, piano glissandi are more limited in their choice since enharmonics are naturally excluded leaving only the glissando on the white or on the black keys. The score will generally indicate which is required:

Ex. 378   Stravinsky, *The Firebird*

but often enough it is obvious. Falla uses both in quick alternation in *El Amor Brujo*:

Ex. 379

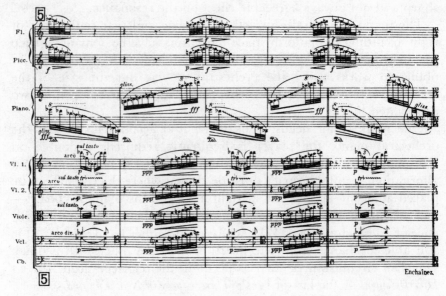

They can moreover be done simultaneously and in *Lulu* Berg goes one better still and plays all the notes simultaneously in block clusters to depict the athlete Rodrigo:

Ex. 380

In contemporary scores, however, clusters are not usually written out in full but are indicated either by solid rectangular black blocks or by arrows between the notes at each extremity. Ives also uses both forearms for a monumental smudge in the last *fff* bars of his *Three Places in New England*.

Shakes

Trills and tremolos are a commonplace on the piano, the action of striking the keys being so much more agile than plucking them. Although normally and readily done by the fingers of a single hand, both hands are called into operation for purposes of a ferocious *fortissimo*:

Ex. 381   Respighi, *Fountains of Rome*

and furthermore for chordal tremolos like the following from Stravinsky's revised version (1947) of *Petrouchka*, which perhaps makes an interesting comparison with the harp tremolo in Honegger's *Horace Victorieux* quoted above on p. 453:

467

Ex. 382

Harmonics

A method of exploiting what are described as harmonics on the piano was invented by Schoenberg and introduced into many works by his pupils and followers. The idea is to put down certain keys so gently that the hammers are not brought into operation: this is indicated by *Tonlos niederdrücken* or similar words and these notes are then shown with diamond note-heads: clusters of lower notes are then struck very strongly and abruptly damped, the strings of the upper held notes can then be heard gently vibrating in sympathy. In chamber music or solo passages the device can be magical, but in orchestral music it has to be conceded that these so-called 'harmonics' are for all intents and purposes inaudible.

Prepared Pianos and Other Extremist Devices

Various types of 'prepared pianos' have been introduced experimentally over the past half century, the first of which is surely Ravel's 'piano (luthéal)' that appears in his *L'Enfant et les Sortilèges*. This seems to have corresponded more or less with a type of piano, usually upright, found occasionally in Britain, that is equipped with an extra pedal converting the sound into a jangling quality not unlike that of the harpsichord. Ravel says that in default of the 'luthéal' an ordinary piano can be fitted, where indicated, with a sheet of paper over the strings 'pour imiter la sonorité de clavecin'. But in the event these indications consist of the encircled numerals ① and ④, alternating with ② and ③ and with appropriate cancellations, that invite speculation on the exact nature of Ravel's instrument which has long since vanished without a trace.

John Cage was the prime mover in popularizing prepared pianos amongst the extreme avant-garde composers. The preparation starts from the Ravel-like stretching of tissue over the strings, but goes much further with the alarming use of drawing-pins, screws, metal bolts, rubber wedges *et alia*. Reginald Smith Brindle gives a full and entertaining account of all this activity in his book *Contemporary Percussion* (the piano being here considered essentially as an instrument of percussion) in which, on pp. 169-72, he also discusses 'pizzicato' (putting the hand inside the instrument and plucking the strings), muting with strips of cloth and various other forms of artificial activities both delicate and brutal. He then adds the following paragraph:

'There are also several other percussive roles for the pianist, of a rather more banal character. For instance, in Maderna's Oboe Concerto the second piano player is instructed to play 'on the surface of the piano' with light sticks; in pieces by John Cage the player has to slam down the piano lid; while in Krenek's Flute Sonata there is a passage where the pianist plays on the cover with a metal coin. None of these effects is particularly ingenious or musical, and care must be taken to reserve such and similar usages for moments when they are apt. Otherwise, from an aesthetic point of view, the result can be catastrophic. However, a touch of humour is certainly welcome occasionally, and Cage manages to introduce entertaining moments of comedy into his works by means which other composers would never deign to use.'

Denis ApIvor created what he terms a Piano-harp by denuding a common-or-garden cottage upright down to its bare strings which are then played directly by the hands in harp position. Again one's mind is sent swiftly to Harpo Marx with a hilarity that the composer in no way intended.

CELESTA

The name of the instrument is universal, even the French form being *célesta*. Strange to say 'celeste', given by Scholes as an alternative and always used in orchestral parlance, is in fact no more than an organ stop.

Tchaikovsky is generally credited with having introduced the celesta into the orchestra, which he did within ten years of the instrument's very invention—not, curiously enough, in the famous 'Dance of the Sugar Plum Fairy' from the *Casse-Noisette* ballet, but in his symphonic poem *The Voyevode* composed the previous year but only published posthumously.

In this splendid but largely unknown work he was still unsure of the style and dynamic possibilities of the instrument, for he wrote an elaborate pianistic part which he then completely swamped with surging tutti orchestration. By the time he came to *Casse-Noisette*, however, he had the full measure of its potential, although he again wrote the part at actual pitch allowing for the substitution of a piano.

The conventional notation of the celesta is on two bracketed staves like the harp and piano but an octave lower than it sounds. This, however, carries the additional and curious complication that not all composers, or conductors for that matter, are any too sure either what octave is required or even what octave is actually being played. The limpid bell-like tones are oddly deceptive and the deep notes of the weak lower register turn out to be unexpectedly high when compared against the piano. A passage often played an octave too high, for example, is the isolated solo in the Ritual Dances from Tippett's *Midsummer Marriage*:

Ex. 383

The actual range of the celesta is usually cited as being the four octaves of the original, and still most commonly found, Mustel instrument:

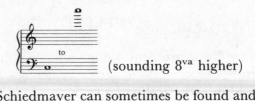

(sounding 8va higher)

but the five-octave Schiedmayer can sometimes be found and it is this instrument, with its fifth octave extending the range to ♪ which is called for in scores such as Mahler's Sixth Symphony[1]. (Mahler indeed calls for two such instruments, as does Strauss in *Die Frau ohne Schatten*, but such extravagance in celesta writing is extremely rare.) When faced with the need for this wider compass, players tend to

---

[1] The original edition added the enigmatic instruction 'in F' but despite the misleading type this must have referred to his wish for the doubling of the celesta in *forte* passages.

adapt the music to fit the available keyboard as best they may with octave transpositions, like the glockenspiel practice described earlier; nor is this necessity uncommon, even as standard a score as Ravel's

Ma mère l'Oye going down to 𝄢.

In the 'Carillon Féerique' from Stravinsky's *Firebird* ballet the celesta is instructed to play 'con moderatore' which can only refer to its single pedal. This, misleadingly known principally as the 'damper pedal' is supposed, on the contrary, to increase the celesta's sustaining power but it has to be admitted that its effect is imperceptible and (perhaps for this reason) instructions for its application are excessively rare.

It is hard to place the celesta to best advantage on the platform; its necessary proximity to the piano (if there is one in the score) has already been discussed; another important consideration is that it should if possible be near the harps with whom it is often closely associated in ensemble work. Yet so long as it is not totally masked from the audience (and conductor) it is surprising how much its tiny voice can tell across the orchestral texture, even though the range of dynamics available to the player using even the strongest wrist action hardly exceeds a *mezzopiano*. Accordingly many celesta parts lack any dynamic marks.

The technique of the celesta corresponds broadly (within obvious limitations) to that of the piano, having equal capacity for tremolos, trills, scales, arpeggios, telling chords, glissandi and the like, all of which can add touches of enchantment to a sensitively laid out orchestral tapestry, and have been widely exploited by composers. Debussy in *La Mer* suggested it as an alternative to the glockenspiel (see p. 407) in the second movement 'Jeu de vagues'. It is certainly more suitable here than the over-bright glockenspiel, which is then held in reserve for greater effect in the succeeding 'Dialogue du vent et de la mer'.

This exceptional instance may explain why the celesta is sometimes wrongly listed among the percussion, even the part being coupled with those of the kitchen department, causing total confusion in rehearsal. Properly the celesta lies within the specialized field of a keyboard player and is in no circumstances handled by the percussion group.

One irritating cross the celesta player has to bear is that the ledge provided to support the music is just about high enough for a miniature score, so that the single sheet of music (which is often all his part consists of) is apt to flop over dismally or even fall to the floor, inevitably while he is executing his one important solo.

HARPSICHORD

The orchestral role of the harpsichord, or *cembalo*, is, like that of the piano, composite but in an entirely different way. Whilst it can, however rarely, be found as an orchestral colour, or more aptly for its period associations—as in Strauss's *Capriccio* and 'Couperin' Suites, or Falla's *El Retablo de Maese Pedro*—its major role lies in the field of continuo.

Both the words *continuo* and *cembalo* need a certain disentangling here. Each is closely associated with the harpsichord though not strictly meaning that specific instrument more than any other. Piano, harp, harpsichord, organ, even harmonium could theoretically all be used to serve as continuo, whose purpose is to support and fill out the harmonies of the musical texture. The bass line itself—in Monteverdi called *bassus generalis*, in baroque music *basso continuo* and often doubled by a solo cello and/or bass— is supplemented by figures printed beneath it in the score; these serve as instructions to the keyboard player in respect of the harmonies he is expected to supply. Where none are required the words *tasto solo* are substituted for the figures and he then merely plays the printed bass line.

A skilled continuo player needs no special part to work from, using for preference a full score identical with that of the conductor. But many editions of Bach, Handel and other popular composers using continuo contain 'realizations' of the figured bass in order to facilitate performance. These fully worked out keyboard parts, though no more than conjectural suggested versions prepared for the publisher by some musicologist, are even incorporated into the scores of what are described as Urtext editions, which correctly should contain nothing beyond the original work.

As for *cembalo*, this is a shortened form of *clavicembalo*[1] and strictly speaking means no more than 'keyboard instrument' in which it is in

---

[1] Not to be confused with the clavichord which is a quite separate instrument with a very very soft tone. Perhaps for that reason the clavichord, which is the instrument for which Bach wrote the '48', has never been used orchestrally.

actual fact synonymous with the German *Klavier* (see p. 456). But in the same way that *Klavier* has come to denote specifically the piano, so *cembalo* has turned into the generally accepted term for harpsichord in all languages except French which has its own term, *clavecin*. In German, for example, Strauss's *Capriccio* uses 'Cembalo' in preference to the dictionary word for the instrument, *Klavizymbel*; and in Stravinsky's *The Rake's Progress*, where the instrument list is given in English, 'cembalo' is used instead of 'harpsichord' even though the latter is wholly established colloquially. The Stravinsky example is of wider interest, however, since the listing also gives 'pianoforte' in brackets. This could imply that Stravinsky was using the word *cembalo* in its broadest sense, the keyboard instrument actually to be used being the piano. His own recordings, however, negate this theory and it is to be understood that the reference to the piano was intended as no more than an emergency replacement. Certainly the piano would be a poor substitute for the eerie effect of the harpsichord in the penultimate scene where poor Tom plays a desperate game of cards with Nick, his soul standing as stake, and the harpsichord has since been frequently used to evoke the supernatural in film music.

The range of the harpsichord varies infinitely from period to period as well as from instrument to instrument, but this diversity is also because of the very nature of the harpsichord. For they come in all sizes and shapes, the smallest being called a 'spinet'. The largest instruments, however, have more than one manual and are equipped with stops and pedals, the latter—unlike the organ—being merely foot-operated stops. The stops have the dual purpose of changing both the quality of the sound and the octave pitch. There are also coupling stops which link the manuals and by this means more than one octave is enabled to sound at a time when the harpsichordist is only playing single notes. This is all patently very closely akin to organ terms, even the pipe lengths being transferred though they have no true application to the harpsichord string-lengths—'8-foot' signifying stops sounding at actual pitch, with '4-foot' an octave higher and '16-foot' an octave lower. Equally, as in organ parlance, the use and handling of these stops is described as 'registration'.

By the use of the many stops and pedals in the largest harpsichords the range can be extended to as much as five octaves from which Strauss typically extends still further to ♯♮ in his 'Couperin' Suites.

Registration indications are very rarely found in harpsichord parts but an outstanding exception is Frank Martin's *Petite Symphonie Concertante*. This gives a variety of instructions, though without mentioning the 'harp-stop', which produces a kind of pizzicato effect, or the 'lute-stop', often asked for in relationship to very soft passages as it greatly reduces the notorious jangling quality described by Beecham as 'skeletons dancing on a tin roof'.

For the harpsichord has virtually no range of expressive dynamics. There is not even an equivalent of the organ's swell box and the harpsichord cannot therefore follow the orchestra's fluctuations of intensity as can the harp and piano. Nor has the very concept of a sustaining pedal any reality when applied to the harpsichord. *Forte* and *fortissimo* are supplied by means of octave couplings (which thicken the texture and so give the impression of loudness), regardless of the notation in the score, and *pianissimo* by whatever variety of stops the instrument may boast. It is therefore still rarely used outside chamber-orchestral combinations despite its spectacular return to favour during the past few decades.

The harpsichord is usually placed fairly centrally, especially when used for the continuo; this is not only to give its tone the best chance to project (the lid is opened to its fullest extent or removed), but also to seat the player as near as possible to the principals, especially the cello whose line he is elaborating. Players often possess and bring their own instruments and may even tune them, for the maintaining of a harpsichord is as exacting a part of the job as playing it. Electrical amplification is sometimes resorted to in larger halls (though more often when the harpsichord is a solo instrument than in ensemble works) but, apart from the unnatural quality such artificial boosting is ever prone to give to the true delicate quality of the instrument, this belies the intimate chamber-music purpose that is integral to its very nature.

ORGAN

The appearance of the organ in orchestral work is always an occasion. Its size, visual impact, potential strength, associations, all mark it as a distinguished visitor and it is in this image that composers have mostly introduced it when using it orchestrally rather than in the role of continuo, a function which it serves equally with the harpsichord.

To take this continuo role first, so primarily is the organ associated with the church and with religious functions that it is in the church music of classical composers up to the time of Beethoven that one looks, to find the organ specified purely as part of the basso continuo and written for only in the manner of a figured bass. So it is in Beethoven's Mass in C, Op. 86, but by the *Missa Solemnis* it already appears fully worked out with its own staves (though with the term *senza org.* sometimes given as the organ's version of *tacet*) and notated higher in the score, i.e. above the strings. Even in a work as late as Brahms's Requiem, the organ part is not absolutely fixed although later full scores, such as the reprinted Peters or the Breitkopf, contain a specific part at the foot of each page that is not to be found in earlier editions or in the miniature score. In the Berlioz sacred choral works, such as the *Te Deum*, the organ part is also put at the foot of the score.

The use of the organ as continuo is not by any means always specified precisely in scores; and according to the conductor's feeling for, or knowledge of, period style, performances are given of, for example, Bach's Passions or Handel's Oratorios in which the organ may supply the continuo for choral movements whilst a harpsichord is used for solo numbers.

Again, as with the harpsichord, realizations of the organ's contribution exist in respect of many well-known works, but an experienced artist will mostly prefer to work from the figured bass in a full score. The choice of registration is also entirely his responsibility, there being no indications whatever of this in the score.

Sometimes, as for example in the recitative section of Mozart's *Exsultate Jubilate*, the orchestral string parts are printed with a full realization of the organ continuo laid out in self-contained harmonies, even though no sign of this exists in the score. Such practice emphasizes the problem, never absent from consideration where the organ is concerned, over the suitability of the instrument in the building where the performance is to take place, or even whether an organ is available at all.

For the pianist's occupational hazard, already referred to—i.e. different instruments he may have to contend with from one location to another—is magnified immeasurably when it comes to organs. The different stops, number of manuals, all the subsidiary extras such as swell box, composition buttons (couplers), mixtures, etc., will vary or some may be lacking in different organs. At the worst the concert may take place in a hall with no built-in organ at all and the question may arise of whether or not an electric organ should be hired, its tubby synthetic tone all too often a dismal substitute for a genuine pipe organ, especially at full volume and with regard to the deeper notes. It is true that very large electric organs do now exist and give a surprising illusion of the right quality, but even these are rare and can be fallible. Small portative organs as well as the similar but not identical Royals, or Positives, also exist, but are very seldom used as replacements for the grand organ; mostly they fulfil a specialized purpose either for old music, such as the Monteverdi *Vespers* which needs a portative as well as a grand organ, or for very new music, such as many works by Peter Maxwell Davies, whose *Five Motets*, as well as his opera *Taverner,* call especially for the delicate, subtle tone of these instruments.

Yet even if the premises boast a grand organ the question of its pitch may be crucial. Organs are all too often tuned to a different pitch from that used by orchestras. If the variation is not too great the orchestra can, though with some difficulty, partially adjust to the point where the performance is at least able to take place. In no case can the organ be retuned for the purpose at the time: if a piano takes hours to tune, a large organ would take days. Hence, before rehearsing or performing any work using an organ, the orchestra takes a new A from that instrument, and even then needs to take care to listen, for an organ always sounds flat when set in abrupt apposition to the combined living tones of massed orchestral players. The following is only one of many contexts which can give the listener an uncomfortable jolt:

476

Ex. 384

Vaughan Williams, *Job*

Heaven is now lit up. The figures throw off their veils and display themselves as Satan enthroned, surrounded by the hosts of Hell

NOTE:— Where there is an Organ with very powerful reeds the bars marked ✦ may be played by Organ and Timpani only

It emerges, therefore, that in certain circumstances plans to include a work containing an organ in the list of instruments may actually have to be abandoned. Or, on the contrary, such a work may be especially included because of the presence of a fine instrument.

Some replacement is more easily tolerated, of course, when the organ is needed as no more than a continuo instrument, though even then an inadequate substitute may seriously mar the success of a major choral work.

Bearing all these considerations in mind, it is understandable that composers do not write lightly or casually for the organ, and that it was not over-protesting to have said that its presence always lends a sense of occasion to a work or performance. The Third Symphony of Saint-Saëns, a pioneer work in this respect (following Liszt's initiative in the symphonic poem *Hunnenschlacht* and the choral epilogue of the *Faust Symphony*), is widely known as the 'Organ Symphony' although the organ is used very sparingly and only in two of the four movements. Similarly, the organ entries in Strauss's *Also sprach Zarathustra*, Janáček's *Taras Bulba*, and Vaughan Williams's *Job* are suprisingly few, but are thus the more dramatically exciting or impressive. Elgar even uses this impressiveness to increase the stature of works like the 'Enigma' Variations and the overture *Cockaigne* by adding optional ('ad lib') organ parts to the closing pages.

Larger opera houses are equipped with organs, for it plays a substantial part in the world of opera, especially in such obvious contexts as the church scenes of Gounod's *Faust*, Massenet's *Manon*, Puccini's *Tosca*, Britten's *Peter Grimes*, etc.

The organ also plays a vital part in large-scale choral works such as Mahler's Eighth Symphony and Janáček's *Glagolitic Mass*, which latter has spectacular solo parts for the instrument, and sacred works from all schools up to the late romantics tend as a matter of course to feature the organ; the Requiems of Fauré and Duruflé are outstanding in this area, the latter (as befits the work of a prominent organist) being full of detailed registration and written out on three staves.

Strictly speaking, this is the way that the organ should always be notated, the manuals sharing the upper two staves and the pedals always having the lowest to themselves. But although all solo organ music is so written, it is by no means always adhered to in orchestral organ parts. These, on the contrary, are regularly shown simply on two staves like piano music, the mode of execution and distribution of the lines between manuals and pedals left to the player, apart from a few scattered indications showing some notes intended for the pedal keyboard.

Liszt in his *Faust Symphony,* Elgar, Strauss, Respighi, Bruckner, Mahler, Vaughan Williams and Britten are all punctilious enough to write their organ parts in full on the three staves, showing that it is not a matter of period or of country but of the individual composer. Nor does the custom give any indication of the extent or importance of the organ part in a given work. Saint-Saëns in his Third Symphony makes a considerable feature of the organ but only notates it on the two staves, as does Holst in *The Planets.* The same is true of most opera organ parts, for example: *La Forza del Destino, Cavalleria Rusticana, Faust, Tosca,* Massenet's *Manon* (the latter having an extended solo representing a Voluntary at the seminary of Saint Sulpice); these all use the organ to represent genuine organ music played in churches, but in every case the composer has only given a two-dimensional figuration of what is essentially three-dimensional music. Yet this restriction cannot be said to imply ignorance on the part of the composers or inadequacy with regard to their music, but rather that they were content to use what amounts to a short score (not perhaps unlike that used for stage bands) in the firm knowledge that their intentions would be fully realized by any competent organist on the basis of the notation supplied.

The most usual manuals of the organ are (from top to bottom): the Swell, specializing in the reeds; the Great, the manual of the diapasons and the loud brassy stops; and the Choir, the softest toned. Above the Swell some larger organs have a fourth manual called the Solo and the largest of all yet a fifth, the Echo manual.

The conventional playing (as opposed to sounding) range of the

manuals in a modern organ is the five octaves from

In general the basic manual stops are the 8-foot and 4-foot stops so called after the length of the largest pipe of the set;[1] the 8-foot plays at pitch and the 4-foot sounds an octave higher than written. Then there are 2-foot stops sounding an octave higher again and two intermediary

---

[1] Organ stops are named in feet even in continental countries using the equivalent (*Fuss, pieds,* etc.) which have long used the metric system in other respects.

stops called the Quint and the Twelve which automatically add consecutive fifths to everything that is played, with polytonal effect.

The playing range of the pedals is two and a half octaves from

$\boxed{9\!:\ \text{to}}$, the stops being 16-foot, sounding an octave lower than

written, while in the largest organs there will be the enormous 32-foot sounding two octaves lower which makes everything vibrate including, it may well be, the very building itself. (The 32-foot stops in the magnificent organ of Lincoln Cathedral were for long actually debarred from use for fear lest the cathedral should shake to the point of actual collapse; nevertheless 64-foot pipes have been installed in the recently completed Anglican cathedral in Liverpool. The notes can hardly be heard at all, but only felt). These low stops, however, are particularly desirable for such opening rumbles as in Strauss's *Zarathustra* and Verdi's *Otello*.

Very little of all this technical detail is indicated in the organ parts of most orchestral scores. This is partly because one of the major specializations of organists is resourcefulness in the art of registration; but also—perhaps primarily—because any registration specified by a composer based on an organ known to him would in any case have to be reorganized by the player according not only to his own personal taste and style, but also in the light of the resources available to him with each instrument and on every occasion. Nevertheless, bearing in mind that a change in registration amounts to no less than the equivalent of a total rescoring of the orchestral wind parts, and that solo organ music is normally published with suggestions for registration, it may well be thought remarkable that not even the choice of manual is normally indicated, Brahms's *man. oben* (i.e. upper manual-—presumably the Swell) in the Requiem, being exceptional.

The term 'full organ' (Ger., *volles Werk*; Fr., *grand jeu*; It., *organo pieno*) is used when maximum tone is required with a ringing diapason supporting reeds and brass-type pipes. In this the doubling of octaves twice and three times above and below the written notes is presupposed.

A curious impediment of the organ is its difficulty in making subtle gradations of dynamics. One can add or reduce the stops but this is stepwise crescendo or diminuendo and the only gradual rise or fall at the player's disposal is the swell box controlled with the feet; and the opening and shutting of a box hardly corresponds with the infinite tonal gradings at the disposal of every orchestral musician.

The platform position of the organ has, of course, generally to be accepted precisely as it stands because in most buildings the console cannot be moved, however inconvenient its placing may be for orchestral purposes. This often means that communication between organist and conductor can only be achieved through a system of mirrors (hence the splendid twist shown in the cartoon by the late Gerard Hoffnung, depicting an alarmed organist interrupted while playing by the view of a cop-car in his mirror). In some cathedrals the organ console is totally hidden from the conductor and vision is only possible on a one-way basis by means of closed-circuit television. But whether the communication is by mirrors, television, or any other such artificial contrivance, it creates so uniquely inconvenient a situation that it is only accepted because of the understood fact that the organist is an exceptionally accomplished specialist in his own field and almost by courtesy, as it were, entering into the conventions of orchestral practices.

HARMONIUM

The name of this instrument is the same in all languages. Even more than the organ the harmonium conjures up associations with religious functions. It is therefore surprising to discover that, for example, the extended part in the 'Purgatorio' movement of Liszt's *Dante Symphony* and, even more extraordinary, the great solo at the end of Tchaikovsky's *Manfred Symphony*, the latter always in fact pealed out in the fullest registration available on the grand organ, are actually given in the printed score to none other than the humble harmonium.

Strauss frequently wrote for harmonium as a support for his orchestral wind, such as the offstage instrument in *Salome*, and in the pit as an important and active member of the orchestra itself in *Ariadne auf Naxos*. This latter may indeed represent the pinnacle of the instrument's orchestral career, for Strauss took the trouble to discuss in detail the stops and colouring he wanted used by the highly complex and developed species of harmonium he had discovered and was writing for. These instructions, however, never reached the full score but reside hidden in the original edition of the player's copy. Moreover they have little more than historical interest, as that specific instrument is now scarcely ever available. Nevertheless the interested player is given much guidance as to the kind of sounds Strauss intended to establish. That Strauss seems to have had an unaccountable affection for the instrument is undeniable, his celebration offering for the wedding of his son being none other than a *Hochzeitspräludium* for two harmoniums.

It is hard nowadays, though not impossible, to find harmoniums of tolerable quality and in any condition of reliability; certainly the usual Moody and Sankey sounds that, with much wheezing and groaning, emerge from the normal run of instruments, hardly fit in with the ethic and atmosphere of a symphonic or operatic performance. There are generally a few stops to change the tone a little, these controlled by hand as the feet are inescapably occupied with the bellows and activity is only relaxed even momentarily at the music's utter peril.

The equivalent to the organ's *grand jeu* is operated by the knee, but the difference is that its effect is dangerously instantaneous in summoning the instrument's maximum volume.

The overall range of the harmonium is usually the five octaves from

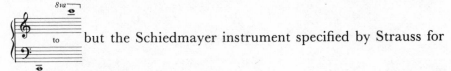

but the Schiedmayer instrument specified by Strauss for

use in *Ariadne* seems to have extended a great deal further in the lower

compass, for Strauss writes down to ⎯⎯ .

Piston states that the harmonium has two manuals, but such instruments are rare, and in any case virtually unknown in Britain. The harmonium has the patent advantage over the organ that it is relatively mobile, but it is usually placed as far to the rear as possible since its bulk is apt to create hazards of visibility.

GUITAR

If the harpsichord suffers by being too soft-toned to compete with a full orchestra, the guitar is still more at a disadvantage even though, theoretically, gradations of expressive dynamics are no problem. But anything less than the sound of fully spread chords over the six strings of the whole instrument is barely audible over an orchestra playing above a *mezzopiano*.

Generally speaking, in spite of two or three popular concertos, the guitar is an even more exclusive world than the organ, star players making their meteoric careers primarily through solo recital. Hence the very occasional importation of guitar players into the orchestral world, since Mahler and the Schoenberg school, has carried with it the hazard of highly accomplished executants who are nevertheless not geared to the need for such meticulous precision, and who are moreover often inexperienced in working under a conductor's beat. A few *routiné* players have now sprung up since a certain demand has been established, but even though the repertoire in which the guitar is required has grown, it remains relatively tiny and a handful of key players naturally control the market.

In the broader world of orchestral ensemble work the enormous subtlety of guitar colours, entirely controlled by the player's fingers and fingernails, is altogether lost and players are content to fill in their lines in a simple firm tone quality. At the same time it should be added that these variations of technique are never discussed or specified in guitar music but represent the resourcefulness of the player's artistry.

Apart from its special and soloistic operatic use, as in Rossini's *Barber of Seville*, the earliest appearance of the guitar in the symphony orchestra is in the second 'Nachtmusik' from Mahler's Seventh

Symphony. The conventional tuning is: and

the normal range is between   (all sounding an octave

lower). The standard notation is on a single line in the treble clef and sounds an octave lower than written, but Mahler takes it into the bass clef for a passage going down to the low C:

Ex. 385   Mahler, Symphony No. 7

Schoenberg, according to his custom from Op. 22 onwards, writes for the guitar in his Serenade, Op. 24 at concert pitch using treble and bass staves and this is also how the player's part is printed. It is accordingly useless and the work is performed from renotated manuscript copies. Schoenberg, unlike Mahler, clearly recognized the standard tuning, as notes lying below E (which he does occasionally include) are put in brackets. He also uses harmonics:

Ex. 386   Schoenberg, Serenade, Op. 24

The guitar is normally placed as near to the audience as possible on account of its very intimate nature, as well as notable lack of volume, and this has also sometimes led to its artificial amplification like the harpsichord, especially for concerto playing. In the case of the guitar, however, the resultant change of character has come to cause a different sub-species of guitar being built with its original source of tone-quality, the hollow resonating belly, itself dispensed with as no longer relevant. So has emerged the electric guitar of the pop world, which has found its way into art music through such avant-garde composers as Stockhausen, in *Gruppen* for example, and is also scored for by Tippett in his opera *The Knot Garden* and its parergon *Songs for Dov*.

MANDOLINE

Mandolines exist in various sizes (I myself possess a score of Cimarosa's overture *Il Matrimonio Segreto* arranged for mandoline orchestra scored for, amongst others, *mandolini soprani*, *mandole tenori*, *mandoloncelli* and *mandolone*). But the only mandoline used orchestrally

is the standard mandoline with a range of three octaves from

the most common Neapolitan instrument, being tuned in fifths like the violin. It is written on one stave in the treble clef at pitch and, unlike the guitar (with which it is in this respect often unfairly coupled) is played with a plectrum, having a strongly penetrating angular quality.

The first orchestral appearance of the mandoline is usually cited as being Mozart's brief use in Don Giovanni's Serenade 'Deh vieni alla finestra' but this is again a special case, analogous with the guitar in *The Barber of Seville* or Beckmesser's lute in *Die Meistersinger*. A more genuine orchestral use of the instrument, though still specialized in the sense of local colour, is that of Respighi's *Feste Romane* composed in 1929, which is always played with the characteristic tremolando though this is not indicated by the notation in the score:

Ex. 387

Indeed the tremolo is so indigenous to the instrument that it is commonly thought that all passages must automatically be played in this way, with ruinous consequences to the other school of orchestral mandoline writing—that inaugurated as long ago as 1908 together with the guitar, by Mahler in his Seventh Symphony and which he pursued in the Eighth and in *Das Lied von der Erde*. In the last two of these he abandoned the guitar, whereas Schoenberg continued to write for both instruments as a pair in his Serenade, as did Webern in his *5 Orchesterstücke*, Op. 10.

In the works of these composers the tremolo is clearly indicated wherever required; though in Mahler's Seventh Symphony some confusion has arisen through the Mengelberg practice, too often followed, of allowing tremolo to intrude everywhere, so that Erwin Ratz—the editor of the Mahler Society Revised Edition—was misled into adding tremolo strokes to almost all notes of longer value (such as minims), even though when Mahler positively wanted the effect he clearly said so—as at Fig. 215. Ratz's preface is interesting in this respect, however, referring to different schools of mandoline playing not otherwise commonly known.

On the platform the mandoline is normally placed side by side with the guitar—when the two are written, as so often, in conjunction. As in the case of the guitar, though to an even greater extent, so few orchestral works include the mandoline that players regard themselves, not without considerable justification, as specialized soloists in a colourful—even exotic—field, and this viewpoint becomes even more applicable to the remaining instruments or artists that follow.

ACCORDION

It cannot be pretended that the accordion forms part of the orchestral scene. Essentially a folk instrument, it does, however, play a lively role in the popular music of many countries, together with its little cousin the concertina, which is a smaller and more limited version of the same species. But whereas there is no instance of a concertina being included in an orchestral score, its sound, like that of the accordion, is often imitated orchestrally in works depicting popular gatherings such as Vaughan Williams's *London Symphony* or Stravinsky's *Petrouchka*. Tchaikovsky, however, actually used two real accordions (or four, including doublings, as detailed in a long preface to the movement on the mode of execution) in the 'Scherzo burlesque' of his Suite No. 2, Op. 53 (see Ex. 388, opposite).

After this stimulating début the accordion languished in near total neglect, orchestrally speaking, until it was revived by Roberto Gerhard in his Second Symphony after an earlier experiment in a chamber ensemble for his *Nonet* with wind instruments.

Although, as can be seen from Ex. 388, Tchaikovsky only used the alternation of two dominant and tonic chords so characteristic of the instrument, it is entirely out of order to suppose that this is all the accordion can do. The 1954 edition of Grove's Dictionary goes so far as to state that '. . . the capabilities of the instrument are extremely limited, as it can only be played in one key, and even in that one imperfectly; it is, in fact, little more than a toy', a statement that must be bitterly resented by accordion players and is totally disproved through Gerhard's extensive chromatic orchestral use of it.

The larger instruments are equipped with a keyboard, not unlike a piano's, and possess a range of just over four octaves; these are indeed known as piano accordions.

The question of notation remains unstandardized orchestrally, though at least it is always written at pitch in the usual treble and bass staves. Tchaikovsky's method, illustrated above, shows the fingered notes in thicker, normal note-heads with the doubling or harmonic extras supplied by studs (much like stops on an organ) in smaller notes. Gerhard did not adopt this method, which had little relevance to his style of writing for the instrument, and experienced some changes of thought on the best notation in consultation, no doubt, with the player, Ivor Beynon, for whom he wrote.

In the *Nonet* of 1956 Gerhard still used the two bracketed staves in

Ex. 388

treble and bass clefs, as for a piano, though curiously adding indications of registration as if for an organ ('8′ only', 'col 16′′ etc.). All this, however, he abandoned in his later orchestral use of the accordion which he now notated on a single stave with changes of clef as required, and no longer making any attempt at guidance on registration; and this, Thea, is the way you too have written for it in your Clarinet Concerto.

CIMBALOM, TYPOPHONE, TUBAPHONE

The cimbalom is a popular Hungarian instrument, still to be found played by virtuosi in every Budapest café and restaurant. Its first appearance in orchestral music is in Liszt's *Hungarian Rhapsody* No. 3 in D, but by far the most famous example of its exploitation is Kodály's *Háry János* Suite. Moreover, during the 1920s Stravinsky used the cimbalom briefly for a little cluster of works, notably *Renard*, *Ragtime* and the pre-1923 orchestral version of *Les Noces*.

Hungarian cimbalom players do not normally use music at all, improvising around well established formulae; but for orchestral purposes the cimbalom is notated much like a piano, with which it used to be replaced on occasions when the popular *Háry János* was programmed even though no cimbalom was available. A recording with piano was once issued but the substitution proved a travesty for two important reasons, apart from the utterly different timbre.

First, the cimbalom is played with sticks, one in each hand, more like a xylophone, though the ends of the wooden sticks are covered in cotton-wool and are struck directly onto the piano-like wire strings. Hence tremolos are a basic method of sustaining the long notes of a melody, and are either notated conventionally:

Ex. 389   Liszt, *Hungarian Rhapsody* No. 3 in D

or as a kind of shake as in the 'Intermezzo' fourth movement of Kodály's suite:

Ex. 390   Kodály, *Háry János*

This latter constitutes a style of playing that cannot be imitated on a piano.

Secondly, the strings of the cimbalom are oddly arranged, so that the highest and lowest registers lie adjacent, with the middle register lying to one side. Thus the quasi-glissando effect in the third movement ('Song') of *Háry János*:

Ex. 391

does not represent a continuous descending row of notes such as it would on a piano, but involves a sudden jump in pitch as the sticks pass from the one group of strings to the other.

Moreover the glissando is executed by continuous hammering between the two sticks and not by sliding the hammer along as on a glockenspiel or xylophone.

The cimbalom is notated at actual pitch but variably on either one stave or two, as necessitated by the style of the music, using treble and bass clefs. Stravinsky, however, adds a third stave for isolated notes in more complicated places in his *Ragtime:*

Ex. 392

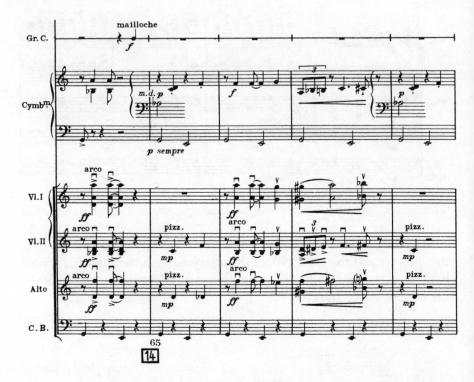

Stravinsky also writes for the cimbalom (which he unusually spells with a 'y') to be played 'près du chevalet' (near the bridge) and even 'derrière le chevalet', some strings being indeed stretched over no less than two bridges. The effect, of course, bears no relationship to *sul ponticello* as applied to the violin family, but produces a hard, even vicious sound.

Modern instruments are fitted with a damping pedal, this being prescribed by Bartók in his First Violin Rhapsody. Bartók also writes 'pizz.', meaning that the player should pluck the strings with the fingertips instead of striking them with the sticks, and in addition instructs that the wooden ends of the sticks should be used. In *Renard*, Stravinsky calls for leather sticks in alternation with wood.

The range of the modern Hungarian cimbalom is usually the five octaves from [musical notation] but Stravinsky adds *ossias* in his *Ragtime*

and *Renard* making provision for 'L'instrument qui a la Ré grave'. The instrument to which Stravinsky referred was one which, although descending chromatically to E, also had the isolated D string—i.e. it had no E♭. The 'Song' in *Háry János* also uses this D, and in the *Kálló Folk Dances* (which is actually scored for two *Zimbalom ungharese*) Kodály writes down to the low C: [musical notation] ; this is because

Hungarian makers are ever building bigger and better instruments.

None, however, has ever gone so low as [musical notation] which Debussy wrote

in his instrumentation of the waltz *La plus que lente*. Made in 1912, this included a part for cimbalom, but it needs some adaptation to become playable. Perhaps Debussy misunderstood something he was told by a Hungarian virtuoso.

Confusion is thrown on the musicological scene by one of the Italian terms for the cimbalom being *cembalo* (see above, p. 472) a fact which has misled Read, in his orchestral thesaurus, into mixing up the instruments.

Although it is as the 'cimbalom' that the instrument is known in orchestral circles, it is actually closely related to the biblical psaltery and also the dulcimer, under which latter name it is mostly to be found in reference books or textbooks of orchestration. This, however, should not cause it to be confused with the dulcitone which is a sort of celesta-like keyboard instrument with a set of tuning forks struck with hammers. The French name for this instrument is *typophone* and it is to be found in the works of French composers such as d'Indy and especially Duparc, in whose beautiful song *L'Invitation au Voyage* it is featured, though the celesta is given as an *ossia*.

The tubaphone, though not properly belonging to this group, may also find a place here, if partially to ensure its distinction from the *typophone*, for in genus it is nearer to the glockenspiel family, consisting as it does of a row of metal tubes arranged horizontally and struck much like a small vibraphone. It appears, suitably translated into Italian as *tubaphono*, in several movements of Khachaturian's *Gayaneh* ballet where it is given a range of [musical notation] sounding an octave higher.

HARMONICA

The greatest problem surrounding this instrument is the basic one of its sheer identity. The 'Harmonika' for which Mozart wrote his *Adagio* and *Adagio and Rondo* shortly before his death was the Musical Glasses, which have in recent years returned to the concert scene through the virtuosity of a single artist, Bruno Hoffman. His instrument, like Mozart's, consists quite simply of a row of glasses variably filled with, or immersed in, water and rubbed with the moistened fingers.[1]

Except for Mr Hoffman's star appearances, however, this is not at all the instrument used when the scores requiring the Harmonica are performed. So many totally different contraptions have been created to serve the purpose that it is no longer at all sure what composers such as Saint-Saëns and Strauss either expected or intended when they wrote for the 'Harmonica' and the 'Glasharmonika' in the *Carnival of the Animals* and *Die Frau ohne Schatten* respectively. The instruments which either are or have been in existence are even as widely varied as harmonicas consisting of glasses struck through the medium of a keyboard (as described by Forsyth), or suspended and played with soft beaters in a manner not unlike tubular bells. Certainly either of these would be suitable, as the true harmonica would not, for the *Carnival of the Animals* which includes glissandi and trills. It is perhaps indicative that Saint-Saëns actually describes the xylophone, in a footnote to the score of the *Danse Macabre*, as 'un instrument . . . analogue à l'Harmonica' which suggests that the glass bars of his instrument were laid flat. Sometimes the suspended type of instrument consists of bars made not of glass at all but of soft wood, which gives a similar gentle resonance.

Although dictionaries insist that the true name is 'armonica' it is as 'harmonica' that the instrument is universally known and written for. Some confusion has been further added by the application of 'harmonica' to the mouth organ, whose proper name probably seems too undignified for its virtuosi; but since the mouth organ has no place whatever within the orchestra (indeed its very appearance on the orchestral platform is limited to a couple of concertos), the conflict is not very important. It was, however, no doubt to avoid any possibility

---

[1] Peter Maxwell Davies resurrects this homespun device in his *Stone Litany*, writing for wine glasses in Eb and C.

of misunderstanding—that 'harmonica' was a misprint for 'har-monium' as it might be—that Strauss added the prefix 'Glas-'.

Mozart wrote for the *Harmonika* on two staves, both mostly in the treble clef with a range of (sounding an octave higher).

Forsyth cites the ranges of the keyboard instrument as:

which is much wider than Saint-Saëns uses, writing only on a single stave. In fact performances of the *Carnival of the Animals* are mostly given using a glockenspiel. Glinka, on the other hand, writes quite an elaborate part for *Harmonika* which really does suggest the necessity of a keyboard:

Ex. 393   *Russlan and Ludmila*

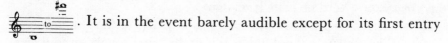

Strauss writes on the two staves like Mozart, but limits himself to using it for simple block chords[1] or slow motifs within a range of . It is in the event barely audible except for its first entry

at the key point in the opera where the Kaiserin receives her shadow, a moment that is admittedly magical:

---

[1] As many of these have eight notes the part is played at Covent Garden on two vibraphones.

Ex. 394   Strauss, *Die Frau ohne Schatten*

ZITHER, ETC.

One would hardly have reckoned the zither an orchestral instrument, but then the same is broadly true of the cimbalom and other such popular instruments which have become accredited members through their use as local colour. Thus too, if to a lesser extent, the zither finds its way into the symphonic world mainly through the great Johann Strauss, for there are substantial solos in his popular waltz *Tales from the Vienna Woods*; though Villa-Lobos has also included a part for it in his *Amazonas* where he calls it 'cytharra'.

It is written at pitch on two staves as in piano or harp notation. A flat box-like instrument not unlike the cimbalom, though without legs, it is plucked with the fingers of one hand as well as with a plectrum held in the other. According to the textbooks the bottom note is: (the tuning of the lowest string) but Strauss writes happily down to the D below the stave:

Ex. 395   J. Strauss, *Tales from the Vienna Woods*

His uppermost note is 𝄞 which is consistent with the tuning of

the top string being: 𝄞 .

As with the cimbalom or bagpipes, a special artist is usually engaged who will often appear dressed in national (e.g. Tyrolean) costume, though it must be admitted that the score disappointingly includes *ossia* lines for a small ensemble drawn from the orchestral strings.

The Banjo has made an occasional appearance in the orchestral world. Delius introduced banjos for local colour in his adaptation of *La Calinda* in the opera *Koanga*. Křenek, on the other hand, actually integrates two banjos into his unusual orchestration of the *Kleine Symphonie*, Op 58 as does Kurt Weill in *Mahagonny*, etc. The banjo, too, is written in the treble clef at pitch. Variants of this instrument such as tenor banjos and even that other popular strumming instrument, the ukulele, have made sporadic appearances in works of contemporary composers such as Henze.

ONDES MARTENOT

Of all the exotic musical instruments that have been contrived since the development of electronic sound during the past half century, the only instrument to survive so far remains the *Ondes* (= waves) invented by M. Martenot in the late 1930s. The reason for its supremacy, whilst no doubt owing much to its intriguing possibilities of varied sonority, must be primarily attributed to the works by important composers that include a part for it.

Honegger's *Jeanne d'Arc au Bûcher* and Messiaen's *Turangalîla-Symphonie* as well as his *Trois Petites Liturgies* are outstanding examples but there are many others, mostly amongst the French school. Koechlin wrote for it in his *Seven Stars Symphony* to describe the film actress Marlene Dietrich.

In character it is like a wild, penetrating, inhuman wailing musical saw; yet it is eerily fascinating and by no means disagreeable.

It is played in two primary ways, described in its notation as *au clavier* and *ruban*. The former uses the keyboard, which is similar to that of the piano, and with its seven octaves: . It

has, however, the additional capability of a very wide vibrato and of quarter tones, both obtained through the flexibility of the keys, which are in this respect unlike those of the piano.

Ruban gives the other style of playing, the ribbon being controlled by a metal ring which the player wears on his right forefinger. With this the keyboard serves as no more than a guide to pitch, every kind of portamento and—above all—glissando being its chief stock-in-trade.

Honegger, like most composers, leaves the many complex details of possible execution to the performer (much like organ registration), at most contenting himself with the primary instructions *au clavier* and *ruban* as just discussed:

Ex. 396   Honegger, *Jeanne d'Arc au Bûcher*

Messiaen, however, is not only well acquainted with Ginette Martenot (the original executant of her husband's creation), but his sister-in-law Jeanne Loriod is also a skilled performer on the Ondes. He was thus able to fill his score with every kind of technical instruction including the variations of tone production (by means of curved arrows), degrees and species of resonance (indicated by numbers and letters corresponding to the controls manipulated with the left hand) and the choice of the three available loudspeakers. These are described as *principal*; *métallique*—this is equipped with an orchestral tam-tam; and *palme* which is a lyre-like object fitted with 24 tuned strings and is visually the most picturesque feature of the whole instrument. Messiaen uses numerous other words and instructions as well, including suggestions for the orchestral tone-colour that should be emulated, as one of the characteristics of the Ondes is the ability to imitate orchestral timbres.

The Ondes Martenot is exclusively a melodic instrument and as such is notated on a single stave, as in this typical solo from the *Turangalîla-Symphonie*:

Ex. 397

VOICES

It may seem odd to include a section on the human voice in a book that is essentially concerned with the orchestra, and indeed there is no intention to treat voices either in their function as soloists or to discuss the wider aspects of choruses or choral writing. Yet not only is the chorus sometimes used as a purely orchestral colour but individual voices also appear in symphonic scores treated almost instrumentally.

By its very nature, as well as through the power of the associations it evokes, the voice inevitably draws attention to itself; nevertheless in some works this is handled in a way that is only an extension of the soloistic style assumed automatically by any woodwind or solo string player where the passage calls for such individual spotlighting.

The Scandinavians seem to have specialized in this kind of treatment; both Nielsen in his *Sinfonia Espansiva* and Alfven in his Fourth Symphony have used a pair of voices, one female and one male, in just such an orchestral style, both cantilenas being wordless throughout. And Vaughan Williams features a wordless chorus in his ballet *Old King Cole* and especially *Flos Campi*. He also introduces a wordless off-stage soprano into both his *Pastoral* and *Antartica* Symphonies, though in the former the voice is isolated against a drum roll (or, at the end, a sustained high note on violins), an effect that could, for example, be compared with Sibelius's long clarinet solo over a drumroll at the beginning of his First Symphony.

Nevertheless, as no singer can, by definition, be an orchestral player, such introduction of voices inevitably entails soloists who must be engaged and treated as such, with consequent organization of rehearsals and acknowledgement at the concert even though the singer's contribution may be vastly less than that of any member of the orchestra.

Choruses are also used quasi-instrumentally as a wordless extra colour in the orchestral spectrum. Debussy's *Sirènes* was a pioneer work in this respect, although his use of a female chorus might be considered as special pleading, suggesting as it does the perilously seductive beauties of nautical legend. The chorus often sings the languorous phrases seated, to preserve the elusive distant character of impressionist tone painting, but this is only one of the many practical decisions that has to be taken by the conductor in planning the presentation of any concert.

In 'Neptune', the last of *The Planets*, Holst took over Debussy's wordless female chorus though he places it off-stage and as far away as practicable, allowing for a final dying-away to total inaudibility for the conclusion of the work:

Ex. 398

*) This bar to be repeated until the sound is lost in the distance.

The full chorus is again used as a wordless colour in Scriabin's *Prometheus*[1] and has also appeared in such works as Bartók's *The Miraculous Mandarin*, Ravel's *Daphnis et Chloé*, Florent Schmitt's *La Tragédie de Salomé* (again women's voices), Delius's *Song of the High Hills* and *Eventyr*—the part in the latter consisting of no more than two wild shouts by twenty men's voices heard off-stage. This marvellously imaginative effect used to cause great hilarity in Beecham's performances, for which it was one of the duties of his various minions or assistants (such as myself at one period) to co-opt the services of the hall attendants and male programme sellers to foregather behind the platform and shout lustily and ferociously on cue at the two relevant places when Sir Thomas shook his baton in our direction.

The *Song of the High Hills* uses the voices in a much more elaborate way, two solo singers, soprano and tenor, being used as well as full chorus divided into as many as eleven parts. It is still entirely wordless and colouristic, nevertheless, and—since it is the Norwegian

[1] This extraordinary work is additionally scored for 'Luce', meaning a colour organ, though what colours of the spectrum this would have projected on the screen in accordance with the musical notation of the part can only be reconstructed through knowledge of Scriabin's personal associations of colour and sound.

hills that Delius was evoking—is once more in the Scandinavian tradition.

If no words are used singers normally vocalize to some syllable such as 'Ah' unless, as for example in *Sirènes*, the instruction is given for closed lips. It is rare, however, to find syllables specified in the score although in *Prometheus* Scriabin does mark some passages 'o . . . ho . . . e . . . a' etc.[1]

In the score the voice or voices are normally placed immediately above the strings. The chorus may be notated either in open score, that is to say with a separate stave for each of the standard voice parts, soprano, alto, tenor, bass; or, if there are not many subdivisions, they can be found condensed on to two staves, although this entails notating the tenors with the basses in the bass clef at pitch. As a result the tenor line will be at variance with the part which is always written, as in most scores, an octave higher in the treble clef (although some composite clef sign is occasionally substituted such as 𝄞𝄞, 𝄞 , 𝄞 , or 𝄞 to indicate that the octave transposition has been made).

When the voices are used as colour the old-fashioned notation using alto and tenor clefs—occasionally even soprano clef[2]—is never found. Nor are the half-way voices, mezzo-soprano and baritone, ever to be found specified in choral writing. The extreme upper or lower register of each voice is usually given to the 1st or 2nds of the respective group, the voice line dividing for the purpose. The range of the voices used by composers are astonishingly wide:

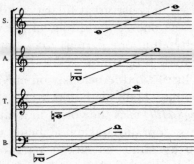

<hr />

[1] Vocalizing on a syllable in this way can also be found as an additional effect in fully choral works, as can be seen in Ex. 396, from Honegger's *Jeanne d'Arc au Bûcher*.

[2] An extraordinary example of the soprano clef can be seen in Mendelssohn's *Die erste Walpurgisnacht* where it is used for both the soprano and alto lines.

but in the instrumental context that is being discussed here such extremes of compass are not used although the *Song of the High Hills* does extend as far as:

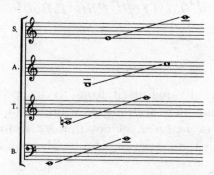

Rehearsal difficulties are often encountered in these kinds of work where the publishers, treating the chorus (conveniently for themselves), as part of the orchestra, print the vocal parts individually exactly like orchestral parts, with bars rests and no more indication of what is going on around them than any orchestral player is used to having. But this cuts against the way choruses operate and ignores the sheer difficulty of picking out of the blue the note on which the singers come in, which can be very demoralizing unless, of course, they happen to have absolute pitch.

Postscript and Envoi

Your book, Thea, divided itself from its inception into chapters comprising the component sections of the orchestra. But there remain certain problems or features, of notation for example, common to them all and which should perhaps find a place before I finally call a halt.

Take the following accentuation or separation symbols:

1) ⸱ ⁣ 2) ⸱ ⁣ 3) ⸱ ⁣ 4) ⸱ ⁣ 5) ⸱ ⁣ 6) ⸱

to which may be added

7) ⸠ ⁣ 8) ⸠ ⁣ and 9) ⸠

(⸠ which is to be found in Busoni's *Tanzwalzer* is meaningless and must be a misprint). To this collection can be further appended Schoenberg's ⸍ ⸌ ! ⸍ ⌣ and ⸱ . There is, however, some difference of opinion over many of these, leading with great frequency to confusion and heated debate.

Essentially I would propose the following:

No. 1 means a simple staccato, a short note, though the degree of shortness is not fixed by definition and when applied to longer value notes such as ♩ or 𝅝 may be open to individual interpretation. There used to be a rule-of-thumb dogma that the value of the note should be halved, but this view is so fallible that it has, happily, come to be discredited.

During a rallentando the question sometimes arises whether it is the notes or the rests that gradually become longer. Stravinsky posed the situation and then solved it in his own typical manner in the various versions of *The Firebird*. The closing passage appears in the 1945 version with re-notations which attempt to set down his own method of interpretation, according to which the notes become increasingly separated by rests, viz:

Ex. 399

(a)   (b)

Players often tend to elongate staccato notes during a crescendo with, one should concede, some justification unless a particularly terse dramatic effect is required.

No. 2 is really another staccato symbol but usually implying an even shorter note; though this is not always what Britten meant by it, and Mozart used it over semibreves. However, it very often carries with it a suggestion of bite in the enunciation of the note taking it into the province of accentuation, and some composers use it nearly synonymously with No. 5 or even No. 6.

No. 3 is the normal stress symbol, i.e. an accent with duration quality, giving the note the character, rather, of a brick, viz: as opposed to a 'placed note' of no deliberate, calculated length, which

might compare with a kind of pear drop: The degree of accent is

small and the function of the stress is more to attach importance to the note that bears it. Where opinions differ most is to what degree the stress affects sheer duration, and the schools of thought vary between those who consider that it implies separation and thus must of necessity shorten the note, and those who, on the contrary, firmly assert that it lengthens it. Certainly context is often a deciding factor and places can be found where each opinion can be proved right, but as always there are countless borderline cases that remain the responsibility of the individual artist.

No. 4 taken at its face value is palpably a short or shortish note played with significance, but again in the very nature of things the length will be affected to an arguable degree. One can spend a happy half-hour trying to play correctly, to the strict meaning of their different notations, the following:

Ex. 400

and so on.

To complicate matters still further. Stravinsky elects to interpret ÷ over a sustained note, as a sharp, firm accentuation:

Ex. 401   Stravinsky, *Orpheus*

No. 5 is the most familiar form of straight accent; and No. 6 is the same but more so, that is to say with the sharpest accentuation.

No. 7 is one of the most controversial signs of all. It really indicates a legato in which the second note is lifted off short: cf. Ex. 401 above, as well as Falla, *Nights in the Gardens of Spain*:

Ex. 402

But it is surprising how many composers clearly mean the second note to be enunciated as in:

No. 8, a sign representing separation rather than accentuation and different only in degree from:

No. 9, where it is clear that the line stresses must also *shorten* the notes at least to some small extent if any separation consistent with the maintaining of tempo is to be achieved at all. (See also No. 3).

Schoenberg's extra symbols are in the main devoted to the dotting of i's and crossing of t's, and are in any case explained carefully in every score in which he uses them (though not in the orchestral parts). Two, however, borrowed from verse scansion are new and interesting, for they indicate rhythmic inflexion, especially where this falls contrary to the natural phrasing within the structure of the bar-lines, as in the following examples from the Violin Concerto:

Ex. 403

The above example also introduces the problem of the symbols Ⱶ and Ⲛ. These were invented by Schoenberg to indicate the principal and secondary strands (the Ⱶ standing for *Hauptstimme*, the Ⲛ for *Nebenstimme*) in the more complicated polyphonic textures. The intention was that this knowledge would affect the players' sensitivity in ensemble playing, the end of the important lines being marked by a kind of close bracket: ⅂. Unfortunately, although interesting, and perhaps enlightening to the conductor, if taken literally by the players these symbols often waste rather than save time in rehearsal as they are apt to contradict dynamic marks, causing instrumentalists to ignore either the one or the other. The relationship of the score to the players' part is a more specialized subject than many composers, publishers and copyists realize.

The significance of a comma, placed variously at the ends of phrases or at the top of the score as a whole, provides another controversial issue; for there is a fundamental difference between the commas used by Stravinsky (which do not hold up the pulse but merely curtail the preceding notes) and those in, for example, Sibelius's First Symphony.

These are admittedly extreme instances that are more generally known and understood, but in the works of many composers it is quite unsure whether a *Luftpause* (one of Mahler's favourite words) is intended or not.

Yet another thorny subject that affects the orchestra as a whole is the question of rehearsal letters or figures. In older editions these are often totally lacking, as in the *Meistersinger* Prelude and the orchestral excerpts from Act 3 of that opera, making one wonder how rehearsals were expected to be conducted. Or rehearsal letters may be so far apart as to be nearly useless, for which reason later printings of the standard repertoire in Breitkopf and Peters editions have bar numberings added at the beginning of every line.

But stemming from this, many composers have come to mark the bar numbers themselves as rehearsal figures. When these come at musically meaningful places as in Bartók this is ingenious, but all too often they appear regularly at ten-bar intervals making the counting —especially of rests—illogical and confusing. Unfortunately nowadays most copyists adopt this method without realizing how much it leads to miscounting and to players losing their places, with severe cost in rehearsal time and frayed tempers.

However, these subjects, as no doubt many others, my dear Thea, could be greatly extended and, as I suggested in your Preface, should perhaps form the basis for another book. Maybe I shall write it for you as well, one day.

INDEX

by Pauline Del Mar

(bold figures indicate the main discussion of the subject, or music example)

509

Tippett, (cont.)
  Orchestra, 458; *Fantasia Concertante on a Theme of Corelli*, 60; *Knot Garden*, 484; *Midsummer Marriage*, 308; *Ritual Dances*, 147, **174**, 441, **470**; *Songs for Dov*, 484; Symphony No.1, 88; Symphony No.2, **195**, Symphony No.3, 329; Symphony No.4, 424
Toch, Ernst, Symphony No.3, 429
Tom-toms, 375, 399, **418–9**
Tonlos niederdrücken (piano harmonics), 468
Toscanini, Arturo, 50, 64, 68, 109, 179, 295, 347, 380
Touche, sur la, *see* Sul tasto
Tovey, Donald Francis, 239
Tre corde, 462
Tremolo dental, *see* Flutter-tonguing
Triangle, 372, **391–2**; muted, 378; Turkish music, 390
Trogxylophones, 411
Tromba, *see* Trumpet
Tromba contralto in F, *see* Contralto trumpet
Tromba da tirarsi, 278
Trombone, 71, 77; Schubert's use of three, 228; their presence constitutes 'Grosses Orchester', 273; doubling on bass trumpet, 275, 289; species in use, 277–9; doubling voice parts, 279; names, 279; notation, 285; range, 296–9; seating position, 303; number in section, 306; order in score, 309; species not indicated, 311; muting, 313; bouché, 316; glissando, 317; flutter-tonguing, 321; off-stage, 323; trombone-à-pistons, 327n; solos and style, 326–7; *see* Contrabass trombone
Trommeln, 419
Trompa, *see* Horn
Trumpet, 173; bumper, 231; valves, 241; always included in brass group, 273; species, 274–7; concert pitch, 276; names, 276; notation, 281–5; lack of key signatures, 285; transposition table, 283; some confusions, 284–5; range, 286–95 (*see* Clarino); seating position, 302; pair in section, 304; other numbers, 305; single, 306; order in score, 232, 309; muted, 312, types of mutes, 313; bouché, 315; tonguing, 320; natural

harmonics, 322; off-stage, 322; nervous element of exposed solos, and style, 324–6; flügelhorn played by trumpeters, 330; posthorn played by trumpeters, 330; correspond to litui, 332
Tuba, seating with Wagner tubas, 269; family, 279–81; notation, 286; range, 301–3; replacement for ophicleide, 308, 335; use of two, 304, 308; without trombones, 309; order in score, 309; shares stave with trombone, 311; confusion with Wagner tubas, 312; mutes, 314; flutter-tonguing, 321; off-stage, 323; solos, 329; plays tenorhorn, 333
Tubaphone, 408, 491
Tubular bells, 372, 377, **402–5**, 408
Tuning, to A, 35, 169, 476; scordatura, 30, 103–4; strings, 100; double bass, 101, **105**; timps, 343, harps, 434; piano, 463; *see* Pitch
Turina, Joachin, *Danzas Fantasticas*, 216
Turkish crescent (pavillon chinois), 422
Tuxen, Erik, 398n
Tympani, *see* Timpani
Typewriters, 429
Typophone (dulcitone), 491

Übrigen (rest of section), 36
Ukulele, 495
Umstimmen nach ..., *see* Muta in
Una corda, 462
Unison, 45, 68
Unisoni, 37

Varèse, Edgar, *Intégrales*, 389, 427; *Ionisation*, 398, 415, 422, 429,
Vaughan Williams, Ralph, 479; Concerto Grosso, 123; *Five Tudor Portraits*, 347; *Flos Campi*, 498; *Job*, 386, **477**, 478; *Old King Cole*, 498; *A London Symphony*, 305, 421, 486; *Pastoral Symphony*, **263**, 322, 388, 449, **450**, 498; Symphony No.4 in F minor, **328**, Symphony No.6 in E minor, 220; *Sinfonia Antartica*, 423, 498; Symphony No.8, 399; Symphony No.9, 329
Vents (French for wind including brass), 139
Verdi, Giuseppe, 217, 273, 308; *Aida*, 378; *Ballo in Maschera*, **120**; *Falstaff*,